The Development Century

This anthology offers a cutting-edge perspective on how development has shaped the history of the modern world. Stephen J. Macekura and Erez Manela have gathered together leading historians to examine development on the international, regional, and national levels as well as local manifestations of development initiatives and transnational organizing on behalf of alternative approaches. Themes include the relationship between empire and development, the role of international organizations, the influence of the Cold War, decolonization and postcolonial development strategies, reform and resistance to development, development and global health, and the ecological effects of development. *The Development Century* examines how ideas and discourses about development have shaped its practices on the ground; explores the ways in which policymakers and experts attempted to implement development through specific institutions and policies; and analyzes development initiatives and their effect on local environments and people.

Stephen J. Macekura is Assistant Professor of International Studies at Indiana University, Bloomington. He is the author of *Of Limits and Growth: The Rise of Global Sustainable Development in the Twentieth Century* (Cambridge, 2015).

Erez Manela is Professor of History at Harvard University, where he also serves as Director of Graduate Programs at the Weatherhead Center for International Affairs and co-chairs the Harvard International and Global History Seminar (HIGHS). He is the author of the prize-winning book *The Wilsonian Moment: Self-Determination and the International Origins of Anticolonial Nationalism* (2007) and co-editor *of The Shock of the Global: The 1970s in Perspective* (2010) and *Empires at War, 1911–23* (2014).

D1444472

Global and International History

Series Editors
Erez Manela, *Harvard University*
John McNeill, *Georgetown University*
Aviel Roshwald, *Georgetown University*

The Global and International History series seeks to highlight and explore the convergences between the new International History and the new World History. Its editors are interested in approaches that mix traditional units of analysis such as civilizations, nations, and states with other concepts such as transnationalism, diasporas, and international institutions.

Titles in the Series

The Development Century

A Global History

Edited by

STEPHEN J. MACEKURA

Indiana University, Bloomington

EREZ MANELA

Harvard University, Massachusetts

CAMBRIDGE
UNIVERSITY PRESS

CAMBRIDGE
UNIVERSITY PRESS

University Printing House, Cambridge CB2 8BS, United Kingdom

One Liberty Plaza, 20th Floor, New York, NY 10006, USA

477 Williamstown Road, Port Melbourne, VIC 3207, Australia

314–321, 3rd Floor, Plot 3, Splendor Forum, Jasola District Centre, New Delhi – 110025, India

79 Anson Road, #06–04/06, Singapore 079906

Cambridge University Press is part of the University of Cambridge.

It furthers the University's mission by disseminating knowledge in the pursuit of education, learning, and research at the highest international levels of excellence.

www.cambridge.org
Information on this title: www.cambridge.org/9781316515884
DOI: 10.1017/9781108678940

First published 2018

Printed in the United States of America by Sheridan Books, Inc.

A catalogue record for this publication is available from the British Library.

Library of Congress Cataloging-in-Publication Data
NAMES: Macekura, Stephen J., editor. | Manela, Erez, editor.
TITLE: The development century : a global history / edited by Stephen J. Macekura and Erez Manela.
DESCRIPTION: Cambridge, United Kingdom ; New York, NY : Cambridge University Press, 2018. | Series: Global and international history | Includes bibliographical references and index.
IDENTIFIERS: LCCN 2018026096 | ISBN 9781316515884 (hbk. : alk. paper) | ISBN 9781108453479 (pbk.)
SUBJECTS: LCSH: Economic development – History. | Economic history. | Globalization – History.
CLASSIFICATION: LCC HD78 .D483 2018 | DDC 338.9009/04–dc23
LC record available at https://lccn.loc.gov/2018026096

ISBN 978-1-316-51588-4 Hardback
ISBN 978-1-108-45347-9 Paperback

Contents

Figures

Contributors

Jeremy Adelman is the author or editor of ten books, including *Sovereignty and Revolution in the Iberian Atlantic* (2006) and *Worldly Philosopher: The Odyssey of Albert O. Hirschman* (2013). He is currently the Henry Charles Lea Professor of History and the Director of the Global History Lab at Princeton University.

Paul Adler is Assistant Professor of History at Colorado College. He previously taught at the Harvard History & Literature concentration. His first book examines how nonprofit advocacy groups in the United States became important players in debates over global economic governance in the late twentieth century.

Nathan J. Citino is Associate Professor of History at Rice University. He is the author of *Envisioning the Arab Future: Modernization in U.S.-Arab Relations, 1945–1967* (Cambridge University Press, 2017).

Alessandro Iandolo is Lecturer in International History in the Department of Politics and International Relations at the University of Oxford. His main research interest is the history of the Soviet Union's economic and technical cooperation with radical states in Africa, Asia, and Latin America during the Cold War. Alessandro published articles on international and economic history in *Cold War History*, *The Journal of Cold War Studies*, *Contemporary European History*, and *Diplomatic History*. He is currently writing a book on the Soviet attempt to export a model of development to Ghana, Guinea, and Mali during the 1950s and 1960s, entitled *Contested Development: The Soviet Union in the Struggle for West Africa's Modernity*.

Julia F. Irwin is Associate Professor of History at the University of South Florida. Her research focuses on the place of humanitarian assistance in twentieth-century US foreign relations. Her first book, *Making the World Safe: The American Red Cross and a Nation's Humanitarian Awakening* (2013), is a history of US international relief efforts during the World War I era. She is now writing a second book, *Catastrophic Diplomacy: A History of U.S. Responses to Global Natural Disasters*, a history of US foreign disaster relief during the early- to mid-twentieth century.

Priya Lal is Associate Professor of History at Boston College. Her first book, *African Socialism in Postcolonial Tanzania: Between the Village and the World* (Cambridge University Press, 2015), tells the story of Tanzania's ujamaa experiment of the 1960s and 1970s. She is currently working on a book tentatively entitled *Human Resources* about the politics of national development, medicine, and higher education in southeastern Africa since independence.

Stephen J. Macekura is Assistant Professor of International Studies at Indiana University, Bloomington. He is the author of *Of Limits and Growth: The Rise of Global Sustainable Development in the Twentieth Century* (Cambridge, 2015).

Erez Manela is Professor of History at Harvard University, where he also serves as Director of Graduate Programs at the Weatherhead Center for International Affairs and co-chairs the Harvard International and Global History Seminar (HIGHS). He is the author of the prize-winning book *The Wilsonian Moment: Self-Determination and the International Origins of Anticolonial Nationalism* (2007) and co-editor of *The Shock of the Global: The 1970s in Perspective* (2010) and *Empires at War, 1911–23* (2014).

Amanda Kay McVety is Associate Professor of History at Miami University. She is the author of *Enlightened Aid: U.S. Development as Foreign Policy in Ethiopia* (2012) and *The Rinderpest Campaigns: A Virus, Its Vaccines, and Global Development in the Twentieth Century*, (Cambridge, 2018).

Edward Miller is Associate Professor of History at Dartmouth College. He is the author of *Misalliance: Ngo Dinh Diem, the United States, and the Fate of South Vietnam* (2013) and *The Vietnam War: A Documentary Reader* (2016).

Timothy Nunan is Wissenschaftlicher Mitarbeiter and Freigeist Fellow at the Center for Global History at the Freie Universität Berlin. He is the author or editor of two books: *Writings on War* (2011), a compendium of Carl Schmitt's interwar writings on international order, and *Humanitarian Invasion: Global Development in Cold War Afghanistan* (2016). His present project, *The Islamic Factor: Socialists, Islamists and the Soviet Union in Cold War Eurasia*, examines the clash between the international Islamist movement and the international socialist movement in the twentieth century.

Thomas Robertson researches the environmental history of international development. His works include *The Malthusian Moment: Global Population Growth and the Birth of American Environmentalism* (2012); *Cold War Landscapes: Toward an Environmental History of U.S. Development Programs in the 1950s and 1960s, Cold War History* (2016); and, co-edited with Jenny Leigh Smith, *Transplanting Modernity: New Histories of Technology, Development, and Environment* (forthcoming). Thomas's current research examines the environmental history of US development projects in Cold War Nepal. Trained at the University of Wisconsin-Madison, he currently directs the Fulbright office in Kathmandu, Nepal.

Cyrus Schayegh (PhD, Columbia University, 2004) was Associate Professor at Princeton before joining the Graduate Institute, Geneva, in 2017. His books include *The Middle East and the Making of the Modern World* (2017) and *The Routledge History Handbook of the Middle East Mandates* (2015), and he has published in *The American Historical Review, Comparative Studies in Society and History*, and *Geschichte und Gesellschaft*, among other journals. His current research projects focus on the interplay between globalization and decolonization after World War II, interwar European inter-imperial cooperation, historiography, and Arab views of Afro-Asian decolonization.

Christy Thornton is Assistant Professor in the Department of Sociology at Johns Hopkins University, and a fellow in the Weatherhead Initiative on Global History at Harvard. She received her PhD from New York University, and she is completing her first book, *Revolution in Development: Mexico and the Governance of the Global Economy*, which is under contract with the University of California Press.

Corinna R. Unger is Professor of Global and Colonial History (19th and 20th centuries) at the European University Institute in Florence, Italy. Her research focuses on the history of development, decolonization, and international organizations in the twentieth century. Among her publications are *International Development: A Postwar History* (2018); *Entwicklungspfade in Indien: Eine internationale Geschichte, 1947–1980* (2015); and, together with Marc Frey and Sönke Kunkel, eds., *International Organizations and Development, 1945–1990* (2014).

Alden Young is a political and economic historian of Africa. He is particularly interested in the ways in which Africans participated in the creation of the current international order. Since 2014, he has been Assistant Professor of African History and Director of the Africana Studies Program at Drexel University. His first book, *Transforming Sudan: Decolonization, Economic Development, and State Formation,* was published by Cambridge University Press in December 2017.

Acknowledgments

The editors would like to thank the Radcliffe Institute for Advanced Study at Harvard University for its generous support of the June 2016 workshop that launched this collaboration, as well as everyone who took part in that workshop. We are also grateful to our editor at Cambridge University Press, Debbie Gershenowitz, and the rest of the staff there for their enthusiasm and expertise in shepherding this volume to publication. We thank, too, the anonymous readers for the press for their excellent feedback, which helped make this a better book. Finally, our greatest gratitude goes to the contributors to this volume, who made this collaboration a true pleasure.

Introduction

Stephen J. Macekura and Erez Manela

International development is everywhere these days. Every year governments, international organizations, private foundations, and even multinational corporations offer billions of dollars to spur economic growth in the "developing" world. Official assistance alone – not including philanthropic or private investment – amounted to $132 billion in 2015.[1] Beyond those formal engagements, consumers in wealthy countries choose to buy products from corporations that claim to donate part of the proceeds to developing countries. Some watch Bono's TED Talks on the importance of eliminating global poverty. Others donate a few spare dollars in the cashier's line at the supermarket to offer "microloans" to a basket weaver in Uganda. Giant philanthropies such as the Bill & Melinda Gates Foundation spend many billions annually on development programs across many countries, as do the international development agencies of numerous rich-country governments. Thousands of students in the Western world enroll in "development studies" courses at universities with an eye toward making an impact on the lives of underserved populations around the globe. International development captivates public and private attention.

However current this focus on development may seem to us today, it has a long history. At least since the eighteenth century, European thinkers and political economists envisioned economic activity and material abundance as "progressing" or "increasing" or "improving" through time. By the late nineteenth century, imperial powers seeking to legitimate

[1] *Development Cooperation Report: The Sustainable Development Goals as Business Opportunities* (Paris: OECD, 2016), 17.

expanding colonial rule began to promote the "development" of their territories and their subjects as a justification, even as nation-building elites throughout the Global North, from the United States to England, Germany, Russia, and Japan, used development as an argument for increasing the power of government. By the early twentieth century, imperial authorities and national leaders alike used the rhetoric of development as a way to galvanize support for large-scale transformations of economic, political, and social life. In practice, under the rubric of development leaders pursued projects that ranged from inoculating populations against disease to constructing new factories, from counterinsurgency operations to building massive dams to produce electricity, irrigate farmland, and settle populations. Increasingly, moreover, powerful governments and wealthy foundations started to foster development not only within their own nations or colonial possessions but also elsewhere. As development shifted from national and imperial formations toward the global arena, the idea of international development was born.

By the middle of the twentieth century, as global decolonization loomed, much of the world sought reconstruction from global war, and the Cold War began, the push for international development – the process wherein a national government or private foundation seeks to promote development elsewhere – intensified. Over the ensuing decades, the United States, Soviet Union, and European powers, as well as nongovernmental bodies usually based in the Global North, ramped up the provision of foreign aid intended to promote the development of the so-called underdeveloped regions of what became known, by the mid-1950s, as the "Third World." The conflict between the two superpowers was in part a competition over differing forms of economic development, with each trying to persuade Third World countries of the superiority of their respective systems and expand their influence worldwide. All the while, Third World countries adopted their own national developmental aspirations and plans. By the mid-1960s, development was a widespread policy-making focus, a subject of academic and philanthropic interest, and a dominant feature of international politics.[2] Development, in other words, has long been the rage in the global arena.

---

[2] On the history of the development idea, see Gilbert Rist, *The History of Development: From Western Origins to Global Faith* (London: Zed Books, 2008); Stephen Macekura, "Development and Growth: An Intellectual History," in *History of the Future of Economic Growth*, ed. Matthias Schmelzer and Iris Borowy (London: Routledge, 2017), 110–128.

Our understanding of its history, however, has trailed behind the ever-growing economic and social scientific literature on how to engineer development in the present and future. *The Development Century* brings together cutting-edge work on the history of national and international development in order to highlight critical themes, approaches, and recent advances in our understanding of this central theme in the history of the twentieth century. This book examines development at various scales, with the more familiar international and national development histories placed alongside studies of local manifestations of development as well as of transnational organizing on behalf of alternative approaches.

What the histories assembled here show is that the very meaning of development has never been fixed or stable for very long. Rather, development in history has amounted to a loose framework for a set of assumptions – that history moves through stages; that leaders and/or experts could guide or direct the evolution of societies through these stages; that some places and people in the world are at more advanced stages than others – that have structured how diverse historical actors understood their place in the world and sought to change it. Part of the historian's task is to retrieve the myriad ways in which the pursuit of development framed (and was informed by) imaginings of the future, how it has reshaped the material world, and how it has drawn on historical narratives to explain and justify contemporary choices. *The Development Century* examines the texts and discourses that have inspired ideas about development and shaped its practices; explores the ways in which policymakers and experts attempted to implement development ideas and plans through specific institutions and policies; and analyzes specific development initiatives and their effect on local environments and people. The diversity of perspectives represented in these pages reflects the many different ways historians have studied development to date and offers a set of methodological and analytical approaches that historians of development, and its practitioners, can expand and build upon in the future.

The Development Century proceeds from the assumption that we should understand and evaluate past development initiatives with full regard to their specific historical contexts. Rather than looking to history to derive specific prescriptions or identify potential variables (such as "inclusive institutions" or geographical and environmental endowments) that might provide a blueprint for future action, we investigate how the history of international development illuminates important aspects of the global history of the modern era and how that broad historical context, in turn, illuminates the evolution of development as idea and practice.³ The global, international, and transnational histories that come together in the pages that follow provide a useful guide for rethinking not only the history of international development but also the history of the twentieth century writ large.

After all, thinking about the twentieth century as "the development century" can help us see the connections and continuities across the chronological divisions that have long constrained how historians have told the story of the recent past. Narratives of twentieth-century international history often focus on the ideological conflict between liberal capitalism and communism that defined the period from 1945 to 1991; they assume a sharp distinction between the East and West, or between the Global North and Global South; they locate the nation-state and its power at the core of global politics. *The Development Century* moves beyond these narratives. It highlights how development became a shared language, an object of governance, a form of political expectation, and a set of practices that transcended the ideological divisions (capitalist/communist) commonly seen as incompatible and operated across the political domains (empire/state/nonstate) that are often seen as separate and distinct. At the same time, studying the history of development in its diverse meanings and experiences around the world allows us to examine the myriad ways people have tried to narrate the past, envision the future, and transform the natural and human world alike in the name of alleviating suffering, engineering progress, and redressing inequalities between and within countries. The chapters herein each offer separate but interconnected entryways into the meanings, practices, and outcomes of the development century.

***

We now have a considerable body of scholarship focused on the history of international development. The first edited volumes appeared in print in the mid-1990s.⁴ Dozens of monographs have been published

---

³ On institutional explanations for global inequality, see, for instance, Daron Acemoglu and James A. Robinson, *Why Nations Fail: The Origins of Power, Prosperity, and Poverty* (New York: Crown Business, 2012). On geographical and environmental explanations, see Jared Diamond, *Guns, Germs, and Steel: The Fates of Human Societies* (New York: W.W. Norton, 1997).

⁴ Jonathan Crush, ed., *The Power of Development* (New York: Routledge, 1995); Frederique Apffel-Marglin and Stephen Marglin, eds., *Decolonizing Knowledge: From Development to Dialogue* (New York: Oxford University Press, 1996); Frederick Cooper and Randall Packard, *International Development and the Social Sciences: Essays on the History and Politics of Knowledge* (Berkeley: University of California Press, 1997).

since.[5] This historical scholarship built on pioneering critiques of development discourse by social scientists such as James C. Scott, Arturo Escobar, Timothy Mitchell, and Frédérique Apffel-Marglin, who critiqued its occlusions of power relations and sought to historicize it in order to examine its origins, evolution, and outcomes.[6] In this, these scholars departed from earlier work that had simply used the history of international development as a collection of case studies or data points in order to build models, theories, or prescriptions for how development should proceed.

The recent historical investigations into international development have yielded many insights. Historians have revealed the power relationships and contentious histories behind the received categories (such as "development," "modernization," or "progress") that continue to shape international development work.[7] Recent scholarship has also elucidated the ideas and motivations behind development and illuminated the key thinkers and theories that shaped major policies, with much of this work focused on the rise and popularity of "modernization theory" in mid-twentieth-century social science and US foreign policy.[8] It has uncovered

---

[5] Frederick Cooper, "Writing the History of Development," *Journal of Modern European History* 8:1 (2010): 5–23; Marc Frey and Sönke Kunkel, "Writing the History of Development: A Review of Recent Literature," *Contemporary European History* 20:2 (May 2011): 215–232; Joseph Morgan Hodge, "Writing the History of Development (Part 1: The First Wave)," *Humanity: An International Journal of Human Rights, Humanitarianism, and Development* 6:3 (2015): 429–463; Joseph Morgan Hodge, "Writing the History of Development (Part 2: Longer, Deeper, Wider)," *Humanity: An International Journal of Human Rights, Humanitarianism, and Development* 7:1 (2016): 125–174.

[6] Nick Cullather, "Development? It's History," *Diplomatic History* 22:4 (2000): 641–653.

[7] Michael Adas, *Machines as the Measure of Men: Science, Technology, and Ideologies of Western Dominance* (Ithaca: Cornell University Press, 1989); James Ferguson, *The Anti-Politics Machine: 'Development,' Depoliticization, and Bureaucratic Power in Lesotho* (Cambridge: Cambridge University Press, 1990); Wolfgang Sachs, ed., *The Development Dictionary: A Guide to Knowledge as Power* (London: Zed Books, 1992); Arturo Escobar, *Encountering Development: The Making and Unmaking of the Third World* (Princeton: Princeton University Press, 1995); Michael Cowen and Robert Shenton, *Doctrines of Development* (New York: Routledge Press, 1996); Cooper and Packard, *International Development and the Social Sciences*; Gilbert Rist, *The History of Development: From Western Origins to Global Faith* (London: Zed Books, 2008).

[8] H. W. Arndt, *Economic Development: The History of an Idea* (Chicago: University of Chicago Press, 1987); Colin Leys, *Rise and Fall of Development Theory* (London: James Murray, 1996); Nils Gilman, *Mandarins of the Future: Modernization Theory in Cold War America* (Baltimore, MD: Johns Hopkins University Press, 2003); David Engerman, *Modernization from the Other Shore: American Intellectuals and the Romance of Russian Development* (Cambridge, MA: Harvard University Press, 2003).

the strategic motivations behind development aid.[9] Development projects rarely achieve their stated goals without unintended social, economic, political, and ecological consequences, and the variety of these short- and long-term aftereffects has been explored in these studies as well.[10]

Historians from many different topical and thematic backgrounds have begun to analyze the history of development, too. Historians of empire have drawn out the continuities of people, practices, and ideas between colonial governance and postcolonial development, and they have drawn connections between development efforts in the colonies and governance at home in the metropole.[11] Historians of science, technology, and the environment have analyzed the relationship between development ideas and practice, technocracy, and ecological change.[12] Scholars have

---

[9] See, for instance, Michael Latham, *Modernization as Ideology: American Social Science and "Nation Building" in the Kennedy Era* (Chapel Hill: The University of North Carolina Press, 2000); Michael E. Latham, *The Right Kind of Revolution: Modernization, Development, and U.S. Foreign Policy from the Cold War to the Present* (Ithaca: Cornell University Press, 2011); Timothy Nunan, *Humanitarian Invasion: Global Development in Cold War Afghanistan* (New York: Cambridge University Press, 2016).

[10] On the limits of development schemes to colonize fully the objects of their control, see Anna Tsing, *Friction: An Ethnography of Global Connections* (Princeton: Princeton University Press, 2005). On the limits of state-led development, see James C. Scott, *Seeing Like a State: How Certain Schemes to Improve the Human Condition Have Failed* (New Haven: Yale University Press, 1998). On this theme, see also, Timothy Mitchell, *Rule of Experts: Egypt, Techno-Politics, Modernity* (Berkeley: University of California Press, 2002).

[11] Helen Tilley, *Africa as a Living Laboratory: Empire, Development, and the Problem of Scientific Knowledge* (Chicago: University of Chicago Press, 2011); Charlotte Lydia Riley, "Monstrous Predatory Vampires and Beneficent Fairy-Godmothers: British Post-War Colonial Development in Africa" (PhD diss., University College London, 2013); Suzanne Moon, *Technology and Ethical Idealism: A History of Development in the Netherlands East Indies* (Leiden: CNWS Publications, 2007); Joseph Morgan Hodge, *Triumph of the Expert: Agrarian Doctrines of Development and the Legacies of British Colonialism* (Athens: Ohio University Press, 2007); Monica van Beusekom, *Negotiating Development: African Farmers and Colonial Experts at the Office du Niger, 1920–1960* (Oxford: Oxford University Press, 2002); Benjamin Zachariah, *Developing India: An Intellectual and Social History, c. 1930–50* (New Delhi: Oxford University Press, 2005).

[12] On science, development, and technocracy, see Nick Cullather, "Development and Technopolitics," in *Explaining the History of U.S. Foreign Relations*, rev. ed. (New York: Cambridge University Press, forthcoming), 102–118; Christophe Bonneuil, "Development as Experiment: Science and State Building in Late Colonial and Postcolonial Africa, 1930–1970," *Osiris* 15:1 (2000): 258–281. See also, Suzanne Moon, *Technology and Ethical Idealism: A History of Development in the Netherlands East Indies* (Leiden: CNWS Publications, 2007); Gabrielle Hecht, "Introduction," in *Entangled Geographies: Empire and Technopolitics in the Global Cold War*, ed. Gabrielle Hecht (Cambridge, MA: The MIT Press, 2011), 1–12; Ross Bassett, *The Technological Indian* (Cambridge, MA: Harvard University Press,

investigated the evolving cultural dimensions of development and modernization theory, as well.[13] In recent years, too, scholars have begun to study the origins and expansion of development thought and practices in international organizations such as the League of Nations and the United Nations, especially its so-called specialized agencies.[14] Historians of US foreign relations have argued that international development policy helped to expand American influence abroad during the twentieth century, particularly during the Cold War when the two rival superpowers competed over whose version of modernity would best serve the emerging nations of the "Third World." These works have often focused on showing how and why US officials came to embrace international development as such an integral part of their foreign policy.[15] Recent research has also

2016); Sigrid Schmalzer, *Red Revolution, Green Revolution: Scientific Farming in Socialist China* (Chicago: University of Chicago Press, 2016); Gabriela Soto Laveaga, *Jungle Laboratories: Mexican Peasants, National Projects, and the Making of the Pill* (Durham: Duke University Press, 2009). On technology and US foreign relations more broadly, see Michael Adas, *Dominance by Design: Technological Imperatives and America's Civilizing Mission* (Cambridge, MA: Harvard University Press, 2006). On development and the environment, see Thomas Robertson, "Cold War Landscapes: Towards an Environmental History of US Development Programmes in the 1950s and 1960s," *Cold War History* (2015): 1–25; Thomas Robertson, *The Malthusian Moment: Global Population Growth and the Birth of American Environmentalism* (New Brunswick, NJ: Rutgers University Press, 2012); David Biggs, *Quagmire: Nation-Building and Nature in the Mekong Delta* (Seattle: University of Washington Press, 2010); Allen F. Isaacman and Barbara S. Isaacman, *Dams, Displacement, and the Delusion of Development: Cahora Bassa and Its Legacies in Mozambique, 1965–2007* (Athens: Ohio University Press, 2013); Daniel Klingensmith, *'One Valley and a Thousand': Dams, Nationalism, and Development* (New Delhi: Oxford University Press, 2007); Stephen Macekura, Of Limits and Growth: The Rise of Global Sustainable Development in the Twentieth Century (New York: Cambridge University Press, 2015).

[13] Peter J. Bloom, Stephan F. Miescher, and Takyiwaa Manuh, eds., *Modernization as Spectacle in Africa* (Bloomington: Indiana University Press, 2014); Christina Klein, *Cold War Orientalism: Asia in the Middlebrow Imagination, 1945–1961* (Berkeley: University of California Press, 2003); Melanie McAlister, *Epic Encounters: Culture, Media, and U.S. Interests in the Middle East since 1945* (Berkeley: University of California Press, 2005).

[14] Amy L. S. Staples, *The Birth of Development: How the World Bank, Food and Agriculture Organization, and the World Health Organization Changed the World, 1945–1965* (Kent: The Kent State University Press, 2006); Michele Alacevich, *The Political Economy of the World Bank: The Early Years* (Stanford: Stanford University Press, 2009); Daniel Maul, *Human Rights, Development and Decolonization: The International Labour Organization, 1940–1970* (London: Palgrave Macmillan, 2012); Eric Helleiner, *Forgotten Foundations of Bretton Woods: International Development and the Making of the Postwar Order* (Ithaca: Cornell University Press, 2014).

[15] Latham, *Modernization as Ideology*; Gilman, *Mandarins of the Future*; David C. Engerman, Nils Gilman, Mark H. Haefele, and Michael E. Latham, eds., *Staging*

explored the relationship between development practice abroad and at home, the varieties of development approaches the United States employed abroad and how they changed over time, and the connections between development and Cold War security imperatives.[16] Scholars have begun to analyze how and why critics challenged US international development policy, as well as how non-Americans shaped the ways the United States conceived and implemented its development aid.[17] Finally, historians have studied how the other Cold War powers, such as the Soviet

Growth: Modernization, Development, and the Global Cold War (Amherst: The University of Massachusetts Press, 2003); Gilman, *Mandarins of the Future*; David Ekbladh, *The Great American Mission: Modernization and the Construction of an American World Order* (Princeton: Princeton University Press, 2010); Latham, *The Right Kind of Revolution*.

[16] On the connections between development at home and abroad, see Daniel F. Immerwahr, *Thinking Small: The United States and the Lure of Community Development* (Cambridge, MA: Harvard University Press, 2015); Sheyda F. A. Jahanbani, *"The Poverty of the World": Discovering the Poor at Home and Abroad, 1935–1980* (New York: Oxford University Press, forthcoming); Amy C. Offner, "Anti-Poverty Programs, Social Conflict, and Economic Thought in Colombia and the United States, 1948–1980" (PhD diss., Columbia University, 2011). On varieties of development, see Nick Cullather, *The Hungry World: America's Cold War Battle against Poverty in Asia* (Cambridge, MA: Harvard University Press, 2011); Nicole Sackley, "Cosmopolitanism and the Uses of Tradition: Robert Redfield and Alternative Visions of Modernization during the Cold War," *Modern Intellectual History* 9:3 (November 2012): 565–595. On development and the Cold War, see Nicole Sackley, "Village Models: Etawah, India, and the Making and Remaking of Development in the Early Cold War," *Diplomatic History* 37:4 (September 2013): 749–778; Gregg Brazinsky, *Nation Building in South Korea: Koreans, Americans, and the Making of a Democracy* (Chapel Hill: The University of North Carolina Press, 2007); James M. Carter, *Inventing Vietnam: The United States and State Building, 1954–1968* (Cambridge: Cambridge University Press, 2008); Larry Grubbs, *Secular Missionaries: Americans and African Development in the 1960s* (Amherst: University of Massachusetts Press, 2009); Amanda Kay McVety, *Enlightened Aid: U.S. Development as Foreign Policy in Ethiopia* (New York: Oxford University Press, 2012); Bradley Simpson, *Economists with Guns: Authoritarian Development and U.S.-Indonesian Relations, 1960–1968* (Stanford: Stanford University Press, 2008); Thomas C. Field, *From Development to Dictatorship: Bolivia and the Alliance for Progress in the Kennedy Era* (Ithaca: Cornell University Press, 2014); Edward G. Miller, *Misalliance: Ngo Dinh Diem, the United States, and the Fate of South Vietnam* (Cambridge, MA: Harvard University Press, 2013). Scholars have also studied the US south as an "underdeveloped region" within the country. Tore Olsson, *Agrarian Crossings: Reformers and the Remaking of the US and Mexican Countryside* (Princeton: Princeton University Press, 2017); Natalie Ring, *The Problem South: Region, Empire, and the New Liberal State, 1880–1930* (Athens: University of Georgia Press, 2012); Andrew Zimmerman, *Alabama in Africa: Booker T. Washington, the German Empire, and the Globalization of the New South* (Princeton: Princeton University Press, 2010).

[17] Macekura, *Of Limits and Growth.*

Union and China, actively promoted and funded their own visions of development abroad, too.[18]

The time is now ripe, therefore, to reflect on where all of this scholarship has led us and what course future research should take. What are the most important insights that we have learned about development history? In what ways has the scholarship on international development challenged or reshaped the dominant narratives of twentieth-century history? And how might historians continue to expand the study of international development in the future in ways that matter to scholars and practitioners alike? Taken together, the chapters in this book seek to expand our perspective on the history of international development in three main ways: by showcasing its thematic and conceptual diversity; by casting it as a fully global story that nevertheless operates on multiple spatial scales, from local to national to regional to international; and by considering it in its full chronological breadth, from its pre-twentieth-century origins to the present day.

First, this book engages a wide range of theories and practices of international development across a broad swathe of time and space. Early histories of development focused on social scientific theories of modernization that became popular in the United States and Western Europe during the 1950s and 1960s. Scholars charted how Cold War geopolitics led policymakers and intellectuals to promote and adopt such theories as the basis for state-to-state foreign aid projects. Here, however, we venture beyond the history of modernization theory and its influence on US foreign policy to explore other traditions – from community development to sustainability and beyond – that have shaped the practices of development from the colonial era to the present day. The actual implementation of development policies and projects rarely matched the grand design or expectations of modernization theorists, and this book captures some of the diversity of development ideas, discourses, and practices on the ground and explores their political, economic, cultural, and environmental dimensions.

---

[18] Sergey Mazov, *A Distant Front in the Cold War: The USSR in West Africa and the Congo, 1956–1964* (Stanford: Stanford University Press, 2010); Oscar Sánchez-Sibony, *Red Globalization: The Political Economy of the Soviet Cold War from Stalin to Krushchev* (Cambridge: Cambridge University Press, 2014); David C. Engerman, "Learning from the East: Soviet Experts and India in the Era of Competitive Coexistence," *Comparative Studies of South Asia, Africa and the Middle East* 33:2 (2013): 227–238; Jamie Monson, *Africa's Freedom Railway: How a Chinese Development Project Changed Lives and Livelihoods in Tanzania* (Bloomington: Indiana University Press, 2009).

This book brings together historians of empire, historians of international relations and international institutions, and scholars of regional and area studies to show how development emerged as a powerful concept that drew from diverse sources and in a variety of locations far removed from elite universities in the United States or Western Europe. For instance, Cyrus Schayegh explores the evolution of developmental thinking and policy among elites across the Ottoman Empire in the nineteenth and early twentieth century. Julia Irwin demonstrates that in the case of many US experts during the early twentieth century, development practices implemented in the Caribbean derived not from high theory but from the experiences on the ground responding to natural disasters, less preplanned programs than ad hoc reactions shaped by encounters with political and institutional arrangements different from those of the United States. Nathan Citino argues that, even at the height of the Cold War, there was rarely consensus about how to pursue development by tracing the wide-ranging debates over the development trajectory of the Middle East during the middle twentieth century, as national leaders and international experts debated how national and regional development goals fit together – if at all. Recovering some of these differing meanings, aspirations, and practices of development throughout its history reveals development not as a universal concept but rather as a contingent, messy, and often-contested process of explaining the past and imagining the future.

Second, the history of development should be viewed as a fully global project, exploring the far-flung and wide-ranging networks of actors, spaces, and institutions that have been involved in it. This requires examining development across the world from multiple perspectives: national and local politics in the Third World; the focus on international development assistance policies from the Soviet Union, Europe, the United States, and even countries within the Third World itself; the role of international organizations and transnational expert networks in defining development ideas, policies, and practice; and the place of private actors, such as philanthropic foundations, in shaping development history. The contributors to this book include scholars with specialties in US, European, African, Middle Eastern, Asian, Latin American, Soviet, and international history, and the chapters rely on a wide range of sources, drawing on archives on four continents and on material in many different languages.[19] Such a global approach to the history of development allows

---

[19] See also, Erez Manela, "Reconceiving International History," *Reviews in American History* 37:1 (March 2009): 69–77. On the opportunities and challenges posed by

us to see it as more than simply a story of the diffusion of theories and practices from the Global North to the Global South. Rather, we adopt a multidimensional and multifocal approach recognizing that ideas and approaches to development emerged and traveled in complex, multidirectional pathways that, while surely inflected and directed by state power in significant ways, also flowed through civil society activist organizations, expert networks, and domestic interest groups.

This book offers multiple entry points toward the sort of global history of development in the modern era that scholars have long called for. Some chapters examine development as a fully global project, a historically contingent idea adopted by a network of experts and officials that, in certain instances, took the entire world as its object of intervention. Erez Manela's contribution, for instance, focuses on the history of global disease control to trace the emergence of a global institutional framework explicitly designed to promote development, or at least one aspect of it, worldwide. By contrast, Timothy Nunan analyzes how a wide range of people and organizations – from German foresters to American nongovernmental organization (NGO) workers to Soviet engineers – tried to develop Afghanistan in the 1960s and 1970s, thus showing how such multivalent interventions are a way to see the global converging within a national framework, namely the history of the construction of a "modern" Afghan nation-state. Other chapters reveal, however, how influence also flowed in the other direction, as national elites often reshaped the ideas and practices of transnational actors and international organizations to fit specific circumstances on the ground. The Sudanese elites analyzed by Alden Young, for example, established a national currency to assert the boundaries of the Sudanese national economy and claim their sovereignty in a tumultuous region and rapidly changing global trading system.

Indeed, in the course of the "development century," actors from around the world learned to speak the vernacular of development and think in terms of development theories and approaches. Corinna Unger's chapter investigates the origins of European development assistance as the

researching and writing transnational and global history in general, see C. A. Bayly et al., "AHR Conversation: On Transnational History," *American Historical Review* (2006): 1441–1464; Sebastian Conrad, *What Is Global History?* (Princeton: Princeton University Press, 2016). This volume builds on a 2009 special issue of the journal *Diplomatic History* to construct a global history of modernization theory and its implementation during the Cold War by studying modernization efforts around the world. See David Engerman and Corinna Unger, "Towards a Global History of Modernization," *Diplomatic History* 33:3 (2009): 375–385.

old empires crumbled during the 1950s and 1960s, while Alessandro Iandolo recounts the rise of Soviet development economics during the Khrushchev years. For the postcolonial world, Ed Miller shows how South Vietnamese state builders linked counterinsurgency strategy and development policy, while Priya Lal analyzes how national development goals in postcolonial southeastern Africa came to shape the gender politics of unwaged work. In all these cases development rarely appears as a clear and linear process, either of a singular national vision or story of diffusion from one country to another, but instead as fractious, negotiated, and multidimensional.

Third, the history of international development extends well beyond the temporal boundaries of the Cold War era; rather, it is a central aspect of global history in the modern era writ large. Though the Cold War superpower rivalry gave the development project added urgency, the project itself stretched back to the colonial era and continues to persist long after the Cold War ended.[20] From programs for humanitarian aid to colonial improvement projects to post–Cold War nation-building schemes, the long history of development tracks the evolution of a set of discourses and practices that continue to shape the contemporary world. As Amanda McVety argues, classical economists in the eighteenth and nineteenth centuries conceived of a linear developmentalism in which societies would progress through set stages of social and economic change, and the belief that imperial rulers have the capability to bring about development elsewhere dated to the late eighteenth century. Christy Thornton uncovers how Mexican intellectuals in the 1920s and 1930s articulated visions of international development and international institution building that prefigured and significantly shaped postwar institutions and debates. Taking the history of development toward the new millennium, Paul Adler demonstrates why activists from the Global North and the Global South came together to argue for an "alternative development"

---

[20] This book follows from the lead of scholars such as Matthew Connelly, who argued historians should remove the "Cold War lens" and view the history of international and transnational themes beyond the temporal and political boundaries of the superpower rivalry. See Matthew Connelly, "Taking off the Cold War Lens: Visions of North-South Conflict during the Algerian War for Independence," *The American Historical Review* 105 (June 2000): 739–769; Matthew Connelly, *Fatal Misconception: The Struggle to Control World Population* (Cambridge, MA: Harvard University Press, 2008). For such a perspective on development in Afghanistan, see Timothy Nunan, *Humanitarian Invasion: Global Development in Cold War Afghanistan* (New York: Cambridge University Press, 2016).

framework in the 1970s and how their activities contributed to the fierce anti-globalization protests of the 1990s.

The chapters in this book draw on insights from numerous fields to explore the history of international development from diverse perspectives. Tom Robertson shows how the history of technology and environmental history can provide a useful lens to examine the lasting impact of development efforts. Manela's chapter links the history of global health with the history of development, just as Irwin draws on the history of humanitarianism and disaster studies to reveal early development practices by the US government. Through such analysis, development becomes much more than a form of competition between the Cold War superpowers. As the framework for pursuing disease eradication to the justification for the vast expansion of fossil fuel use, the long-term effects of development shaped many aspects of twentieth-century life and will continue to do so long into the future.

There remains, though, much work to be done on the development century. Scholars have only recently begun, as Thomas Robertson does here, to examine the environmental history of development. Likewise, additional scholarship that incorporates insights from fields such as cultural and spatial history would aid our understanding of how development related to the organization of lived space and the nature of day-to-day living for billions of people worldwide. In addition, greater focus on business and the private sector as key actors in global and local development initiatives, on the ways race and gender have profoundly shaped the history of development, and on connections within and among the countries of the Global South in development thought and practice would all greatly enhance our understanding of the development century. This book seeks to offer a starting point for such research by linking the history of international development with other fields of historical inquiry, thus highlighting the advantages of thinking about its subject using multiple theoretical frameworks and methodological approaches.

***

This book is organized into four main sections. The first explores the long origins of development as a global idea and a global practice. The chapters tackle these themes in a number of ways. Amanda McVety's chapter argues that the intellectual genealogy of development assistance stretched back to the Scottish enlightenment. Though thinkers such as Adam Smith spoke in terms of "improvement" rather than "development," McVety suggests that they, too, held that societal change derived from an economic process driven by capital investment and that wealthy nations had a responsibility and strategic interest in helping their poorer counterparts. Julia Irwin expands on this line of inquiry by demonstrating how the specific practices that shaped US international development activities often owed their origins less to abstract theory and more to the practical experiences involved in the provision of humanitarian relief during the early twentieth century. Throughout the Caribbean Basin, US officials hoping to provide relief cultivated habits, skills, and institutions that later shaped how the United States would try to organize development efforts. Erez Manela analyzes how global health experts constructed international organizations with global scope that eventually carried out a worldwide campaign against smallpox. Understanding development as a global phenomenon, he suggests, requires an analysis of how experts imagined and built institutions that sought to mimic the power and reach of the nation-state, but on a global scale. Cyrus Schayegh explores late Ottoman development initiatives to reveal how Ottoman officials embraced development as a way to strengthen the empire and build a bulwark against its powerful European neighbors. Taken together, these essays highlight some of development's origins – as a set of ideas, as embedded in institutions, and as learned in on-the-ground practice.

The chapters in the second section of the book show how the interrelated processes of global war, decolonization, national state building, and development assistance reshaped the mid-twentieth-century world. Central to their analysis is the study of development as a contest of envisioning time and managing space. Thomas Robertson's chapter suggests that four mass industrial technologies employed during World War II – DDT, aerial photography, bulldozers, and hybrid seeds and chemical fertilizers – contributed heavily to the development, and the ecological degradation, of the tropics during that conflict. Yet after the war development experts redeployed all of these technologies, as part of development projects, which expanded the scale and increased the intensity of development policies' deleterious environmental effects. In his in-depth study of South Vietnamese counterinsurgency strategies, Edward Miller focuses on how President Ngô Đình Diệm and like-minded officials sought to manage the fight against communist insurgents through the construction and control of various spaces in the Bến Tre province. While their efforts did not achieve their goals, they nonetheless reshaped the land and water environments in the process and altered the patterns of settlement and resource use for the local population. Alden Young's chapter, which focuses on postcolonial Sudan, argues that while the postcolonial government was of one mind about the need to pursue economic development there were divergent views over the territorial unit that needed to be developed. Young depicts a competition between imperial British, regional, and national ideas over whether to adopt a national currency, and then shows how Sudanese officials struggled to support their national economic goals in the face of regional rivalries and an increasingly competitive world economy. Priya Lal, in turn, examines the gendered nature of work in East African development politics and state building. She argues that the workers necessary for the developmental welfare states established in postcolonial Tanzania and Zambia were both the subjects and the objects of development projects – people who were needed in order to develop the country's resources while also those who needed to be formed through education to meet the state's needs. Part Two thus explores postcolonial struggles over both narrative and resources as new states sought to define the terms and parameters of developmental change.

Part Three focuses on the wide varieties of expert knowledge and practice that shaped international development in the Cold War world. Timothy Nunan hones in on the contested terrain of Cold War–era Afghanistan to highlight how the West and the Soviet bloc competed for influence and presented overlapping and often frustrated attempts to graft particular visions of modernity onto Afghan society. Far from being merely a site for the rivalry between the two superpowers, he reveals Afghanistan as a crossroad of overlapping contests between diverse actors – such as humanitarian NGOs, West German foresters, political Islamists, and Pashtun nationalists – to transform the physical and human landscape of the country. Alessandro Iandolo shows how global decolonization and Cold War geopolitical imperatives pushed the Soviet leadership to empower economists to conceive of theories of economic change that more closely resembled contemporary development economics than classical Marxism. Corinna Unger brings the Western Europeans more fully into the story by analyzing how Cold War concerns, decolonization, and the economic integration shaped the production of European expertise on international development and its deployment to the Global South. Each chapter in this section highlights the growing imbrication between experts and the state in the mid-twentieth century, and shows how global trends such as decolonization helped to reshape and redirect the role of experts and expertise in international development.

The fourth and final section examines the relationship between development and international society during the twentieth-century world, focusing on international institutions, expert communities, and nonstate activism. Christy Thornton uncovers a network of postrevolutionary Mexican officials who pursued development as an international program that they hoped would overcome and redress the distress that unfettered capitalism had brought to Latin America in the nineteenth and early part of the twentieth century. Nathan Citino reveals how Egyptian President Gamal 'Abd al-Nasser's vision for Egypt's national development contrasted with UN Secretary-General Dag Hammarskjöld's aspirations for regional development of the Middle East. These two approaches to development, Citino argues, reveal divergent political purposes. Nasser emphasized national development to create a story of shared struggle in order to minimize potential class conflict and consolidate his rule, while Hammarskjöld hoped regional economic integration would replace persistent international conflicts after the Suez Crisis. Finally, Paul Adler's chapter analyzes the role of NGOs of the Global North and activists and reform movements in the Global South in forging a global civil society committed to "social justice development." This idea of an "NGO International," he argues, challenges standard depictions of Northern NGOs as neo-imperial or paternalistic by showing how, by the 1970s, activists around the world committed to linking national politics of distribution with global socioeconomic justice found common cause across political and social boundaries.

***

This book is not designed as a complete or comprehensive global history of development. What it seeks to do is to help scholars and practitioners alike to think of the history of development as a fully global story and to show how the broad expanse of the twentieth century was shaped by the visions, desires, and pursuits of development. As a master concept of the modern era, development has framed and constructed much of what we think of as the modern world: as a story of how to explain the past; a rhetoric for making claims on resources and power in the present; and a vision for structuring the future that has persisted from the origins of eighteenth- and nineteenth-century imperial politics to our present age of post–Cold War neoliberalism. To understand the pervasive role of international development in today's world – from counterinsurgency in Afghanistan to promoting entrepreneurship in Accra to analyzing financial rescue packages for Argentina – we must examine the thought and practice of development in its various manifestations from numerous perspectives and scales. The fifteen chapters that follow, taken together, seek to offer a robust starting point for reconsidering this history. We hope that they will point the way and serve as a foundation for further scholarship on global histories of the "development century."

PART I

ORIGINS OF DEVELOPMENT AS A GLOBAL PRACTICE

2

Wealth and Nations

The Origins of International Development Assistance

Amanda Kay McVety

In 1919, Sun Yat-sen, the Premier of the Chinese Nationalist Party, sent a "sketch project for the international development of China" to the US Secretary of Commerce, William C. Redfield. Sun sent the sketch to other people as well, including the head of the US Legation in Peking. He was particularly concerned in making sure that the US government received his plan. Redfield wrote back that he agreed "that the economic development of China would be of the greatest advantage, not only to China, but to the whole of mankind," but the plan that Sun envisioned would "take billions of dollars" and China was already burdened with debts that it could not pay. No doubt disappointed by the response, Sun turned his sketch into a book, *The International Development of China*. His plan, he argued, was one for global peace. "Since President Wilson has proposed a League of Nations to end military war," he wrote, "I propose to end the trade war by cooperation and mutual help in the development of China." The nations who participated in this effort, he predicted, would not only benefit financially from a strong China, they would also help "strengthen the Brotherhood of Man," creating the "keystone in the arch of the League of Nations."[1]

Sun's plan was innovative in its call for international assistance for development. China needed "foreign capital" above all, he wrote, but if that could not be obtained, then it would "at least have to use their experts

---

[1] Sun Yat-sen, *The International Development of China*, 2nd ed. (New York: G. P. Putnam's Sons, 1929), xi, 8–9, 257–258; C. Martin Wilbur, *Sun Yat-sen: Frustrated Patriot* (New York: Columbia University Press, 1976), 96–111.

and inventors to make for us our own machinery."[2] He hoped to get it by tapping into the Western power's major concern of the day: repairing the war's economic and political damages via expanded international cooperation. In 1919, however, as Redfield's letter made clear, the world's wealthiest nations had no interest in expending significant funds for China's economic development. That would change, however, in the aftermath of the next global war.

A 1947 United Nations Relief and Rehabilitation Administration (UNRRA) report explained that its efforts in China were "different in character" from the European programs "because of the depressed state of the Chinese economy before the war." In consequence, "greater effort was therefore expended to provide rehabilitation through new economic development in the hope of alleviating the chronic need for relief." Initial UNRRA activities in China had – as they had in most places – revolved around securing "relief" and "rehabilitation" through the bringing in of supplies: food, medicine, tools, livestock, etc. But now in China UNRRA was directing its efforts toward establishing "projects" explicitly initiated in the name of meeting "the need for new economic development."[3] Concern reached beyond China. At a 1947 conference hosted by the Institute of Pacific Relations, participant H. Belshaw warned, "Reconstruction policies which express too great a nostalgia for the *status quo ante bellum* are likely to do damage to the prospect of an expanding world economy." It is now clear, he continued, that "the expansion of production, purchasing power and trade in other, poorer countries is conducive to their own welfare, and to the peace of the world." When we talk of "reconstruction" today, he insisted, we should understand it to mean *"the continuous process of economic progress and development, as it is with this long-run objective, covering at least several decades, that we shall mainly be concerned."*[4]

Belshaw was correct. Economic development became one of the central concerns of the global community in the second half of the twentieth

---

[2] Ibid., 198. For more on Sun's modernization vision, see Marie-Claire Bergère, *Sun Yat-sen*, trans. Janet Lloyd (Stanford: Stanford University Press, 1998), 246–291 and Margharita Zanasi, *Saving the Nation: Economic Modernity in Republican China* (Chicago: University of Chicago Press, 2006).

[3] *12th Report to Congress on Operations of UNRRA*, as of June 30, 1947 (Washington, D. C.: U.S. Government Printing Office), 9–12.

[4] Emphasis original. H. Belshaw, "Agricultural Reconstruction in the Far East" (September 1947); Tenth Conference of the Institute of Pacific Relations; International Secretariat, Institute of Pacific Relations.

century, as subsequent chapters in this volume will show. This chapter is an attempt to explain, in part, why that happened. It focuses on the time span between Sun's failed 1919 call for international aid for China and the creation exactly thirty years later of the United Nations Expanded Program of Technical Assistance for Economic Development of Underdeveloped Countries and the United States Point Four Program. International assistance for development would take many more forms in the late 1940s and early 1950s, but those two were particularly widely celebrated and became potent symbols of the institutionalization of international assistance for development.

Sun Yat-sen had been ahead of his time when he constructed his plan for China's economic development. By 1949, the global community had caught up with him, agreeing that development was an international issue that warranted international action, but the members of that community were not in complete agreement on why that was the case. People rallied to development from a variety of places for a variety of reasons. This chapter looks primarily at three of them: the emergence of the idea of "the economy" and the rise of national income accounting during the interwar period; the massive devastations of World War II, which triggered international action for relief and reconstruction on a previously unimaginable level; and the outbreak of the Cold War. Together, these three factors helped make international assistance for development a standard part of post–World War II international relations. In the process, they popularized a specific narrative of development as a fundamentally economic process driven by capital investment and technological innovation – exactly what Sun had described back in 1919.

That development narrative had roots that stretched back to an eighteenth-century interpretation of human history as a story of social progress through material change. Baron de Montesquieu laid the groundwork by arguing that underlying structures drove the historical development of societies, but it was the Scottish philosophers – Adam Smith in particular – who gave it structure. Smith narrated a history of progress based on the improvement of land, manufacturing, and trade – through the expansion of economic relationships. That path was, he firmly believed, open to all nations, though success was dependent in part upon luck in terms of geography and resources. It was a compelling vision.[5]

---

[5] Emma Rothschild, *The Inner Lives of Empires* (Princeton: Princeton University Press, 2011), 132–133; Emma Rothschild, *Economic Sentiments* (Cambridge, MA: Harvard University Press, 2001), 40; Jonathan Israel, *Enlightenment Contested* (Oxford: Oxford

Smithian ideas about national improvement through economic expansion flourished in the nineteenth century and people began using the word "development" to describe the process he had narrated.[6] In 1828, the French historian François Guizot wrote that "the first fact comprised in the word civilization is the fact of progress, of development; it presents at once the idea of a people marching onward, not to change its place, but to change its condition."[7] In Latin America, many governments created new departments dedicated to promoting national improvement, often including the word "*fomento* – translated as development, improvement, or promotion" – in their names. Mexico's Ministry of Fomento, Colonization, Industry and Commerce, founded in 1853, was described by its secretary as directed toward "the happiness of those peoples who want to advance, marching forward with civilization and taking advantage of the triumphs of science and industry."[8] This narrative that expressly tied progress in science and industry to "development" did not have to become racist and exclusionary, but a significant branch of it did during the nineteenth century as political leaders and influential academics in Europe and in the United States used it to justify imperialism and slavery as part of the West's "civilizing mission."[9] Japan's rise to

University Press, 2006), 22–23; Anthony Brewer, "Adam Ferguson, Adam Smith, and the Concept of Economic Growth," *History of Political Economy* 31:2 (1999): 237–254; Anthony Brewer, "The Concept of Growth in Eighteenth-Century Economics," *History of Political Economy* 27:4 (1995): 609–638. For more on the universality of Smith's thought, see Jennifer Pitts, *A Turn to Empire* (Princeton: Princeton University Press, 2005), 41–42.

[6] "By 1830, the works of the French and Scottish philosophers could be found in public libraries from Madras to Penang to Sydney, and in places where the concept of the public, the library, or even the book was entirely new" (C. A. Bayly, *The Birth of the Modern World 1780–1914* [Malden, MA: Blackwell Publishing, 2004], 119). David Armitage's point about liberalism provides a helpful guide for thinking about the global spread of the idea of development during this period: "Liberalism in Britain was not the same as liberalism in India, each developed within its own ecological niche, yet they did not emerge in ignorance of each other, but rather in dialogues mediated by local conditions of the reception, circulation and hybridization of arguments" (David Armitage, *Foundations of Modern International Thought* [Cambridge: Cambridge University Press, 2013], 30).

[7] François Guizot, *The History of Civilization in Europe*, trans. William Hazlitt, ed. Larry Siedentop (London: Penguin, 1997), 16.

[8] Casey Marina Lurtz, "Developing the Mexican Countryside: The Department of Fomento's Social Project of Modernization," *Business History Review* 90:3 (Autumn 2016): 431–455. See also, Teresa Cribelli, "'These Industrial Forests': Economic Nationalism and the Search for Agro-Industrial Commodities in Nineteenth-Century Brazil," *Journal of Latin American Studies* 45:3 (August 2013): 545–579.

[9] Pitts, *A Turn to Empire*; Thomas McCarthy, *Race, Empire, and the Idea of Human Development* (Cambridge: Cambridge University Press, 2009); Michael Adas, *Machines*

power at the end of the nineteenth century dramatically challenged the racist aspects of the development narrative, but helped to solidify the idea that states needed to take "advantage of the triumphs of science and industry" if they wanted to become significant players on the global stage.[10]

This was the "development" that Sun would call for in 1919, and he was not alone. In 1923, *Ras* Tafari (later Haile Selassie) wrote to the League of Nations requesting membership so that Ethiopia could "govern its people in peace and tranquility" and "develop its country under prosperous conditions." Tafari had no interest in a so-called civilizing mission for Ethiopia; he wanted capital and technology.[11] Sun and Tafari made their requests at a moment when what "international" itself meant was changing. They and others saw new possibilities in the creation of the League of Nations. And the League answered some of those hopes: it sent health "experts" abroad and funded a small number of "technical and humanitarian activities." The initial emphasis of this work was to improve the international state system itself by curtailing the international drug trade, slavery, and trafficking in women and children, but the League's involvement in the question of "international development" soon expanded in response to new ideas in economics that the League helped foster.[12]

---

as the *Measure of Men: Science, Technology, and Ideologies of Western Dominance* (Ithaca: Cornell University Press, 1990); Michael Adas, *Dominance by Design: Technological Imperatives and America's Civilizing Mission* (Cambridge, MA: Harvard University Press, 2006); Paul A. Kramer, "Power and Connection: Imperial Histories of the United States in the World," *The American Historical Review* 116:5 (December 2011): 1348–1391; Daniel R. Headrick, *Power over Peoples: Technology, Environments, and Western Imperialism, 1400 to the Present* (Princeton: Princeton University Press, 2010); Emily S. Rosenberg, *Spreading the American Dream: American Economic and Cultural Expansion, 1890–1945* (New York: Hill and Wang, 1982); Merle Curti and Kendall Birr, *Prelude to Point Four: American Technical Missions Overseas, 1838–1938* (Madison: University of Wisconsin Press, 1954).

[10] Cyrus Veeser, *Great Leaps Forward: Modernizers in Africa, Asia, and Latin America* (Boston: Prentice Hall, 2010).

[11] Harold G. Marcus, *Haile Selassie I* (Berkeley: University of California Press, 1987), 53–54. Notably, at that moment, the League itself was still arguing for the necessity of "civilization" to guide the "well-being and development" of some peoples via the mandate system (Marc Frey, Sönke Kunkel, and Corrina R. Unger, "Introduction: International Organizations, Global Development, and the Making of the Contemporary World," in *International Organizations and Development, 1945–1990*, ed. Marc Frey, Sönke Kunkel, and Corinna R. Unger [New York: Palgrave Macmillan, 2014], 1–22).

[12] For information about League development initiatives, see Secretariat of the League of Nations, *The Aims, Methods and Activities of the League of Nations* (Geneva: Secretariat

In 1926, the president of the League's Economic Committee announced that the League's future lay in the "new paths ... opening out before it" in the field of economics. A few years later, a report to the Economic Committee described a "world-wide movement of economic thought destined to substitute for the 'hit or miss' of laissez-faire economics a planned and scientifically ordered progress towards higher levels of material prosperity."[13] This movement in thought was partially the outcome of what Timothy Mitchell has dubbed "the realization of the economy." The concept that had remained vague since Smith was gradually becoming understood to be "a self-contained structure or mechanism whose internal parts are imagined to move in a dynamic and regular interaction," which could, therefore, be manipulated into growth with beneficial consequences for the nation.[14] What was at first an interesting idea quickly became perceived to be a vital one. The Great Depression, which put a quarter of the working population in the United States,

---

of the League of Nations, 1935); Thorvald Madsen, "The Scientific Work of the Health Organization of the League of Nations," *Bulletin of the New York Academy of Medicine* 13:8 (August 1937): 439–465; Tomoko Akami, "A Quest to Be Global: The League of Nations Health Organization and Inter-Colonial Regional Governing Agendas of the Far Eastern Association of Tropical Medicine 1910–25," *The International History Review* 38:1 (2016): 1–23; Sunil Amrith and Patricia Clavin, "Feeding the World: Connecting Europe and Asia, 1930–1945," *Past and Present*, Supplement 8 (2013): 29–50; Sunil Amrith, *Decolonizing International Health: India and Southeast Asia, 1930–1965* (London: Palgrave Macmillan, 2006); Stefan Hell, "The Role of European Technology, Expertise and Early Development Aid in the Modernization of Thailand before the Second World War," *Journal of the Asia Pacific Economy* 6:2 (2001): 158–178; Daniel Gorman, *The Emergence of International Society in the 1920s* (Cambridge: Cambridge University Press, 2012), 52–108; Margherita Zanasi, "Exporting Development: The League of Nations and Republican China," *Comparative Studies in Society and History* 49:1 (2007): 149; Jürgen Osterhammel, "'Technical Co-Operation' between the League of Nations and China," *Modern Asian Studies* 13:4 (1979): 661–680; John Farley, *To Cast Out Disease: A History of the International Health Division of the Rockefeller Foundation (1913–1951)* (Oxford: Oxford University Press, 2002); Paul Weindling, "Philanthropy and World Health: The Rockefeller Foundation and the League of Nations Health Organization," *Minerva* 35 (1997): 269–281.

[13] Quoted in JoAnne Pemberton, "New Worlds for Old: The League of Nations in the Age of Electricity," *Review of International Studies* 28 (2002): 317–318.

[14] Timothy Mitchell, *Rule of Experts* (Berkeley: University of California Press, 2002), 82–83; Matthias Schmelzer, *The Hegemony of Growth: The OECD and the Making of the Economic Growth Paradigm* (Cambridge: Cambridge University Press, 2016); H. W. Arndt, *Economic Development* (Chicago: University of Chicago Press, 1987). For examples of key works in this transformation, see Allyn A. Young, "Increasing Returns and Economic Progress," *The Economic Journal* 38:152 (December 1928): 527–542 and Charles Frederick Roos, *Dynamic Economics* (Bloomington, IN: Principia Press, 1934).

Germany, Britain, and France out of work, made economic growth the central political preoccupation of the 1930s.[15]

The Depression gave the League a new agenda that was most evident in the creation in 1935 of the "Mixed Committee on the Problem of Nutrition," which brought together people from several new organizations associated with the League to analyze the global food situation.[16] The resulting report highlighted global inequality in access to food and "in the process created a new language for discussing poverty and consumption on a global scale."[17] That work complemented the LNHO's *International Health Yearbook*, which provided "a survey of the progress made by the various countries in the domain of public health."[18] The League also supported efforts to collect and publish comparative data on standards of living – a concept "that became a lens through which to see the world as an object to be improved by liberal capitalism, western science, and international organization."[19] These efforts were aided by the concurrent efforts of individual economists to compile and publish national income estimates.[20] A 1939 League report explained that the work was "making men and women all over the world more keenly aware of the wide gap between the actual and potential conditions of their lives," which, in turn, was making them "impatient to hear that some real and concerted effort is being made to raise the standard of their lives nearer to what it might become."[21]

The new data about global inequality changed what people demanded from their governments, be they national or imperial. In the British

---

[15] Thomas Piketty, *Capital in the Twenty-First Century*, trans. Arthur Goldhammer (Cambridge, MA: Harvard University Press, 2014), 136.

[16] Patricia Clavin, *Securing the World Economy: The Reinvention of the League of Nations, 1920–1946* (Oxford: Oxford University Press, 2013), 8–9, 161.

[17] Amrith and Clavin, "Feeding the World," 42; Iris Boroway, *Coming to Terms with World Health: The League of Nations Health Organization* (Frankfurt am Main: Peter Lang, 2009), 379–394; Nick Cullather, *The Hungry World: America's Cold War Battle against Poverty in Asia* (Cambridge, MA: Harvard University Press, 2010), 32–33, 38.

[18] A.G.N., "The International Health Year-Book of the League of Nations, 1928," *Canadian Medical Association Journal* 22:1 (January 1930): 93; Boroway, Coming to Terms with World Health, 177–183.

[19] Clavin, *Securing the World Economy*, 172–179.

[20] Colin Clark, *The Conditions of Economic Progress* (London: Macmillan, 1940); Arndt, The Rise and Fall of Economic Growth, 5–23; Daniel Speich, "The Use of Global Abstractions: National Income Accounting in the Period of Imperial Decline," *Journal of Global History* 6:1 (March 2011): 7–28.

[21] Quoted in Amrith and Clavin, "Feeding the World," 35.

Empire, "the impetus for a dramatic reworking of earlier assumptions about imperial development" would manifest itself in the Colonial Development and Welfare Acts of the 1940s. For the French, too, the old "civilizing mission" gave way to "an imperialism of knowledge and planning as well as of capital."[22] The data also changed ideas about the purpose of international cooperation. By the end of the 1930s, the League was insisting that the "really vital problems" facing the world did "not lend themselves to settlement by formal conferences and treaties" and, therefore, "the primary object of international co-operation should be rather mutual help than reciprocal contract – above all, the exchange of knowledge and the fruits of experience."[23] There was a bit of self-interest in the argument: the League had clearly failed in its original purpose of preventing another global war and it was looking for a way to remain relevant. But the decision to emphasize the exchange of knowledge and technical skill was more than just a defensive maneuver; it was the outcome of a decade-long shift in priorities at Geneva toward "positive security" that sought peace through higher living standards, and higher living standards through technical and scientific cooperation for the expansion of human welfare.[24]

By 1939, interest in global security through economic development had spread beyond the League of Nations. That year, Eugene Staley, an economist at Tufts, wrote that we are "well into the era of planetary economy," and we can achieve much more growth together than we can apart. We must, he insisted, launch "a development program designed to carry modern capital equipment and technical knowledge into parts of Asia, South America, and Africa." Nationalism, Staley worried, was currently threatening the "disintegration of the world economy"; it must

---

[22] Joseph Hodge, "Writing the History of Development (Part 2: Longer, Deeper, Wider)," *Humanity* 7:1 (Spring 2016): 131; Frederick Cooper, "Development, Modernization, and the Social Sciences in the Era of Decolonization: The Examples of British and French Africa," *Revue d'Histoire des Sciences Humaines* 10 (2004): 9–38. See also, Suke Wolton, *Lord Hailey, the Colonial Office and the Politics of Race and Empire in the Second World War* (New York: St. Martin's Press, 2000); Joanna Lewis, *Empire State-Building: War & Welfare in Kenya, 1925–52* (Oxford: James Currey, 2000); Michael Havinden and David Meredith, *Colonialism and Development: Britain and Its Tropical Colonies, 1850–1960* (London: Routledge, 1993); Joseph Morgan Hodge, *Triumph of the Expert: Agrarian Doctrines of Development and the Legacies of British Colonialism* (Athens: Ohio University Press, 2007).

[23] Quoted in Clavin, *Securing the World Economy*, 231.

[24] Ibid., 231–240. See also, Randall M. Packard, *A History of Global Health: Interventions in the Lives of Other Peoples* (Baltimore, MD: Johns Hopkins University Press, 2016), 51–90.

not be allowed to do so.[25] Notably, as David Ekbladh has shown, Staley "acknowledged that modernization was a political and social process as much as an economic and technological one," but he believed "technical assistance was foundational" and even "pointed to Sun Yat-sen's *The International Development of China* as a template."[26] Staley helped to popularize the idea that development was something that could and should be shared through capital investment and technical assistance.

The US government embraced the idea on a limited scale, looking not at the entire world, but at the entirety of the Americas. In 1939, Harry Dexter White, who worked in the Treasury Department, sent a memo to Treasury Secretary Henry Morgenthau warning that without US action, the arm of Axis power would reach Latin America. To stop it, he argued for a "bold program" of financial aid. "Only capital and technical skill are needed to develop the area," he insisted, "so that it could provide for a much larger population, for a higher standard of living and a greatly expanded foreign trade." The following year, Nelson Rockefeller sent President Franklin D. Roosevelt a proposal for "Hemispheric Economic Defense" that called for economic development in Latin America via capital investments and technical assistance. Roosevelt seized on the idea and made economic development part of his regional diplomacy. In July of 1941, a Treasury official reported that "if one goes around Washington now I think he will hear more often than any other one word in the vocabulary of the Good Neighbor enthusiasts with which that city abounds the word 'developmental' or 'development.'"[27] It was a short conceptual leap from that hemispheric concern to a global one. "Development" was soon on the lips of more people in Washington than just those working in Latin America. Roosevelt himself led the way.

In his 1941 Annual Message to Congress, Roosevelt famously announced that he wanted to secure "four essential human freedoms" worldwide, including "freedom from want." Roosevelt had added the "everywhere in the world" part to the speech himself, responding to the concern of one of his speechwriters that worldwide "covers an awful lot of territory," with the quip that "the world is getting so small that even the

---

[25] Eugene Staley, *World Economy in Transition*, reissue (Port Washington, NY: Kennikat Press, 1971), 19, 283, 332–333.

[26] David Ekbladh, *The Great American Mission: Modernization and the Construction of an American World Order* (Princeton: Princeton University Press, 2010), 74–75.

[27] Eric Helleiner, *Forgotten Foundations of Bretton Woods* (Ithaca: Cornell University Press, 2014), 40–51.

people in Java are getting to be our neighbors now."[28] When he met with Prime Minister Winston Churchill that August to discuss war aims, the two agreed that they hoped to secure a peace that would "afford assurance that all the men in all the lands may live out their lives in freedom from fear and want" and ensure the "fullest collaboration between all nations in the economic field with the object of securing, for all ... economic advancement and social security."[29] What achieving all that would require was not completely clear at the time, but the words themselves unleashed calls for action all over the world.[30] People already wanted development assistance; the Atlantic Charter gave them hope that the Allied powers would give it to them.

In 1943, Yilma Deressa, Ethiopia's finance minister, told US officials that foreign assistance for development was "implied in the Atlantic Charter."[31] Harry White, who had been asked by the White House to create a plan for a "United Nations Stabilization Fund and a United Nations Bank," reported in his first draft that the fund was designed to assist with "the attainment of the economic objectives of the Atlantic charter." White told Roosevelt that one of the main purposes of the bank would be "to supply the huge volume of capital that will be needed abroad for relief, for reconstruction, and economic development essential for the attainment of world prosperity and higher standards of living."[32] He got support for his argument from the League (still "soldier[ing] on in a variety of guises and locations"), which, in 1942, circulated among Allied officials a "manifesto" whose principal purpose, Patricia Clavin has argued, was "to shape policy, notably American, on reconstruction and international relations."[33] *The Transition from War to Peace Economy*, which was officially published in 1943, argued that "Relief, to be effective, must not simply fill the human belly for a short period of time, but must enable the individuals who require it to continue that process themselves in the future." Avoiding a repeat of the economic anarchy of the 1930s required a commitment "to ensure that the fullest possible use was made of the resources of production, human and material, of the skill and enterprise of the individual, of available scientific

---

[28] Quoted in Elizabeth Borgwardt, *A New Deal for the World: America's Vision for Human Rights* (Cambridge, MA: Harvard University Press, 2005), 20–21.
[29] The Atlantic Charter (August 14, 1941), available at http://avalon.law.yale.edu/wwii/atlantic.asp.
[30] Borgwardt, *A New Deal for the World*, 46–86.
[31] Helleiner, *Forgotten Foundations*, 228.   [32] White quoted in ibid., 109, 121.
[33] Clavin, *Securing the World Economy*, 251, 285–294.

discoveries and inventions so as to attain and maintain in all countries a stable economy and rising standards of living."[34] Peace, in other words, required economic growth.

The idea of a global economy changed the stakes of war "relief." It was readily apparent that the humanitarian operations that had followed World War I were not going to be enough, though they would, as Julia Irwin demonstrates in Chapter 3, provide a critical foundation for the way the Allies approached "relief and rehabilitation" during World War II. The US government had created the Office of Foreign Relief and Rehabilitation Operations (OFRRA) back in 1941. OFRRA soon gave way to the UNRRA, which would be headed by the same man who had led OFRRA and dedicated to a similar mission: provide immediate aid in the form of "food, clothing and shelter, aid in the prevention of pestilence and in the recovery of the health of the people," followed by assistance for "the return of prisoners and exiles to their homes" and for "the resumption of urgently needed agricultural and industrial production and the restoration of essential services."[35] UNRRA, Roosevelt explained, was designed to help people "so that they can help themselves; they will be helped to gain the strength to repair the destruction and devastation of the war and to meet the tremendous task of reconstruction which lies ahead." Their own governments, a UNRRA report to Congress explained, will have the "major responsibility for seeing to it that the peoples liberated from the enemy will be able to liberate themselves also from the hunger and disease that the enemy left behind among them."[36] Assistance for relief and rehabilitation had been internationalized, but the United States and Great Britain remained leery about internationalizing assistance for reconstruction, let alone development. But the demand was growing louder from a number of quarters.[37]

---

[34] League of Nations, Report of the Delegation on Economic Depressions, Part I, *The Transition from War to Peace Economy* (Geneva: League of Nations, 1943), 14, 75–76.

[35] Agreement for the United Nations Relief and Rehabilitation Administration (November 9, 1943); available online at www.loc.gov/law/help/us-treaties/bevans/m-us t000003-0845.pdf

[36] *First Report to Congress on United States Participation in Operations of UNRRA*, as of September 30, 1944 (Washington, D. C.: U.S. Government Printing Office), 5, 8.

[37] For more discussion of the terminology, see Ben Shephard, "'Becoming Planning Minded': The Theory and Practice of Relief 1940–1945," *Journal of Contemporary History* 43:3 (July 2008): 405–419; Jessica Reinisch, "'We Shall Rebuild Anew a Powerful Nation': UNRRA, Internationalism and National Reconstruction in Poland," *Journal of Contemporary History* 43:3 (July 2008): 451–476; Jessica Reinisch, "Internationalism in Relief: The Birth (and Death) of UNRRA," *Past*

In 1943, when in preparation for the conference at Bretton Woods Chinese officials received American and British proposed plans for what would eventually become the International Monetary Fund (IMF) and the International Bank for Reconstruction and Development (IBRD), some immediately noted that "neither plan gives sufficient consideration to the development of industrially weak nations." To help ensure that the final plans did so, they constructed their own draft to take to the conference. In addition, the head of the delegation, Hsiang-Hsi Kung, told the press, "America and others of the United Nations, I hope, will take an active part in aiding the post-war development of China." We want development, he told fellow delegates, not in order "to compete," but "for the purpose of raising the standard of living of our people." China's efforts, combined with the concomitant efforts of several other countries, helped ensure that "the encouragement of the development of productive facilities and resources in less developed countries" became one of the official purposes of the IBRD.[38]

In 1943, reflecting on the forthcoming Bretton Woods Conference, the Hot Springs conference that created the Food and Agriculture Organization (FAO), and UNRRA, the Commission to Study the Organization of Peace declared that the world was creating "the international mechanisms that will be needed to achieve what the great Chinese leader Sun Yat-sen once described as 'the principle of livelihood' – what we now call 'freedom from want.'"[39] It got those mechanisms, US Treasury Secretary Henry Morgenthau later explained, speaking specifically about Bretton Woods, because of the "realization that it is to the economic and political advantage of countries such as India and China, and also of countries such as England and the United States, that the industrialization and betterment of living conditions in the former be achieved with the aid and encouragement of the latter."[40] That realization

---

and Present, Supplement 6 (2011): 258–289; Jessica Reinisch, "'Auntie UNRRA' at the Crossroads," *Past and Present*, Supplement 8 (2013): 70–97; Andrew J. Williams, "'Reconstruction' before the Marshall Plan," *Review of International Studies* 31:3 (July 2005): 541–558.

[38] Helleiner, Forgotten Foundations, 9, 191–200. Also see Daniel Speich Chassé, "Technical Internationalism and Economic Development at the Founding Moment of the UN System," in *International Organizations and Development, 1945–1990*, 23–45.

[39] Commission to Study the Organization of Peace, Fourth Report, Part II: The Economic Organization of Welfare (November 1943) in *Building Peace: Reports of the Commission to Study the Organization of Peace 1939–1972* (Metuchen, NJ: The Scarecrow Press, Inc., 1973), 127.

[40] Quoted in Helleiner, *Forgotten Foundations*, 132.

had been a long time coming, but it had arrived, aided by the new hard data about global standards of living, the idea of the economy, and the global devastations of the war, which made efforts to relieve and rehabilitate Europe far from enough to fulfill the promises of the Atlantic Charter. People asked the dominant Allied powers for development and, convinced that it was in their economic and political interest to do so, the Allies created the "international machinery for the promotion of the economic and social advancement of all people" that the United Nations would promise to employ in its 1945 charter.[41]

That machinery marked a revolution in international affairs, but it was, nevertheless, far more modest in scope and action than its supporters had hoped it would be. It was designed (and funded) to enable a vision of development via primarily the transfer of "expertise" as opposed to development via the transfer of significant amounts of capital and technology. FAO, for example, began with a $5 million budget.[42] In a 1945 message to President Truman about the new agency, the Department of Agriculture explained that "FAO will be an expert consulting agency operating on a modest budget, with nothing to give away free except advice." But that advice would be "the kind that gets results. It will stimulate research and development and the rapid spread of use of knowledge in all its various fields of work."[43] The argument was not disingenuous. People had faith in technological expertise, but political leaders in the world's wealthiest nations – notably the United States – also particularly wanted to have that faith, in the hope that it meant that they would not have to spend too much money on the effort to raise standards of living and strengthen the global economy. The hopes of 1945, however, would give way by 1947. Europe's stalled recovery from the war crushed

---

[41] Charter of the United Nations (June 26, 1945), available at www.un.org/en/sections/un-charter/preamble/. See also, Daniel Maul, "'Help Them Move the ILO Way': The International Labor Organization and the Modernization Discourse in the Era of Decolonization and the Cold War," *Diplomatic History* 33:3 (June 2009): 387–404 and Amy L. S. Staples, *The Birth of Development: How the World Bank, Food and Agriculture Organization, and World Health Organization Changed the World, 1945–1965* (Kent, OH: Kent State University Press, 2006).

[42] United Nations Interim Commission on Food and Agriculture, Facts about FAO (September 11, 1945); United Nations Food and Agriculture Organization, 121–128; President's Secretary's Files; Papers of Harry S. Truman; Harry S. Truman Presidential Library.

[43] Suggested Remarks, G. H. (September 24, 1945); United Nations Food and Agriculture Organization, 121–128; President's Secretary's Files; Papers of Harry S. Truman; Harry S. Truman Presidential Library.

American dreams that the global economy would expand without significant additional effort on its part.

In a June 1947 commencement address, Secretary of State George
Marshall warned his audience that Americans, "distant from the troubled
areas of the earth," did not comprehend how much people were still
suffering and could not, therefore, comprehend the gravity of the threat
it posed to peace. The Allied powers had not been prepared for the extent
of the damage. "In considering the requirements for the rehabilitation of
Europe," Marshall explained, "the physical loss of life, the visible destruction of cities, factories, mines and railroads was correctly estimated, but it
has become obvious during recent months that this visible destruction was
probably less serious than the dislocation of the entire fabric of European
economy." This rehabilitation will take more time and more effort than
we ever imagined, he admitted, and "any assistance that this Government
may render in the future should provide a cure rather than a mere pallia-
tive." And it needed to provide it. The "consequences to the economy of
the United States" of not doing so, Marshall warned, "should be apparent
to all."[44]

Marshall insisted that this new assistance would be "directed not
against any country or doctrine but against hunger, poverty, desperation
and chaos," but that was not true. The United States shut UNRRA down
(with a bit of a delay for the China program) and created the Marshall
Plan to fight the spread of communism.[45] That was a war that it was
willing to put a great deal of effort and money into. Congress brought the
Marshall Plan to life with the creation of the Economic Cooperation
Administration (ECA) in April of 1948 with a budget of about
$4 billion a year. Its creation helped the "development" cause in several
ways. In November of 1947, the president of the IBRD, which, despite its
name, had that year only given out loans to European nations for reconstruction purposes, told the board of executive directors that they "were
going to be driven into a very different field sooner than [he] thought, into
the development field." Forced "to reinvent itself in order to survive,"
development "abruptly became [the bank's] *raison d'être*." It sent its first

---

[44] George C. Marshall, Address at Harvard (June 5, 1947), available at www
.marshallfoundation.org/library/MarshallPlanSpeechfromRecordedAddress_000.html
[45] On the politics of the decision to terminate UNRRA, see Reinisch, "Internationalism in
Relief." The United States, Melvyn Leffler has shown, "launched the Marshall Plan to
arrest an impending shift in the correlation of power between the United States and the
Soviet Union." Melvyn P. Leffler, *A Preponderance of Power* (Stanford, CA: Stanford
University Press, 1992), 163.

General Survey Mission to Colombia in July of 1949 to formulate a "development program designed to raise the standard of living of the Colombian people."[46] In January of 1949, *Pravda* announced the creation of a new Council for Mutual Economic Assistance to help participants in "speeding up the reconstruction and development of their national economies." Comecon would become the foundation of the Soviet Union's international development outreach.[47]

The Marshall Plan also paved the way for the establishment of a new American development program. In his memoirs, Truman wrote that the Marshall Plan and the Greek-Turkish aid program "hinted a new concept which was to be enunciated two years late – the idea of a continuing and self-perpetuating program of technical assistance to the underdeveloped nations of the world which would enable them to help themselves to become growing, strong allies of freedom."[48] In his 1949 inaugural address, Truman announced that the United States was going to "embark on a bold new program for making the benefits of our scientific advances and industrial progress available for the improvement and growth of underdeveloped areas."[49] The Truman administration sold the subsequent program, known as Point Four, as "bold" and "new." As a State Department official readily admitted at the time, the "idea of exchanging knowledge and skills is not new." What was "new and essential," he argued, was the "emphasis on the great importance of economic development in underdeveloped areas and on the concept of an expanded and coordinated approach to the stimulating of technological exchange and capital investment."[50] With Point Four, the United States dedicated itself to strengthening the economies of countries around the world both to

---

[46] Michele Alacevich, "The World Bank and the Politics of Productivity: The Debate on Economic Growth, Poverty, and Living Standards in the 1950s," *Journal of Global History* 6:1 (March 2011): 55–56; Michele Alacevich, *The Political Economy of the World Bank* (Stanford: Stanford Economics and Finance, 2009), 1–15.

[47] Elena Dragomir, "The Formation of the Soviet Bloc's Council for Mutual Economic Assistance," *Journal of Cold War Studies* 14:1 (Winter 2012): 34–36. For a US government perspective of the Council, see CIA, Soviet Economic Assistance to the Sino-Soviet Bloc Countries (June 13, 1955), CIA/SC/RR 103, available at www.cia.gov/library/readingroom/docs/DOC_0000496610.pdf

[48] Harry S. Truman, *Memoirs by Harry S. Truman*, vol. 2 (Garden City, NY: Doubleday & Company, Inc., 1956), 230.

[49] Harry S. Truman, Inaugural Address (January 20, 1949), available at www.trumanlibrary.org/whistlestop/50yr_archive/inaugural20jan1949.htm

[50] State Department, "Building the Peace," *Foreign Affairs Outline* 21 (Spring 1949); Near Eastern and African Staff subject files 1951–1953; Technical Cooperation Administration; RG 469; National Archives College Park.

fight the spread of communism and to expand the global economy. It is, Secretary of State Dean Acheson explained to Congress, "a security measure ... for our military and economic security is vitally dependent on the economic security of other peoples." Point Four's aid, he continued, will help "the people of the underdeveloped areas" not only to develop but to "associate economic progress with an approach to the problems of daily life that preserves and enlarges the initiative, dignity, and freedom of the individual." It would, in other words, convince them not to turn to communism for help.[51]

Point Four was both proactive and reactive. Many of the world's "underdeveloped countries" had expressed "dissatisfaction ... with the American thesis that priority for reconstruction and recovery in Europe was justified because the rest of the world would benefit from the revival of world trade and by the provision of European capital for economic development." They wanted direct, not indirect, aid.[52] They had made their voices heard in several ways, including at the UN General Assembly, which had, in December 1948, passed a resolution calling for the allocation of funds to provide "technical assistance for economic development" all over the world.[53] In the aftermath of its Point Four promise, the US government encouraged this call. In March of 1949, the US delegate to the United Nations proposed the creation of "a comprehensive plan for an expanded cooperative programme of technical assistance for economic development through the United Nations and its specialized agencies."[54]

---

[51] Hearings before the Committee on Foreign Relations on an Act for International Development, United States Senate, 81st Congress, Second Session, March 30 and April 3, 1950 (Washington, D. C.: U.S. Government Printing Office, 1950), 5. For more on Point Four, see Amanda McVety, *Enlightened Aid: U.S. Development as Foreign Policy in Ethiopia* (New York: Oxford University Press, 2012), 83–120; Amanda McVety, "Pursuing Progress: Point Four in Ethiopia," *Diplomatic History* 32:3 (June 2008): 371–403; Stephen Macekura, "The Point Four Program and U.S. International Development Policy," *Political Science Quarterly* 128:1 (Spring 2013): 127–160.

[52] William Adams Brown, Jr. and Redvers Opie, *American Foreign Assistance* (Washington, D. C.: The Brookings Institution, 1953), 389.

[53] UN General Assembly, 3rd session, Resolution 200 (III). Technical assistance for economic development (December 4, 1948); available at www.un.org/documents/ga/res/3/ares3.html

[54] Samuel P. Hayes, Jr., "Truman's 'Bold New Program,'" draft attached to letter from Hayes to Carter (August 26, 1949); Point 4 Memoranda – Miscellaneous; Box 109, NEA-Memoranda, Notes, etc. to UNESCO, 1946–1950; Subject Files of the Chief, 1945–1951; Bureau of Public Affairs, Office of Public Affairs, Division of Public Liaison, Lot File 53D387; RG 59; National Archives and Records Administration, College Park.

The General Assembly, "impressed with the significant contribution to economic development that can be made by an expansion of the international exchange of technical knowledge through international cooperation among countries," adopted resolution 222 that fall, establishing the United Nations Expanded Program of Technical Assistance for Economic Development of Underdeveloped Countries.[55]

In 1950, the United Nations held a Technical Assistance Conference in which fifty countries pledged $20 million for the effort. The United States provided 60 percent of the total.[56] The United Nations FAO was delegated 29 percent of the first $20 million to expand its technical assistance programs. The year before, it had had $1.2 million for that work. In 1952, it received $6.2 million.[57] At the end of that year, its director general reported that "he believed that during the past year FAO had made more progress in its work than in the previous five years of its existence, adding that this was mainly because nations were 'moving ahead more rapidly in the program of technical assistance for economic development.'"[58] And FAO was just one of many organizations that benefited from the shift to technical assistance. Looking back, UN Secretary General Trygve Lie wrote that the American commitment to funding technical assistance gave the UN specialized agencies "new life."[59]

---

[55] Committee on Expenditures in the Executive Departments, *Research Summary on Technical Assistance Proposals of the Food and Agriculture Organization of the United Nations*, House Report no. 670, 82nd Congress, 1st session (Washington, D. C.: U.S. Government Printing Office, 1951), 1–2, 13. On changes in economic thinking at the United Nations during this period, see John Toye and Richard Toye, "How the UN Moved from Full Employment to Economic Development," *Commonwealth and Comparative Politics* 44:1 (March 2006): 16–40.

[56] David Owen, "The United Nations Expanded Program of Technical Assistance – A Multilateral Approach," *Annals of the American Academy of Political and Social Science* 323 (May 1959): 28.

[57] Gove Hambidge, *The Story of FAO* (Toronto: D. Van Nostrand Company, Inc., 1955), 83–84; Richard Jolly, Louis Emmerij, Dharam Ghai, and Frédéric Lapeyre, *UN Contributions to Development Thinking and Practice* (Bloomington, IN: Indiana University Press, 2004), 68–73; P. Lamartine Yates, *So Bold an Aim: Ten Years of International Co-operation Toward Freedom from Want* (Rome: FAO, 1955), 119–121; Francis O. Wilcox, "The United Nations Program for Technical Assistance," *Annals of the American Academy of Political and Social Science* 268 (March 1950): 45–53.

[58] "Food and Agriculture Organization," *International Organization* 7:1 (February 1953): 131.

[59] Trygve Lie, *In the Cause of Peace: Seven Years with the United Nations* (New York: 1954), 146.

That commitment also inspired new forms of organization for development assistance, both to bolster the UN effort and to counter it. Participants at the 1950 Commonwealth Conference on Foreign Affairs in Colombo, Sri Lanka, agreed to create the Colombo Plan for Cooperative Economic Development in South and Southeast Asia. That same year, Britain, France, Belgium, South Africa, Portugal, and Southern Rhodesia launched the Combined Commission for Technical Co-operation in Africa South of the Sahara "to secure," British officials privately explained, "effective arrangements for the co-ordination of action in the technical field between countries having responsibilities in the area, as a substitute for the setting up of bodies for this purpose by the United Nations."[60]

Influenced by the onset of the Cold War and decolonization, postwar international development assistance would not look exactly like interwar international development assistance. It would be far more expansive and far more politically charged.[61] It would also come in a multitude of forms, as later chapters in this volume will show, as people hotly contested what "development" meant and what assistance for it should look like. Despite the differences, however, postwar international development assistance retained much of its prewar origins. The idea that development was essentially about national economic growth and that it could be measured through increased standards of living remained the dominant paradigm.[62] Even initiatives to improve health internationally were often justified as efforts to increase national economic growth.[63] Development remained strongly linked to the wealth of nations, whether people embraced it in the

---

[60] John Kent, *The Internationalization of Colonialism* (Oxford: Clarendon Press, 1992), 264–267. See also, Isebill V. Gruhn, "The Commission for Technical Co-Operation in Africa," *The Journal of Modern African Studies* 9:3 (October 1971): 459–469.

[61] For recent thoughts on this, see David C. Engerman, "Development Politics and the Cold War," *Diplomatic History* 41:1 (January 2017): 1–19. For the classic work on this, see Odd Arne Westad, *The Global Cold War: Third World Interventions and the Making of Our Times* (Cambridge: Cambridge University Press, 2005).

[62] For more on this, see Schmelzer, *The Hegemony of Growth;* Alacevich, "The World Bank and the Politics of Productivity"; Alexander Nützenadel and Daniel Speich, "Editorial – Global Inequality and Development after 1945," *Journal of Global History* 6:1 (2011): 1–5.

[63] See Erez Manela's essay in this volume; Thomas Zimmer, "In the Name of World Health and Development: The World Health Organization and Malaria Eradication in India, 1949–1970," in *International Organizations and Development*, 126–149; Sunil S. Amrith, "Internationalizing Health in the Twentieth Century," in *Internationalisms: A Twentieth-Century History*, ed. Glenda Sluga and Patricia Clavin (Cambridge: Cambridge University Press, 2017), 245–264; Randall M. Packard, "'Roll Back Malaria, Roll in Development': Reassessing the Economic Burden of Malaria," *Population and Development Review* 35:1

hope of bolstering national security, holding together a crumbling empire, improving international welfare, or, indeed, as Sun Yat-sen had argued in 1919, improving the world itself. The extent to which the post–World War II expansion of development assistance actually did improve the world is open to debate, but it is impossible to deny that that assistance has played and continues to play a vital role in international relations. There is no better example of this than China. The nation that in the first half of the twentieth century played a leading role in the effort to convince the international community of the necessity of embracing development in the hope of getting aid became in the twenty-first century one of the world's most influential aid donors.[64]

(March 2009): 53–87; Sanjoy Bhattacharya, *Expunging Variola: The Control and Eradication of Smallpox in India 1947–1977* (New Delhi: Orient Longman, 2006).

[64] Gregg A. Brazinsky, *Winning the Third World: Sino-American Rivalry during the Cold War* (Chapel Hill: University of North Carolina Press, 2017); Giovanni Arrighi, *Adam Smith in Beijing: Lineages of the Twenty-First Century* (London: Verso, 2007); John F. Copper, *China's Foreign Aid and Investment Diplomacy*, vols. 1–3 (New York: Palgrave Macmillan, 2016).

3

The "Development" of Humanitarian Relief: US Disaster Assistance Operations in the Caribbean Basin, 1917–1931

Julia F. Irwin

As categories of international aid, "relief" and "development" might appear to be discrete – analogous in certain respects, but ultimately distinct in form, and driven by a very different set of concerns and objectives. At least, this is how they tend to be treated throughout much of the relevant scholarship. In her survey of twentieth-century foreign aid, for instance, Carol Lancaster defines "aid for relief" as "temporary, aimed at returning people to a situation in which they could provide for their own sustenance." Humanitarian relief, she asserts, is "never intended to bring about 'development' – that is, long-term improvements in economic and social well-being in other countries."[1] In a similar vein, Michael Barnett divides humanitarian assistance into two broad categories, "emergency" and "alchemical," which adhere to a similar definitional logic. The former "concerns the provision of relief to those in immediate peril," while the latter "address[es] the root cause of suffering" by "transform[ing] social, political, economic, and cultural relations so that individuals can lead more productive, healthy, and dignified lives."[2] If relief, according to these definitions, focuses on the *restorative* – saving lives, reducing suffering, and returning societies to a precrisis state – then development emphasizes the *transformative* – the construction of a better future.

To be sure, not all scholars hew to such strict definitions. Even so, many of the most important and influential histories of global development in

[1] Carol Lancaster, *Foreign Aid: Diplomacy, Development, Domestic Politics* (Chicago: University of Chicago Press, 2006), 26.
[2] Michael Barnett, *Empire of Humanity: A History of Humanitarianism* (Ithaca: Cornell University Press, 2013), 37, 39.

recent years tend to reinforce the relief/development dichotomy by focusing predominantly on longer-term technical, agricultural, economic, and military assistance projects, while devoting considerably less attention to short-term, emergency aid efforts for disasters and other humanitarian crises.[3]

But are the divides really so stark? Does it make sense to draw such a solid conceptual line between the temporary, emergency, and restorative nature of humanitarian relief and the long-term, alchemical, and transformative character of development assistance? The answer, as this chapter will argue, is no – at least not in such absolute terms. For in the wake of past humanitarian crises, the boundaries between these two forms of international assistance have regularly blurred. In the course of providing international relief, donor countries and institutions have routinely attempted to effect more comprehensive social, political, and economic changes in the nations receiving their assistance. Far from distinctive, the discourses, practices, and genealogies of relief and development are more deeply intertwined than we may acknowledge.

To demonstrate and substantiate these claims, this chapter presents a case study of the disaster relief operations of one nation, the United States, in three Caribbean Basin countries – Guatemala, the Dominican Republic, and Nicaragua – between World War I and World War II. During these years, the US government and US citizens provided money, material aid, and military assistance to dozens of disaster-stricken countries throughout the world. Among the most intensive and invasive, in terms of their duration and the degree of US involvement, were the US responses to earthquakes in Guatemala (1917–1918) and Nicaragua (1931), and to a hurricane in the Dominican Republic (1930). In each case, US disaster relief efforts evolved into months-long undertakings,

---

[3] See, for example, Nathan Citino, *Envisioning the Arab Future: Modernization in US-Arab Relations, 1945–1967* (New York: Cambridge University Press, 2017); Nick Cullather, *The Hungry World: America's Cold War Battle against Poverty in Asia* (Cambridge: Harvard University Press, 2010); David Ekbladh, *The Great American Mission: Modernization and the Construction of an American World Order* (Princeton: Princeton University Press, 2011); David Engerman et al., eds., *Staging Growth: Modernization, Development, and the Global Cold War* (Amherst: University of Massachusetts Press, 2003); Daniel Immerwahr, *Thinking Small: The United States and the Lure of Community Development* (Cambridge, MA: Harvard University Press, 2015); Michael Latham, *Modernization as Ideology: American Social Science and "Nation Building" in the Kennedy Era* (Chapel Hill: University of North Carolina Press, 2000); Amanda McVety, *Enlightened Aid: U.S. Development as Foreign Policy in Ethiopia* (New York: Oxford University Press, 2012).

designed and administered by committees of US diplomatic, military, and American Red Cross (ARC) officials. During their respective tenures of operation, these individuals not only secured considerable power over relief operations, but also wielded this clout to promote more lasting reforms.

Through a close analysis of the policies and activities of these relief committees, and of the language, rhetoric, goals, and ideology of the US officials who carried them out, this chapter examines the conceptual and material links between relief and development. Outwardly, the members of all three US relief committees defined their work as a temporary mission to save lives and reduce immediate suffering, not as a transformative enterprise. And yet, in the process of organizing and overseeing relief operations, US officials also made a number of subtle (and sometimes not so subtle) attempts to shape local behaviors, decisions, and institutions. Through particular humanitarian activities, they tried to influence existing ideas about health and sanitation, economic and financial policies, and cultures of labor in the nations they assisted. In assuming such extensive authority over other countries' disaster relief operations in the first place, moreover, US relief committees endeavored to model a very specific system of disaster response, one based squarely on their own experiences and precedents. Confident in the superiority of the United States' methods and practices of disaster relief, they imagined that the governments they assisted would learn from their examples and adopt similar approaches in the case of future catastrophes. Beyond simply assisting in the restoration of predisaster conditions, in other words, US officials endeavored to effect permanent, structural changes through their humanitarian aid.

In their transformative ambitions, long-term duration, and emphasis on outside expertise, these three US disaster relief operations thus bore notable parallels to what we more commonly identify as "development assistance." In advancing this claim, it is not my intent to argue that the US relief committees' efforts constituted an active, concerted program of development. Nor do I mean to imply that either US officials or the individuals they assisted would have viewed US disaster aid as a formal development program. Rather, and more modestly, I am proposing a more nuanced reading of these humanitarian activities and the ideologies that underlie them, and suggesting that relief and development overlap much more closely, and in many more respects, than we often recognize. Tracing these points of intersection has much to tell us about the histories of both global humanitarianism and global development.

Indebted to much of the recent historiography of global development, my analysis also builds on the work of Kevin Rozario, Mark Healey, Stuart Schwartz, and other disaster studies scholars. Collectively, their research examines how politicians, military personnel, corporate leaders, and social scientists have embraced disasters as opportunities for implementing or reinforcing desired political, economic, and social policies and practices in catastrophe-stricken societies. Their work also reminds us that the events we call "natural disasters," though routinely termed "acts of God," are in fact always the product – at least in part – of human actions and choices. These insights provide a useful framework for interrogating the "development" of US disaster relief in the Caribbean Basin.[4]

Examining the early twentieth-century history of US relief operations in this region, this chapter also joins many scholars in working to trace the pre–Cold War antecedents of US and global development.[5] Along with Amanda Kay McVety's chapter in this book, it proposes an earlier starting point for the development story. Decades before a more formal modernization theory propelled the Alliance for Progress in Latin America, disaster relief operations gave US actors a pretext for intervening in, and attempting to influence, Caribbean and Central American affairs. If, as Emily Rosenberg, Mary Renda, and others have argued, US dollar diplomacy and military occupations in the Caribbean Basin were the precursors to the United States' post–World War II development discourses and practices, this chapter makes an equivalent case for US-led disaster aid.[6]

---

[4] Kevin Rozario, *The Culture of Calamity: Disaster and the Making of Modern America* (Chicago: University of Chicago Press, 2007); Mark Healey, *The Ruins of the New Argentina: Peronism and the Remaking of San Juan after the 1944 Earthquake* (Durham: Duke University Press, 2011); Stuart Schwartz, *Sea of Storms: A History of Hurricanes in the Greater Caribbean from Columbus to Katrina* (Princeton: Princeton University Press, 2015); Andrea Rees Davies, *Saving San Francisco: Relief and Recovery after the 1906 Disaster* (Philadelphia: Temple University Press, 2011); Naomi Klein, *Shock Doctrine: The Rise of Disaster Capitalism* (New York: Picador, 2008); J. Charles Schencking, *The Great Kanto Earthquake and the Chimera of National Reconstruction in Japan* (New York: Columbia University Press, 2013); Michele Landis Dauber, *The Sympathetic State* (Chicago: University of Chicago Press, 2012).

[5] Michael Adas, *Dominance by Design: Technological Imperatives and America's Civilizing Mission* (Cambridge: Belknap Press, 2009); Ekbladh, *The Great American Mission*; McVety, *Enlightened Aid*; Joseph Morgan Hodge, *Triumph of the Expert: Agrarian Doctrines of Development and the Legacies of British Colonialism* (Athens: Ohio University Press, 2007).

[6] Emily Rosenberg, *Financial Missionaries to the World: The Politics and Culture of Dollar Diplomacy, 1900–1930* (Durham: Duke University Press, 2004); Mary Renda, *Taking*

While tracing the genealogical links between interwar US disaster relief efforts and later development initiatives, finally, this chapter remains attuned to their shared intellectual and cultural roots and their common historical lineage. Domestically, the progenitors for both disaster relief and development assistance can be found in Anglo-US citizens' longstanding and repeated efforts to reform or "civilize" populations they deemed inferior, among them American Indians, African Americans, and immigrants.[7] They can be located, too, in the histories of US welfare and scientific charity, whose middle- and upper-class proponents sought to distinguish the "deserving" from the "undeserving" poor when providing benevolent assistance.[8] Internationally, precursors to disaster relief and development assistance appear time and again throughout the far-flung corners of the US empire. In US territories like the Philippines, Puerto Rico, and the Panama Canal Zone, and in other contemporaneous sites of US involvement, intervention, and occupation – including China, Cuba, Haiti, and Mexico, among others – US Americans engaged in a collective mission to uplift and improve (in their minds, at least) other societies, cultures, and governments.[9] To fully appreciate the connections between interwar disaster aid and later development efforts, it is essential to situate them in these broader historical and historiographical contexts.

THE CATASTROPHES IN GUATEMALA, THE DOMINICAN REPUBLIC, AND NICARAGUA AND THE US RESPONSES TO THEM

On December 25, 1917, a major earthquake struck Guatemala City and its environs. The city had been experiencing smaller tremors since mid-November, but the Christmas Day earthquake proved especially powerful and destructive, leveling hundreds of buildings and rendering thousands

---

Haiti: Military Occupation and the Culture of U.S. Imperialism, 1915–1940 (Chapel Hill: University of North Carolina Press, 2001).

[7] For an introduction, see Ann Laura Stoler, ed., Haunted by Empire: Geographies of Intimacy in North American History (Durham: Duke University Press, 2006); Alyosha Goldstein, ed., Formations of United States Colonialism (Durham: Duke University Press, 2014).

[8] Linda Gordon, Pitied but Not Entitled: Single Mothers and the History of Welfare 1890–1935 (Cambridge, MA: Harvard University Press, 1998); Brent Ruswick, Almost Worthy: The Poor, Paupers, and the Science of Charity in America, 1877–1917 (Bloomington: Indiana University Press, 2012).

[9] For an introduction, see Alfred McCoy and Francisco Scarano, eds., Colonial Crucible: Empire in the Making of the Modern American State (Madison: University of Wisconsin Press, 2009).

homeless. Over the next few weeks, several additional severe shocks occurred, further contributing to the devastation. While relatively few Guatemalans died as a result of the extended period of seismic activity, the material losses were enormous.[10] By the time the quakes subsided, more than 100,000 Guatemalans had lost their homes. The city's hospitals, orphanages, and existing sanitary infrastructures, moreover, were almost entirely destroyed.[11]

While many countries responded to the crisis in Guatemala with gifts of cash or material aid, the response from the United States was particularly noteworthy in its magnitude. On December 28, the ARC – the voluntary organization chartered by Congress to serve as the nation's official international disaster relief agency[12] – wired an initial $5,000 contribution to the US Legation in Guatemala City, raising this contribution to $200,000 a few weeks later.[13] These funds, though amassed from private donations, underwrote a sizable program of US governmental assistance. During the first two weeks of January, US Naval ships carried in large quantities of food, medical supplies, and tents from US bases in the Canal Zone and Key West.[14] US troops and advisers soon appeared on the scene as well. On January 11, a team of US officers, medical professionals, and enlisted men arrived in Guatemala City. Together with the US Chargé d'Affaires, Walter Thurston, and several prominent US nationals in Guatemala, they organized a committee to oversee the US disaster response.[15] Dr. Alvin Struse, head of the Rockefeller Foundation's International Health Board in Guatemala, joined the committee as its medical director. Subsequently, the ARC sent several of its personnel from the United States to assume long-term direction of the committee, including an "experienced relief administrator," John O'Connor, and a sanitary engineer, Edward Stuart.[16] Arriving in

---

[10] William Leavell to Secretary of State [SoS], February 11, 1918, file 814.48/69, Central Files [CF] 1910–1929, Record Group [RG] 59, National Archives [NARA].

[11] Alvin Struse to W. Frank Persons, March 5, 1918, file 891.4/508, box 703, RG 200/2, NARA.

[12] For the ARC's unique quasigovernmental status in foreign aid, see Julia Irwin, *Making the World Safe: The American Red Cross and a Nation's Humanitarian Awakening* (New York: Oxford University Press, 2013).

[13] Minutes of American Red Cross [ARC] Executive Committee Meeting [1918], file 891.4, box 703, RG 200/2, NARA.

[14] Robert Lansing to American Legation in Guatemala, January 9, 1918, file 814.48/27, CF 1910–1929, RG 59, NARA.

[15] Walter Thurston to SoS, January 9, 1918, file 814.48/44, CF 1910–1929, RG 59, NARA.

[16] Persons to Alfred Clark, January 17, 1918, file 814.48/35, CF 1910–1929, RG 59, NARA.

Guatemala in late January, they remained to supervise the committee's relief efforts until early June.[17]

During the US relief committee's roughly six months in operation, its members wielded tremendous influence over aid operations in Guatemala – not only over the United States' contributions, but indeed the entire disaster response. They did so, significantly, with the consent and express authorization of Guatemala's President, Manuel Estrada Cabrera. Shortly after the US relief committee formed, Estrada Cabrera granted its members "full and unquestioned powers" and "supreme control of the city."[18] The President went on to declare existing relief organizations subordinate to the US committee and placed the Guatemalan military at its disposal.[19] Although Estrada Cabrera and other Guatemalan government officials remained closely involved in the disaster response themselves, they had ceded considerable control to US military and diplomatic officials and to ARC and Rockefeller Foundation personnel.

This was not the only instance in which US officials secured such broad authority in the aftermath of a natural disaster in the Caribbean Basin. Thirteen years after the earthquakes in Guatemala, US officials obtained comparable powers over a second regional relief operation, this time in the Dominican Republic. On September 3, 1930, the San Zenon Hurricane made landfall near Santo Domingo, the nation's capital. One of the most destructive Atlantic hurricanes ever recorded, it left as many as 6,000 dead while injuring thousands more. Roughly 70% of the buildings inside Santo Domingo's city walls experienced damage; just outside, that number neared 100%.[20] As in Guatemala, the US response to this catastrophe was swift and substantial. Ships and a new innovation, aircraft, transported US food and other material aid, as well as personnel, from the United States and its Caribbean military outposts to the devastated city. By September 4, the day after the hurricane hit, two US Army officers stationed in Puerto Rico, Major Cary Crockett and Captain Antonio Silva, had arrived in Santo Domingo by plane. Joining them on September 7 was US Naval Commander and surgeon Lucius Johnson, dispatched to Santo Domingo from Haiti, where he had been

---

[17] John O'Connor to the Executive Committee of the ARC Relief Committee, June 11, 1918, file 891.4/08, box 703, RG 200/2, NARA.
[18] Thurston to SoS, January 12, 1918, file 814.48/30, CF 1910–1929, RG 59, NARA.
[19] Thurston to SoS, January 9, 1918, RG 59, NARA.
[20] Ernest Swift to J. Arthur Jeffers, October 8, 1930, file FDR-65.08, box 713, RG 200/2, NARA.

part of the ongoing US Marine occupation. Ernest J. Swift, the ARC's Assistant Director of Insular and Foreign Operations, flew in from Washington the following day.[21]

When the disaster occurred, Rafael Trujillo had recently consolidated his control over the Dominican Republic, having been inaugurated President just weeks before the hurricane struck. Though his relations with the US State Department and the US minister, Charles Curtis, remained icy, Trujillo eagerly accepted US military and ARC assistance.[22] Not only did he welcome US troops and ARC advisers to the country, but he also delegated significant powers to them. In the early days after the hurricane, Trujillo cooperated closely with the ARC's Ernest Swift to devise plans for the relief operation. Upon Swift's return to Washington, Trujillo appointed Major Thomas Watson, a Marine Corps officer and the US Naval Attaché, to head the relief effort. He also named Johnson, the US Naval surgeon, as director of medical relief, and put Crockett in charge of the docks and unloading of relief supplies. Working closely with Trujillo, and financed by a $220,300 appropriation from the ARC, the relief committee would remain in operation for nearly two months, until November 1.[23]

Just a few months later, a similar pattern unfolded yet again in Nicaragua, where a major earthquake occurred on March 31, 1931. The quake and a resulting fire destroyed 90% of Nicaragua's capital city, Managua. Over 1,000 people died, and many thousands more were injured and left homeless.[24] Once again, US ships ferried in supplies and military personnel from US bases in the Caribbean Basin, this time from the Canal Zone and Guantánamo Bay.[25] Unlike in Guatemala and the Dominican Republic, however, the disaster itself did not serve as a catalyst for the US military to intervene, for US Marines were already occupying Nicaragua, and had been since 1927. Although the US government had

---

[21] Swift to James Fieser, September 19, 1930, Folder 9, Box 998, Presidential Foreign Affairs [PFA], Herbert Hoover Presidential Library [HHPL].

[22] Eric Roorda, *The Dictator Next Door: The Good Neighbor Policy and the Trujillo Regime in the Dominican Republic, 1930–1945* (Durham: Duke University Press, 1998), 54–59.

[23] ARC, Press Release, November 16, 1930, file FDR-65.72, box 713, RG 200/2, NARA; ARC Relief Committee, "Report of Relief Work Carried on in Santo Domingo," file FDR-65, box 713, RG 200/2, NARA.

[24] ARC, "Managua Earthquake: Official Report of the Relief Work in Nicaragua after the Earthquake of March 31, 1931," 1931, Correspondence File [CoF] 848, Diplomatic Posts Pre-1936 [DPP-1936] (Nicaragua), RG 84, NARA.

[25] Memorandum, "Assistance the Navy has thus far rendered in Nicaragua disaster," April 1, 1931, file 817.48/61, CF 1930–1939, RG 59, NARA.

announced its intention to withdraw earlier in the year, roughly 1,000 US Marines still remained in Nicaragua at the time of the earthquake.[26] Together with US diplomats and ARC officials, they exercised significant authority over disaster relief efforts.

The day after the quake occurred, the US Minister to Nicaragua, Matthew Hanna, organized meetings with Nicaraguan President José Maria Moncada and the heads of the US Marines and *Guardia Nacional*. As in Guatemala and the Dominican Republic, they quickly established a committee to over-see the relief effort. Chairing it was Hanna, with Moncada assuming the post of Honorary Chairman. Filling out the committee's ranks were then Undersecretary of Foreign Affairs, Anastasio Somoza; the Commander of the US Marines' Second Brigade, Colonel Frederic Bradman; the US Commander of *Guardia Nacional*, Brigadier General Calvin Matthews; and the head of the US Army Engineers in Nicaragua, Lieutenant Colonel Dan Sultan.[27] Once more, the ARC's Ernest Swift flew in from Washington to help plan the relief operations, arriving in Managua on April 3. Supported by a $100,000 appropriation from the ARC, the US-led relief committee oversaw various facets of the Nicaraguan relief effort for more than four months, until mid-August 1931.[28]

THE "DEVELOPMENT" OF US DISASTER RELIEF IN THE CARIBBEAN BASIN

In Guatemala, the Dominican Republic, and Nicaragua, US diplomatic, military, and ARC officials thus assumed substantial and prolonged authority over postcatastrophe assistance. On the surface, all three of these interventions might logically be classified as "humanitarian relief" rather than "development assistance" for at least two reasons. First, all three operations prioritized restorative, rather than transformative, forms of aid. During their respective tenures of operation, US-led relief commit-tees established field kitchens and food distribution centers, which pro-vided cooked and raw food to tens of thousands of disaster survivors. They organized large tent camps to shelter the thousands of homeless

[26] Alan McPherson, *The Invaded: How Latin Americans and Their Allies Fought and Ended U.S. Occupations* (New York: Oxford University Press, 2014), 231; Michel Gobat, *Confronting the American Dream: Nicaragua under U.S. Imperial Rule* (Durham: Duke University Press, 2005), chs. 8 and 9.

[27] Matthew Hanna to SoS, April 3, 1931, file 817.48/53, CF 1930–1939, RG 59, NARA.

[28] Hanna to Swift, July 21, 1931, file FDR-73.08, box 714, RG200/2, NARA; Hanna to José Maria Moncada, August 29, 1931, file FDR-73.67, box 714, RG200/2, NARA.

refugees in each country, and they constructed and staffed temporary hospitals to treat the ill and wounded. They extinguished fires, developed emergency water supply systems, dug latrines, helped bury the dead, and cleared away debris. Collectively, these activities shared the goals of saving lives, meeting basic needs, and returning disaster-stricken societies to some semblance of normalcy. Second, all three US-led relief operations, while lengthy, remained decidedly temporary affairs, officially executed as humanitarian responses to states of emergency. Once US officials determined that immediate needs had been met, US-led relief committees disbanded, expecting local governments to assume responsibility for the longer-term processes of recovery and reconstruction, as well as for more comprehensive social and economic reforms.

Yet if we analyze more closely the nature of these relief activities – and the language, rhetoric, assumptions, and beliefs of the US officials who administered them – a more nuanced and complicated picture begins to emerge. While providing relief, US officials simultaneously attempted to influence disaster-stricken societies and to sway individual behaviors and beliefs. Through *restorative* forms of assistance, in short, US relief committees also endeavored, whether consciously or not, to *transform* the nations they assisted. In both form and underlying ideology, the US relief efforts in Guatemala City, Santo Domingo, and Managua bore a resemblance – sometimes faint, sometimes more discernible – to many of the twentieth century's more familiar global development projects.

At the most fundamental level, these operations mirrored development projects in the sense that US officials in all three countries were guided by the objective of improving existing approaches to disaster response. Highly skeptical of the individuals they assisted, US officials believed that Guatemalans, Dominicans, and Nicaraguans were incapable of carrying out effective disaster relief operations themselves. In Guatemala City, the members of the US legation disparaged the "native relief committee" for its "grafting and inefficiency," informing the State Department that, "with the leisurely ways and the inadequate methods of these people it will take months to clear away the debris."[29] Similarly in Santo Domingo, the US Minister complained that most local officials had "shown the lack of competence which was to be expected in the handling of the situation created by the terrible disaster," adding that they had

---

[29] Thurston to SoS, January 12, 1918, RG 59, NARA; Leavell to SoS, February 11, 1918, RG 59, NARA.

"proved themselves thoroughly incompetent and often dishonest."[30] Deeply distrustful of Latin American capabilities, US officials emphasized "the necessity of placing the whole situation in the hands of people who would impartially and drastically handle it," insisting, "it is absolutely essential that we strictly supervise the distribution of all ... money, medicines, food and shelter."[31]

With broad authority over aid operations, US committees employed their own methods and practices of disaster relief. As they did so, they modeled a system that was invariably based on approaches then considered best practices in the United States. Beginning in the late nineteenth century, but particularly in the years following the 1906 San Francisco earthquake, US social scientists and ARC officials – so-called "disaster experts" – had developed a common, standardized set of assumptions about what constituted a proper and effective response to catastrophe.[32] These "principles of relief," influenced by the era's scientific charity movement, emphasized the importance of careful record keeping and audits, as well as oversight by experienced professionals who were trained to provide relief "calmly, systematically and expeditiously." Additionally, fearing the potential of aid to "lessen the sense of responsibility ... and encourage idleness and dependence," US disaster experts stressed that relief should be extended only to those judged truly deserving, and then for as short a duration as possible.[33]

Well entrenched in US culture by World War I and into the 1930s, these principles of relief infused the US disaster responses in Guatemala, the Dominican Republic, and Nicaragua. By organizing their aid according to these precepts, US relief committees believed, they stood to improve the local approaches that they had judged so inferior. To underscore the importance of technocratic, medical, and social scientific professionals to administering an effective disaster response, they provided the "expert advisory assistance" of ARC disaster management specialists, US physicians and surgeons, and

---

[30] Charles Curtis to SoS, September 15, 1930, CoF 848/174, DPP-1936 (Dominican Republic), RG 84, NARA.

[31] Thurston to SoS, January 9, 1918, RG 59, NARA.

[32] Scott Knowles, *The Disaster Experts: Mastering Risk in Modern America* (Philadelphia: University of Pennsylvania Press, 2013); Jones, *The American Red Cross*, chs. 6–9; Davies, *Saving San Francisco*, chs. 2 and 4.

[33] Ernest Bicknell, "Relief Measures and Methods in Times of Disaster," 1913, file 494.1, box 34, RG 200/1, NARA; Edward Devine, *The Principles of Relief* (New York: The Macmillan Company, 1904).

US sanitary engineers.[34] To counter the perceived threat of graft and ensure that relief reached only those they deemed "deserving," the three US relief committees established ration card systems, which allowed them to strictly control and monitor survivors' access to food supplies. To document their efforts, they compiled numerous, lengthy reports, where they narrated progress and results and provided detailed financial accounting.[35] By adhering to these and other procedures, relief committees endeavored to export the principles of US disaster experts to the Caribbean Basin.

Confident in the superiority of their methods, the members of the three US relief committees lauded the effectiveness and professionalism of their assistance. In Guatemala City, US officials declared that thanks to their system, disaster survivors had been "protected against the abuses of the petty officials," while in Nicaragua, they avowed that "the possibility of abuse was eliminated or minimized" due to their procedures.[36] US officials also took pride in the belief that aid recipients sought and valued their expertise. Relief committee members in Guatemala were gratified that government officials "are turning to us more and more for expert advice."[37] In the Dominican Republic, they commended Trujillo for having "had the courage to give such wide powers and such firm support to foreigners."[38] Buoyed by the influence they felt they had exerted, US officials envisioned that the principles and practices of disaster relief they endorsed would take hold permanently, improving the response to future catastrophes in the region.

Thus, just as they assumed an obligation to teach Latin American peoples "to elect good men" and to manage their finances and customs houses, US officials saw it as their responsibility to influence existing methods, practices, and principles of disaster relief in the Caribbean Basin. In this more general sense, US disaster relief operations in Guatemala, the Dominican Republic, and Nicaragua arguably manifested

---

[34] J. O'Connor to Persons, February 5, 1918, file 814.48/93, CF 1910–1929, RG 59, NARA.

[35] See, for example, J. O'Connor to Persons, February 5, 1918, RG 59, NARA; ARC Relief Committee, "Report of Relief Work Carried on in Santo Domingo," RG 200/2, NARA; and William Beaulac, "Report on the Work of the American Red Cross to Relieve Distress in Nicaragua," September 1931, file 817.48/193, CF 1930–1939, RG 59, NARA.

[36] Herbert Apfel, "Report of the Camp Department," June 5, 1918, file 891.4/68, box 703, RG 200/2, NARA; ARC, "Managua Earthquake," 1931, RG 84, NARA.

[37] J. O'Connor to Persons, February 5, 1918, RG 59, NARA.

[38] Curtis to SoS, September 22, 1930, CoF 848/181, DPP-1936 (Dominican Republic), RG 84, NARA.

the transformative aspirations inherent in many development assistance projects. But in addition to this broader, more far-reaching goal of inculcating new methods and practices of relief, these three US interventions paralleled development assistance in another way as well: underlying many relief activities was a desire (if sometimes tacit) to influence specific beliefs, behaviors, and institutions. As Andrea Davies, Kevin Rozario, and other disaster studies scholars have argued, authorities and elites have historically used relief as a tool for compelling desired behaviors. By controlling the way relief was designed and distributed, those in charge of aid operations have held great power to reinforce existing social and economic hierarchies and expectations; alternatively, they have used their positions to dismantle predisaster structures and practices and to cultivate new ones in their place.[39]

In Guatemala, the Dominican Republic, and Nicaragua, both of these dynamics came into play, most notably in the fields of health and sanitation, on the one hand, and labor and economics, on the other. In these two areas, US committees wielded relief as an instrument to promote ideas and practices they considered desirable and to discourage those they deemed backward or improper. In so doing, they further mirrored the discourses, ideologies, and practices common to more identifiable development projects.

In the fields of health and sanitation, US relief committee members attempted to influence the societies they aided in several ways. One such channel was through the medical institutions they established. In Guatemala City, for example, US relief committee members constructed and ran a temporary hospital for earthquake survivors. From the beginning, however, US officials saw the hospital as more than a place for providing medical care; they also envisioned it as a site for demonstrating new medical approaches to Guatemalan physicians. As the Rockefeller Foundation physician in charge of the institution put it, much of the hospital's value lay in "stimulating the Guatemalan [medical] profession" to adopt new methods of care and prevention.[40] In addition to targeting medical professionals, they also attempted to reach ordinary citizens. Through an outpatient Children's Department connected to the hospital, US officials provided food to infants while "teach[ing] the mothers proper methods to prepare and administer food to their dying children." Through

[39] See footnote 5.
[40] Struse to Persons, April 2, 1918, File 814.48, CF 1910–1929, RG 59, NARA.

such efforts, US officials boasted, the "improvement in baby feeding and baby care could be easily accomplished."[41]

Hoping to maintain the influence of these institutions long after they had departed, US relief committee members in Guatemala later purchased and donated all the equipment required for a new 600-bed general hospital. By outfitting the city's general hospital, committee members reasoned, they stood to "leave a permanent stamp" on Guatemalan medical practices.[42] Similarly in Nicaragua, the US relief committee persuaded the ARC to fund the construction and outfitting of a brand new leper hospital. Noting that the conditions in Managua's current leper colony were "indescribably horrible" and "not suitable for a modern pig sty," they determined to replace it with "adequate hospital facilities" that would provide continuing medical care once the relief committee disbanded.[43] Through these various medical institutions, both temporary and permanent, US officials aspired to shape health outcomes in the Caribbean Basin well into the future.

While hospitals presented US relief committees with specific sites for influencing physicians and patients, scientific and social surveys represented a second, broader channel through which US officials tried to transform health and hygienic conditions. The activities undertaken by the US relief committee in Guatemala provide a good illustration of these types of projects. There, the head of the relief committee's engineering division, US sanitary engineer Edward Stuart, undertook a thorough study of Guatemala City's existing water supply. Determining that "the present systems are not clean and healthful, and the population of the city are not as happy and healthy as they would be with a good water supply," Stuart prepared detailed plans for a permanent, up-to-date water treatment and distribution system, which he subsequently presented to the Guatemalan government.[44] Other members of the committee, meanwhile, conducted a comprehensive social survey of the roughly 1,200 families living in the US-administered tent camp. Upon discovering "appalling" conditions,

---

[41] "Hospital Report," May 22, 1918, in *Report of the Medical Relief of the American Red Cross in the Catastrophe of Guatemala City*, 1918, file 891.4/508, box 703, RG 200/2, NARA; Louise O'Connor to ARC Executive Committee, June 1, 1918, file 891.4/08, box 703, RG 200/2, NARA.

[42] Struse to Persons, April 2, 1918, RG 59, NARA; Minutes of ARC Executive Committee Meeting [1918], RG 200/2, NARA.

[43] Hanna to Swift, August 22, 1931, file FDR-73, box 714, RG 200/2, NARA; Hanna to Moncada, August 29, 1931; file FDR-73, box 714, RG 200/2, NARA.

[44] Edward Stuart, "Recommendations Regarding a Permanent Water Supply for the City of Guatemala," June 1, 1918, file 891.4/51, box 703, RG 200/2, NARA.

including an infant mortality rate of 60% and widespread evidence of "insufficient and improper nourishment," the relief committee reported their findings to Guatemalan government officials, recommending that "it will be necessary ... to give state aid in this matter, which is of vital importance for the future of the country." By making such investments, US officials stressed, "the power of the country both economically and otherwise would be greatly enhanced."[45] US officials, it bears noting, did not commit additional resources toward improving Guatemala City's water supply or infant mortality rates, deeming these more comprehensive reform projects the Guatemalan government's responsibility. Nonetheless, they understood their surveys as a necessary first step in developing the nation's health.

In addition to analyzing public health concerns through surveys, the members of the three US relief committees also employed compulsive and coercive measures, a third form of intervention, in their quest to inculcate new medical beliefs and hygienic behaviors. In Guatemala, the US relief committee advised the government to adopt a wide slate of new sanitary laws, making compulsory such things as smallpox and typhoid vaccination, underground burials, and the use of latrines, and mandating "the imprisonment of any person guilty of soil pollution."[46] While the Estrada Cabrera administration did not enact all of these suggestions, it did implement many of the committee's recommendations. To enforce these new laws, again at the US relief committee's urging, Estrada Cabrera established a sanitary police force, led by an American "soldier of fortune" named General Lee Christmas, and granted its members broad authority over alleged offenders.[47]

In the Dominican Republic and Nicaragua, US relief committees found their own mechanisms for compelling consent. In Santo Domingo, the relief committee mandated that all Dominicans receive a typhoid inoculation before they would be eligible for any food rations, and required relief recipients to present a certificate of inoculation in order to receive food aid. Within just four days, due in part to such pressure tactics, they administered over 12,000 vaccinations.[48] In Managua, meanwhile, the US commander of the *Guardia Nacional* declared martial law on the day

[45] L. O'Connor to ARC Executive Committee, June 1, 1918, RG 200/2, NARA; Apfel, "Report of the Camp Department," June 5, 1918, RG 200/2, NARA.
[46] "Preventive Medicine," in *Report of the Medical Relief of the American Red Cross*, 1918, file 891.4/508, box 703, RG 200/2, NARA.
[47] Stuart to Persons, February 11, 1918, file 814.48/61, CF 1910–1929, RG 59, NARA.
[48] Swift to Fieser, September 19, 1930, PFA, HHPL.

of the earthquake, proclaiming broad powers for many US officials in Nicaragua.[49] Among its many effects, this order gave the head of the emergency sanitary service – Colonel Gordon Hale, part of the *Guardia Nacional*'s Medical Corps and a US Naval Commander – wide (if temporary) latitude to police the hygienic behaviors of Nicaraguan disaster survivors.[50] While the primary and stated intent of these various regulations and policies was to reduce the immediate risk of postdisaster epidemics, US relief committee members also understood that these emergency measures, policies, and legislation all held the potential to leave lasting effects on the public's health.

If endeavoring to influence health and sanitation represented a central and persistent concern of the US relief committees in Guatemala, the Dominican Republic, and Nicaragua, US officials also devoted significant attention to issues of labor and economics in all three countries. As Emily Rosenberg has persuasively shown in her work on dollar diplomacy, US political elites in the early twentieth century regarded the promotion of capitalism itself as a tool of civilization and development. Throughout the Caribbean Basin, US officials had worked to spread capitalist values and institutions through such channels as international lending and financial advising.[51] Disaster relief operations would serve a similar function in the region, in several implicit ways.

First, through the design and implementation of their food relief programs, US officials strove to promote a culture of work and labor discipline. In the minds of many contemporary US Americans, Caribbean and Central American populations proved deficient in these values even in normal times, and all the more so in the aftermath of major catastrophes. Of particular concern to the members of the three US relief committees was the belief that providing food to disaster survivors would encourage dependency and idleness. In the Dominican Republic, US officials argued that the "continued issue of free food would tend to keep some of the people from going to work."[52] In Nicaragua, likewise, they stressed "the necessity of reducing and eventually discontinuing the free distribution" in order to avoid "the creation of a beggar class."[53] Given these fears, committee members in both countries opted to discontinue most food

---

[49] Hanna to Moncada, April 14, 1931, CoF 848, DPP-1936 (Nicaragua), RG 84, NARA.
[50] ARC, "Managua Earthquake," 1931, RG 84, NARA.
[51] Rosenberg, *Financial Missionaries to the World*.
[52] ARC Relief Committee, "Report of Relief Work Carried on in Santo Domingo," RG 200/2, NARA.
[53] Hanna to Moncada, April 30, 1931, CoF 848, DPP-1936 (Nicaragua), RG 84, NARA.

rations just weeks after the disasters struck. While admitting that such steps might seem "very drastic measures," as the US relief committee in Santo Domingo put it, US officials nonetheless deemed them "necessary to force the people, as a whole, to understand that free food was not going to be available for them forever."[54]

In place of free food distributions, US officials in the Dominican Republic and Nicaragua instead instituted programs of labor relief. Under these programs, US relief committees compensated men, and some women, for clearing streets, hauling away debris, repairing roads and buildings, and performing other tasks related to recovery and rebuilding. Workers in Santo Domingo received "three meals a day and some cigarettes" for their labor, while their counterparts in Managua earned forty cents per day.[55] As Mary Renda has argued in her work on US-occupied Haiti, US authorities believed that employing Latin American civilians in public works projects would instill appreciation for wage labor and serve as a "means to economic development."[56] The same held true, in US officials' minds, with respect to Dominican and Nicaraguan disaster survivors. US officials in both countries heralded work relief programs for their ability to stimulate industrious behavior. In Nicaragua, moreover, they regarded labor relief as a "vitally necessary" tactic in the Marines' and *Guardia Nacional's* ongoing counterinsurgency operations. Warning that "the germs [of disorder] are present and are spreading and may easily become dangerous if not stamped out," the chair of the US relief committee, US Minister Matthew Hanna, insisted that "employment for those out of work ... as a consequence of the disaster will help to prevent such disorder."[57] Speaking for many US officials, in both Nicaragua and the Dominican Republic, Hanna judged "the employment of labor ... our principal and most beneficial form of relief."[58]

While US officials worked to reinforce capitalist values among disaster survivors by limiting the distribution of free food and instituting work relief programs, they also attempted to influence the economic policies of Latin American governments by giving them frequent financial advice.

---

[54] ARC Relief Committee, "Report of Relief Work Carried on in Santo Domingo," RG 200/2, NARA.

[55] ARC Relief Committee, "Report of Relief Work Carried on in Santo Domingo," RG 200/2, NARA; Swift, "Managua, Nicaragua Earthquake," Annex to League of Red Cross Societies Circular Letter, May 1931, file FDR-73.08, box 714, RG 200/2, NARA.

[56] Renda, *Taking Haiti*, 117–118.

[57] Hanna to SoS, April 10, 1931, file 817.48/114, CF 1930–1939, RG 59, NARA.

[58] Hanna to Swift, June 6, 1931, CoF 848, DPP-1936 (Nicaragua), RG 84, NARA.

In Guatemala, for example, members of the US relief committee "suggested that the government tax each property owner according to the number of carts of debris" it hauled away. They also advised government officials to finance such civic improvements as the laying down of rail tracks, the construction of public toilets, and various other public health and sanitary reforms.[59] In the Dominican Republic, the US government intervened even more actively in the country's financial affairs. Three weeks after the San Zenon Hurricane struck, President Herbert Hoover sent Eliot Wadsworth, a long-time member of the ARC's governing Central Committee and former Assistant Secretary of the Treasury, to Santo Domingo on an economic mission. Explaining that "questions of reconstruction of the city of San Domingo and readjustment of San Domingo finances call for careful planning and first-hand knowledge," Hoover dispatched Wadsworth with instructions "to advise [the Trujillo] Government on those subjects."[60] Twenty-six years after Theodore Roosevelt first seized the Dominican customs houses, the Hoover administration had found, in the aftermath of disaster, an opportunity to exert its own sway on the Dominican Republic's economic affairs.

***

In a variety of ways – through their attempts to influence labor and economics, health and sanitation, and the system of disaster assistance more generally – US officials had attempted to leave their mark on Guatemalan, Dominican, and Nicaraguan affairs through the channels of humanitarian relief. While primarily and ostensibly focused on providing restorative forms of assistance, they had also endeavored, through those same relief activities, to effect changes of a more transformative nature. Operating with the consent of, and in collaboration with, Latin American governing elites and strong-armed rulers, US relief committees assumed significant powers and influence over disaster-stricken populations. As their words and actions made clear, they also believed they had an obligation to do so. Driving their relief efforts was a conviction that the United States not only could, but indeed must, help steer the internal affairs of other nations. Bolstering them was a confidence in US expertise over disaster management, paired with a deep distrust in Latin American countries' disaster response capabilities.

---

[59] O'Connor to Persons, February 5, 1918, RG 59, NARA.
[60] Herbert Hoover, Draft of Press Statement, September 22, 1930, Folder 9, Box 998, PFA, HHPL.

Although this chapter has focused on the ideologies, rhetoric, and exploits of the US officials involved in these aid efforts, its findings also compel us to consider how Guatemalan, Dominican, and Nicaraguan disaster survivors understood the US relief efforts detailed in the preceding pages. How did the survivors of catastrophic earthquakes and hurricanes – many of them homeless, hungry, wounded, and in real need of relief – respond to US aid and its accompanying exercises of social control and coercion? In a region marked by decades of US invasions and occupations, how did these same men and women react to the extended presence of US officials – many of them uniformed troops, many of them in positions of direct authority over aid recipients – in their ruined and recovering cities? While the answers to these questions are beyond the scope of this article, I invite and encourage future researchers to study how the residents of disaster-stricken countries experienced, to borrow Timothy Nunan's provocative term, these U.S. "humanitarian invasions."[61]

CONCLUSION: BRIDGING THE RELIEF/DEVELOPMENT DIVIDE

US disaster relief operations in the interwar Caribbean Basin thus resembled, in key respects, many of the twentieth century's more familiar development projects. To be sure, neither the members of the US relief committees nor the individuals they aided necessarily considered their activities "development assistance." Yet in hindsight, and through closer analysis, clear parallels materialize. Even if many of these parallels were admittedly implicit, moreover, at least one US official at the time was beginning to think more consciously about the relationship between disasters, emergency relief, and long-term development. Having witnessed the earthquakes and ensuing relief effort in Managua, US Minister Matthew Hanna arrived at a sober conclusion. "When I try to differentiate between distress resulting from the earthquake and from some other cause," he admitted, "I am at a loss to know where to draw the line."[62] Disasters and development, as Hanna had started to appreciate, were in fact intimately intertwined. Perhaps, it followed, disaster relief and development assistance should be more closely aligned as well.

Today, a century later, practitioners and policymakers have gained an increasingly nuanced and sophisticated understanding of the links

---

[61] Timothy Nunan, *Humanitarian Invasion: Global Development in Cold War Afghanistan* (New York: Cambridge University Press, 2015).
[62] Hanna to Swift, July 21, 1931, RG 200/2, NARA.

between disasters, disaster management, and global development – and they have come to appreciate several unfortunate truths. First, the economic, environmental, and human costs of disasters are borne most heavily by the world's poorest, least developed countries, and among the most marginalized populations within those nations. Second, in order to finance postdisaster relief, recovery, and reconstruction, states are often compelled to divert funds from ongoing development activities, thus slowing poverty reduction efforts, infrastructural improvements, and other related projects. Third, complicating matters further, the process of development itself often increases vulnerability to disasters by damaging local ecosystems and by encouraging migration into hastily and poorly constructed urban areas, where large populations are put at risk. For these reasons, "disasters," as a 2013 Oxfam report puts it succinctly, "have a devastating impact on development."[63]

As awareness about these interconnected issues has grown in recent years, however, the international community has also taken more concerted action to address them, and has begun to actively incorporate disaster management into development planning. In 2001, United Nations (UN) Secretary-General Kofi Annan called on member states to "intensify our collective efforts to reduce the number and effects of natural and man-made disasters," declaring this a necessary step toward achieving the UN's Millennium Development Goals.[64] More recently, in 2015, the UN General Assembly pledged "to promote resilience and disaster risk reduction" as part of its 2030 Agenda for Sustainable Development.[65]

Following the international community's lead, we scholars of global assistance would do well to consider more critically the links between disasters and development, and between humanitarian relief and development assistance. For as this chapter has sought to demonstrate, the discourses, ideologies, and practices of relief and development are not discrete, but in fact deeply interconnected. At the same time, we should

---

[63] Debbie Hiller and Katherine Nightingale, *How Disasters Disrupt Development* (Oxford: Oxfam International, 2013). https://www.oxfam.org/en/research/how-disasters-disrupt-development.

[64] Report of the Secretary-General A/56/326, "Road map towards the implementation of the United Nations Millennium Declaration," September 6, 2001, p. 33, www.un.org/documents/ga/docs/56/a56326.

[65] United Nations General Assembly Resolution A/70/1, "Transforming Our World: The 2030 Agenda for Sustainable Development," October 21, 2015, p. 9, http://www.un.org/ga/search/view_doc.asp?symbol=A/RES/70/1.

cast our gazes further back in time, before the Cold War era, to search for earlier chapters in the development story. If we are to better understand the origins of development as a global practice, in short, it would behoove us to devote further attention to the years before 1945, and to the "development" of humanitarian relief.

As we do so, we should also reflect on the lessons that both scholars and practitioners can draw from this history. Specifically, we should think more critically about the profoundly unequal power dynamic that so often exists between donors and recipients of international aid. We should consider, too, how to supplant coercion and control in the distribution of aid with more cooperative and collaborative approaches. Achieving these outcomes, and ensuring the humanity and respect of aid recipients, would indeed be a positive development.

4

Imperial and Transnational Developmentalisms: Middle Eastern Interplays, 1880s–1960s

Cyrus Schayegh

In the past two decades, development historians have expanded their field with works that are "longer" in time, "deeper" actor-wise, and thematically "wider" than earlier analyses, which defined development rather ahistorically as a hegemonic "intellectual and ideological project" producing and dominating the postcolonial Third World.[1] Even so, this chapter argues, the development literature continues to rest on a twofold tacit assumption. The world of development is composed of Western imperial metropoles and their overseas colonies, and (postcolonially and during the Cold War) of nation-states in the Global North and Global South. In consequence, while multiple groups were negotiating development, they were basically situated in Western imperial metropoles and their overseas colonies or, postcolonially, in nation-states in the Global North and Global South.[2]

---

[1] Quote: Joseph Hodge, "Writing the History of Development (Part I: The First Wave)," *Humanity* 6 (2015): 438; see also, Hodge, "Writing the History of Development (Part II: Longer, Deeper, Wider)," *Humanity* 7 (2015): 125–174.

[2] Examples include Joseph Hodge and Gerard Hödl, "Introduction," in *Developing Africa: Concepts and Practices in Twentieth-Century Colonialism* (Manchester: Manchester University Press, 2014), 1–34; Joseph Hodge, *Triumph of the Expert: Agrarian Doctrines of Development and the Legacies of British Colonialism* (Athens: Ohio University Press, 2007); Suzanne Moon, *Technology and Ethical Idealism: A History of Development in the Netherlands East Indies* (Leiden: CNWS Publications, 2007); David Biggs, *Quagmire: Nation-Building and Nature in the Mekong Delta* (Seattle: University of Washington Press, 2010); Helene Tilley, *Africa as a Living Laboratory: Empire, Development, and the Problem of Scientific Knowledge* (Chicago: University of Chicago Press, 2011); Benjamin Zachariah, *Developing India: An Intellectual and Social History, c. 1930–1950* (New Delhi: Oxford University Press, 2012); and Allen F. Isaacman and Barbara S. Isaacman, *Dams, Displacement, and the Delusion of Development:*

To be sure, recent historians of development have become interested in international organizations linking up Northern and Southern countries. And historians of colonial development are now treating colonies as spaces, not simply of development domination, but of negotiations between colonial subjects and bureaucrats who interpreted policies issued by metropolitan centers. In effect, they use development as a case study: as a meeting area of metropolitan and colonial actors.[3]

Spatially, however, recent studies mirror earlier texts' view of the world of development as being constituted by colonies/postcolonial countries and imperial/postimperial metropoles. Symptomatically, many a development history centers on, or at least deals with, Africa. Recent interest in the question of continuity and change from colonial to postcolonial times, although well taken, inadvertently keeps our eyes glued on colonies/postcolonial countries and Northern imperial metropoles. And historians interested in international development organizations linking Northern and Southern countries see the objective of those organizations as the Global South.[4]

This does not quite do. First, from the nineteenth century, development – broadly defined as state and society improving people's material conditions and seeking to strengthen economic power underpinning those conditions – was seen also by non-Westerners as a key reason, yardstick, and/or proof of Western empires' global dominance. In conjunction, the world economy became quite firmly Eurocentric. In consequence, development was not simply a colonial issue but a global one – one molded by the world's uneven power constellation.[5] On a related note,

---

Cahora Bassa and Its Legacies in Mozambique, 1965–2007 (Athens: Ohio University Press, 2013).

[3] In effect, this approach adopts views, especially in British Empire studies, of the empire not as hub-and-spokes, and not as metropole here and colony there, but as an asymmetrical web whose study ought to integrate colonial and metropolitan actors in one analytical frame. Antoinette Burton and Tony Ballantyne, "Introduction," in *Bodies in Contact: Rethinking Colonial Encounters in World History* (Durham: Duke University Press, 2005), 3, talk of "webs of trade, knowledge, migration, military power, and political intervention that allowed certain communities to assert their influence and sovereignty over other groups." Related, John Darwin, *The Empire Project: The Rise and Fall of the British World-System, 1830–1970* (Cambridge: Cambridge University Press, 2009), 1, calls the empire a "far-flung conglomerate." And Darwin, "Imperialism and the Victorians: The Dynamics of Territorial Expansion," *English Historical Review* 112 (1997): 629, asks historians to investigate "bridgeheads" in which metropole and colony interact.

[4] For literature, see, for example, Hodge, "Writing," 2:164n39–41.

[5] See Martin Thomas and Andrew Thompson, "Empire and Globalisation: From 'High Imperialism' to Decolonisation," *International History Review* 36 (2014): 142–170; Christopher Bayly, *The Birth of the Modern World, 1780–1914* (Malden: Blackwell,

self-development, i.e., individuals' attempt to become more productive, was a global trend, too, but assumed special significance among non-Westerners. Derisively othered as unproductive or wrongly productive, the latter othered themselves while rejecting Western claims of being barely or not reformable.

Moreover, the pre–Cold War modern world included polities that were neither simply a Northern imperial metropole nor a European colony created before or during the peak of European imperial expansion in the later nineteenth century. A case in point was Asian empires. These included the Ottoman Empire and its League of Nations Mandate successors – British Palestine and Transjordan and Iraq, and French Lebanon and Syria, all formed in the late 1910s and independent in 1930–1932 (Iraq) and the mid- to late 1940s (all others) – on which this chapter will focus.

Last, those polities were not neatly wedged between Northern imperial metropoles on the one side and, on the other, European colonies. Put differently, they were not homogeneous, airtight, unified spaces. In consequence – and to stay with this chapter's case – development projects were not simply devised within, and for, each Ottoman and post-Ottoman polity. Rather, these lands and populations nurtured various development projects, which were mutually linked and tied into a globalizing, unevenly structured world.

Specifically, this Ottoman/post-Ottoman case study evinces three interplaying dimensions, which can also be tracked through time across the Ottoman/post-Ottoman break. The first dimension is vertical intraimperial: subimperial developmentalist projects whose actors situated themselves within a broader imperial project. The second dimension is horizontal intraimperial, i.e., from the late 1910s Middle-East-wide transnational. It refers to how subimperial developmentalist projects interplayed, and how those interplays persisted after 1918. And the third dimension is transnational/transimperial; it concerns the flux into and out of Ottoman and post-Ottoman polities of developmentalist ideas devised in empires around the world. In all dimensions, developmentalists were not only empire and/or nation-state builders.

In what follows, I first lay out Ottoman imperial developmentalism, and then present interplays between the above three dimensions through

2004); Jürgen Osterhammel, *The Transformation of the World. A Global History of the Nineteenth Century* (Princeton: Princeton University Press, 2014).

a study of developmentalism in, across, and beyond the Ottoman and post-Ottoman "new Yishuv" (the Zionist settlement in Palestine that started in 1882) and the port city of Beirut.

LATE OTTOMAN DEVELOPMENTALISM

Post-1905 Japan aside, Asian empires were (and were seen as) weaker than European empires in the nineteenth century until World War I. But some, like Iran, the Ottoman Empire, or China, were not weak or malpositioned enough to be entirely pulled to pieces and/or to be colonized.[6] Thus, the Ottoman Empire was not simply "the sick man of Europe," a rather self-serving epithet that Europeans flung at it from the mid-nineteenth century. Rather, it was "a major, albeit weak, actor in European diplomacy . . . [and] European and Ottoman political practices and ideas were inextricably intertwined."[7] Even when, or rather precisely when, it was on the back foot – bit by bit losing provinces in Europe and Africa, though not in Asia – Istanbul tried to play the empire game in foreign policy, seeking to expand into Africa, push back against Russia, blunt British rule in Egypt, and be recognized as a fellow empire by Europeans. Further, exploiting the fact that the sultan was also the Sunni world's caliph, Istanbul nurtured pan-Islamic and pan-Asian ideas, especially the latter in contact with Japan, to counteract Western discourses of superiority and undermine Western colonies with Muslim populations.[8]

---

[6] Historians indeed have called for analyzing Asian and European empires together, for they were incessantly, systemically interacting. See Michael Adas, "Imperialism and Colonialism in Comparative Perspective," *International History Review* 20 (1998): 371–388; Kenneth Pomeranz, "Empire and 'Civilizing Missions,' Past and Present," *Daedalus* 134 (2005): 34–45; Dina Khury and Dane Kennedy, "Comparing Empires: The Ottoman Domains and the British Raj in the Long Nineteenth Century," *Comparative Studies of South Asia, Africa, and the Middle East* 27:2 (2007): 233–244.

[7] Aimee Genell, "Empire by Law: Ottoman Sovereignty and the British Occupation of Egypt, 1882–1923" (PhD diss., Columbia University, 2013), 6.

[8] Mostafa Minawi, *The Ottoman Scramble for Africa: Empire and Diplomacy in the Sahara and the Hijaz* (Stanford: Stanford University Press, 2016); Michael Reynolds, *Shattering Empires: The Clash and Collapse of the Ottoman and Russian Empires, 1908–1918* (Cambridge: Cambridge University Press, 2011); Cemil Aydin, *The Politics of Anti-Westernism in Asia: Visions of World Order in Pan-Islamic and Pan-Asian Thought* (New York: Columbia University Press, 2007); Genell, "Empire by Law;" Azmi Özcan, *Pan-Islamism: Indian Muslims, the Ottomans, and Britain (1877–1924)* (Leiden: Brill, 1997).

Most crucial for our purposes, though, Istanbul endeavored to socio-economically buffer its realms against European powers that posed a twin existential threat, politically and economically. James Gelvin has called that Ottoman approach "defensive developmentalism." Territorial losses like those in the Balkans and the Caucasus resultant of the Russo-Ottoman War of 1877–1878, while painful and disruptive, stiffened Istanbul's resolve to develop its remaining lands. In Asian interior and frontier areas, Ottoman state officials creatively adapted European Orientalist and related colonial civilizational discourses to reframe populations as people in need of development guidance. This excluded those populations in some new ways – they were tagged as the most under-developed Ottomans – but as importantly included them within an imperial project. Late Ottoman developmentalism, while related to European colonialism, was not identical with it, then. It was not really structured by race. It was shaped by a shared majority Muslim religion, which became more and more important as the empire was losing its majority Christian lands in the Balkans. And the empire did not seek to simply exploit interior and frontier areas or force them into a dependent relationship, but to socioeconomically develop them to strengthen itself against European political and economic pressure. Moreover, it invested in infrastructures and administrative restructuration also in certain coastal regions, for instance Palestine and Lebanon.[9]

European political and economic pressure preoccupied Ottoman officialdom all the way up to the highest office. Western powers, sultan Abdul Hamid II (r. 1878–1909) stated in an 1895 memorandum, had forced the empire to accept low customs that underpinned a liberal economic system supported by Ottoman politicians and economic thinkers from the 1830s to 1840s – when Istanbul signed low-tariff agreements with several

---

[9] Quote: James Gelvin, *The Modern Middle East: A History* (New York: Oxford University Press, 2005), 73. See also, Sabri Ateş, *The Ottoman-Iranian Borderlands: Making a Boundary, 1843–1914* (Cambridge: Cambridge University Press, 2013); Thomas Kühn, *Empire, Islam, and the Politics of Difference: Ottoman Rule in Yemen, 1849–1919* (Leiden: Brill, 2011), esp. 201–246; Eugene Rogan, *Frontiers of the State in the Late Ottoman Empire: Transjordan, 1850–1921* (Cambridge: Cambridge University Press, 1999); Ussama Makdisi, "Ottoman Orientalism," *American Historical Review* 107 (2002): 768–796; Selim Deringil, "'They Live in a State of Nomadism and Savagery': The Late Ottoman Empire and the Post-colonial Debate," *Comparative Studies in Society and History* 45 (2003): 311–342. For three typological areas constituting the empire's Asian lands – coast, interior, and frontier – see Cem Emrence, "Imperial Paths, Big Comparisons: The Late Ottoman Empire," *Journal of Global History* 3 (2008): 289–311.

European powers – until the 1860s. In consequence, Westerners outcom-
peted Ottomans. They also, the sultan added, used their might to make
Istanbul preserve a system of economic capitulations and had enticed it to
accept loans; in 1875, Istanbul was bankrupt and had to accept
a European-controlled Ottoman Public Debt Administration (OPDA),
a "state within the state controlling around one-third of the state revenue." To Abdul Hamid II, then, the root problem of what he called
Ottoman backwardness was the world's West-centric political and economic order.[10]

Ottoman thinkers concurred with what present-day historians, too,
would argue was a fundamentally correct analysis.[11] "Consider[ing] the
'science' of economics as an indispensable instrument for the salvation of
the empire," from the 1880s many called on the state to support the economy
to buffer the effects of that West-centric order. In textbooks and popular
magazines in various languages, thinkers like Ahmed Midhat (1844–1912),
Mustafa Nuri Bey (1844–1906), and Musa Akyiğitzade (1865–1923)
rejected laissez-faire economics as unsuitable for the Ottoman Empire.
Liberalism may work in the future. But for now Istanbul had to be protectionist, nurturing agriculture and manufacturing, just like European countries had done earlier and Germany and the United States were doing now.
European claims that economic laws were universal, and that those laws
command freedom from state intervention, were false. Those laws were
contingent. Just as false were European beliefs that a passion for labor was
culturally specific, i.e., European, and hardly replicable elsewhere. Rather,
those thinkers argued, that passion is a universal human instinct, though one
that the Ottoman state and its citizens should foster through education, just
as European countries had done. The end goal of these thinkers, then, was
a productive "homo ottomanicus" through self-development. Such
a citizen's work ethic would, collectively, help develop the Ottoman
Empire. Here, then, "development" had not only an economic meaning
but also – because of the grave political-strategic consequences of being

---

[10] Quote: Murat Birdal, *The Political Economy of the Ottoman Public Debt: Insolvency and European Financial Control in the Late Nineteenth Century* (London: Tauris, 2010), 7. See also, Deniz Kılınçoğlu, *Economics and Capitalism in the Ottoman Empire* (London: Routledge, 2015), 146, 152.

[11] Reşat Kasaba, *Ottoman Empire and the World Economy* (Albany: State University of New York Press, 1988); Şevket Pamuk, *The Ottoman Empire and European Capitalism, 1820–1913* (Cambridge: Cambridge University Press, 1987); Roger Owen, *The Middle East in the World Economy 1800–1914* (London: Tauris, 1981); Turan Kayaoğlu, *Legal Imperialism: Sovereignty and Extraterritoriality in Japan, the Ottoman Empire, and China* (Cambridge: Cambridge University Press, 2010).

under economic pressure from Europe – an existential personal and collective dimension.[12]

Regarding state policies, while Istanbul was unable to disband the OPDA before 1914 or raise tariffs, it did implement development measures. In Asian interior and frontier lands, especially in Syria and Iraq, Abdul Hamid II adopted a "systematic colonization" policy of purchasing land, which he opened to peasants, nomads, and migrants, most importantly Muslim refugees from North Africa, the Balkans, and Caucasus, to stem Western economic inroads and expand agricultural output. The empire also aided merchants and manufacturers in interior cities like Damascus to make it difficult for European merchants to penetrate from coastal cities. It gradually improved security in rural areas, attracting peasants and helping to settle nomads. And it invested in infrastructures like telegraphs, roads, and railways. Thus, the Damascus-Hijaz Railway, built in 1900–1908, while facilitating troop movements, also had development aims. It was billed accordingly. The intellectual Muhammad 'Arif's *The Book of the Increasing and Eternal Happiness: The Hijaz Railway* extolled its "many obvious advantages for populating the country, restoring life to the servants [of Allah], serving the two shrines [Mecca and Medina], assisting those desirous to visit both of them, promoting the scope of profitable commerce, [and] bolstering the planning of superior agriculture." By the turn of the century, a generation of protectionist, economic nationalist thought popularized in print, together with Ottomans' acute sense of the threat of European powers, had crystallized into bottom-up action. From the 1890s, urban consumers especially made a slow, partial "move away from imports and toward local manufacturers," paralleled by a "move toward buy-Ottoman and then buy-Muslim promotions in the late-Hamidian press." And when in 1908 Austria-Hungary annexed Bosnia, which it had occupied in 1878, Ottoman citizens readily followed the call by the newly ruling Committee of Union and Progress (CUP) regime to boycott Austro-Hungarian goods.[13]

---

[12] Quotes: Kılıncoğlu, *Economics*, 72, 101. See also, ibid., esp. 47, 50, 51, 56–57, 66–67, 90–93, 97–102. For Ahmed Midhat, see also, François Georgeon, "L'économie politique selon Ahmed Midhat," in *Première Rencontre Internationale sur l'Empire Ottoman et la Turquie Moderne*, ed. Edhem Eldem (Istanbul: ISIS, 1992), 461–479. For analyses also of non-Turkish Ottoman sources, see Ileana Moroni, *O Ergatis, 1908–1909: Ottomanism, National Economy and Modernization in the Ottoman Empire through a Greek-Language Newspaper of Izmir* (Istanbul: Libra Kitap, 2010).

[13] Quotes: François Georgeon, *Abdülhamid II. Le sultan caliphe (1876–1909)* (Paris: Fayard, 2003), 166; Jacob Landau, *The Hejaz Railway and the Muslim Pilgrimage: A Case of Ottoman Political Propaganda* (Detroit: Wayne State University, 1971), 42

Ottoman developmentalism did not stop in 1914. Despite organizational problems, Istanbul sustained related policies for its war efforts. In Greater Syria – present-day Syria, Lebanon, Israel/Palestine, and Jordan – for instance, Jamal Pasha (1872–1922), a CUP leader and general, maintained "the broader political and ideological goals of the Ottoman government ... [with] a comprehensive program aimed at developing the Syrian infrastructure." This transcended wartime military needs. In extended conversations Jamal Pasha had with a German-Ottoman delegation, "a main topic was Syria's economic future." He told a German visitor that economic undertakings "will endure long after the war." And determined to collect data, he ordered a Greater Syria-wide economic survey. This formed the base for a lengthy publication in 1917, *Syrien als Wirtschaftsgebiet [Syria as an Economic Region]*, directing future development for the "state's interest," *maslahat*, as the travel laissez-passer issued to the head of the survey noted.[14]

THE YISHUV

That head was Arthur Ruppin (1876–1943), the German Jewish director of the World Zionist Organization's (WZO) Palestine Office, opened in 1908 in Jaffa, next to today's Tel Aviv. An economist, Ruppin wrote in the belief that Germany and its Ottoman ally might win World War I. He did not simply survey Greater Syria's economy. He also argued that "The Jewish colonies are models of their kind, and ... the colonists,

---

(translation of 'Arif's text); and Elizabeth Frierson: "Cheap and Easy: The Creation of Consumer Culture in Late Ottoman Society," in *Consumption Studies and the History of the Ottoman Empire, 1550–1922*, ed. Donald Quataert (Albany: State University of New York Press, 2000), 256. See also, Pierre Bardin, *Algériens et Tunisiens dans l'Empire Ottoman de 1848 à 1914* (Paris: CNRS, 1979), esp. 5–8, 15–17, 128–132; Feroz Ahmad, "War and Society under the Young Turks, 1908–18," *Review* (Fernand Braudel Center) 11 (1988): 268; and Mahmoud Haddad, "Ottoman Economic Nationalism in the Press of Beirut and Tripoli (Syria)," in *The Economy as an Issue in the Middle Eastern Press*, ed. Gisela Procháska-Eisl and Martin Strohmeier (Berlin: LIT, 2008), 75–84.

[14] Three quotes: Hasan Kayalı, "Wartime Regional and Imperial Integration of Greater Syria during World War One," in *The Syrian Land Processes of Integration and Fragmentation*, ed. Thomas Philipp and Birgit Schäbler (Stuttgart: Steiner, 1998), 296; Willhelm Feldmann, *Reise zur Suesfront* (Weimar: Kiepenheuer, 1917), 82; and Max Übelhör, *Syrien im Krieg* (Berlin: Deutsche Verlags-Anstalt, 1917), 39. Arthur Ruppin, *Syrien als Wirtschaftsgebiet [Syria as an Economic Region]* (Berlin: Kolonial-Wirtschaftliches Komitee, 1917). For the laissez-passer, see Siyahat-waraqasi #748, A107/631, Central Zionist Archives, Jerusalem (hereafter, CZA).

through their initiative and enterprise have not only organized the sale of their products in a new and efficient way, but ... have made their colonies into real oases of civilization, thanks to the schools, physicians, druggists, and water-works they have introduced."[15]

In claiming that Yishuvi developmentalism aided the Ottoman economy, Ruppin inscribed the former as a pioneer into Istanbul's imperial project of surviving in a global West-centric political-economic order. Indeed, Zionists were not yet wedded to the idea of a fully independent nation-state. Many worked vertically intraimperially, within a broader Ottoman framework. To be sure, Istanbul did not create in Palestine a frontier for Zionist settlement the same way London, for instance, did for European migrants in white dominions and some colonies like Kenya, or as Washington did in the US West. It did not make land available at low prices, and did not remove or kill locals. But Ottoman legislation like the 1858 land law, which unintendedly concentrated land titles in the hands of urban notables and merchants in Palestine and adjacent places like Beirut, and efforts to secure the countryside for agriculture, were structural preconditions for Zionist and other Jewish philanthropists and organizations to buy, at however high prices, private land and keep it. Further, politically, especially from the 1908 Young Turk Revolution that reinstalled parliamentarism, "the pursuit of Jewish nationalism within the Ottoman framework was largely accepted among wide segments of the yishuv." And the Yishuv felt confident that its technical knowledge could be of use to the empire. As Jamal Pasha's and Ruppin's wartime collaboration shows, some Ottoman officials agreed.[16]

But those officials distrusted Zionists' separatist intentions and ties with European empires, too. This worry rose against the background of European powers widening their political-consular, cultural-religious, and economic influence in Palestine from the mid-nineteenth century. The worry peaked during the war. Jamal Pasha executed several Palestine-based

[15] Quote: Arthur Ruppin, *Syria: An Economic Survey* (New York: The Provisional Zionist Committee, 1918), 32.

[16] Quote: Yuval Ben Bassat, "Rethinking the Concept of Ottomanization: The *Yishuv* in the Aftermath of the Young Turk Revolution of 1908," *Middle Eastern Studies* 45 (2009): 461. More broadly for Jews, also non-Zionists, in Palestine, and beyond, see Michel Campos, *Ottoman Brothers: Muslims, Christians, and Jews in Early Twentieth-Century Palestine* (Stanford: Stanford University Press, 2011); and Julia Phillips Cohen, *Becoming Ottomans: Sephardi Jews and Imperial Citizenship in the Modern Era* (New York: Oxford University Press, 2014). For structural preconditions, see Gershon Shafir, *Land, Labor, and the Origins of the Israeli-Palestinian Conflict, 1882–1914* (Berkeley: University of California Press, 1996), 23–24, 30–36, 41–42.

Zionists, spies for Britain who were seen with alarm doubly because some Zionists had convinced Britain to allow the establishment in Egypt and deployment against the Ottoman Empire of two however minute forces, the Zion Mule Corps (1915–1916) and Jewish Legion (1917–1918). Zionist activities did not only have an Ottoman framework, then. As Gershon Shafir has argued, "we must place Zionism in [the] broader context of the intervention and penetration of outside forces into the Ottoman Empire." This showed discursively, too. Ruppin's "oases of civilization" exemplified how Zionists sidelined Arabs developmentally – although agriculture, including export crops, and Ottoman development efforts had been expanding in Palestine before Zionists arrived from the 1880s.[17]

With the British Balfour Declaration's promise of a "national home for the Jewish people" in 1917 and definitely with the defeat, in 1918, and subsequent dismemberment of the Ottoman Empire, Zionism was uncoupled from Istanbul's imperial developmentalism. But still not sovereign, and poor in land and people, the Yishuv could not stand on its own feet. Rather, another vertical intraimperial link, to Britain, was solidified as Britain's 1917–1918 occupation of Palestine became a Mandate. Four decades of Zionist settlement, from the 1880s, caused influential British imperial policy makers to see Jews in general and the Yishuv in particular as "agents of development" for the empire. This vision was reinforced by Zionists' global self-promotion. A case in point is my above quote from Ruppin's book, which I did not translate from the 1917 German edition but copied from a 1918 English translation. A first abortive try occurred before the war: the so-called "Uganda Plan," the offer to settle Jews in East Africa that British Colonial Secretary Joseph Chamberlain (1836–1914) made in 1903 to Theodor Herzl (1860–1904), the founder, in 1897, of the WZO. Later, imperial development visions caused British officials like Leo Amery (1873–1955), William Ormsby-Gore (1885–1964), and Alfred Milner (1854–1925) to support the Balfour Declaration and, during the Mandate, hold an "imperial shield" over the Yishuv. This showed also legally. The Balfour Declaration was integrated into the 1922 League of Nations Palestine Mandate charter.[18]

---

[17] Quote: Shafir, *Land*, 22. For Ottoman reactions to European powers in Palestine, see Johann Büssow, *Hamidian Palestine: Politics and Society in the District of Jerusalem, 1872–1908* (Leiden: Brill, 2011). For agricultural expansion, see Alexander Schölch, *Palästina im Umbruch, 1856–1882* (Stuttgart: Steiner, 1986).

[18] Quotes: Jacob Norris, *Land of Progress: Palestine in the Age of Colonial Development, 1905–1948* (Oxford: Oxford University Press, 2013), 63; and Bernard Wasserstein,

On the one hand, then, "British emphasis on Palestine as an arena for colonial development was essentially a continuation of older Ottoman practices" – though Britain called its rule a total break with that past. On the other, London's "predilection for Jews as the sole agents of that development represented a significant break from the past." Britain claimed to treat Palestine's inhabitants equally, but did not. London and its High Commissioners in Jerusalem favored the Yishuv – often openly, sometimes not; in certain fields without a hitch, in others despite question marks – politically and economically, in areas as different as land and agriculture, industry, and immigrant worker quotas. Zionist developmentalism's intraimperial British setting continued even when political ties with London started fraying after the 1939 White Paper limited immigration and, ineffectively, land purchases. In World War II Britain invested in Yishuvi industries, which had been rapidly growing since the 1930s, to help sustain its troops in the Middle East. Meanwhile, Jewish manufacturers and the Jewish Agency, the Yishuv's proto-state, regularly published English articles for British eyes and in 1941 even launched a new magazine, *Palestine and the Middle East.* Its "Home Front" section's name echoed British wartime parlance, and it fed British views of the Yishuv's imperial usefulness with assertions that tiny Palestine had a "significant place in the planned war economy" of the empire.[19]

The British in Palestine: The Mandatory Government and the Arab-Jewish Conflict, 1917–1929 (Oxford: Blackwell, 1991), 157, quoted in Norris, *Land,* 65. For the Uganda Plan, see Adam Rovner, *In the Shadow of Zion: Promised Lands before Israel* (New York: New York University Press, 2014), 45–78. Earlier nineteenth-century philanthropic activities and calls to action within an emerging Jewish transnational public sphere, which built on and remolded older diasporic networks, had to rely on European empires' support, too. See Carole Fink, *Defending the Rights of Others: The Great Powers, the Jews, and International Minority Protection, 1878–1938* (Cambridge: Cambridge University Press, 2004); and Abigail Green, *Moses Montefiore: Jewish Liberator, Imperial Hero* (Cambridge, MA: Harvard University Press, 2010).

[19] Quotes: Norris, *Land,* 66, 66; and Dr. K. Mendelsohn, "Economic Mobilization," *Palestine and the Middle East* 9: xiii (1941): 166–167. For self-serving claims about British rule breaking with the Ottoman past, see, for example, "Speech Delivered by the Right Hon. Sir H. Samuel," July 1920, in *Political Diaries of the Arab World. Palestine and Jordan,* vol. 1: 1920–1923, ed. Robert Jarman (Slough: Archives Edition, 2001), 4–5, 7. For British policies, e.g., regarding land and agriculture, see Barbara Smith, *The Roots of Separatism in Palestine: British Economic Policy, 1920–1929* (Syracuse: Syracuse University Press, 1993); Kenneth Stein, *The Land Question in Palestine, 1917–1939* (Chapel Hill: University of North Carolina Press, 1984); Amos Nadan, *The Palestinian Peasant Economy under the Mandate: A Story of Colonial Bungling* (Cambridge, MA: Distributed for CAMES by Harvard University Press, 2006); and Martin Bunton, *Colonial Land Policies in Palestine, 1917–1936* (New York: Oxford University Press, 2007).

Yishuvi developmentalism cannot be solely situated vertically intraimperially within the Ottoman or British empires, though. As Zionism formed
part of a broader world of dominant European empires, Zionist developmentalism was involved in transimperial transmissions of developmentalist
ideas, particularly in agriculture. WZO technocrats studied agriculture
around the world, and some worked for imperial bodies. Otto Warburg
(1858–1938), a doctor of botany, explored the South Pacific and Southeast
Asia in 1885–1889, then taught at the University of Berlin. Finding "in the
fertile soil of the tropics a perfect opportunity to promote the growth of
useful plants," he was a cofounder in 1896 of the Colonial Economic
Committee (CEC). ". . . Warburg continued to participate in colonial projects while working on behalf of Zionist settlement:" he was the founder, in
1903, of the WZO's Palestine Commission, where he until 1907
"implanted into the WZO German colonialism's celebrated commitment
to scientific research and experimentation." And Selig Soskin (1872–1959),
born in the Russian Crimea, studied agronomy in Berlin, where he met
Warburg. He then "traveled through Africa and South America, familiariz-
ing himself with the colonial practices of all the Great Powers, especially
Germany;" and after working in Palestine in 1896–1902 and in Berlin for
German colonial projects and for Warburg, in 1906–1918 served in
German West Africa as an agricultural advisor.[20]

Zionist developmentalism's transimperial dimension did not simply and
fuzzily amount to technocrats visiting a motley crew of European colonies,
helping to develop a mix of ideas, and bringing these somehow to bear on
Palestine. Rather, specific models rose to dominance at particular junctures;
and as none disappeared, they formed a multilayered developmentalist
landscape in the Yishuv. From the early 1880s Europe-based colonization
societies bought land for a few *moshavot* (sing., *moshava*), settlements of
often rather religious farmers working independent plots, often vineyards.
They maintained the *moshavot* with donations and had them use methods
developed mostly in French Algeria and France and imported into Palestine
starting with the establishment, in 1870 by French Jewish philanthropists,
of an agricultural school, *Mikveh Israel*. From 1903 the *moshavot*'s continued unrentability, and from 1904 Herzl's failure to realize Zionist aims
through diplomacy with various empires, helped bring to the fore the
"national institutions:" the WZO and its technocratic branches, most

[20] Quotes: Derek Penslar, *Zionism and Technocracy: The Engineering of Jewish Settlement
in Palestine, 1870–1918* (Bloomington: Indiana University Press, 1991), 60, 61, 66. There
are many similar biographies; for another, of engineer Joseph Treidel, see ibid., 67.

importantly the Jewish National Fund (1901), Palestine Office (1908), and Palestine Foundation Fund (1920).[21]

Although the *moshavot* persisted – also after 1903, new immigrants joined them – their landscape was from 1903 overlaid with a newly dominant, more systematically developmentalist latticework of cooperative *moshavim* (sing., *moshav*). These were farmed by Eastern European and Russian secular, socialist-nationalist pioneers like David Ben-Gurion, who by the 1920s led Labor Zionism and in 1948 became Israel's first Prime Minister. In turn, these women and men were guided by WZO technocrats, mainly German and German-educated Eastern European agricultural specialists like Warburg and Soskin. These "desire[d] to study the Palestinian ecology in a global context, in order both to contribute to and benefit from the international scientific discourse on agriculture in arid regions." They also adapted to the Yishuv settlement ideas developed for the prewar German Empire's European east. They worked with "a theory of public ownership of land and cooperative settlement" and developed a "'pure settlement theory' [that] drew on liberal socialist, national liberal, and conservative attempts to deal with the 'agrarian problem' of Germany and the experience of national conflict between the German-speaking and Slavic peoples on the historical frontiers of German expansion. Its basic principle was that the political questions would find their solution once most of the land in Palestine was in Jewish hands, most of the population was Jewish, the Jews dominated the economy, especially agriculture, and the Jewish residents demanded autonomy." Rooted in the last prewar decade, this approach shaped Zionist agricultural developmentalism throughout the Mandate period. Key postwar shifts were, from the 1920s, the establishment of collective kibbutzim; their paramilitarization and push into Palestine's southwestern and northern frontiers from the 1930s; and the fine-tuning, by the 1920s, of the smallest viable land-to-farmer ratio. The latter was a key issue: Palestine was small and private land expensive, Jewish immigration became pressing when European fascism flourished in the 1930s, and Palestinian resistance grew over time.[22]

Finally, from the late 1910s, private farmers – some in *moshavot*, others on individual plots mainly on the coast between Tel Aviv and

---

[21] Penslar, *Zionism*, 13–40; S. Ilan Troen, *Imagining Zion: Dreams, Designs, and Realities in a Century of Jewish Settlement* (New Haven: Yale University Press, 2003), 3–14.

[22] Quotes: Penslar, *Zionism*, 67; Shafir, *Land*, 151, 154. See also, Troen, *Imagining Zion*, 15–84.

Haifa – started adopting citrus growing methods developed in the US West, especially California. Long neglected by historians who were focused on the pioneers forming the hard core of Labor Zionism, this process was not as directly supported by the WZO as the *moshavim* and kibbutzim. In this sense, it is less fully part of parastate Zionist developmentalism. But it mattered greatly: citrus agriculture, developed from the late nineteenth century by Palestine's Arabs, became the Yishuv's, and Palestine's, key export from the 1920s. It also shows again that Yishuvi developmentalism unfolded transimperially. US agricultural expertise was part of a worldwide transimperial network, and had grown together with the United States' imperial push westwards, from the Atlantic coast to California and then across the Pacific to Hawaii and the Philippines.[23]

But why did the US agricultural model arrive in the Yishuv "only" in the 1910s? A key answer to this question – the rising influence of US Jewry after World War I – also points to another issue. While the nature of specific developmentalist models flowing into and out of the Yishuv was transimperial, timing had to do with the relative power of national populations within the Zionist movement. First out of the block were French Jews whose civilizational mission crystallized in 1860 in the non-Zionist *Alliance Israélite Universelle* and who influenced also the moshavot; from the 1890s through the 1910s followed German-speaking Jews; then came US and British Jews.[24] At the same time, the argument of historians like Abigail Green – that premodern diasporic networks were in the nineteenth century transformed into a complex transnational Jewish public sphere[25] – matters also for Zionist developmentalism. It helps explain why no uniformly "national" developmentalist layer displaced all others and why, in consequence, the Yishuv's developmentalist landscape was so multilayered.[26]

---

[23] Nahum Karlinsky, *California Dreaming: Ideology, Society, and Technology in the Citrus Industry of Palestine, 1890–1939* (Albany: State University of New York Press, 2005). For the failed attempt, led by US Jews, to shift the WZO's agricultural developmentalism closer to the US capitalist model, see Troen, *Imagining Zion*, 29–34.

[24] Politically, the elite of Labor Zionism, which dominated Zionism from the 1920s, was mainly from Russia; the Zionist masses, too, were mostly from there and Eastern Europe.

[25] Abigail Green, "Nationalism and the 'Jewish International': Religious Internationalism in Europe and the Middle East, c.1840–c.1880," *Comparative Studies in Society and History* 50 (2008): 535–558.

[26] To complete this account, one would need to add the developmentalist notions behind the industrialization drive of the 1930s and after. See Arie Krampf, "Reception of the Developmental Approach in the Jewish Economic Discourse of Mandatory Palestine, 1934–1938," *Israel Studies* 15 (2010): 80–103; Cyrus Schayegh, *The Middle East and the Making of the Modern World* (Cambridge, MA: Harvard University Press, 2017), chs. 4–5.

As for self-development, the productivization of the Jewish self, it was if anything more important to Zionist than to Ottoman nationalists. At the 1898 Zionist Congress, the German Zionist and physician Max Nordau (1849–1923), author of the famous 1892 monograph *Entartung [Degeneration]*, coined the term *Muskel-Judenthum*, muscular Judaism. Since then, it has "always been associated with the opposite of the typical *Galut* (diaspora) Jew: weak, frail, despised, doing his *Luftgeschäfte* (unproductive business)." Indeed, although building on an almost century-long central European gymnastic tradition, *Muskel-Judenthum* had a racial twist. It turned at the Jewish self the anti-Semitic gaze that othered Jews as weak and unproductive or as abnormally productive, i.e., parasitic. Physical productivization through sports and/or hard agricultural work was seen to improve also one's moral fiber. The Jewish body was a central space for the collective Zionist politics of national regeneration.[27] It was not by chance, then, that *the* motto of secular pioneers was *livnot we-lehibanot*, "to build and be built," and that the women and men adored as leading the Yishuv's collective development were also venerated for being ready to defend the Yishuv with their very own bodies. They were "the silver platter / upon which you will have the State of Israel," to quote a famous poem that Nathan Alterman penned in 1947, or to quote another one, from 1934:

> Rest has come to the weary,
> Comfort to the laborer.
> Pale night spreads forth
> Upon the fields of the Valley of Jezreel.
> ...
> Darkness upon Mount Gilboa,
> A horse gallops from shadow to shadow,
> The sound of a cry flies upward
> Upon the field of the Valley of Jezreel.
> Who fired? And who fell there,

[27] Quote: Moshe Zimermann, "Muscle Jews versus Nervous Jews," in *Emancipation through Muscles: Jews and Sport in Europe*, ed. Michael Brenner and Gideon Reuveni (London: University of Nebraska Press, 2006), 13. The last sentence's final formulation draws on the title of a monograph by Todd S. Presner, *Muscular Judaism: The Jewish Body and the Politics of Regeneration* (New York: Routledge, 2007). See also, H. Kaufman, "The National Ideas of the Term Muscle Judaism," *Movement* 3 (1996): 261–268; and more broadly, Oz Almog, *The Sabra: The Creation of the New Jew* (Berkeley: University of California Press, 2000).

Between Beit Alpha and Nahalal?
What, what, from night to night?
Silence in the Valley.
Sleep, Valley, land of glory,
We stand guard over you[28]

BEIRUT

By the early 1930s Beirut counted a good 200,000 inhabitants including,
among others, a multiconfessional middle class and mercantile elite whose
tastes – "toujours de la nouveauté en stock" from Galeries Lafayette in Paris;
"vins [et] liqueurs des meilleures marques" – bore scant resemblance to the
Yishuv pioneers' rather ascetic tastes. This was because Beirut from the mid-
nineteenth century had become *the* connector between global economic and
cultural networks and Greater Syria and, hence, the region's economic and
cultural gravitation point: a port city whose better-offs and even middling
classes by the later 1800s took to leading the good life and appreciating the
arts privately and publicly. Istanbul's and Paris's decisions in 1888 and
1918–1920 to make it a provincial capital and the Mandate capital, respectively, solidified the port city's hub function; so did Ottoman and French
infrastructure investments in its harbor and in telegraphs, roads, and rails.[29]

In education and knowledge production, too, Beirut was a regional-
global connector. Besides numerous private confessional, Ottoman state,
and foreign secondary schools, the city boasted two colleges, the
US Syrian Protestant College [from 1920, American University of Beirut
(AUB)] and the French Catholic Université de Saint Joseph, founded in
1866 and 1875, respectively. Especially AUB soon attracted students from
across Greater Syria as well as from adjacent countries, in particular Egypt
and Iraq. Following World Wars I and II, political changes in the Middle
East and the world won AUB new funders. In 1928 it accepted
a Rockefeller Foundation (RF) offer to finance a Social Science Research
Section (SSRS), and in 1952 the Ford Foundation (FF) funded an
Economic Research Institute (ERI). These and similar AUB creations

---

[28] Quotes: from Nathan Alterman, "The Silver Platter" and "Song of the Valley," translated
in *The Origins of Israel, 1882–1948*, ed. Eran Kaplan and Derek Penslar (Madison:
The University of Wisconsin Press, 2011), 345, 109.

[29] Quotes: "Galleries Lafayette," *L'Orient*, January 17, 1925, 3; and "Carnet mondain,"
L'Orient January 9, 1925, 2. See also, Samir Kassir, *Beirut* (Berkeley: University of
California Press, 2010), 279–326; Toufoul Abou-Hodeib, *A Taste for Home:
The Modern Middle Class in Ottoman Beirut* (Stanford: Stanford University Press, 2017).

sought to guide new (first European-ruled, then postcolonial Cold War) nation-states in the Middle East.[30]

Developmentalist institutions, AUB's SSRS and ERI, mirrored the fact that Beirut was a powerful port city and a regional-global hub, and that the global networks in which it operated were uneven and bent by Western imperial powers, in its case most centrally the United States.

In the case of AUB's post–World War I developmentalist institutions, the transimperial/transnational and horizontal intraimperial dimensions were not simply overlapping, but tightly linked if not blurred. That is because the empire in the horizontal intraimperial dimension was the United States, which rarely ensured imperial interests by territorial conquest. Rather, from World War I the United States had a "broadly internationalist vision linking US security to the global environment;" and especially in the interwar years but also thereafter wealthy US foundations played a considerable role in this regard. Thus, from 1924 the RF developed "a closely articulated program in social sciences of international scope," mainly in Europe but also beyond.[31]

At AUB, this "intensely [US] nationalist internationalism" was particularly felt because the university was a US institution: Presbyterian founded, accredited in New York, and mainly US funded. The US focus of AUB's global developmentalist network showed not only in large US foundations making large donations from the 1920s or in foreign institutional and personal connections being by far most dense with US academia. It was manifest also in a fundamentally shared analysis of contemporary political-economic challenges. In the 1920s–1930s, the RF and SSRS had matching visions of contemporary political problems: the irrational, emotional behavior of leftist and rightist nonliberals in Europe and of rising national(ist) elites in Western colonies. The solution in the Middle East, SSRS held, was to

---

[30] For details, see Cyrus Schayegh, "The Inter-war Germination of Development and Modernization Theory and Practice: Politics, Institution Building, and Knowledge Production between the Rockefeller Foundation and the American University of Beirut," *Geschichte und Gesellschaft* 41 (2015): 649–684; Schayegh, "The Man in the Middle: Developmentalism and Cold War at AUB's Economic Research Institute in-between the U.S. and the Middle East, 1952–1967," in *150 Years AUB. Commemorative Volume*, ed. Nadia El Cheikh and Bilal Orfali (Beirut: AUB Press, 2016), 105–119.

[31] Quotes: Michael Latham, *The Right Kind of Revolution: Modernization, Development, and U.S. Foreign Policy from the Cold War to the Present* (Ithaca: Cornell University Press, 2011); and "From the Report of the Executive Committee and Director to the Board of Trustees for the Year 1924–1925," p. 26, Folder 10, Box 2, Series 910, Record Group 3/FA112, Rockefeller Archives Center, Sleepy Hollow, New York, Rockefeller Foundation Collection.

guide Arab college students and to train them in applied sociological methods, helping them to develop their selves and become "native leaders who in
turn can solve other local questions." And in the early 1950s, AUB won
an FF grant for the ERI by stressing the need to educate economists from the
Middle East and to carry out thorough statistical analyses of the region as
a precondition for the development of its newly independent countries.[32]

But SSRS and ERI were not simply appendices of metropolitan
US academia and foundations, and they did not see their research as
simply derivative of US models. Rather, they made universalist claims
about their developmentalist research. A case in point was SSRS village
analyses, which were meant to diagnose villagers' problems and find
solutions so they would not migrate to cities. These analyses were
described as an integral part of rural and community sociology studies
not only on the United States but also on non-Western countries like
China and India. SSRS also claimed that the post–World War I Middle
East's relative underdevelopment, colonial type of government, and feudal land ownership permitted its social scientists to exert a remarkable
laboratory-like control over its research environment, their village studies.
This gave SSRS researchers a methodological edge over peers working in
the West, which in turn meant that to them their research findings were
universally applicable.[33]

This universalist claim, however, contradicted AUB's culturalist claim
of having special knowledge about, and geographical access to, the
Middle East. The university made this claim vis-à-vis the RF in the late
1920s. And applying for United Nations and FF grants following World
War II for the ERI, AUB Economy Department professor Albert Badre
noted that AUB "has correspondents in the Arabic-speaking countries,"
underlined the importance of "promoting such regional contacts," and
emphasized that a regionally based economic institute would be "much
more effective and much less costly than sending out large teams of
experts" to the Middle East.[34]

This tension between AUB's universalist and culturalist claims –
between being part of a developmentalist world and knowing "its" region

---

[32] Quotes: Sondra Herman, *Eleven against War: Studies in American Internationalist
Thought, 1898–1921* (Stanford: Hoover Institution Press, 1969), 34; and Schayegh,
"Germination," 664, quoting a 1931 letter by AUB president Bayard Dodge. See also,
Schayegh, "Man," 106–110, 118n67.

[33] Schayegh, "Germination," 679–681.

[34] All quotes from Schayegh, "Man," 109, quoting FF files. See also, Schayegh,
"Germination," 663.

best – reflected its location in a supranational, regional center, Beirut, in an age of rising nation-states. Through the 1960s, in a deeply nationalist world, Beirut's AUB and its developmentalist institutions were able to survive, indeed thrive, by *not* being nationalist, by capturing a presumably neutral space, by being *the* connector between West-centric global circuits and a multinational region.

This special position was reflected in SSRS's and ERI's kind of developmentalist work, too. Neither implemented projects that were nationwide or were meant to develop an entire economic sector. Rather, they prepared state-led development, by collecting data across the region. There cannot be progress (in the interwar period) or planning (after World War II), they argued, without proper prior knowledge. This approach helps us see development as more than either on-the-ground projects or the theoretical basis laid in the 1950s–1960s by modernization theorists in the United States. There was also data collection, after World War II in increasingly statistical form. This approach fit AUB's supranational, non-nation-state nature best, and also allowed it to claim knowledge dominance in the region.

But Beirut was not alone in Greater Syria. It entertained transnational developmentalist links – including with the Yishuv. It was already in the late Ottoman period that the city's cultural and economic centrality in Greater Syria radiated also to its south. The Yishuv imported certain goods, for instance US drilling machines for Ruppin's Palestine Office projects, through the big port city to its north. The Zionist Anglo-Palestine Bank Beirut, founded in 1902, opened its only non-Palestine Arab branch there. Zionist publications like *Palästina* and *Altneuland* followed the city's economy with interest. And until Israel's independence in 1948, hundreds of Yishuvi Jews enrolled at AUB; its proximity to Palestine, educational excellence, English-language instruction, and the British Mandate's recognition of its degrees made it highly attractive.[35]

Even when the Arab-Yishuvi conflict really took off after World War I, a distinct if precarious sense continued to exist that personal contacts could survive political disagreements. In the case of AUB, this sense turned around professional expertise, *inter alia* about Greater Syria's development. The Yishuv, too, had economic interests here. And although – unlike in Beirut's case – its interests were those of an emerging nation-state, this did not necessarily have to come between Yishuvi

---

[35] Schayegh, *Middle East*, 78–79, 220–221, 385n114.

economic specialists and AUB's interest in the economic study of the
region. Thus, B. Veicmanas, in the Yishuv, wrote on "internal trade" for
The Economic Organization of Palestine, an edited volume published by
AUB economist Sa'id Himadeh in 1938, i.e., at the very peak of the
Palestine Revolt of 1936–1939. Similarly, AUB professors were in contact with the German Jewish economist Alfred Bonné who in 1931
founded the Economic Archives for the Near East. Funded by the
Hebrew University and from 1935 the Jewish Agency, its "double task
was . . . establishing a central collection of economic material for the use
of scientific research, and of supplying the public with reliable information." From 1935 to 1937, it was visited by AUB scholars including
Himadeh and Dodd, Political Science professor Ritcher, Dean of School
of Arts and Sciences Nicholy, and SSRS assistant Amin Himadeh.
To them and Bonné, it went without saying that they shared research
interests. When in 1935, Bonné invited AUB Economics professor
George Hakim to contribute an article to the Archives' new quarterly,
he underlined that the "postwar development of the Near East has
created, in practically all the countries concerned, a number of major
economic and social problems." (Hakim accepted.) And Dodd, preparing in 1936 for his first visit to Bonné, wrote that "[I]it is possible that
our little Social Science Research Section here at the University, and your
Institute, may cooperate in various ways in the future, at least to the
extent of our not duplicating things which we discover you are doing."
Such contacts continued well into the 1940s.[36]

   At the same time, the hardening of Jews' and Arabs' positions toward
the Zionist/Palestine Question from the 1929 Wailing Wall/*Buraq* riots –
arguably the point of no return in (the violent management of) that
question[37] – sometimes affected Beiruti-Yishuvi transnational contacts
regarding development knowledge. A fascinating example was the fate
of a chapter for *The Economic Organization of Palestine* that Himadeh
asked Bonné to write in 1936. From the start, while discussing chapter
drafts, the two argued over the hierarchy and hence legitimacy of different
data producers (the Jewish Agency *versus* the Mandate government) and

---

[36] Quotes: Alfred Bonné, "Memorandum" (1933), 1, A473/7, CZA; and Bonné to Hakim,
   Jerusalem, August 12, 1935, and Dodd to Bonné, Beirut, February 10, 1936, both in
   A473/1, CZA. See also, B. Veicmanas, "Internal Trade," in *Economic Organization of
   Palestine*, ed. Sa'id Himadeh (Beirut: AUB Press, 1938), 343–384. For the 1940s, see
   Schayegh, *Middle East*, 296.
[37] Hillel Cohen, *1929: Year Zero of the Arab-Israeli Conflict* (Waltham, MA: Brandeis
   University Press, 2015).

over formatting (the body of the text *versus* footnotes). That is, they faced off over the political "who" and "how'" underpinning the scientific text. For Bonné, politics was about existential interests. He wished to prove that many Jews could settle in Palestine without damaging Arabs. Hence, he "regard[ed] the question of the *cultivatable area* in Palestine as the point of departure and as the main subject for a discussion of natural resources," the theme of his chapter. By contrast, Himadeh wanted to "avoid discussions of the economic conditions of the country in terms of sects or nationalities .... Any diversion from this policy would, in our belief, involve the university in controversial questions of a political nature." While he was willing to compromise on Jewish Agency, not only government, data being used in the body of the text, he insisted on a hierarchy of sources. He wished to move some information from the body of the text into a footnote, "to avoid undue emphasis on the Jewish Agency's estimate as against that of the Government." Bonné first acceded, then retracted. And his last draft – written following the publication, in July 1937, of the British Peel Commission Report on the revolt that was rocking Palestine since 1936 – moved the signposts. Although, as agreed referring to that report, Bonné selected what "support[s] the figures of the Jewish Agency experts, and disregards the comments which depreciate [them,] ... giv[ing] the chapter a tone of partisanship." Himadeh insisted he would accept the chapter only after correction. There was no agreement. *The Economic Organization of Palestine* appeared without Bonné's chapter.[38]

CONCLUSION

Using the late Ottoman Empire and the early post-Ottoman Middle East as its case, this chapter has illustrated that developmentalism has had different dimensions, including vertical intraimperial, horizontal intraimperial/regionwide transnational, and transnational/transimperial ones; and that these dimensions have interplayed in various ways.

In other cases, too, presumably nation-state-bounded developmentalisms in actual fact did not simply unfold within nation-state borders. Iran's and Turkey's economic nationalist credos developed in parallel and partially borrowed from each other. Both were rooted in comparable late-

---

[38] Quotes: Bonné to Vitales, Jerusalem, May 23, 1937, Himadeh to Vitales, Beirut, June 3, 1937, Himadeh to Bonné, Beirut, July 16, 1937, and Himadeh to Bonné, August 16, 1937, all in box A473/1, CZA.

nineteenth-century experiences within a West-centric global economy; both peaked in the 1930s in reaction to the Great Depression; and both included a heavy dose of state-driven industrialization. Another instance was the accentuation of Yishuvi and Syrian economic nationalism in the 1930s. The two polities in the making used the same voluntarist economic weapon, a boycott, against each other to develop their national economy under political conditions – lacking sovereignty – that ruled out state protectionism. Further, both sought the same supranational end, i.e., to help their economies withstand outside regional competition and obtain regional dominance. (Both ultimately failed.)[39]

In a modern world that is globally interdependent yet very uneven, in which not only empires and nation-states but also cities and regions matter, and in which empires like the British, Ottoman, and American ones assumed different yet interrelated forms, the history of development transcends the metropole-colony and Global North-South dyads and the story of international organizations linking them.

---

[39] Şevket Pamuk, "Intervention during the Great Depression: Another Look at the Turkish Experience," *The Mediterranean Response to Globalization before 1950* (London: Routledge, 2000), 330–332; Ayhan Aktar, "Economic Nationalism in Turkey: The Formative Years, 1912–1925," *Boğaziçi Journal* 10 (1996): 263–290; Schayegh, *Middle East*, chs. 3–4.

5

Smallpox and the Globalization of Development

Erez Manela

In May 1806, US president Thomas Jefferson wrote to Edward Jenner, the English physician who had developed the new smallpox vaccine a decade earlier. "Having been among the early converts, in this part of the globe, to its efficiency," Jefferson wrote to Jenner about the vaccine, "I took an early part in recommending it to my countrymen." He continued:

I avail myself of this occasion of rendering you a portion of the tribute of gratitude due to you from the whole human family. Medicine has never before produced any single improvement of such utility. ... You have erased from the calendar of human afflictions one of its greatest. Yours is the comfortable reflection that mankind can never forget that you have lived.

The discovery, Jefferson concluded, would ensure that "future nations will know by history only that the loathsome small-pox has existed."[1] The Sage of Monticello, as it turned out, was prescient if somewhat premature. It was only 171 years later, in 1977, that the last naturally occurring human smallpox infection abated. Three years later, in May 1980, the World Health Organization (WHO), an institution that Jefferson could scarcely have imagined, held a ceremony at its Geneva headquarters to certify that smallpox, an infectious disease that

---

[1] Thomas Jefferson to Edward Jenner, May 14, 1806, The Thomas Jefferson Papers, Series 1, General Correspondence, Library of Congress, Washington, D. C. The practice of using material from infected individuals to induce immunity to smallpox in others, known as variolation, had been prevalent across Asia since ancient times and had been introduced in Europe through the Ottoman Empire in the early eighteenth century. Jenner's innovation was to use instead material from cows infected with a related disease, cowpox, which also had an immunizing effect but carried a much lower risk to humans. This procedure was named *vaccination* after the Latin word for cow.

had killed hundreds of millions throughout history, had been eradicated worldwide.[2]

How and when did development become global? For this to happen, it was not sufficient for historical actors such as Jefferson simply to imagine the possibility of ameliorating disease on a worldwide scale. The globalization of development required imagining the improvement of human well-being globally, yes. But it also had to wait for the emergence of organizations that defined action on a global scale as their mission and then developed the institutional structures and professional methodologies that allowed development projects of worldwide scope to be conceived, planned, and pursued. It required, too, the resources to animate such institutions into action and allow them to carry out their plans. The field of global health is one in which the emergence of such organizations over the course of the twentieth century is among the most notable, both in terms of the worldwide scope of their ambitions and, no less important, in terms of their actual impact on human lives globally. Within that field, moreover, the success of the WHO's global Smallpox Eradication Program (SEP), launched in 1965, is a central landmark. This chapter shows how development became a global practice through the lens of global health, tracing this history from the earliest days of the institutionalization of disease control as a state function and focusing in particular on the rise of organized efforts to control smallpox and, eventually, to eradicate it globally.

For much of the twentieth century, the concept of "development" was most closely associated with the idea of economic growth. Development of this sort was often imagined as calling for high-modernist infrastructure projects such as the construction of massive dams or heavy industry such as steel and measured with econometric yardsticks such as gross domestic product (GDP). In this scheme, "developed" nations were defined by high GDP figures and "underdeveloped" nations by low ones.[3] At least since the 1970s, however, the view of development as economic growth has

---

[2] *The Global Eradication of Smallpox: Final Report of the Global Commission for the Certification of Smallpox Eradication* (Geneva: World Health Organization, 1980).

[3] The view of development as a high-modernist project is most famously critiqued in James C. Scott, *Seeing Like a State: How Certain Schemes to Improve the Human Condition Have Failed* (New Haven: Yale University Press, 1998). While the high-modernist approach to development predominated for much of the twentieth century, there was always also a countervailing approach that centered development on small-scale, community projects. See Daniel Immerwahr, *Thinking Small: The United States and the Lure of Community Development* (Cambridge, MA: Harvard University Press, 2015).

been criticized as self-defeating and too narrow, with the former critiques giving birth to ideas about "sustainable development" and the latter to the rise, beginning in the 1980s, of the related concept of "human development." These days, many in the development community talk about their mission in the broad terms of increasing the well-being of communities or nations, and measures reflecting quality of life have taken their place alongside GDP per capita as important yardsticks of development.[4]

While development as measured by GDP does not directly account for health outcomes, development in the broader sense of human well-being has improvement in human health at its heart. After all, the stuff of "traditional" development projects – the dams, the rail, the steel mills – are related only indirectly to improvements in human well-being. Build a dam, and you still require several complex steps and additional infrastructure to turn its mere existence into an improvement in well-being. But administer medicine that cures disease or a vaccine that prevents it and, if all goes well, the improvement in well-being is immediate and direct. This chapter sheds light on the long history of the globalization of development by examining how the control of infectious disease, particularly smallpox, was institutionalized as a development practice, first among modernizing states and then in international, transnational, and finally global spaces. It focuses in particular on the contentious processes through which global health institutions emerged, came to conceive of their roles as agents of development, and finally managed to recruit the resources to turn their institutional missions, the ideas upon which they were founded, into epidemiological practices implemented on the ground, on a global scale.

THE REASON OF STATES: CONTROLLING DISEASE ACROSS NATION AND EMPIRE

State efforts to preserve and improve the health of inhabitants go back to the ancient world, perhaps most famously with the Roman projects to

[4] On the rise of "sustainable development," see Stephen J. Macekura, *Of Limits and Growth: The Rise of Global Sustainable Development in the Twentieth Century* (New York: Cambridge University Press, 2015). The recent emphasis on development as "well-being" may be seen as a return to older, preeconometric notions. The goal of promoting "the well-being of mankind throughout the world" was defined as the central mission of the Rockefeller Foundation (RF) as outlined in its original charter in 1913, and Article XXII of the 1919 League of Nations Covenant defined the Mandates as designed to promote the "well-being and development" of the populations under their purview. RF charter found at https://assets.rockefellerfoundation.org/app/uploads/20150530122332/Rockefeller-Foundation-Charter.pdf

provide the population of the republic, and later the empire, with clean water, public baths, and other services of sanitation and hygiene. Beyond such measures of public health, political authorities in premodern times also engaged in direct prophylaxis against infectious diseases, often involving the isolation of individuals marked as contagious. One of the best known examples in the West of the use of isolation as a public health measure is the banishment of lepers practiced in medieval Europe. This practice was often implemented by church officials, who drew authority and inspiration from precepts laid down in the Old Testament decreeing the segregation of "impure" individuals from the community on a temporary or permanent basis. Early Christian councils placed restrictions on the association of lepers with healthy individuals in the community, and such procedures were further developed by religious and secular authorities in subsequent years. "Leper houses" appeared outside communities throughout much of Western Europe, and such practices persisted until leprosy largely disappeared as a public health problem in Europe in the sixteenth century.[5]

The same principle of segregating suspected agents of contagions from the community was implemented on a larger scale when quarantine came to be used widely in Western Europe with the great outbreak of plague, the Black Death, in the middle of the fourteenth century. Plague, which is caused by the *Yersinia pestis* bacterium and is transmitted to humans most commonly through the bite of an infected rat flea, was a deadly disease in the age before antibiotics. The fourteenth-century pandemic is estimated to have killed between 75 and 200 million people worldwide; in Europe, 30–60 percent of the population died. The medieval pandemic, which likely originated in central Asia, moved westward to the Black Sea, and then spread by sea to major European ports including Constantinople, Genoa, and Venice. It arrived in Europe in early 1348 and within a few years ravaged much of the continent. The terror of the plague led to the development of isolation techniques and the rise of quarantine (derived from the phrase meaning "forty days," the typical duration of isolation, in the Venetian dialect) as a public health measure.[6] Still, until the rise of modern states around the turn of the nineteenth century, the application of such direct prophylactic measures on a large scale by official authorities in the name of public health remained limited to times of crisis.

---

[5] George Rosen, *A History of Public Health*, exp. ed. (Baltimore, MD: Johns Hopkins University Press, 1993), 38–40.
[6] Rosen, *History of Public Health*, 41–45.

The nineteenth-century rise of regular medical prophylaxis as a state function, particularly in Europe and its colonial (or former colonial) off-shoots in North America and elsewhere, was tied with the contemporaneous rise of scientific medicine and of industrial capitalism, with its attendant social dislocations and the large labor force it required. Gradually, it came to be seen as insufficient to isolate individuals seen as contagious or seek to prevent contagion from the outside through quarantine. Instead, states grew interested in applying direct preventive measures to the bodies of healthy individuals to ward off contagion before it appeared. It was during this period that stewardship over public health generally, and the control of infectious disease more specifically, came to be viewed as a responsibility of emerging nation-states and became a component of the state's claim to legitimacy and authority, at once reflecting and shaping the state-building projects that sought to delineate and control borders and to render populations more legible and productive.[7]

Within the broad narrative of the construction of modern state authority in Europe and its colonial possessions around the globe, the evolution of smallpox prophylaxis presents an intriguing subplot. Unlike cholera, which for Europeans was the paradigmatic external contagion coming from the East and which therefore was the target of new regimes of quarantine, smallpox was in that era in Europe an endemic disease. It was always present in cities and among dense rural populations, often as the most feared, most dangerous, and, for those who survived, one of the most disfiguring of childhood diseases. And while various techniques for its prevention had long been practiced in Europe and elsewhere, it was not until the appearance of Jenner's vaccine during the time of the rise of modern nation-states in Europe and elsewhere that prophylaxis against smallpox shifted from a matter for families and local communities to one that concerned national authorities and became subject to projects of national control.[8]

In Britain, for example, the landmark 1898 Vaccination Act was a culmination of a decades-long struggle between the efforts of the state to propagate and regulate the practice and to manage resistance to it among the populace. Legislation passed in 1840 and 1841 made the

---

[7] Peter Baldwin, *Contagion and the State in Europe, 1830–1930* (Cambridge: Cambridge University Press, 1999).

[8] William L. Langer, "Immunization against Smallpox before Jenner," *Scientific American* 234:1 (1976); Baldwin, *Contagion and the State*, 526–527.

vaccination of children free and universal, and in 1853 it was made compulsory for children within the first year of life. A succession of further legislation in the 1860s and 1870s tightened enforcement by compelling local governments to appoint vaccination officers and allowing authorities to levy repeated fines on parents until they produced their offspring for vaccination. Resistors were sometimes jailed and their possessions confiscated to cover outstanding fines. These acts of state coercion led to fierce resistance among civil libertarians and the general populace, resistance that by the 1870s became organized in a number of anti-vaccination groups that objected to state compulsion in the matter. In addition, some advocates of sanitary and hygienic reforms resented the state's focus on vaccination since they worried, in an early echo of later tensions between "vertical" and "horizontal" (or narrowly targeted vs. broad-based) interventions in public health, that this focus would relax official vigilance on broader measures such as improving the quality of air, water, and living accommodations, especially for the poor.[9]

Despite the resistance it engendered within Europe itself, Jenner's innovation spread around the world as vaccination presented itself to modernizing states and medical experts as an instrument for establishing and extending their authority and legitimacy. Smallpox had had a major presence in South Asia for centuries, and it remained endemic in the densely populated subcontinent as the British established and expanded their authority there in the course of the eighteenth century. British physicians in India "ranked smallpox as among the most prevalent and destructive of all epidemic diseases," accounting on average for more than one hundred thousand fatalities annually.[10] In the Dutch East Indies, where smallpox had been present at least since the sixteenth century, the authorities introduced vaccination in 1804, only two years after its arrival in British India. The practice spread steadily and by the 1870s was established across much of the archipelago. As a result, smallpox, though not entirely eliminated, largely disappeared from the region by the 1920s,

---

[9] While the anti-vaccination movement in Britain failed to get compulsory vaccination abolished entirely, its efforts led to the introduction in 1907 of a "conscientious objection" clause allowing parents to opt out. By then, however, vaccination had become nearly universal in Britain, smallpox largely disappeared as a public health problem, and the debate petered out. Dorothy Porter, *Health, Civilization and the State: A History of Public Health from Ancient to Modern Times* (London: Routledge, 1999), 128–130; R. M. MacLeod, "Law, Medicine, and Public Opinion: The Resistance to Compulsory Health Legislation 1870–1907," *Public Law* (1967): 107–128, 189–211.

[10] David Arnold, *Colonizing the Body: State Medicine and Epidemic Disease in Nineteenth-Century India* (Berkeley: University of California Press, 1993), 116.

with the last major outbreak in Java recorded in 1913.[11] France, too, used vaccination to assert and institutionalize the authority of modern biomedicine in its colonial territories, and by the mid-twentieth century such campaigns had reduced the significance of smallpox as a public health problem.[12]

GERMS WITH BORDERS: DISEASE CONTROL AND THE RISE OF INTERNATIONAL INSTITUTIONS

Even as nation-states and colonial regimes adopted smallpox vaccination in the nineteenth century, institutions for international coordination on disease control also began to emerge. The direct impetus for the rise of institutionalized international arrangements to prevent disease was not smallpox, long an endemic problem in Europe, but rather the appearance of a new threat to the health of European populations: cholera. This disease, unknown in Europe before the nineteenth century, arrived there in a series of epidemics that swept Europe and North America between the 1830s and the 1890s and helped galvanize a succession of international sanitary congresses beginning in Paris in 1851. These congresses saw clashes between the powers most dependent on maritime trade, namely Britain and (to a lesser extent) France, who wanted looser quarantine regulations, and those who had less to gain from the free flow of goods across borders and therefore supported tougher quarantine regulations not only to protect anxious populations but also to frustrate the free-trading ambitions of their rivals. These tensions intersected with rancorous arguments among physicians about the role of contagion in the spread of disease, with the "contagionist" position (that favored quarantine) pitted against the arguments of those, especially among the British sanitary reformers, who argued that improvements in hygiene (better sewage, clearer water and air, personal hygiene) were far more important than quarantine at the border for improving population health.[13] Eventually,

---

[11] The upheaval of World War II, however, reintroduced the disease into the archipelago, and so, when the global eradication campaign began in the 1960s the now independent Indonesia was counted among the endemic regions for the disease. Vivek Neelakantan, "Eradicating Smallpox in Indonesia: The Archipelagic Challenge," *Health & History* 12: 1 (2010): 61–87.

[12] Christopher Ellis Hayden, "Of Medicine and Statecraft: Smallpox and Early Colonial Vaccination in French West Africa (Senegal-Guinea)" (Phd diss., Northwestern University, 2008).

[13] The classic analysis of this debate is Erwin H. Ackerknecht, "Anticontagionism between 1821 and 1867," *Bulletin of the History of Medicine* 22 (1948): 562–593. See also,

however, participants concluded treaties that for the first time established and regulated quarantine regimes at the international level rather than just a national one.[14]

The fifth sanitary conference, held in 1881, marked a turning point of sorts as the first to be held in the western hemisphere, in Washington, D. C. Reflecting the recent emergence of the United States as a major world power, the conference also included more participants than any of the previous ones, with representatives of the European powers joined not only by delegates from seven Latin American states but also from China, Japan, Liberia, Haiti, and Hawaii (then still an independent kingdom). One notable participant was Cuban-born Dr. Carlos Finlay, there to represent the interests of Cuba and Puerto Rico, then still both Spanish possessions. Finlay had been working to discover the method of transmission of yellow fever, one of the deadliest infectious diseases in the tropical regions of the Americas since its introduction from the Old World. Referencing the ongoing debate between contagionsists and anticontagionsists, Finlay asserted that there was a third element, independent of both the agent causing the disease and the humans susceptible to it, which must be present for transmission of yellow fever to occur. Six month later he suggested, for the first time, that a mosquito was that missing link.[15]

After 1881 there followed, in quick succession, several more conferences before century's end, all of them in Europe and all still mostly concerned with debating and establishing measures to prevent outbreaks of cholera.[16] At the same time, understandings of disease causation, or etiology, were undergoing a revolution as germ theory emerged as the dominant paradigm of infectious disease, gradually sidelining alternative explanations that focused on environmental causes. By the turn of the twentieth century, the growing acceptance of the germ theory introduced a range of new methods of disease control. These new discoveries were disseminated around the world, often by colonial powers eager to make newly acquired tropical territories safe for their personnel and to

Charles E. Rosenberg, "Commentary: Epidemiology in Context," *International Journal of Epidemiology* 38 (2009): 28–30.

[14] Norman Howard-Jones, "Origins of International Health Work," *British Medical Journal* (May 1950): 1: 1032–1046; Norman Howard-Jones, *The Scientific Background of the International Sanitary Conferences, 1851–1938* (Geneva: WHO, 1975).

[15] Howard-Jones, *The Scientific Background*, 42–45.

[16] Rome in 1885, Venice in 1892, Rome again in 1893, Paris in 1894, and Venice again in 1897.

demonstrate the "civilizing" effect of their rule. The United States, for example, moved to tackle yellow fever and malaria in Cuba and other tropical territories it acquired after the Spanish-American War of 1898. Building on Finlay's earlier insights, US Army surgeons Walter Reed and William C. Gorgas concluded that the two diseases were transmitted by specific species of mosquitoes and set in place programs to target these insect vectors, draining ponds and swamps and deploying fumigation and mosquito netting. In 1904, Gorgas also instated such measures in the Panama Canal Zone, making the work of constructing the canal project possible. In the Philippines, too, US colonial officials put in place programs of sanitation and disease control.[17]

Still, what is perhaps most notable about the development of international health regimes from the first sanitary conference of 1851 to the eve of World War I is the apparent disconnect between the transformation in the scientific understanding of the causes and modes of transmission of infectious diseases, on the one hand, and the limited, narrow responses to it on the international level. Granted, in the history of global health the international sanitary conferences are often seen as steps toward the eventual development of international and global health regimes. But while they established mechanisms for international coordination in disease control, they still construed it as primarily a task of the nation-state. The treaties, after all, simply aimed to help each contracting government ensure that its own territory remained contagion-free, suggesting that the existence of disease outside the boundaries of the state was important only to the extent it could travel and endanger the populations or possessions of that state. For the idea of confronting disease on a truly global scale to be institutionalized and implemented, the task of disease control would have to transcend the boundaries of the "prophylactic state" and move into transnational and global realms.

TRANSCENDING THE INTERNATIONAL: PHILANTHROPIC FOUNDATIONS AND TRANSNATIONAL NETWORKS

The idea that disease control was a global problem, rather than a national or even international one, began to take root not within formal national or international institutions but rather among emerging transnational networks of physicians and public health experts

---

[17] Warwick Anderson, *Colonial Pathologies: American Tropical Medicine, Race, and Hygiene in the Philippines* (Durham: Duke University Press, 2006).

working across government, academia, and private foundations.[18] These networks stretched across numerous countries, but a central node in them was the Rockefeller Foundation (RF), established in 1913 by the oil tycoon John D. Rockefeller in order to promote – in an echo of more recent rhetoric about development – "the well-being of mankind." The foundation's International Health Division, which operated from 1913 until 1951, was the single most influential actor in the field of global health in the first half of the twentieth century, and its ideology, outlook, and approach continue to permeate the global health establishment to this day. The RF's first foray into public health was a campaign against hookworm, an intestinal infection, in the US South, intended to help lift the region out of its perceived "backwardness." The hookworm campaign, begun in 1910, soon led to the internationalization of the foundation's health efforts, with programs directed at yellow fever, malaria, tuberculosis, and other infectious diseases that spread in the ensuing decades to dozens of countries across the Americas and around the world. From the outset, the foundation adopted a "scientific philanthropy" model that called for specific, defined interventions that had concrete goals and measurable results. Over the course of the first half of the twentieth century, the foundation's work with governments, international organizations, universities, and research institutes was instrumental in creating the transnational expert networks that would make up the global health establishment.[19]

The outbreak of World War I in August 1914 stalled international health collaboration while helping to create massive epidemics, including the global influenza pandemic of 1918 and the epidemics of typhus and other diseases that ravaged much of Eastern Europe, particularly after the collapse of the Russian Empire in 1917 and the ensuing civil

---

[18] Martin David Dubin has called this network the "biomedical/public health episteme." Martin David Dubin, "The League of Nations Health Organisation," in *International Health Organisations and Movements 1918–1939*, ed. Paul Weindling (Cambridge: Cambridge University Press, 1995), 56–80.

[19] John Farley, *To Cast out Disease: A History of the International Health Division of the Rockefeller Foundation, 1913–1951* (New York: Oxford University Press, 2004); Anne-Emanuelle Birn, *Marriage of Convenience: Rockefeller International Health and Revolutionary Mexico* (Rochester: University of Rochester Press, 2006); Marcos Cueto, *Missionaries of Science: The Rockefeller Foundation and Latin America* (Bloomington: Indiana University Press, 1994); Anne-Emanuelle Birn and Elizabeth Fee, "The Rockefeller Foundation and the International Health Agenda," *The Lancet* 381 (2013): 1618–1619.

war.[20] After the armistice, campaigns launched to stem these epidemics were part of efforts to ameliorate the devastation of the war and the ongoing mass violence, in Eastern Europe in particular.[21] These concerns were on the table at the 1919 Paris Peace Conference and thus Article 23 in the League of Nations Covenant announced that the members of the League would "endeavour to take steps in matters of international concern for the prevention and control of disease," while Article 25 added that they would "encourage and promote the establishment and co-operation of duly authorised voluntary national Red Cross organisations having as purposes the improvement of health, the prevention of disease and the mitigation of suffering throughout the world."[22] These declarations took institutional form soon thereafter, mainly through the establishment of the League of Nations Health Organization (LNHO).

Throughout most of its life, the main force behind the LNHO was its medical director, the Polish physician Ludwik Rajchman. Rajchman was born in Warsaw, then part of the Russian Empire, in 1881 to an assimilated family of Jewish origin, and received a medical degree from the University of Kraków in 1906. His activities and connections in socialist circles attracted the attention of the tsarist police and encouraged him to leave for Paris, where he studied at the Institut Pasteur, and then to the Royal Institute of Public Health in London, where he taught bacteriology and assisted in laboratories from 1910 to 1913. Energetic, charming, and possessed of a broad vision for the role of medicine in the improvement of society, Rajchman made inroads into transnational health circles. Arriving back in Warsaw just as the armistice was declared, he played a major role in devising Poland's response to the typhus epidemic, enlisting western assistance for the effort, and establishing an epidemiological and bacteriological infrastructure in the new state. He became a member of the League of Nation's Epidemic Commission, the forerunner to the LNHO, and impressed health officials and experts with his passion and efficiency. In October 1921, therefore, he was appointed LNHO medical

---

[20] On the influenza pandemic, see John M. Barry, *The Great Influenza: The Epic Story of the Deadliest Plague in History* (New York: Viking Penguin, 2004). On typhus, Paul Weindling, *Epidemics and Genocide in Eastern Europe, 1890–1945* (Oxford: Oxford University Press, 2000), esp. chap. 4.

[21] On the postarmistice violence in Europe, see Robert Gerwarth, *The Vanquished: Why the First World War Failed to End* (New York: Farrar, Straus, and Giroux, 2016). On the relief efforts, see Julia Irwin, *Making the World Safe: The American Red Cross and a Nation's Humanitarian Awakening* (New York: Oxford University Press, 2013).

[22] Covenant text at http://avalon.law.yale.edu/20th_century/leagcov.asp.

director, responsible for the daily management and operations of the organization.[23]

Rajchman had great ambitions for the LNHO, and the staff he gathered around him in the LNHO secretariat shared his views. One key to his success in battling the postwar epidemics in Eastern Europe and the Balkans, including the epidemics caused by the massive dislocations and population transfers that attended the conflicts in post-Ottoman territories, was his ability to collaborate with the new Soviet leaders, who saw in him something of a kindred spirit.[24] At the same time, Rajchman was also able to work closely with the Rockefeller Foundation, with the LNHO often serving as a surrogate for the foundation, functioning for example as a clearinghouse for governments requesting RF grants for physician training and other health-related purposes. From 1922 until the mid-1930s, the RF transferred more than 2 million dollars to the LNHO, accounting for a substantial proportion of its budget in those years.[25]

The establishment of the LNHO marked a crucial stage in the emergence of disease control as a task amenable to global action, not least since its leadership imagined its responsibilities as global. The professional cohort that formed around the organization helped to knit more tightly the transnational networks of public health experts, an epistemic community that was central in the postwar establishment of the World Health Organization (WHO) and, more generally, in the rise of the postwar global health establishment.[26] As the institutionalization of international health entered a new phase in the wake of World War II, the WHO emerged from the ashes of the LNHO even more ambitious than its predecessor. Indeed, its founders chose the term *world*, rather than international, for its name as a conscious reflection of their global ambitions: to serve not nations, but humanity itself.

---

[23] Marta A. Balińska, *For the Good of Humanity: Ludwik Rajchman, Medical Statesman.* Trans. Rebecca Howell (Budapest: Central European University Press, 1998). Originally published in French in 1995; Dubin, "The League of Nations Health Organisation," 65–69.

[24] Amy L. S. Staples, *The Birth of Development: How the World Bank, Food and Agriculture Organization, and World Health Organization Changed the World, 1945–1965* (Kent: The Kent State University Press, 2006), 129–132.

[25] Dubin, "The League of Nations Health Organisation," 72–73.

[26] Neville M. Goodman, *International Health Organizations and Their Work* (London: J. & A. Churchill, 1952); Norman Howard-Jones, *International Public Health between the Two World Wars – The Organizational Problems* (Geneva: WHO, 1978).

LAUNCHING A GLOBAL CAMPAIGN: PROFESSIONAL
NETWORKS MEET COLD WAR IRONIES

By the time the WHO's constitution was ratified in 1948, however, the Cold War was in full force. The Soviet Union and the other Eastern Bloc countries refused to join the organization, suspicious of its intentions. This meant that the WHO's first major global campaign, the Malaria Eradication Program (MEP) launched in 1955, was primarily a US-backed initiative with no Soviet participation. It was, moreover, designed to reflect US strategic concerns, focusing on regions, such as Southeast Asia, where Washington wanted to increase its influence and marginalizing those, such as sub-Saharan Africa, that were deemed less strategically important.[27] In this way, the MEP resembled colonial disease control efforts in that its public health goals were secondary to broader concerns related to promoting economic development and political stability and allegiance.[28] The smallpox campaign, launched a decade later in a different international environment, would instead come to center obsessively on the goal of global eradication seeking, in effect, to reproduce the capacity of the modernizing, prophylactic state, but do so on a global scale.

By the early 1960s, it had become clear the MEP was in trouble. The program's basic method was to seek to interrupt the transmission of the malaria parasite by targeting its mosquito vector with synthetic residual insecticides, chief among them dichlorodiphenyltrichloroethane, or DDT. But the massive worldwide use of DDT spraying for malaria control since World War II had caused the emergence and proliferation of resistant mosquito populations; the more DDT was used, the more prevalent resistance became. In addition, DDT had come under attack for its environmental effects as it reverberated up the food chain and disrupted ecosystems.[29] Thus, despite significant early successes in some regions the malaria eradication campaign was fast approaching its limits, and those limits lay well short of worldwide eradication.[30]

---

[27] Javed Siddiqi, *World Health and World Politics: The World Health Organization and the UN System* (London: C. Hurst: 1995), 104–109, 141–145.

[28] Randall M. Packard, "Visions of Postwar Health and Development and Their Impact on Public Health Interventions in the Developing World," in *International Development and the Social Sciences*, ed. Frederick Cooper and Randall M. Packard (Berkeley: University of California Press, 1997), 93–118

[29] This was, most famously, the focus of Rachel Carson's *Silent Spring* (1962), a seminal text of the environmental protection movement.

[30] Staples, *Birth of Development*, 161–171. As of late 2017, the WHO still does not expect the worldwide eradication of malaria in the foreseeable future. Instead, it has set a goal of

As the prospects for the global eradication of malaria waned, epidemiologists in the United States and elsewhere began to seek a more promising target for their efforts. When Dr. James Watt, then Chief Assistant to the US Surgeon General and director of the Office of International Health at the US Public Health Service, wrote in 1962 to fellow members of the American Public Health Association to solicit suggestions for disease eradication programs that the US health establishment could undertake, several proposed smallpox as the leading candidate.[31] There was a vaccine with a long history of use with few side effects, and unlike the malaria pathogen the virus that caused smallpox had no animal vector; instead, it moved directly from one human to another through close contact. Fighting it, therefore, would not require a wider ecological intervention. Moreover, success would have broad positive implications for the international standing of public health experts: "We must face the cold sober fact," wrote one respondent, "that no communicable disease has ever been eradicated throughout the world to date through man's conscious efforts. It would certainly be a salutary thing to prove just once that one communicable disease can be eradicated through man's conscious efforts. Smallpox is my nominee for such a global program."[32]

By the early 1960s, then, the public health establishment had smallpox clearly in its sights. But how could it recruit the political support needed to get the funding for such an ambitious eradication program for a disease that, after many decades of large-scale vaccination, was no longer seen as a major public health threat in the developed world? A window of opportunity opened in early 1965, with the approach of World Health Day, celebrated by the WHO each year on April 7. For that year, the WHO had chosen the theme of "Smallpox—Constant Alert," a reminder for governments to remain vigilant against the threat of the importation of the disease from the world's endemic areas – that is, much of the Global South. At the same time, to mark the twentieth anniversary of its

---

substantially reducing its incidence and mortality by 2030. http://www.who.int/malaria/about_us/en/.

[31] James E. Perkins, managing director of the National Tuberculosis Association, to Ernest S. Tierkel, Sept. 26, 1962. A memorandum by the prominent epidemiologist T. Aidan Cockburn, Sept. 12, 1962, also ranked smallpox as the top candidate for global eradication. United States National Archives (USNA), RG 90, Box 22, Folder "Association – APHA – Committee on Disease Eradication."

[32] Perkins to Watt, Aug. 28, 1962. Underlined in original. USNA, RG 90, Box 22, Folder "Association – APHA – Committee on Disease Eradication."

founding, the United Nations had declared 1965 as International Cooperation Year. Washington took notice, and with the escalating war in Vietnam damaging the US reputation around the world the White House was searching for ways to display its support for international cooperation.[33]

This was the opening the public health establishment needed. Why not have the president, proposed an official from the US Department of Health, Education, and Welfare (HEW), issue a statement for World Health Day highlighting the success of smallpox control in the Global North and expressing US support for the idea of launching a campaign to eradicate it globally?[34] For the Johnson administration, smallpox eradication seemed to be exactly what the doctor ordered: an inexpensive and relatively uncontroversial way to demonstrate US commitment to international cooperation. Thus, as the World Health Assembly, the WHO's governing body, gathered for its annual meeting in Geneva in May, the White House released a statement declaring that "as long as smallpox exists anywhere in the world, no country is safe from it." Summarizing the recently established expert view, the statement asserted that the "technical problems" of global eradication were "minimal," while the "administrative problems," including assuring vaccine supplies, personnel, and coordination, could be solved through international cooperation. The United States, it concluded, was therefore "ready to work with other interested countries to see that smallpox is a thing of the past by 1975."[35]

From the outset, the push for global smallpox eradication was presented to the public as a shining example of international collaboration amid Cold War conflict. But while the White House announcement to the world framed the US decision to support international health initiatives as a move toward transcending Cold War tensions, US officials tasked with justifying these programs domestically often fell back on traditional Cold War rhetoric, presenting them as an opportunity to showcase the superiority of American science and as an antidote against the spread of communism among the world's poor and downtrodden. Such a program, argued one official memorandum, would be a tool that could "penetrate

[33] "President Johnson on International Cooperation Year," Department of State, *Foreign Affairs Outline, 1965: International Cooperation Year,* in USNA, RG 90, Box 42, Folder "International Cooperation Year."

[34] Levy to Holborn, n.d., and Holborn to Horowitz, March 12, 1965, Lyndon Baines Johnson Library [LBJL], White House Central Files, Ex HE/MC, box 6.

[35] White House press release, May 18, 1965, LBJL, White House Central Files, Ex HE/MC, Box 6.

any Iron or Bamboo curtain to reach the minds and the hearts of man." It would promote world peace, showcase the United States as "the fountainhead of medicine," and help US allies combat the temptations of communism.[36] Washington's support for the push to eradicate smallpox globally, then, could have conflicting justifications for different audiences. For the international community and domestic internationalists, it was about transcending the Cold War. To hard-line anti-communists, it was about winning it.

GLOBAL HEALTH IN PRACTICE: MIMICKING THE PROPHYLACTIC STATE ON A WORLD SCALE

For those who needed to do eradication on the ground, however, political considerations of a different sort of took precedence. For one, the SEP required vast quantities of vaccine – more than two billion doses, it turned out – and only the USSR initially had the infrastructure in place to produce that many doses.[37] So when Donald A. Henderson, head of the Epidemic Surveillance Section at the Communicable Disease Center (CDC), moved to the WHO's Geneva headquarters in 1966 to lead the program, his first priority was to ensure an ongoing Soviet vaccine supply.[38] His task was complicated by the fact that the Soviets, who had been first to call on the WHO to undertake a worldwide campaign against smallpox, thought that one of their own should have been appointed to

---

[36] Undated memorandum, LBJL, Office Files of Joseph A. Califano, Box 29 (1737), Folder "Health." Underlined in the original.

[37] F. Fenner et al., *Smallpox and Its Eradication [SAIE]* (Geneva: WHO, 1988), 469, 564. This volume, a detailed institutional account of the SEP, is also available online through the WHO website. Other published participant accounts of the SEP include D. A. Henderson, *Smallpox: The Death of a Disease* (New York: Prometheus Books, 2009), William H. Foege, *House on Fire: The Fight to Eradicate Smallpox* (Berkeley: University of California Press, 2011), and Larry Brilliant, *Sometimes Brilliant: The Impossible Adventure of a Spiritual Seeker and Visionary Physician Who Helped Conquer the Worst Disease in History* (San Francisco: HarperOne, 2016). See also, Sanjoy Bhattacharya and Sharon Messenger, eds., *The Global Eradication of Smallpox* (New Delhi: Orient Blackswan, 2010), Erez Manela, "A Pox on Your Narrative: Writing Disease Control into Cold War History," *Diplomatic History* 34:2 (April 2010): 299–323, and Bob H. Reinhardt, *The End of a Global Pox: America and the Eradication of Smallpox in the Cold War Era* (Chapel Hill: The University of North Carolina Press, 2015).

[38] Confidential memorandum from Chief SE to Director CD, Oct. 28, 1968, WHO Archive, Smallpox Eradication Program papers [WHOA-SEP], Box 303, Folder 30. The CDC was later renamed the Centers for Disease Control and Prevention, though the acronym CDC was kept.

lead it. So when Henderson approached the head of the Soviet delegation, Dmitry Venediktov, at the World Health Assembly meeting to ask for an ongoing supply of vaccine, he was somewhat apprehensive. The Russian, however, explained that though he could not officially guarantee vaccine donations more than one year at a time, the nature of the Soviet-planned economy was such that once a certain annual production quota was in place, it was likely to be met, like clockwork, each year. As it turned out, it was.[39]

Even with such superpower collaboration, however, how could the program vaccinate billions of individuals across dozens of nations and in some of the world's most impoverished, inaccessible regions? One of the SEP's defining characteristics, after all, was the imposition of a homogenized, scientific procedure, that of vaccination, in place of a diverse array of local practices that were still prevalent across the Global South, where many communities already had long-standing traditions designed to ameliorate the encounter with smallpox. Indeed, the standardization of such things as vaccine production and quality, vaccination techniques, and methods of epidemic surveillance and control stood at the center of the program's *raison d'être* and constituted for its leaders a *sine qua non* of global eradication. In other words, in order to succeed, the SEP had to mimic the authority and reach of the modern prophylactic state, but on a global scale.

In numerous regions SEP personnel, working in conjunction with national and local health officials, therefore worked to sideline our long-standing indigenous modes of understanding and dealing with smallpox. In parts of West Africa, for example, this meant negotiating the cooperation or acquiescence of priests of the smallpox deity *Sopona*, while in India the program had to contend with the veneration of the smallpox goddess *Sītalā mata* and the practices associated with it.[40] In rural Afghanistan, vaccinators had to find ways to work around traditions of purdah that rendered their access to women and children difficult.[41] They also had to convince practitioners of the long-established methods of smallpox

---

[39] Donald Henderson, "Smallpox Eradication—A Cold War Victory," *World Health Forum* 19 (1998): 115–116.

[40] *SAIE*, 716, 887–888. For a critical approach to the interaction of vaccination and other practices in India, see Frédérique Apffel Marglin, "Smallpox in Two Systems of Knowledge," in *Dominating Knowledge: Development, Culture, and Resistance*, ed. Frédérique Apffel Marglin and Stephen A. Marglin (Oxford: Clarendon Press, 1990), 102–144.

[41] Henderson to Millar, May 29, 1967, WHOA-SEP, Box 159, Folder 378.

inoculation, a pre-vaccination prevention practice that was still widely used there, to quit their trade or else give up their powdered-scab material for SEP-supplied vaccine. This effort involved a push for legislation and enforcement but also outreach to the community, for example the circulation of a pamphlet entitled "A Variolator Gives Up His Profession and Encourages His Son to Become a Vaccinator."[42]

The absolute nature of the program's goal – smallpox was to be not simply controlled within the boundaries of a given state but eradicated worldwide – meant that resistance to its homogenizing requirements had to be overcome, either negotiated away or, if necessary, broken by force. Pressure on individuals who resisted vaccination took various forms: insistent verbal persuasion, the application of social and legal pressure, offers of payment, and, at the extreme, forcible vaccination conducted through military-style raids. In one well-known example, a top international SEP official in India recalled how he had led a team of vaccinators that, accompanied by Indian military troops, broke in the dead of night into the home of a village elder in a remote locale in what was then southern Bihar state. The man, who believed it was his religious duty to resist vaccination, was vaccinated only after a violent struggle. After that, the rest of the village inhabitants submitted to the procedure.[43]

While various degrees of resistance shadowed the program in many regions, on the whole such resistance took the form of small-scale acts of defiance rather than a well-organized or widespread movement. Nowhere across the vast and varied terrain of the program did it encounter the broad resistance to smallpox vaccination such as had been common in North America and Europe in the nineteenth century, or like the movement that arose in India against tuberculosis immunization in the 1950s.[44] Such broad popular acquiescence was indispensable to the SEP's eventual

---

[42] An undated narrative by A. G. Rangaraj, SEP chief in Afghanistan. On the program's battle against variolation, see also, Chief SE/HQ to Regional Director, SEARO, Oct. 30, 1967, where Henderson complains that the Afghan government had not yet outlawed the practice; Henderson to Khwaja-Waisuddin, 17 Jan. 1969; Henderson to Rangaraj, Nov. 17, 1969; and an undated report on "Variolation in Afghanistan" by Vladimir Sery, Svend Brøgger, Amin Fakir, and Aminullah Saboor. All in WHOA-SEP, Box 159, Folder 378.

[43] Paul Greenough, "Intimidation, Coercion and Resistance in the Final Stages of the South Asian Smallpox Campaign, 1973–1975," *Social Science & Medicine* 41 (1995): 633–645. Lawrence Brilliant with Girija Brilliant, "Death for a Killer Disease," *Quest* (1978): 3–10.

[44] Michael R. Albert, Kristen G. Ostheimer, and Joel G. Breman, "The Last Smallpox Epidemic in Boston and the Vaccination Controversy, 1901–1903," *New England Journal of Medicine* 344:5 (2001): 375–379; Christian W. McMillen and Niels Brimnes, "Medical Modernization and Medical Nationalism: Resistance to Mass

success, as was its work with all levels of government in the target countries across the Global South and the large-scale recruitment of local labor and expertise. After all, the international officials and experts who ran the program – many of them North Americans but many others coming from the USSR, Europe (east and west), Latin America, Asia, and Africa – were all together always a tiny minority of the program's overall staff. The overwhelming majority of SEP field workers, more than 150,000 health personnel in all, were drawn from the local populations in target countries.[45]

In part due to such integration, the program displayed a flexibility in adapting its methods to local conditions, whether political, administrative, epidemiological, or cultural, not often associated with international development programs. When, soon after it was launched, the initial goal of 100 percent vaccination proved impractical, the program moved to focus on a method dubbed "surveillance and containment" that sought to identify outbreaks early and concentrate on vaccinating those living within a certain radius around them in order to prevent transmission beyond the outbreak area.[46] The SEP proved resilient enough to survive the bloody wars that erupted in some of its main regions of operation, including Nigeria, Bengal, and the Horn of Africa, often negotiating vaccinator access to conflict zones with the various state and nonstate parties involved. Finally, unlike many of the projects that populate the historiography of international development in the Cold War era, the SEP succeeded in achieving its stated goal, reaching "smallpox zero" worldwide by the end of 1977, only two years beyond the time frame that had been envisioned when the global program was launched in 1965. No naturally occurring infections have been recorded since, though the smallpox virus continues to live on in two official repositories in the United States and Russia and, possibly, in unofficial ones elsewhere.[47]

Tuberculosis Vaccination in Postcolonial India, 1948–1955," *Comparative Studies in Society & History* 52:1 (2010): 180–209.

[45] Jonathan Tucker, *Scourge: The Once and Future Threat of Smallpox* (New York: Grove Press, 2001), 3.

[46] On the emergence of the surveillance/containment strategy, see Foege, *House on Fire*, esp. ch. 4, and D. A. Henderson, "Surveillance – The Key to Smallpox Eradication," WHO document no. WHO/SE/68.2. On the program's adaptability, see Sanjoy Bhattacharya and Rajib Dasgupta, "A Tale of Two Global Health Programs: Smallpox Eradication's Lessons for the Antipolio Campaign in India," *American Journal of Public Health* 99:7 (2009), and Reinhardt, *The End of a Global Pox*, esp. ch. 4.

[47] These repositories have been the subject of a contentious debate as to whether the remaining virus should be destroyed or preserved for future scientific research. See, for

CONCLUSION

The eradication of smallpox was facilitated by an unusual, perhaps unique convergence of factors that came together in international society from the mid-1960s to the mid-1970s. In the wake of the Cuban Missile Crisis, the two superpowers had entered an era of détente. At the same time, rapid decolonization fostered competition over the "hearts and minds" of newly independent peoples, competition that could, in the right circumstances, turn into collaboration when both sides wanted to be seen as doing something for the world's poor and neither was willing to abandon a promising arena of development aid to the other. This period also saw a high point in the status of the UN specialized agencies such as the WHO, a golden age of sorts that began with the Soviet reengagement in the late 1950s and came to an end with the US disengagement some two decades later under the influence of the rising neoliberal wave. The transnational networks of public health experts, formed over the previous decades, craved a dramatic achievement that would bolster their professional standing, and they won political backing by proposing smallpox as a uniquely eradicable scourge and the SEP as an inexpensive way for the two superpowers, as well as for newly installed postcolonial leaders, to demonstrate their developmental bone fides.

In the time since, with smallpox still the only major infectious disease of humans to have been eradicated, the SEP has come to represent the paradigmatic success in the history of global health, and perhaps even of international development writ large.[48] But the meanings and implications of the SEP's success have remained contested within the global health community and beyond. Was it a model for the eradication of the many other infectious diseases – polio, tuberculosis, malaria, yellow fever, perhaps even AIDS – that still plague humanity? Or was it a singular event made possible by the unique epidemiological characteristics of smallpox and the specific confluence of international conditions in an era of superpower détente and postcolonial optimism? The answer, no doubt, lies somewhere in between.

---

example, Raymond S. Weinstein, "Should Remaining Stockpiles of Smallpox Virus (Variola) Be Destroyed?" *Emerging Infectious Diseases* 17:4 (April 2011) http://dx.doi .org/10.3201/eid1704.101865.

[48] The global eradication of rinderpest, an infectious disease of cattle, was achieved in 2001 and certified in 2011. See Amanda McVety, *The Rinderpest Campaigns: A Virus, Its Vaccines, and Global Development in the Twentieth Century* (New York: Cambridge University Press, forthcoming).

Moreover, even if the SEP success in implementing development on a global scale could be repeated with other diseases – and, at the time of this writing, the poliomyelitis virus may well be on the cusp of global eradication – there still remain the horizontalist critiques that argue that the focus on the eradication of individual pathogens is in any case misguided since it takes resources away from broader efforts to improve the health of the world's poor, especially the improvement in the delivery of primary health care. The globalization of development, reflected in the coalescence of ideologies and methodologies, the establishment of international institutions and transnational networks and, through them, the mobilization of resources around the idea of improving human well-being on a planetary scale, may have helped Jefferson's long-ago prediction to come true. Still, the contentious debates around questions of global development, debates that in the end center, just as they do in national contexts, on the allocation of scarce resources, remain very much with us.

PART II

DEVELOPMENT IN A DECOLONIZING WORLD: BETWEEN LOCAL AND GLOBAL

6

New Frontiers: World War II Technologies and the Opening of Tropical Environments to Development

Thomas Robertson

"In the desperation of a fight to survive, miracles have been wrought in laboratories and with machines. Seeing the reality of things they had never dreamed could happen, men have been deeply stirred; now almost nothing seems impossible."

–David Lilienthal, 1944[1]

"The future, good or bad, will be the work of man and not the result of physical constraints."

–Pierre Gourou, 1954[2]

Many, if not most, international development projects, particularly in the second half of the twentieth century, emphasized transferring knowledge and technological tools from the world's temperate zones to tropical and subtropical areas, and often aimed explicitly at transforming nature, sometimes radically so. These technologies reflected their socio-environmental origins, played out in environments that shaped their success or failure, often decisively so, and, through intended or unintended consequences, forged landscapes that have to be included among development's most lasting changes. Nature both shaped development projects and was shaped by them. Today, much of the world's population lives in "development landscapes" created by big projects.

---

[1] David Lilienthal, *TVA: Democracy on the March* (New York: Harper & Brothers, 1944), 4.
[2] Pierre Gourou, "The Quality of Land Use of Tropical Cultivators," in *Man's Role in Changing the Face of the Earth*, ed. William Thomas (Chicago: University of Chicago Press, 1956), 346.

Development projects surged after World War II, bolstered by a strong wave of technological enthusiasm. "We must embark on a bold new program," Truman announced in his famous 1949 inaugural address launching US "Point Four" international development programs, "for making the benefits of our scientific advances and industrial progress available for the improvement and growth of underdeveloped areas." He added, "Our imponderable resources in technical knowledge are constantly growing and are inexhaustible . . . . We should make available to peace-loving peoples the benefits of our store of technical knowledge in order to help them realize their aspirations for a better life."[3]

Although a long-standing part of Western culture, technological confidence reached unprecedented heights in the United States in the 1950s and 1960s – what Michael Adas has called "technological triumphalism."[4] "For the first time in history," the historian Arnold Toynbee noted in 1951, the "ideal of welfare for all" – meaning international development programs – had become "a practical objective instead of a mere utopian dream." What explained this, he said, was a "sudden vast enhancement of man's ability to make nonhuman nature produce what man requires from her."[5]

Previously, hopes for development stood much lower, especially in the world's "tropical" environments. In the nineteenth century, as Paul Sutter has written, the tropics were seen as "a place that, most importantly, seemed to resist all efforts by temperate Europeans and North Americans at settlement, control, and development."[6] They were landscapes rich in resources but undevelopable. For Benjamin Kidd, writing in *The Control of the Tropics (1898)*, the tropics were "the region most richly endowed by nature on the face of the globe." But for centuries, Europeans had expanded into the temperate areas of the world – North

---

[3] Harry S. Truman, Inaugural Address, January 20, 1949, Harry S. Truman Library and Museum, http://www.trumanlibrary.org/whistlestop/50yr_archive/inagural20jan1949 .htm, accessed January 5, 2011.

[4] Michael Adas, *Dominance by Design: Technological Imperatives and America's Civilizing Mission* (Cambridge, MA: Harvard University Press, 2006), 243. For earlier ideas of technology, see Michael Adas, *Machines as the Measure of Men: Science, Technology, and Ideologies of Western Dominance* (Ithaca: Cornell University Press, 1989).

[5] Arnold Toynbee, "Not the Age of Atoms but of Welfare for All," *New York Times*, October 21, 1951.

[6] Paul Sutter, "The Tropics: A Brief History of an Environmental Imaginary," in *The Oxford Handbook of Environmental History*, ed. Andrew C. Isenberg (New York: Oxford University Press, 2014), 178.

America, parts of Argentina and Chile, Australia and southern Africa – but tropical areas had mostly resisted such development.[7]

Ideas of what was possible in tropical environments changed dramatically over the course of the twentieth century. A new confidence developed – a "tropical triumphalism" in Sutter's words.[8] American success in building the Panama Canal in the 1910s showed the efficacy of American engineering and tropical medicine.[9] US commercial interests – mining, banana, and coffee companies – began expanding widely into tropical areas.[10] As Julia Irwin shows in this book, the United States responded to disasters in the tropics, out of which often grew haphazard and uneven developmental missions. By 1939, the Australian Grenfell Price, writing in *White Settlers in the Tropics*, argued that science could create opportunities for European settlement and development throughout the tropics.[11] "The early history of white settlement in the tropics was a story of wasted lives, wasted efforts, and wasted resources, but the recent years go with achievement," Price wrote the following year. "The scientific world has at last glimpsed the vastness and complexity of the problem. In the hands of scientific workers lies the solution."[12]

Nonetheless, at World War II's outset, doubts still remained about tropical development. "Some scientists still fear that the climate, even in the moderate tropics," Price noted in a 1940 article, "is psychologically and physiologically enervating for white persons."[13] "Many old-fashioned and exaggerated ideas still exist regarding the difficulties of working in tropical climates," William Rudolph wrote in a 1943 article on highway construction. But these ideas were changing. As Rudolph noted, they were "old fashioned" and "exaggerated." Neither disease nor climate, he observed, need undermine either local residents or

---

[7] Alfred W. Crosby, *Ecological Imperialism: The Biological Expansion of Europe, 900–1900* (Cambridge: Cambridge University Press, 1986).

[8] Sutter, "The Tropics: A Brief History of an Environmental Imaginary," 2014, 192.

[9] Adas, *Dominance by Design*, ch. 4.

[10] Richard P. Tucker, *Insatiable Appetite: The United States and the Ecological Degradation of the Tropical World* (Berkeley: University of California Press, 2000); John Soluri, *Banana Cultures: Agriculture, Consumption, and Environmental Change in Honduras and the United States* (Austin: University of Texas Press, 2006).

[11] A. Grenfell Price, *White Settlers in the Tropics* (New York: American Geographical Society, 1939).

[12] Price, 238.

[13] A. Grenfell Price, "Refugee Settlement in the Tropics," *Foreign Affairs* 18:4 (July 1940): 659–670, 670.

outsiders. "Natives work without disadvantage in the climates to which they are accustomed, and foreigners can usually do so too if their food and living conditions are right."[14]

This chapter argues that World War II was a turning point in the history of development. As many chapters in this book show, key elements of postwar international development had earlier roots. World War II vastly accelerated the tropical triumphalism that had first emerged in earlier decades. Unprecedentedly global – fought in places like the South Pacific and North Africa – the war demanded technologies to deploy in some of the world's most far-flung, varied, and unfamiliar environments. "The Second World War was unique," one historian has written, "in the variety of the terrain and climate in which it was waged. Mountain, jungle, and desert, intense heat and extreme cold all required specialist skills and these were often employed as much in a battle with the elements as against the other side."[15] Millions of dollars flowed into tropical research and development and tens of thousands of Americans worked in such regions. Military progress depended upon technological adaptation. In this great effort to develop and adapt American "know how" for tropical areas, the United States capitalized on what historian Robert Gordon has called the "big leap" in American productivity from 1928 to the 1940s: the massive growth that came from electricity, the internal combustion engine and fossil fuels, modern communications, and modern chemistry.[16]

Historically, three barriers had blocked tropical development: disease, the combination of geographical remoteness and poor information, and infertile soil.[17] This chapter traces the World War II development and eventual application in postwar international development programs of four technologies to solve these problems: 1) DDT to prevent diseases such as malaria; 2) bulldozers, trucks, and highways to improve transport; 3) aerial photography to facilitate rapid geographical reconnaissance over inhospitable terrain; and 4) "green revolution" agricultural technology to make up for poor soils. Developed or vastly advanced in large part during and because of the war, these technologies – and the confidence they

---

[14] William E. Rudolph, "Strategic Roads of the World: Notes on Recent Developments," *Geographical Review* 33:1 (January 1, 1943): 114.

[15] Charles Messenger, "Land Power" in *The Oxford Companion to World War II*, ed. I. C. B Dear and M. R. D Foot (Oxford: Oxford University Press, 2011).

[16] Robert J. Gordon, *The Rise and Fall of American Growth: The U.S. Standard of Living since the Civil War* (Princeton: Princeton University Press, 2016), 564.

[17] Sutter, "The Tropics: A Brief History of an Environmental Imaginary," 2014, 194.

spurred – eventually played transformative roles in postwar development programs, adding to both the scale and intensity of development's environmental impact.

Scholars of development have noted the political consequences of postwar technological triumphalism. Michael Adas has examined the logic of cultural and racial superiority that interwove with European and American ideas of technology.[18] According to the anthropologist James Ferguson, development often resembled an "anti-politics" machine that defined poverty as a narrow technical problem, often the absence of a particular technology, thereby justifying unwanted state intervention while disregarding political problems of class exploitation, governmental rent-seeking, and incompetence. More generally, sometimes the availability of certain overhyped technological tools drove the defining of problems and projects, to the exclusion of addressing the underlying social, political, or economic problems – the so-called "when you have a hammer, everything looks like a nail" critique. Similarly, the political scientist James Scott has analyzed how state-centered, authoritarian, technocratic development programs are forced on local communities and environments to render them more standardized – more "legible" – and thus more easily monitored and controlled by the state. The four technologies described in this chapter often formed part of anti-political, high-modernist development projects.[19]

But these are not the only story to tell. Because of their wartime development, the technologies outlined in this article – and, importantly, the conventions surrounding their use – shared several characteristics that gave them an unprecedented environmental scale and intensity, which in turn usually carried large social and political consequences. First, to cover a lot of ground quickly, they were produced in large quantity and/or designed to work on a broad scale. Second, they were designed to have universal application, often encouraging a one-size-fits-all approach that made tailoring to particular environments unnecessary and difficult. Third, they tended to gobble lots of energy, particularly fossil fuels. Fourth, they emerged during a crisis atmosphere of extreme urgency, where normal precautions were downplayed and corners cut in the rush to find solutions. Few worried about worker safety or long-term

---

[18] Adas, *Machines as the Measure of Men*; Adas, *Dominance by Design*.

[19] James Ferguson, *The Anti-Politics Machine: "Development," Depoliticization, and Bureaucratic Power in Lesotho* (New York: Cambridge University Press, 1990). For high modernism, see James C. Scott, *Seeing Like a State: How Certain Schemes to Improve the Human Condition Have Failed* (New Haven: Yale University Press, 1998).

environmental sustainability. The goal was taking territory and defeating the enemy, not cultivating local skills, protecting ecosystems, or creating sustainable, inclusive institutions. The goal was legibility and centralized power, not empowerment. Because of these characteristics, the four technologies described in this article dramatically remade environments and, through them, social and political landscapes.[20]

When the first plans for international development emerged after the war, critics warned about severe environmental problems. Indeed, as the great push for international development first coalesced in the late 1940s, Americans fiercely debated technological and environmental limits. For some, the Great Depression had indicated ecological limits pushed too far, limits that World War II confirmed on a global scale.[21] In *The Great Frontier* (1952), historian Walter Prescott Webb contended that the age of discovery that had opened a world frontier in the late fifteenth century, unleashing "a sudden, continuing, and even increasing flood of wealth" for the Western world, had crashed to a halt. The American frontier had closed during the 1890s and the Depression and war had demonstrated limits reached. In 1951, Webb published an article titled "Ended: Four Hundred Year Boom."[22] In *Road to Survival* (1948), conservationist William Vogt added to this thinking an ecological understanding of the world's limited carrying capacity, warning about the environmental repercussions of newly planned development programs. To anyone who "thinks in terms of the carrying capacities of the world's lands," he stressed, the American promise of a higher standard of living through international development was "a monstrous deception."[23] Overconfidence in technologies and disregard for natural processes would create massive ecological problems. Vogt's ecological warnings went mostly ignored by policymakers in the 1950s and 1960s, but they would gain greater traction, despite their

---

[20] For an overview of recent environmental history of development, see Thomas Robertson, "Cold War Landscapes: Towards an Environmental History of US Development Programmes in the 1950s and 1960s," *Cold War History* 16:4 (2016): 417–441. Also see Robertson and Smith, eds., *Transplanted Modernity? New Histories of Technology, Development and Environment* (Pittsburgh: University of Pittsburgh Press, forthcoming).

[21] Thomas Robertson, *Malthusian Moment: Global Population Growth and the Birth of American Environmentalism* (New Brunswick: Rutgers University Press, 2012), chs. 1 and 2; Alison Bashford, *Global Population: History, Geopolitics, and Life on Earth* (New York: Columbia University Press, 2014).

[22] Walter Prescott Webb, *The Great Frontier* (Boston: Houghton Mifflin, 1952), 13; Walter Prescott Webb, "Ended: Four Hundred Year Boom," *Harper's* 103:1217 (October 1951): 25–35.

[23] William Vogt, *Road to Survival* (New York: William Sloane Associates, 1948), 44.

flaws, during the environmental movement of the late 1960s and 1970s, by which time the spread of wartime technologies around the developing world had created severe environmental problems.

HEALTHY LANDSCAPES: DISEASE & DDT

Before the early twentieth century, widespread infectious disease had long slowed development in the tropics. "While an Edenic view of the tropics had prevailed from Columbus on," Paul Sutter writes, "by the nineteenth century the tropics took on a more ominous cast, particularly as disease decimated outsiders on a larger scale. Well into the twentieth century, a negative [view of] tropicality dominated."[24] Diseases such as malaria, yellow fever, and cholera plagued not just temperate zone visitors but also local populations. (These disease environments were not always "natural," sometimes stemming directly from western interventions, as with sugar plantations in the Caribbean or canal building in India.[25]) But in the late nineteenth and early twentieth centuries scientists discovered that parasites, often carried by mosquitoes, spread diseases. Vast advances in tropical medicine resulted, as well as several pioneering public health efforts, often coordinated by nongovernmental organizations (NGOs) such as the Rockefeller Foundation. World War II not only consolidated and spread these efforts, but also spurred its own remarkable surge of innovation. Antibiotics, synthetic anti-malaria medicine, as well as residual insecticides such as DDT – all developed during the war – brought enormous changes.

Few technologies did more to dispel fears of living and working in the tropics than DDT, which owed its widespread use to World War II. During the war, diseases such as typhus and malaria had incapacitated whole platoons of American soldiers in the Mediterranean and South Pacific. Malaria was a particular problem. At the war's outset, eight to ten times more soldiers died of malaria than actual combat. Malaria plagued the Mediterranean area but especially the South Pacific. In the first offensive on the Solomon Islands, the Allies suffered 10,635 casualties: 1,472 from gunshot wounds but over 5,500 hospitalizations from malaria.[26] "Malaria," *National Geographic* noted in 1943," is proving an

---

[24] Sutter, "The Tropics: A Brief History of an Environmental Imaginary," 186.
[25] Sutter, "The Tropics: A Brief History of an Environmental Imaginary," 184.
[26] David Kinkela, *DDT and the American Century: Global Health, Environmental Politics, and the Pesticide That Changed the World* (Chapel Hill: The University of North Carolina Press, 2011), 29.

even worse menace than the enemy himself."[27] "Disease was a sure and more deadly peril to us than enemy marksmanship," noted a government report.[28] "This will be a long war," General Douglas MacArthur proclaimed, "if for every division I have facing the enemy I must count on a second division in hospital and a third division convalescing from this debilitating disease."[29] Because of problems like malaria, the war became, in Surgeon General Thomas Parran's words, "a public health war."[30]

War made the most common form of malaria control – pyrethrum, an extract of chrysanthemum petals grown mostly in Japan and Kenya – hard to come by. In response, American researchers improved chemical prevention and treatment of malaria and developed a powerful insecticide to fight its mosquito carriers: DDT. Scientists tested DDT's efficacy at a USDA lab in Florida and through field experiments in Mexico, Trinidad, Brazil, and Egypt.[31] In the Nile River Valley, because of his successful malaria eradication work, Fred Soper became known as the "General Patton of entomology."[32] New techniques such as spray guns and airplane broadcasting helped spread DDT over wide areas. It seemed a miracle chemical.

An emergency mentality surrounded the development of these technologies, as historian David Kinkela has noted. Wartime officials deployed chemicals without broad testing. Mexican civilians involved in trials, for instance, were not told of the risks. Scientific warnings about possible health and ecological problems were ignored or downplayed. During the war, risk "was calculated differently," Kinkela writes. "Officials and entomologists believed their job was to help win the war, not make long-term decisions regarding the ecological safety of pesticides."[33]

DDT production skyrocketed from 1,000 pounds per month in April 1943 to 200,000 pounds in early 1944 to 2 million pounds in

---

[27] Albert W. Atwood, "The Healing Arts in Global War," *National Geographic*, November 1943, 609.

[28] Robert L Eichelberger, *Our Jungle Road to Tokyo* (New York: Viking Press, 1950), 43.

[29] Russell, *Introduction to Preventative Medicine in World War II*, 2, as quoted in Kinkela, *DDT and the American Century*, 13.

[30] Thomas Parran, "Public Health Implications of Tropical and Imported Diseases: Strategy against the Global Spread of Disease," *American Journal of Public Health and the Nation's Health* 34:1 (January 1944): 1–6, as quoted in Kinkela, *DDT and the American Century*, 14.

[31] Kinkela, *DDT and the American Century*, 25.

[32] Timothy Mitchell, *Rule of Experts: Egypt, Techno-Politics, Modernity* (Berkeley: University of California Press, 2002).

[33] Kinkela, *DDT and the American Century*, 32.

1945. Prices declined almost 60 percent.[34] Conversion to agricultural uses, as an insecticide to protect crops, came easily.

DDT was only one of several transformative wartime medical advances. Surveying health conditions around the world, the US military poured millions into research and development. Perhaps the greatest advance was penicillin, which was discovered in the United Kingdom in 1928 and, crucially, converted for mass production in the United States by 1942. The war also led to a new, cheaper vaccine for rinderpest, a disease that decimates cattle populations, because of concerns about a biological attack on North America's large herds. (It would become the basis of a postwar international eradication program, an effort to remake livestock in tropical areas.) Because of these changes, confidence in the ability to create healthy landscapes worldwide mushroomed during the war. "It seems highly probable," a 1943 *National Geographic* article on wartime medical advances concluded, "that we may push new frontiers of health in far-distant lands, thus widening the very bounds of civilization itself."[35]

High hopes surrounded all of the wartime medical advances, but especially DDT.[36] DDT, health officials noted in 1947, is "an almost perfect insecticide."[37] During the late 1940s, as part of the Marshall Plan, the United States, the Rockefeller Foundation, and the Italian government joined forces to use DDT to attack malaria on Sardinia, an island viewed as an underpopulated, underutilized frontier zone. Ceylon and India started similar programs. The United States aided programs in

[34] U.S. War Production Board, *War Production in 1944* (Washington, D.C.: U.S. Government Printing Office, 1945), 42.

[35] Albert W. Atwood, "The Healing Arts in Global War," *National Geographic*, November 1943, 618.

[36] Kinkela, *DDT and the American Century*. Other sources on malaria programs include Javed Siddiqi, *World Health and World Politics: The World Health Organization and the UN System* (Columbia: University of South Carolina Press, 1995); Socrates Litsios, "Malaria Control, the Cold War, and the Postwar Reorganization of International Assistance," *Medical Anthropology* 17:3 (1997): 255–278; Mitchell, *Rule of Experts: Egypt, Techno-Politics, Modernity*; Amy L. Sayward, *The Birth of Development: How the World Bank, Food and Agriculture Organization, and World Health Organization Changed the World, 1945–1965* (Kent: Kent State University Press, 2006); Frank M. Snowden, *The Conquest of Malaria: Italy, 1900–1962* (New Haven: Yale University Press, 2006); Randall M. Packard, *The Making of a Tropical Disease: A Short History of Malaria* (Baltimore, MD: Johns Hopkins University Press, 2007); James Webb, *Humanity's Burden: A Global History of Malaria* (Cambridge: Cambridge University Press, 2009).

[37] Fred L. Soper, W. A. Davis, F. S. Markham, and L. A. Riehl, *The American Journal of Hygiene*, 194, as quoted in Kinkela, *DDT and the American Century*, 12.

a score of countries around the world. In 1955, the World Health Organization launched a global Malaria Eradication Program, the greatest public health undertaking of the time, eventually involving over 50 countries. Although these programs did not always completely eliminate malaria, by reducing it they often opened up large new territories to resource development. "The public health worker," US development chief Stanley Andrews noted in 1953, "often precedes the tractors and the plow. There are many areas … which are unavailable for cultivation until the malaria mosquito is licked."[38]

Kinkela argues that these programs suffered from a crucial flaw: they placed so much faith in technological solutions – the eradication of mosquito vectors by DDT – that they overlooked the larger social and environmental context that more subtle, multidimensional approaches might have addressed. "Rather than define the world's malaria problem as part of a political, cultural, or ecological process, one shaped by a long history of human and nonhuman actors," he argues, "eradicators understood the disease through an ever-narrowing lens of vector control. By funnelling time, resources, and human energy into the single (and universal) strategy of eradication, public health experts demonstrated their belief in the power of human technologies."[39] "The solutions to complex problems," he stresses, "were always found at the end of the spray gun."[40] Other options besides DDT were overlooked, and few considered the long-term environmental consequences of chemical dependence and of opening new areas quickly.

RAPID TRANSPORT: THE WAR OF MOVEMENT AND POSTWAR PROJECTS

For centuries, moving around much of the tropics had posed daunting obstacles. Though not impossible, terrain and disease made travel difficult and relatively uncommon. Europeans looking to make inroads into tropical economies couldn't go much beyond coastlines. In Africa, a particular problem was the lack of navigable rivers. Railroads helped, but required vast sums for construction and reached only certain stations. Another package of World War II technologies – advances in bulldozers,

---

[38] Stanley Andrews, "Address to the Southern Branch of the American Public Health Association Conference, Atlanta, Georgia," April 25, 1953, Box 10, Stanley Andrews Papers, Truman Library, 6.
[39] Kinkela, *DDT and the American Century*, 104.   [40] Kinkela, 105.

trucks, and heavy-duty roads – accelerated a revolution in transport. To be sure, none was invented during the war, but they were produced in awesome numbers and spread widely, particularly in subtropical and tropical areas.

If World War I was defined by stagnant trench warfare, World War II was known for mobile combat. One historian has called it a "war of motion."[41] Battles involved hundreds of tanks, trucks, and airplanes. Maintaining supply lines required hundreds more. Thousands of combat engineers maintained mechanized tanks and artillery – and, crucially, built bridges strong enough to support them.[42]

Trucks and roads took on particular importance. Huge quantities of people and materials had to reach battlefields scattered across the planet. Ships and rail could do some of this, but increasingly trucks and roads became indispensable. During the 1930s, larger tires, better roads, and bigger engines had enabled American trucks to catch up with rail as a mover of freight.[43] "In the theaters of this war of movement, with its demand that land forces be mobile, trucks have been essential to victory," noted the US War Production Board in 1945.[44] All-season roads also became important. In peacetime, seasonal roads tended to be good enough, but defense required year-round roads.[45]

Trucks were important, but the "magic instrument" of American military engineering, according to famed war correspondent Ernie Pyle, was the bulldozer.[46] Allied troops deployed over 100,000 tractors, many with bulldozer blades, and 20,000 each of large scrapers, cranes, and shovels.[47] "Always there were bulldozers," another observer noted of the Pacific War. "You saw them everywhere, hacking out ditches and carving roads and building ramps for seaplanes. Sometimes you'd come across an army of them busily digging a coral pit or maybe you'd find them slicing off the top of a mountain. You never knew what you'd see a bulldozer do."[48]

---

[41] Daniel Yergin, *The Prize: The Epic Quest for Oil, Money and Power* (New York: Free Press, 1991), 382.

[42] Barry W. Fowle, *Builders and Fighters: U.S. Army Engineers in World War II* (Fort Belvoir, VA: Office of History, U.S. Army Corps of Engineers, 1992).

[43] Gordon, *The Rise and Fall of American Growth*, 561.

[44] George W. Auxier, *Truck Production and Distribution Policies of the War Production Board and Predecessor Agencies, July 1940 to December 1944* (Washington, D.C.: Civilian Production Administration, Bureau of Demobilization, 1946), preface.

[45] Rudolph, "Strategic Roads of the World," 110.

[46] Ernie Pyle, *Brave Men* (New York: H. Holt and Co., 1944), 40.

[47] Francesca Ammon, *Bulldozer: Demolition and Clearance of the Postwar Landscape* (New Haven: Yale University Press, 2016), 11.

[48] Van Rensselaer Sill, *American Miracle: The Story of War Construction around the World* (New York: Odyssey Press, 1947), 3.

Dozers were a case of a prewar technology produced in large numbers and perfected during the war. Horse-drawn scrapers emerged in the 1880s, but only in the late 1920s did large infrastructure projects like dams use mechanical power. Automobiles, trucks, and agricultural tools like tractors made bulldozers possible. In the 1930s big New Deal projects helped spread the technology.[49] During the war, the need for heavy-duty roads for trucks and tanks spurred demand. Above all, the war showed the tremendous flexible utility of the bulldozer.

There was nothing subtle about the bulldozer's wartime work. In European cities, bulldozers cleared mountains of rubble. In the Pacific, their job – in the hands of the Seabees, American construction battalions whose motto was "can do" – was to "move hills, fill valleys, make roads, change the course of rivers, build harbors, pave airstrips in the jungle, build anything anywhere."[50] Sometimes that meant clearing native housing to make way for a road or camp.[51] Bulldozers, historian Francesca Ammon notes, were far more than an isolated tool; they embodied a new mindset stressing large-scale landscape "clearance."[52] Build anything, anywhere. In the South Pacific, *National Geographic* pointed out, Army Engineers and Navy Seabees using bulldozers "literally 'changed the face of Nature' on Pacific islands."[53]

As the war progressed, confidence grew that engineering and "know-how" could overcome tropical nature. They used to say, one roads expert noted in 1943, "that transportation in undeveloped regions is governed by the natural conditions imposed by topography and climate." But modern engineering, he continued, "has now solved most of the problems posed by topography and climate."[54] By the war's midpoint, Americans had built roads on six continents, "tracking through wilderness and desert, defying extremes of heat and cold, overcoming nature's obstacles of whatever kind." Most famously, Americans built the Alcan Highway in Alaska, the Pan-American Highway in Central and South America, and the Ledo Road, a ribbon of roadway cut through the jungles and mountains dividing northeast India from northern Burma. Technology appeared invincible:

---

[49] Thanks to Linda Nash for this information.
[50] Edmund L Castillo, *The Seabees of World War II* (New York: Random House, 1963), 17.
[51] Ammon, *Bulldozer: Demolition and Clearance of the Postwar Landscape*, 11.
[52] Ammon, 10.
[53] F. Barrows Colton, "Winning the War of Supply," *National Geographic* 88 (December 1945): 705.
[54] Rudolph, "Strategic Roads of the World," 113.

"Engineering science," the transport expert noted in 1943, "has established that man may have whatever he wishes."[55]

Press accounts highlighted the daunting natural hurdles confronting builders, but stressed man's ability to conquer nature. The Pan-American route presented an "uncharted jungle" that "had not even been surveyed," cutting through "a great diversity of terrain and climate, arid desert country, tropical rain forest, and alpine scenery."[56] Yet impenetrable forest, beating rain, mud, feral animals, leeches, and mosquitoes could not stop the Americans. Instead, these obstacles created material for a more important story: the conquest of nature achieved by American technology and the "can-do" spirit. The motto of one commanding officer in Southeast Asia was "Rain, mud, and malaria be damned."[57]

After the war, transportation projects – railways, ports, and especially highways – formed an important part of US strategy in the developing world. "An adequate transportation network," a 1957 report to Congress on US development explained, "is the backbone of a country's economy, servicing all elements of its productivity complex. Without it, no country can prosper."[58] The United States provided substantial funding. In 1956 alone, it assisted 182 transportation projects, spending over $130 million. In places like Thailand, where the United States helped build a national road system from near scratch, new roads fueled agricultural development in new frontiers but also massive deforestation.[59]

RAPID KNOWLEDGE: AERIAL PHOTOGRAPHY
IN WAR AND PEACE

A third wartime technology that expanded the impact of development projects after World War II was aerial photography.

---

[55] Rudolph, 130.

[56] Richard Tewkesbury, "Jungle Journey for a Hemisphere Highway," *Scholastic* 40 (May 18, 1942): 28; Walter Holbrook, "The Pan-American Highway Nears Completion," *Popular Science* 139 (August 1941): 33, Herbert Charles Lanks, "The Pan American Highway," *Canadian Geographical Journal* 26 (April 1943): 162. Thanks to Chris Wells for this material.

[57] James W. Dunn, "Building the Ledo Road," 327–347 in Fowle, *Builders and Fighters*.

[58] International Cooperation Administration, "How Mutual Security Funds Are Used, Part V, Transportation," August 1957, Document PD-ACP-794, USAID Development Clearinghouse Online Database.

[59] Pasuk Phongpaichit and Christopher John Baker, *Thailand, Economy and Politics* (New York: Oxford University Press, 1995), 63.

Air photography grew dramatically during the 1920s and 1930s, but became a widely used "invaluable ally" to military planners during World War II.[60] "With operations of present warfare taking in vast territories as it does," one expert explained, "it is only through the use of aerial photography that reconnaissance can be accomplished and details of operations be planned."[61] By 1943 and 1944, the Allies and the Germans competed for air supremacy not just for direct military control but also to take pictures to plan for future battles. Ninety percent of military intelligence came from aerial photographs. Photography "furnishes a fast and easy means of obtaining military information concerning enemy movements and methods of attack."[62] Aerial photography aided the invasions of Italy and France and the island-hopping campaign in the South Pacific.[63] The US Army Air Forces (the precursor to the Air Force) took almost 175 million photographs during the war.[64] So many "millions of square miles were surveyed in an incredibly short time," a geographer wrote in 1948, that the photos "literally covered acres at the offices in Washington."[65] New wartime technological advances helped spread the use of aerial photography.[66]

During the war years, aerial photos and surveys also shaped activities far from combat. Aerial survey aided the planning of Alaska's Alcan Highway, which was hacked through very rugged terrain.[67] In other parts of Alaska, airplanes helped the US Department of the Interior manage salmon runs as part of an effort to guarantee wartime food supplies.[68] In a different but similarly challenging environment, airplanes helped US biologists conduct "rapid surveys of large, nearly unknown areas of the American tropics," in the hopes of finding strategic materials

---

[60] Earl Church and Alfred O. Quinn, *Elements of Photogrammetry* (Syracuse: Syracuse University Press, 1948), 4.

[61] Benjamin Branche Talley and Paul H. Robbins, *Photographic Surveying* (New York: Pitman Publishing, 1945), preface.

[62] Talbert Abrams, *Essentials of Aerial Surveying and Photo Interpretation* (New York: McGraw-Hill, 1944), preface.

[63] Denis E. Cosgrove and William L. Fox, *Photography and Flight* (London: Reaktion, 2010), 55.

[64] Daniel L. Leedy, "Aerial Photographs, Their Interpretation and Suggested Uses in Wildlife Management," *The Journal of Wildlife Management* 12:2 (April 1, 1948): 191.

[65] Erwin Raisz, *General Cartography* (New York: McGraw-Hill Book Co., 1948), 185.

[66] "Aerial Strip Camera," *Flying* 37 (August 1945): 58–59.

[67] Rudolph, "Strategic Roads of the World," 130. Department of Interior, *Annual Report, 1946* (Washington D.C.: U.S. Government Printing Office, 1946), 155.

[68] Department of Interior, *Annual Report, 1941* (Washington D.C.: U.S. Government Printing Office, 1941), 192.

such as rubber trees, which were needed in part for airplane tires and parts.[69]

After the war, as the United States turned to international development efforts, government officials increasingly turned to the airplane as a planning tool. Wartime improvements in flight, photography, and photographic interpretation created great confidence in aerial images to reveal essential truth about the often bewildering complexity that tropical geographies presented. Mosaics and maps, a 1945 training manual noted, "possess the advantage, unusual in maps made by ordinary ground survey methods, of representing the surface of the earth and its culture as it actually is."[70] Writing about Southeast Asia in 1950, Secretary of State Dean Acheson emphasized that survey maps from aerial photography are "of great basic value to all ECON[omic] development planning."[71] In 1952, the Paley Commission (the President's Materials Policy Commission) stressed that airplane surveys could be a "significant tool" in the global search for desperately needed strategic minerals: "Aerial photography ... can be used widely, quickly, and relatively inexpensively in any programs of mineral discovery." The Commission recommended that "every major mineral search" begin with "detailed aerial photographic study."[72] It singled out the magnetometer as an "efficient low-cost exploration tool of high accuracy even in areas of difficult accessibility" which can be combined with aerial mapping.[73]

In addition to mineral surveys and large construction projects such as roads and dams, aerial surveys and photographs also helped with vegetation surveys, soil surveys, hydrological and landform inventories, building and construction, agriculture, transportation, industry, and wildlife studies.[74] They were probably most widely used for forestry. In general, aerial surveys furnished the same advantages as in the United States: less cost, greater speed, and capacity to access remote areas – particularly important in developing world contexts often lacking basic

[69] Dale W. Jenkins, "Use of the Airplane in Vegetation Surveys," *Ecology* 26:4 (October 1, 1945): 413.

[70] Talley and Robbins, *Photographic Surveying*, 179.

[71] Acheson to American Embassy, Bangkok, July 14, 1950, Mutual Security Agency. Office of the Director of Administration. Administrative Services Division. Communications and Records Unit, 1951–1953, RG 469, NARA II (College Park, Maryland).

[72] President's Materials Policy Commission, *Resources for Freedom*: Vol. 4, *The Promise of Technology* (Washington, D.C.: U.S. Government Printing Office, 1952), 27–28.

[73] Ibid., 29.

[74] *The Application of Aerial Photography and Interpretation to Development Planning Programs*, September 27, 1963 (Palo Alto, CA: Vidya, Itek Corp., 1963), 2.

infrastructure. One 1963 report described maps from aerial photographs as "essential to efficient development."[75]

Aerial photography not only facilitated rapid, large-scale resource development, it also changed the structure and reliability of the knowledge undergirding projects. In early postwar geographical science, as Stephen Bocking has documented for arctic regions (another area opened by World War II), the use of aviation distanced "the field from the site of knowledge production." It separated map making and other information gathering from the actual place being studied. Aerial survey appeared to provide a more complete, accurate, and objective set of data, but in fact, Bocking notes, it was better at some forms of information gathering and worse at other forms. Ground-based survey, which relied heavily on local networks of informants, including indigenous people, had its blind spots, too, but also yielded more accurate information about some parts of the landscape. When using planes, such local knowledge was often lost.[76] Something similar often happened with overseas development programs. A good example is the wildly unsuccessful early postwar British groundnut scheme in Tanzania, which, as Corinna Unger describes in this book, met failure in part because it relied heavily upon hasty air surveys.

MORE FOOD: WARTIME SEEDS AND FERTILIZERS

For many years, noting the abundant and dense vegetation, Westerners predicted that the tropics could produce tremendous agricultural yields. They assumed that tropical land surged with fertility. "By 1900," Paul Sutter writes, "it was a commonplace that, once rid of disease, the tropics would become a cornucopia of global food production."[77] But this view changed in the early twentieth century as tropical agronomists began to learn about the relative infertility of tropical soils, creating what Sutter calls "the paradox of tropical soils": "While many early tropical observers had assumed that the 'luxuriant' vegetation of the hot, humid tropics reflected the high productivity of tropical soils, twentieth-century soil scientists quickly concluded that tropical soils were poor as a rule."[78]

---

[75] Teodoro Moscosa, Coordinator, Alliance for Progress, March 15, 1963, "Photogrammetric Survey" folder, Box 13, Subject Files, 1962–1963, USAID Mission to Uruguay/Executive Office, RG 286, NARA II (College Park, Maryland).

[76] Stephen Bocking, "A Disciplined Geography: Aviation, Science, and the Cold War in Northern Canada, 1945–1960," *Technology and Culture* 50:2 (2009): 265.

[77] Sutter, "The Tropics: A Brief History of an Environmental Imaginary," 193.

[78] Sutter, 194.

American experiments with crops in Mexico during World War II appeared to solve this problem, launching a revolution in developing world agriculture. While combat was exploding across Europe and the South Pacific, researchers from the Rockefeller Foundation, first encouraged by US Secretary of Agriculture Henry Wallace, investigated ways to modernize Mexico's agriculture. The program yielded the "Green Revolution" – the program of hybrid seeds, chemical pesticides, and chemical fertilizers that recast postwar agriculture and rural environments across the developing world.[79] The Green Revolution helped remedy the problem of soil infertility blocking tropical development.

In 1940, as part of the Roosevelt administration's efforts to pull Latin American governments and their resources away from Germany, Henry Wallace traveled to Mexico. Extending New Deal ideas of social welfare to the larger world, Wallace hoped to improve the welfare of farmers, prop up the government, and ultimately aid American war efforts. Seeing Mexican farmers working hard for low harvests, he decided to push for new technology to increase yields. His vision carried tremendous consequences. "Wallace's visit," David Kinkela has written, did nothing less than "set in motion a process that dramatically transformed how humans grew food."[80]

Back in the United States, Wallace convinced the Rockefeller Foundation to launch a major program of agricultural research in Mexico. If the United States did not help the peoples of poor nations "to read and write and improve their agriculture become mechanically literate," Wallace told the foundation, the Germans and Japanese would.[81] The resulting plan was to modernize practices through the new technologies then reshaping American agriculture: hybrid seeds, tractors, chemical pesticides, and fertilizers.[82] A survey team left for Mexico in 1942. "The most acute and immediate problems," they discovered, were poor seeds and pests. They called for "the introduction, selecting, or breeding

---

[79] See John H. Perkins, *Geopolitics and the Green Revolution: Wheat, Genes, and the Cold War* (New York: Oxford University Press, 1997); John Robert McNeill, *Something New under the Sun: An Environmental History of the Twentieth-Century World* (New York: W.W. Norton & Co., 2000), 219–225; Nick Cullather, *The Hungry World: America's Cold War Battle against Poverty in Asia* (Cambridge, MA: Harvard University Press, 2010); Kinkela, *DDT and the American Century*.

[80] Kinkela, *DDT and the American Century*, 62.

[81] Elizabeth Cobbs Hoffman, *The Rich Neighbor Policy: Rockefeller and Kaiser in Brazil* (New Haven: Yale University Press, 1992), 46.

[82] Kinkela, *DDT and the American Century*, 63.

of better-adapted, higher-yielding and higher quality crop varieties [and a] more rational and effective control of plant diseases and insect pests."[83]

As part of the resulting program, the Mexican Agricultural Program, Norman Borlaug began researching new wheat varieties in Mexico in 1944. He developed a disease-resistant variety that used large amounts of water and chemical fertilizers to create larger yields. At the time, the role of chemical fertilizers was expanding rapidly in US agriculture. Before World War I, German scientists had learned how to extract nitrogen from the atmosphere – the Haber-Bosch Synthesis. In the 1930s, US government scientists encouraged chemical fertilizer use of all kinds as part of conservation programs. But it wasn't until World War II that nitrogen fertilizers really took off. "Fertilizers," a 1944 USDA report noted, "are of greater importance to agriculture now than ever before."[84] This was because the war had created "increased demands on this country for food, feed, and other crops" but also "took part of the best manpower off the farm." Better fertilizers helped pick up the slack. At first, demand far outstripped supply, as ammonia flowed to the wartime munitions industry. But new factories were constructed, and by 1943, the munitions need had been met and conversion to peacetime use had commenced, now with far greater amounts available. As with DDT, trucks and bulldozers, and aerial photography, the vast productive infrastructure created during the war proved important. In addition, during the war the United States discovered effective new ways to prevent the caking of the ammonium nitrate during transport, a discovery that the USDA would rank as one of the "outstanding developments" of the war.[85] Despite the shortages, agricultural use of nitrogen fertilizer doubled between 1939 and 1945.[86]

Some questioned Borlaug's approach. Visiting his Mexican research site, the conservationist William Vogt critiqued the use of chemical fertilizer, preferring instead organic methods that preserved soil quality. But Rockefeller scientists pushed forward, supported by Mexican officials, who encouraged the program with lower tariffs, state-financed loans, and

[83] Kinkela, 64–65.

[84] A. L. Mehring, Hilda M. Wallace, and Mildred Drain, *Consumption and Trends in the Use of Fertilizer in the Year Ended June 30, 1944* (Washington, D.C.: U.S. Dept. of Agriculture, 1946), 2.

[85] United States Department of Agriculture, *Fertilizer Resources and Requirements of the United States* (Prepared for the President's Materials Policy Commission) (Washington, 1952), 5.

[86] U.S. Congress, *House Committee on Appropriations, Hearings on Agriculture Department Appropriation Bill, 1947* (Washington, D.C.: United States GPO, 1946), 248.

FIGURE 6.1. Ammonia Plant during World War II. James Rorty, *Soil . . . People and Fertilizer Technology* (Washington, GPO, 1949).

government subsidies.[87] The programs, David Kinkela writes, "served the interests of Mexico's political and economic elite, who often had greater access to capital and owned better agricultural lands."[88]

By the late 1940s, production levels had soared. In the mid-1950s, Borlaug was bragging that in just a decade, agricultural methods that dated "back more than three thousand years" had been replaced by the "most modern tractors and self-propelled combines of the twentieth century... Today virtually all of the wheat plantings ... have been mechanized."[89] For Borlaug, the Rockefeller Foundation, and many agricultural modernizers, Kinkela writes, the Green Revolution symbolized "the triumph of human technology."[90]

Success in jacking up wheat yields spurred similar efforts around the developing world. In 1960, the Rockefeller Foundation and Ford

[87] Kinkela, *DDT and the American Century*, 71.   [88] Ibid., 63.   [89] Ibid., 79.
[90] Ibid., 61.

Foundation established the International Rice Research Institute in the Philippines. In 1963, Borlaug led a team to India to devise better varieties. From 1965 to 1968, areas of Asia planted with Green Revolution seeds increased from almost nothing to 38 million acres. By 1990, the new varieties covered 70 percent of the developing world's wheat and rice fields.

Concern about spreading the Green Revolution around the world helped spur the environmental movement of the 1960s. "Our problems would be much simpler if we needed only to consider the balance between food and population," Stanford biologist Paul Ehrlich wrote in *The Population Bomb* (1968), "But in the long view the progressive deterioration of our environment may cause more death and misery than any conceivable food-population gap." In particular, Ehrlich worried about the DDT and other synthetic chemicals that the Green Revolution relied upon: "It is difficult to predict the results of another 25 years of application of DDT and similar compounds," he wrote, "especially if those years are to be filled with frantic attempts to feed more and more people."[91] The new hybrid seeds also demanded extraordinary amounts of water, draining water tables.[92]

CONCLUSION

Historically, the United States had often displayed faith in technology, but not always toward the world's tropical regions. That began shifting in the early twentieth century, yet doubts still lingered. "White men," an American commander in the Pacific early in World War II commented, "can't . . . exist in the jungle without help."[93] But changes in the works since early in the century accelerated greatly with the war, particularly through innovations in health, transportation, and knowledge-gathering technologies – areas that had previously hampered tropical development.

Postwar development programs displayed a faith in technology that ran counter to William Vogt's and Walter Prescott Webb's pessimistic late 1940s claims that global limits had been reached. Perhaps no one

---

[91] Paul Ehrlich, *The Population Bomb* (New York: Ballantine, 1968), 53. See Robertson, *Malthusian Moment.*

[92] For the environmental problems of the Green Revolution, see Perkins, *Geopolitics and the Green Revolution.*

[93] Eichelberger, *Our Jungle Road to Tokyo*, 123.

elaborated the optimistic technology-driven faith in international development in the 1950s more profoundly than the historian David Potter. In 1954, Potter converted a series of late 1940s lectures into a widely read book, *People of Plenty*. Countering Webb's and Vogt's concern about global limits, Potter wrapped together a powerful reinterpretation of America's own frontier history with ideas of technology to make what he believed should be the governing logic of American development policy overseas – what he called the "mission of America."[94] It was an argument that, as had President Truman with the American Point Four development program, placed almost unbounded faith in technology's ability to transform nature into resources, without geographic bounds.

The United States, Potter noted, had too often met utter failure in efforts to spread democracy. It spent too much time "applauding revolutions conducted in the name" of democracy, when, instead, it should impart "the means that we have developed for raising the standard of living."[95] Spreading economic growth was the answer. During the war, Americans had shown the world "the variety and magic of the new abundance" but not how to achieve it, and thus had done nothing but spread envy and disillusion.[96] Instead, to foster democracy, it needed to pass along the recipe for this economic abundance: modern technology.

Technology had created American prosperity, Potter argued, not abundant land. As had Frederick Jackson Turner before him, Walter Prescott Webb had mistakenly exaggerated the importance of "free" frontier land. True, American abundance had been "in part freely supplied by the bounty of nature." But American abundance was also, Potter insisted, "created by an advancing technology," not just resources. It was Americans' "ability to convert these resources into socially useful form" that made them the "people of plenty." "What really happened" as the frontier spread, he argued, "was that an advancing technology opened up a whole new range of potentialities."[97]

In the 1950s, technology could again open new potentialities, including in the developing world. New frontiers awaited, Potter believed, wherever technology could be applied. "Science has its frontiers, industry its frontiers, technology its frontiers," Potter wrote. "In terms of abundance,

[94] David Potter, *People of Plenty: Economic Abundance and the American Character* (Chicago: University of Chicago Press, 1954). For more on Potter and on the critics of Vogt's criticism, see Robertson, *Malthusian Moment*.
[95] Potter, *People of Plenty*, 139.   [96] Ibid., 136.   [97] Ibid., 161–163.

Turner was correct in saying, 'Never again will such gifts of free land offer themselves,' but his implication that nature would never again offer such bounty is open to challenge, for the frontiers of industry, of invention, and of engineering have continued to bring into play new resources quite as rich as the unbroken sod of the western frontier." In particular, in the 1950s, the world's poor nations – its underdeveloped economic frontiers – possessed many resources awaiting America's transformative technology. Developing them, Potter stressed, was now America's "mission."[98]

Importantly, Potter said nothing about the tropics. His argument about bringing prosperity to the developing world almost completely cut the physical landscape out of the picture. Gone was the logic that had governed understanding of these parts of the world for centuries. Potter writes about the world's poor regions as if the particulars of their natural settings mattered not at all. Nature was no unsurmountable barrier to development, but instead a storehouse of resources waiting to be tapped – a frontier. Technological tools could be easily transferred from one place to the other, including from temperate areas to the "tropics."

In subsequent years, Kennedy administration advisor and "modernization" guru Walt Rostow made a similar argument. For Rostow, poverty stemmed not from racial biology or environment, but from backward cultural traditions. Technology was the answer. "It is, therefore, an essential condition for a successful transition [to prosperous modernity] that investment be increased and – even more important," Rostow wrote in *The Stages of Economic Growth* (1960), "that the hitherto unexploited back-log of innovation be brought to bear on a society's land and other natural resources."[99] "Above all," Rostow wrote, "the concept must be spread that man need not regard his physical environment as virtually a factor given by nature and providence, but as an ordered world which, if rationally understood, can be manipulated in ways which yield productive change and, in one dimension at least, progress."[100] Once a barrier, nature had become universally malleable, an inert stage on which humans could do as they wished.

This was a dramatic change from earlier decades, when the "tropics" had been a place defined by natural barriers – disease, poor soil, and

[98] Potter, 157, 128.
[99] W. W Rostow, *The Stages of Economic Growth, a Non-Communist Manifesto* (London: Cambridge University Press, 1960), 22.
[100] Rostow, 19.

difficult geography. New technologies and technological triumphalism explain this shift. The shift began early in the twentieth century with the building of the Panama Canal, but accelerated significantly during World War II, when the United States, forced by military imperative to engage in tropical and subtropical areas around the world on an unprecedented scale, developed and refined a number of unprecedentedly powerful technologies to manage and remake this hitherto intractable space.

7

A Currency for Sudan: The Sudanese National Economy and Postcolonial Development

Alden Young

Over the last two decades, there has been an explosion of literature on the origins of the economy. In everyday discourse, we take for granted that the economy is governed either by politicians, experts, or of course the ubiquitous self-governing subjects termed market actors.[1] Economic discourse permeates our daily lives. During the second half of the twentieth century, perhaps no indicator came to represent the power of the economy and economic thinking over our collective political, cultural, and social imaginations as much as the GDP.[2] The GDP, based on the System of National Accounts propagated by the United Nations during the 1950s, tied the

---

[1] Recently there have been a number of influential review essays describing the evolution of "the history of the economy" as a field. Kenneth Liparito, "*Reassembling the Economic: New Departures in Historical Materialism,*" *American Historical Review* 121:1 (2016): 101–139. For a discussion of the different ways in which the economy is being studied as an object of historical inquiry, see Quinn Slobodian, "*Which 'the Economy'? Complicating the Timothy Mitchell Thesis,*" *Comment at Historicizing "the Economy" Workshop* (Harvard University, September 2016), https://www .academia.edu/28948215/Which_the_Economy_Complicating_the_Timothy_Mitchell_ Thesis, accessed: November 25, 2017. Timothy Mitchell, "Fixing the Economy," *Cultural Studies* 12:1 (1998): 82–101.
[2] For an excellent discussion of the rise and fall of the Gross Domestic Product in the African context, see the work of Morten Jerven, *Poor Numbers: How We Are Misled by African Development Statistics and What to Do about It* (Ithaca: Cornell University Press, 2013). See also, Daniel Speich, 2008. "Travelling with the GDP through Early Development Economics' History," in *Working Papers on The Nature of Evidence: How Well Do Facts Travel?* No 33/2008, London School of Economics, Department of Economic History and Daniel Speich, "The Use of Global Abstractions: National Income Accounting in the Period of Imperial Decline," *Journal of Global History* 6 (2011): 7–28.

economy to the nation-state.[3] During the 1950s, the collection of the information, the development of the statistics, and finally the production of national income accounts became requirements for new states in order to qualify for membership in the General Assembly of the United Nations and the Bretton Woods organizations such as the IMF and the World Bank Group (WBG).[4]

National economies became ubiquitous as their organization became the price of membership in the international order after World War II for political elites all around the globe. The confluence between the economy and the nation-state led Timothy Mitchell to write:

... one important contribution to the making of the economy was the collapse of a global network of European and other empires. Before the 1930s it would have been difficult to describe something called the "British economy," for example, in part because the forms of trade, investment, currency, power, and knowledge that might be constituted as an economy were organized on an imperial rather than a national scale.[5]

For Mitchell, the nation-state was a necessary precursor for the economy. Yet, as early as 1994 the cultural theorist Stuart Hall argued that:

... globalization is not a recent phenomenon per se. We could say it was inaugurated in the moment at the end of the fifteenth century when Europe, having expelled its others—Jews and Muslims—turned outward and the Euro-imperial adventure we call modernity began on a global scale. The dislocation of a world composed of settled, kin-bound, territorially unified peoples began, then, with exploration and conquest, colonization and slavery ... The first tentative formation of a capitalist and commodity-based market economy took the form of a global rather than regional or continental phenomenon.[6]

---

[3] Beginning in 1947, the United Nations sought to create a system of national income accounts that could be standardized and deployed by all member states in order to further the project of international comparison. In 1953, these standards were finally enshrined in a manual, which could be followed by the statistical offices of various states.

For a basic timeline of the development of national income accounts, please see the website of the United Nations Bureau of Economic and Social Affairs, "Historic Versions of the System of National Accounts," (2012): http://unstats.un.org/unsd/nationalaccount/hsna.asp, accessed: November 25, 2017.

[4] Paul Studenski, *The Income of Nations, Theory, Measurement, and Analysis: Past and Present: A Study in Applied Economics and Statistics* (New York: New York University Press, 1958).

[5] Timothy Mitchell, *Rule of Experts: Egypt, Techno-Politics, Modernity* (Berkeley, University of California Press, 2002), 6.

[6] Stuart Hall, *The Fateful Triangle: Race, Ethnicity, Nation*, ed. Kobena Mercer (Cambridge, MA: Harvard University Press, 2017), 110–111.

If the economic imagination was global from its inception, then what began to change during the middle decades of the twentieth century?[7] Reframing Mitchell's provocation in this way allows us to view the mid-century project to divide the world into a system of national economies as an attempt to domesticate what postwar elites understood as unruly global markets, prone to dramatic peaks and troughs. The architects of the postwar global community hoped to design a system where responsibility for economic regulation could be located at the national level.[8] New types of regulation required new types of surveillance and accountability.

Development narratives encouraged both the colonizers and the colonized to seek their political futures through economic analysis.[9] The ways in which development measured as the expansion of the state's economic capacity was taken up by everyone from Adam Smith to nineteenth-century Ottoman elites interested in defensive modernization can be seen in the chapters by Amanda McVety and Cyrus Schayegh. Recent scholarship by Frederick Cooper and Gary Wilder has demonstrated that even the leaders that we usually associate with the independence movements that swept across much of Africa during the 1950s and 1960s frequently strove for alternatives to the nation-state.[10] Yet, Nathan Citino's chapter in this book argues that it was the potency of development narratives when attached to the image of the nation that guaranteed the victory of the national economy over its other possible forms.

---

[7] Quinn Slobodian, "How to See the World Economy: Statistics, Maps, and Schumpeter's Camera in the First Age of Globalization," *Journal of Global History* 10:2 (2015): 307–332.

[8] Jamie Martin, *Governing Global Capitalism in the Era of Total War* (Cambridge, MA: Harvard University Press, forthcoming). For a view of the negative aspects of "self-determination" as a strategy of organizing international relations, see Timothy Mitchell, *Carbon Democracy: Political Power in the Age of Oil* (New York: Verso Press, 2011); Sudan Pedersen, "Getting Out of Iraq—in 1932: The League of Nations and the Road to Normative Statehood," *The American Historical Review* 115: 4 (October 2010): 975–1000.

[9] Mahmood Mamdani, "Beyond Settler and Native as Political Identities: Overcoming the Political Legacy of Colonialism," *Comparative Studies in Society and History* 43:4 (October 2001): 651 and Frederick Cooper, "Modernizing Bureaucrats, Backward Africans, and the Development Concept," in *International Development and the Social Sciences: Essays on the History and Politics of Knowledge*, ed. Frederick Cooper and Randall Packard (Berkeley: University of California Press, 1998), 64–84.

[10] Frederick Cooper, *Citizenship between Empire and Nation: Remaking France and French Africa, 1945–1960* (Princeton: Princeton University Press, 2014) and Gary Wilder, *Freedom Time: Negritude, Decolonization, and the Future of the World* (Durham: Duke University Press, 2015).

One of the initial tools for the territorialization of the economy was the creation of national currencies. A focus on the tangible elements of the national economy such as its currency makes the large amounts of work that are involved in "enframing" a national economy visible.[11] Attention to case studies of economy formation allows the historian to separate the creation of an economy from teleological narratives of development.[12] For instance, during the 1960s, at the very moment that the national economy was becoming a universal form, economic policymakers in countries such as Sudan began to question its utility. They believed that the development of a national economy neither held out the possibility of remaking the world economy nor of protecting nation-states from its headwinds.[13] This fact is highlighted in the cases of Equatorial Guinea and Southern Rhodesia (now Zimbabwe), societies that possessed all of the symbols of highly formalized national economies only to lose those markers and then to reestablish them.[14] The viability of small economies as autonomous entities has been endlessly debated. In its 1960 report, "Fund Policies and Procedures in Relation to the Compensatory Financing of Commodity Fluctuations," the IMF argued that "a number of small countries like Ghana, Haiti, and Sudan, that are largely dependent on a single product the output of

---

[11] For an excellent discussion of the analytics of "enframing" and "overflowing" in Timothy Mitchell's 2001 classic *Rule of Experts,* see M. Callon, "Egypt and the experts," *Annales des Mines – Gérer et comprendre* 100:2 (2010): 82–95. doi:10.3917/geco.100.0082.

[12] The uneven and interrupted spread of processes such as manufacturing in Africa frequently associated with economic transformations such as industrialization and economic development is captured in the recent essay by Gareth Austin, Ewot Frankema, and Morten Jerven, "Patterns of Manufacturing Growth in Sub-Saharan Africa: From Colonization to the Present," in *The Spread of Modern Industry to the Periphery since 1871,* ed. Kevin H. O'Rourke and Jeff G. Williamson (New York: Oxford University Press, 2017), 345–375.

[13] Alden Young, *Transforming Sudan: Decolonization, Economic Development and State Formation* (New York: Cambridge University Press, 2017) and Alden Young, "African Bureaucrats and the Exhaustion of the Developmental State: Lessons from the Pages of the Sudanese Economist," *Humanity: An International Journal of Human Rights, Humanitarianism, and Development* 8:1 (2017): 49–75.

[14] Hannah Appel, "Towards an Ethnography of the National Economy," *Cultural Anthropology* 32:2 (2017): 294–322; Tinashe Nyamunda, "Money, Banking and Rhodesia's Unilateral Declaration of Independence," *The Journal of Imperial and Commonwealth History* 45:5 (2017): 746–776; and Tinashe Nyamunda, "British Sterling Imperialism, Settler Colonialism and the Political Economy of Money and Finance in Southern Rhodesia, 1945–1962," *African Economic History* 45:1 (2017): 77–109.

which is subject to wide fluctuations from year to year" could not be expected to effectively manage their economies.[15]

Despite the fact that Sudan was in geographical terms the largest country in Africa from its independence in 1956 until the partition of the country into Sudan and South Sudan in 2011, the IMF's concerns that Sudan was either too small or in some other way unsuitable to constitute an independent economy had been echoed by financial and economic experts since the conclusion of World War II. The Colonial Development and Welfare Act of 1940 created a mechanism whereby particularly Britain's Africa colonies began to plan for themselves as independent economies under the banner of development.[16] Mitchell has provocatively argued that the origin of the contemporary international order based on a system of international economies was created during the early twentieth-century debates about whether the Indian and British economies were truly separate. Similar debates took place about whether Egypt constituted a national economy, but Sudan's peculiar status as the Anglo-Egyptian Condominium made it more complicated to think of an autonomous Sudanese economy, because the Sudan Convention of 1899 divided sovereignty between Britain and Egypt and therefore complicated nationalist demands for the reckoning of Sudan's economic performance.[17]

The Condominium was an awkward arrangement involving tons of overlapping authorities. By the 1940s, the deteriorating relationship between Egypt and Britain was making their shared sovereignty over Sudan increasingly contentious. This hostility spilled over into economic and financial questions once Egypt decided to leave the Sterling Zone, which raised questions about whether the Egyptian pound could continue to be the currency in circulation in Sudan even as British officials controlled the Sudan's economic policy as part of the imperial trading zone. This discussion took place in the context of larger debates during the first half of the 1950s over whether Sudan was economically part of a united Nile Valley as the Egyptian governments of King Farouk and Gamal

---

[15] IMF Archive, "Fund Policies and Procedures in Relation to the Compensatory Financing of Commodity Fluctuations" (March 4, 1960), 10.

[16] Wm. Roger Louis, *The British Empire in the Middle East, 1945–1951: Arab Nationalism, The United States, and Postwar Imperialism* (Oxford: Clarendon Press, 1984), 181.

[17] For a discussion of the Sudan Convention of 1899 between Great Britain and Egypt, see the third appendix in Winston Churchill, *The River War: An Account of the Reconquest of the Sudan* (London: Eyre & Spottiswoode, 1933) and Timothy Mitchell, *Rule of Experts*, 80–121.

Abdel Nasser claimed or if it was a part of an imperial trading system based on its cotton exports to the United Kingdom.[18] Ultimately, the debate on whether Sudan should have its own currency was a proxy discussion for the viability and orientation of the Sudanese economy.

THE SUDANESE CURRENCY DISPUTE

Until self-governance was achieved in 1954, the British finance officials in Khartoum were content to leave questions about Sudan's currency unsettled, preserving Sudan's ambiguous economic relationship with both Egypt and Britain, despite the need to employ ad hoc agreements allowing Khartoum to occupy a status outside of the sterling area but with some of the privileges of membership. Officials in Khartoum preferred political flexibility to economic clarity. After 1954, the first Sudanese officials who ascended to the leadership of the Finance Ministry decided that an independent Sudan would need its own currency. Policymakers within the finance department were committed to separating the Sudanese economy from the Egyptian economy, breaking the currency link. They believed that an independent Sudanese currency would legitimate the independence of the state, allowing Sudan to become a full member of international financial institutions such as the IBRD and the IMF.

In 1955, Sudanese officials wanted to create an independent currency, officially within the sterling area. Political factionalism within Sudan, which was divided between those who supported Britain and those who supported Egypt, prevented such a definitive move at the time. Instead, Sudanese officials were left in limbo for several more years, negotiating year-by-year, ad hoc agreements with the Bank of England to be treated as though they were in the sterling area, even as they officially remained outside of the area. Though a Sudanese currency was finally announced in 1957, it would take until 1958 for an agreement between Britain and Egypt to be worked out providing the financial cover to make an independent Sudanese currency a reality.[19]

---

[18] Alden Young, "Accounting for Decolonization: The Origins of the Sudanese Economy, 1946–1964" (PhD diss., Princeton University, 2013), 78–137.

[19] In part, this section benefits from correspondence with Frank J. Kennedy of the London School of Economics and Political Science, Department of Economic History. July 4, 2012.

After 1954, even as political independence gradually became a reality, navigating the international implications of Khartoum's economic strategy remained difficult. As Sudanese officials tried to orient the economy, they found that the politics of the Cold War meant that they were unable to make clear decisions about questions such as whether an independent Sudan should be economically aligned with Britain or Egypt and consequentially how to plan the Sudanese economy, should it look to Britain, Egypt, or the United States for foreign aid and trading partners.

THE CREATION OF THE EGYPTIAN CENTRAL BANK AND THE CURRENCY DISPUTE: 1951–1953

Discussions about the creation of a Sudanese currency began in 1951. The background of this debate was the struggle between Britain and Egypt over control of Egypt's sterling balances. While Britain acknowledged the vast debt that it owed Egypt as a result of the war, it insisted that it should control the rate at which Egypt was allowed to access its credit. During the immediate postwar years, an agreement for Egypt to actively participate in managing its sterling accounts broke down.[20]

During the 1940s, officials in London and Khartoum assumed that they would be able to muddle through the dispute over Egypt's sterling reserves. However, the prospect of a shift in the structure of the National Bank of Egypt's (NBE) management in 1951 meant that officials in London felt the issue of Sudan's monetary relationship to Egypt had to be resolved. The first concern was to define on what terms Egyptian or Sudanese officials would be able to access Sudan's sterling reserves, which were held in London, and whether those reserves could be distinguished and released separately from Egypt's sterling reserves.[21] At stake in these discussions were the terms under which Egypt's own reserves would be released by Britain, and Sudan's future relationship with Egypt.[22]

These seemingly technical discussions were already charged as a result of Egyptian feelings of economic exploitation, but to further complicate matters they took place against the backdrop of increasingly violent confrontations between British forces located within the Suez Canal

---

[20] Bank of England officials were concerned by the absence of exchange controls in Egypt. John Fforde, *The Bank of England and Public Policy, 1941–1958* (Cambridge: Cambridge University Press, 2012), 114–117.

[21] J. A. Cook to The Finance Secretary, November 26, 1949, SAD 732/8/1–162.

[22] Foreign Office Minute. From Mr. Stewart, June 27, 1950, *The National Archives in Kew Gardens, UK* (TNA) FO 371/80387.

zone and the irregular forces of Egyptian liberation groups during 1951. These confrontations reflected the souring of the Anglo-Egyptian relationship, and gave rise to long dismissed fears among some British officials and business interests that their country's commercial position might be sacrificed in a confrontation with Egyptian nationalists.[23] In this context, the transformation of the National Bank of Egypt from a private bank into the Central Bank of Egypt on March 29, 1951 caused concern in both London and Khartoum. There was a fear among officials within the Office of the Sudan Agent in London, and the British Treasury, that the Sudanese government's savings would be held hostage in a potential future confrontation, as well as exaggerated claims that the Bank might be politicized as a weapon in the struggle between Egypt and Britain.[24]

Concerns were raised first by members of the Sudan Agency, the independent office in London that managed the Sudan government's affairs in both Britain and Egypt.[25] In particular there were concerns about the safety of the LE 29,568,000 of the government of Sudan's money held in the Exchange Control Account. The fear was that the Egyptian government would use its voting majority within the Supreme Committee of the NBE to enact decisions that were unfavorable to

[23] Robert L. Tignor, *Capitalism and Nationalism at the End of Empire: State and Business in Decolonizing Egypt, Nigeria, and Kenya, 1945–1963* (Princeton: Princeton University Press, 1998), 45–61.

[24] The transformation of the NBE into the official central bank of Egypt meant that 85 percent of the profits from notes issued would now go to the Egyptian government and 15 percent of the profits would go to the NBE. The bank would continue to operate as the government's banker and it would be capable of providing a cover for budgetary deficits of up to 10 percent of the average budgetary revenue of the preceding three years. The bank would also set interest rates in coordination with a higher council. FO Minute Number 17. "Banking and Credit Operations in Egypt," April 11, 1951, TNA FO 407/230.

[25] The Sudan Agency evolved out of the Egyptian Army's Department of Military Intelligence. The post's original duties were largely confined to collecting information about Sudan, preparing publications, and disseminating that information to the correct officials within the British and Egyptian governments. The stationing of an agent in Cairo was considered necessary as early as 1901, because of the cumbersome nature of dual sovereignty between Britain and Egypt. Officially, the Sudan Agent was to be the channel of communication between the outer world and the Civil Secretariat of the Sudan government. The Sudan Agent also had special responsibilities over personnel matters. He became the primary representative of the Governor-General first in Cairo and then in London. Gradually, the Sudan Agents in Cairo and then London evolved into semiofficial ambassadors for the increasingly independent government of Sudan. M. W. Daly, *Empire on the Nile: The Anglo-Egyptian Sudan, 1898–1934* (Cambridge: Cambridge University Press, 1986), 55–57, 276.

Sudan in retaliation for pressure that Britain might place on Egypt elsewhere.[26]

Sudan Agency officials, as well as members of the Foreign Office, stationed in London were deeply concerned. Officials in Khartoum, however, were far less worried that Egypt would risk an open break with Khartoum by threatening the government's reserves. Financial Secretary A. L. Chick assured the Sudan Agent in London that "Egypt will not do anything that would endanger the use of Egyptian currency in Sudan." In addition, the Finance Department in Khartoum was loath to accept the less favorable commercial terms offered by banks such as Barclays DCO if the government of Sudan were to transfer its investments from the NBE.[27] An additional advantage was that because the NBE was not a bank seeking commercial advantage, it was willing to provide constant streams of funding to other banks in Sudan.[28]

Yet, assurances from Chick and other Finance Department officials in Khartoum did not ease the concerns of Foreign Office officials in London. In response, the Sudan Agent, C. G. Davis, communicated a desire to make the funds stored in the Exchange Equalization Account less fluid.[29] It was in this context that Davis first suggested that Sudan should issue its own currency.[30] However, he added that under no circumstances would

---

[26] C. G. Davis to A. L. Chick, October 23, 1951, SAD 732/8/1–162 G. D. Lampen.

[27] A. L. Chick to C. G. Davis, "Sudan Sterling Balances," October 28, 1951, SAD 732/8/1–162 G. D. Lampen.

[28] Chick's dilemma was that lacking a local capital market, banks in Sudan constantly transferred their funds out of the country, typically depositing them in Cairo, where they could earn more interest. The end result was that when merchants and farmers in Sudan seasonally needed financing there was a scarcity. For instance, the Khartoum branch of Barclays DCO maintained credits of upwards of LE 14 million pounds in Cairo. However, because the NBE was not a bank seeking commercial advantage, its Khartoum branch was willing to provide constant streams of funding to other banks in Sudan. A. L. Chick to C. G. Davis, "Sudan Sterling Balances," November 28, 1951, SAD 732/8/1–162/.

[29] The Sudan Agent in both London and Cairo served many of the functions of a government of Sudan embassy abroad, consular functions as well as political intelligence. Agents after 1945 were exceptionally loyal to the government in Khartoum and according to M.W. Daly, often attempted to advocate the position of senior officials in Khartoum abroad. M. W. Daly, *Imperial Sudan: The Anglo-Egyptian Condominium, 1934–56* (Cambridge: Cambridge University Press, 1991), 248.

[30] Herman Van Der Wee, *Prosperity and Upheaval: The World Economy, 1945–1980* (Berkeley: University of California Press, 1984), 423.

the Bank of England support the government of Sudan by putting British pound sterling notes directly into circulation in the country.[31]

The implication was clear; London was agitating for Khartoum to strike out on its own without offering Sudan financial shelter underneath the imperial umbrella. Chick responded that while Davis's call for Sudan to issue its own currency might be desirable, it was premature. Chick was concerned that the introduction of Sudan's own currency would imply that Anglo-Sudanese officials in Khartoum wished to influence discussions about the political fate of Sudan. The danger was that Sudanese nationalists and Egyptian officials would interpret the introduction of a new currency as a move toward independence without the input of the Sudanese electorate. Chick possessed more familiarity with his Egyptian counterparts such as Fuad Serag el-Din, Minister of Finance and Secretary General of the Wafd Party, than British officials based in London. Therefore, he understood that his Egyptian associates were extremely unlikely to break international norms and violate the claims of the Sudanese government to its reserves and in the process risk economic retaliation.[32]

Still, Finance Department officials began to contemplate measures to separate the new Sudanese currency from the Egyptian currency. For example, they studied the possibility of holding their reserves of dollars with Barclays DCO rather than with the NBE.[33] One possibility was that this reserve of dollars would eventually serve as part of the backing for an independent Sudanese currency. And in the Finance Department, even though its members did not order the new currency, Chick and Carmichael had completed the design of its notes by December of 1952.[34] However, the introduction of a new currency and the formal separation of the Sudanese economy from the Egyptian economy

---

[31] Though it should be mentioned that even Davis thought the outright seizure of Sudan's sterling balances was a remote possibility, considering that Egypt remained a substantial creditor with Britain. C. G. Davis to A. L. Chick, November 2, 1951, SAD 732/8/1–162/ G. D. Lampen.

[32] For instance, Egypt was dependent on Sudan and the other countries of the Nile Basin for access to Nile water, which was vital to the country's economy. A. L. Chick to C. G. Davis, "Sudan Sterling Balances," November 14, 1951, SAD 732/8/1–162/.

[33] A. L. Chick to Serpell, October 16, 1952, TNA FO 371/96947/.

[34] Another detail was that the introduction of a new currency would mean that the Egyptian notes in circulation in Sudan valued at between LE 18 and 20 million would have to be repatriated to Egypt. Fredric Milner to David Serpell, December 10, 1952, TNA FO 371/ 96947/.

remained a bridge too far for Anglo-Sudanese officials. They were afraid to get publicly ahead of the political leadership, even though in their private opinion, separation was inevitable.

In the final analysis, the British Treasury agreed with Chick that for the immediate future, Sudan should continue to use the Egyptian currency and remain in the Sterling Transferable Account Area with Egypt. The rationale was that any move to change the status quo would upset the legitimacy of the British officials in Khartoum by undermining their claim to be custodians of the interests of the Sudanese people.[35] Since 1947, when Egypt left the sterling area, it had been a member of the Sterling Transferable Account Area, which meant that it would have access to only a portion of its reserves for fixed purposes, and only bilaterally negotiated access to the remainder of its reserves. The Bank of England and Treasury regulated the extent to which these reserves could be exchanged into dollars, limiting the possibility that Cairo could unilaterally seize Khartoum's sterling reserves and secretly transfer the reserves into dollars.[36] Despite Foreign Office fears of economic retaliation by the end of 1951, the Governor General's Executive Council in Khartoum had decisively scuttled the idea of a separate currency.[37]

In 1951, despite their support for the continued use of the Egyptian currency, Finance Department officials in Khartoum were in a different economic position than their Egyptian peers. While Khartoum was generating significant current account surpluses as a result of strong export earnings during the late 1940s and early 1950s, it lacked both significant financial reserves that could easily be converted into American dollars and strong prospects for earning dollars through significant exports to the American Accounting Area (the dollar area). Sudanese officials were also forced to spend significant amounts of their dollar earnings outside

---

[35] Serpell to C. G. Davis, "Letter of 4th December enclosing a copy of Mr. Chick's letter 28th of November," December 21, 1951, TNA FO 371/96947/.

[36] Tignor, *Capitalism and Nationalism*, 36–40; Van Der Wee, *Prosperity and Upheaval*, 435.

[37] "A strong political demand for a separate currency may well arise; and if we had our own currency we should be able to keep in check Egyptian propaganda money which will clearly be poured into this country in much greater amounts than in the past." A. L. Chick to C. G. Davis. "Sudan Sterling Balances," October 20, 1951. SAD 732/8/1–162/ G. D. Lampen; The government of Sudan and their contractors estimated that it would take nine months for them to introduce a new currency. Serpell to D. A. H. Wright, January 9, 1952, TNA FO 371/96947; A. L. Chick to C. E. Loombe, January 7, 1952, TNA FO 371/96947.

of the sterling area to purchase staple goods for immediate consumption.[38] It would have been in the economic interest of Sudanese cotton exporters, of which the state was the largest, for the government to issue its own currency and to rejoin the sterling area. A formal position within the sterling area would secure Sudanese exporters' access to the British system of imperial preference and stabilize access to the empire's markets.

The British Treasury acknowledged the precariousness of Sudan's position. After all, Sudan was dependent on its ties to the sterling area because of its trade relationships. Finance Department officials within the government of Sudan wished for Treasury and Bank of England officials to treat the government of Sudan as if it was an ad hoc member of the sterling area. They pushed for the privileges that the British government occasionally granted other states. However, these requests fell on deaf ears. For instance, there was little enthusiasm among British Treasury and Bank of England officials to apportion part of their dollar reserve to be managed locally by officials in Khartoum.[39] Meanwhile, the local management of dollar reserves was becoming a symbol of sovereignty.[40]

While the initial discussions about a Sudanese currency were taking place, Egypt's position on Sudan was undergoing a transition from one of intransigence to support for a plebiscite on the fate of the country in 1953, following the withdrawal of all British and Egyptian troops from Sudan.[41] Additionally in 1951, an agreement was reached between Egypt and Britain over their outstanding sterling balances. The Sterling Release Agreement of July 1951 established that aside from a one-time payment of LE 50 million in 1951, the remainder of Britain's outstanding debts to

---

[38] Import quotas governed the sale of long-staple cotton to the United States. A. L. Chick to Serpell, October 16, 1952, TNA FO 371/96947. In 1952 Sudan also earned dollars from countries outside of the American Accounting Area such as Israel and Bulgaria. But the country was forced to spend dollars on wheat from Canada and coffee from Brazil and Ethiopia. W. J. F. McEwan to G. D. Lampen, "Hard Currencies Budget, 1952." April 1, 1952, TNA FO 371/96947.

[39] By 1952, India, Pakistan, Ceylon, and Iraq had all been allowed by the Bank of England to manage small pools of dollars locally. Minute. From Treasury, October 21 until 23, 1952, TNA FO 371/96947/; and D. R. Serpell to C. E. Loombe, October 21, 1952, TNA FO 371/96947/.

[40] P. E. Ramsbotham to D. R. Serpell, November 3, 1952, TNA FO 371/96947/.

[41] Mr. Creswell to Anthony Eden, "General Political Review of Egypt for 1951, including an Appendix on the Sudan and an Economic Section. Copied D.M.E.O. and Khartoum," June 26, 1952, TNA FO 371/96845/.

Egypt would be paid down at regular, but negotiated intervals, until a balance of LE 80 million remained in 1961.[42]

By 1952, the sense of urgency which had initially gripped officials in London began to subside. The dispute about Egypt's sterling holdings had once again been placed within a negotiated framework, and both Britain and Egypt were entertaining the idea that Sudan might separate itself from their economies, even as such an outcome remained slightly unsatisfactory to both parties.[43] The fight shifted to a dispute about how Sudan would function as a peripheral part of either a British or Egyptian-centric economic system. Political maneuvering revolved around not only which economic sphere appeared more enticing, but also over the terms of membership. Even Governor-General Robert Howe was uncertain about whether Britain would support Sudan economically after independence. In 1953, Howe nervously wrote to the British Foreign Minister Anthony Eden to request a treaty of friendship between Britain and Sudan, only to find his pleas rebuffed.[44]

As politicians within the Anglo-Egyptian Sudan prepared to assume the responsibilities of self-governance in 1954, British holdovers such as Carmichael, who continued to work at the Department of Finance, and his new Sudanese peers, found themselves lacking the political surety of their link to Britain as well as secure economic links to the sterling area. At the same time, their economic policies continued to assume that their privileged access to British markets would remain unaltered. These privileges were negotiated though a series of informal agreements between British and Sudanese officials, which provided very little long-term stability. These agreements, principally long-term purchase agreements for cotton, gave Sudanese exporters a degree of stability, but left Sudan vulnerable to British officials not renewing those agreements.[45] Maintaining informal monetary ties to Britain and formal ties to Egypt also magnified the potential vulnerabilities of Sudanese traders to

---

[42] Mr. Creswell to Anthony Eden, "General Political Review of Egypt for 1951, including an Appendix on the Sudan and an Economic Section. Copied D.M.E.O. and Khartoum," June 26, 1952, TNA FO 371/96845/.

[43] General Neguib was quoted as saying that the only way that Sudan could resist Egyptian encroachment was as a member of the British Commonwealth. From Selwyn Lloyd to Mr. Eden, "Conversation between the Minister of State and General Neguib in Cairo, 28th March, 1953," March 30, 1953, TNA FO 407/232/.

[44] R. G. Howe to Secretary of State Anthony Eden, March 16, 1953, TNA FO 371/102752/.

[45] R. G. Howe to Acting Secretary of State, August 25, 1953, TNA FO 371/102759/.

exchange rate fluctuations. One of the allegations of British foul play leading up to the referendum in 1953 was that British officials spread rumors that the Egyptian pound might suddenly depreciate in value.[46]

Before 1953, within the upper ranks of the Finance Department, creating a Sudanese currency did not enjoy much support.[47] Chick recognized the extent to which a new currency would be seen as a symbol of political independence, and wished to avoid inserting the Finance Department into the ongoing dispute about Sudan's political future. Consequentially, he was willing to sacrifice the increased control and surveillance of Sudan's monetary and financial transactions that an independent currency would grant policymakers in Khartoum. However, moves toward political independence beginning in 1954 meant that Sudan would need its own financial institutions, and that the Sudanese economy could no longer be represented as an appendage of the Egyptian and British economies.

INTRODUCING A SUDANESE CURRENCY: 1954–1955

Britain was reluctant to provide the necessary dollar or sterling cover to support an independent Sudanese currency, and there was little enthusiasm in London for pushing forward Sudan's application to become a scheduled territory within the sterling area.[48] Once negotiations with Egypt were concluded, establishing a formula to resolve Sudan's political future, Britain was reluctant to discuss the issue of a Sudanese currency without Egypt's prior agreement.[49]

By 1955, Sudanese officials began to reexamine the currency question, arguing that an independent Sudan needed its own currency. One reason was that Sudanese economic policymakers increasingly saw themselves in competition with Egypt for markets for their cotton exports, and without an independent currency they would remain vulnerable to swings in the value of the Egyptian pound and attached to a currency designed to support Egyptian, not Sudanese, economic policy. Another reason to support an independent currency was that Sudan could not obtain

[46] Muhammad Neguib to H.E., The Governor-General, August 30, 1953, TNA FO 371/102759/.
[47] A. L. Chick to C. G. Davis, "Sudan Sterling Balances," October 28, 1951, SAD 732/8/1–162/ G. D. Lampen.
[48] John Carmichael to D. R. Serpell, September 24, 1953, SAD 732/8/1–162/ G. D. Lampen.
[49] John Carmichael, "Introduction of Currency," October 19, 1953, SAD 732/8/1–162/ G. D. Lampen.

membership in either the IMF or the International Bank of Reconstruction and Development without its own currency. In addition, an independent currency would allow Sudan to borrow from international lenders, without the limits placed on the country by Egypt or Britain, which were hesitant to extend their own development assistance.[50]

However, even after the achievement of self-governance in 1954, officials within the Sudanese Ministry of Finance wanted a new Sudanese currency to be automatically convertible into sterling at a fixed rate.[51] Sudanese officials sought to ensure that even if they could not become formal members of the sterling area, their preferred choice, then they could remain de facto members, preserving preferential trade access to sterling area markets against stiff competition from cotton producers outside the monetary union, such as the United States and Egypt.

The sharp decline in Sudan's export income during the 1954–1955 cotton season demonstrated to finance officials the extent to which Sudan's economic health depended on its relationships with its former colonial powers. Sudan suffered from losing its privileged access to former cotton markets such as India in 1954, as British authorities began to restrict Sudan's preferential access to sterling area markets. Even when Sudanese officials attempted to construct novel economic arrangements that would facilitate trade with rivals like Egypt, such as bilateral currency swaps, or the exchange of Indian rupees for Egyptian pounds, these agreements often inadvertently redirected trade away from Sudan. Sudan was beginning to find that outside the hallowed halls of managed trade its exports were not very competitive.[52]

The problems associated with introducing a new currency were not simply issues of expertise or technical maneuvering, but rather questions about the orientation of the Sudanese economy. In the minds of both senior Sudanese officials and the few British officials staying on in Khartoum, Sudan was a small and economically vulnerable commodity

---

[50] Ministry of Finance, "The Separate Currency Problem," March 17, 1955, SAD G//S 1166/4/6/.

[51] The basic principle of establishing a currency board was to achieve automaticity. For example, the issuing and redemption of a local currency is made directly against an equivalent amount of a strong universal currency. In this case that currency was expected to be sterling. John Carmichael, "Operation of a Currency Board," (1954) SAD G//S 1166/4/7/ J. Carmichael.

[52] J. C. to Claude, April 17, 1955, SAD G//S 1166/4/6/.

producer with only one or two profitable crops.[53] Therefore, even as Sudanese officials debated the process of introducing their own currency in the months before independence, there was a growing anxiety about whether or not the country would be forced to stand alone economically. The Sudanese Department of Finance recognized that continuing to use the Egyptian currency was unsatisfactory. Egypt had designed a system of import entitlements and special discounts that favored Egyptian cotton at the expense of Sudanese cotton. The continued use of Egyptian pounds as legal tender also meant that money could be transferred between Sudan and Egypt without regard to the rules of the Sudan Exchange Control regulations. These regulations were designed to encourage the accumulation of capital reserves within the country.[54]

As officials in Khartoum strengthened ties with the sterling area, as the best means for Sudan to preserve access to its traditional imperial markets, the limits of informal membership were becoming clearer. Between 1945 and 1955 the government of Sudan budgeted LE 52 million for development, and of this sum, all but LE 2 million was raised from internal sources. Not only was Her Majesty's Government hesitant to provide more aid for development, but British officials also suggested that the price of membership in the sterling area would be restricting Sudan's payment agreements with Eastern Bloc countries and Saudi Arabia. These agreements allowed Sudan to barter directly with those countries in order to avoid having to clear transactions in US dollars or another mutually agreed currency.[55] Aside from the officials in the Bank of England and the Treasury's desire to manage trade within the sterling area, and their reticence to provide development aid to non-Commonwealth or imperial countries, the British economy's capacity to be a market of last resort for cotton was also in decline by the mid-1950s.[56]

In this context, Sudanese officials commissioned two Indian experts to write an extensive report on the relative merits of Sudan joining various currency blocs. The 1955 report by V. K. Nehru and J. P. Jeejeebhoy

---

[53] "Minutes of the Meeting of the Steering Committee," International Cotton Advisory Committee, Washington, D. C., May 17th, 1956, NRO Finance 3-A/28/8/29.

[54] J. Carmichael, "Notes on Financial Problems in the Sudan which are of Interest to HMG," July 21, 1955, SAD G//S 1166/4/6/.

[55] These agreements were common in the 1950s. India and Egypt had just signed an agreement; Britain and Argentina had one in place, as did Britain and Pakistan in which textiles were exchanged for American cotton. Memo. J. Carmichael, "Notes on Financial Problems in the Sudan which are of Interest to HMG," July 21, 1955, SAD G// S 1166/4/6/.

[56] John Carmichael, "Budget 1955–1956," SAD G//S 1166/3/1/.

outlined three options for Sudan.[57] It could become independent, it could become a member of the dollar area, or it could become a member of the sterling area. Fulfilling the hopes of Anglo-Sudanese officials, the Indian delegation argued that Sudan should pursue *de jure* membership in the sterling area. Their rationale was developed as follows: in order to become independent of both the sterling and the dollar area, Sudan would have to negotiate "a series of trade and payment agreements or complicated import or export entitlement accounts" that could debase the currency. These arrangements would allow Sudan to trade freely, the downside being that Sudanese officials would then have to be much more vigilant in ensuring that their trade balanced out with each trading partner.

Another alternative was for Sudan to attempt to join the dollar area. Here the challenge was for Sudan to accumulate a sufficient reserve of dollars in order to allow the country to adopt a nondiscriminatory import policy. Exports would then be directed primarily to countries that could pay in dollars. The primary drawback with this strategy was that Sudan's trade with dollar countries was only one-twentieth the size of its trade with countries whose currencies could not be freely exchanged with dollars.

The third possibility was for Sudan to become a formal member of the sterling area. The main dilemma was whether or not Sudan would cease contributing to the dollar pool or whether Sudan would continue to surrender its dollars to London. Countries that joined the sterling transferable account area were free to trade without regulations from London. Those countries that remained committed to the dollar pool could exchange their sterling for dollars at a favorable exchange rate, but at the same time, they had to coordinate their purchases from the dollar area with central authorities in London.[58] One alternative for Sudanese officials was to turn to international financial institutions to make up its dollar shortfalls.

Once the Sudanese parliament declared independence on January 1, 1956, finally dashing the hopes of Nasser's regime that Sudan would vote

---

[57] V. K. Nehru and J. P. Jeejeebhoy, "The Sudan's External Payments Agreements," 1955, SAD G//S 1166/2/7/.

[58] "The benefit was that the dollar pool was a ready source of hard currency. The fear was that for a relatively small country such as Sudan, if it departed from the dollar pool, then it would not be able to manage its foreign exchange reserves independently in order to successfully carry out its trade." V. K. Nehru and J. P. Jeejeebhoy, "The Sudan's External Payments Agreements," 1955, SAD G//S 1166/2/7/.

for unity with Egypt, Egyptian, Sudanese, and British finance officials began to negotiate about how to introduce a Sudanese currency. Sudan's currency would continue to be supported by sterling, and transactions in dollars would require a government license. In the next two years after independence, the viability of a Sudanese currency was held hostage to decisions made in Cairo and London. In particular, each of these capitals had to resolve competing claims to Egypt's sterling balances, and whether or not and on what terms Sudan would be allowed to access its share of Egypt's sterling. Sudan's share ultimately came to roughly 15 million sterling pounds. Eighteen to twenty million Egyptian pounds were also circulating within Sudan and would have to be redeemed by Egypt in any deal to introduce a separate Sudanese currency. By 1957, it finally began to appear as though a deal might be possible: Britain would release a portion of its sterling reserves and Egypt would redeem its currency circulating in Sudan.[59]

By the end of October 1957, Sudan had essentially completed the process of substituting Egyptian pounds for its own currency.[60] However, in order to support the currency's exchange value, Sudan developed a restrictive system of exchange that was in many ways similar to that practiced by other sterling area countries. A fixed rate of exchange was established between the Sudanese pound and the US dollar. The rate was $ 2.87 for one Sudanese pound.[61] Imports from soft currency countries could be conducted under a general license, while imports from dollar area countries had to obtain specific import licenses. These licenses were only granted up to a specific amount. In 1957, Sudanese authorities budgeted $4 million in order to provide a cover for trade with the dollar area.[62] Sudan maintained bilateral trade agreements, which were designed to increase sales of Sudanese cotton and to allow those countries to pay for these goods in a currency other than sterling.[63]

---

[59] No. 18, "Redemption of Egyptian Currency in Sudan: Foreign Office to Certain HM Reps," April 6, 1957, TNA FO 407/236l.

[60] Staff Report. Prepared by Staff Representatives for 1958 Consultations with Sudan, "Staff Report and Recommendations—1958 Consultations," June 24, 1958, IMF, p 7, Download Date: 4/27/2009.

[61] Lacking a central bank this rate was subject to fluctuations, because it had to be determined by buyers and sellers on the London capital markets. The Sudanese pound was pegged at a rate to the dollar that was only slightly lower than that of the British pound, which in 1957 was at 1 GBP to 2.94 American dollars.

[62] Staff Report. Prepared by Staff Representatives for 1958 Consultations with Sudan, "Staff Report and Recommendations—1958 Consultations," June 24, 1958, IMF, p 11, Download Date: 4/27/2009.

[63] Perhaps the most import bilateral payment agreement was with Egypt. This agreement stipulated that any payment in excess of LS 500,000 would be settled only at preordained

CONCLUSION

The debates surrounding the creation of a currency for Sudan as it became an independent republic highlight some of the paradoxes surrounding the dream of a world of nation-states and national economies. Even though the presence of a national currency served as a hallmark of what it meant to be an independent state and economy, implementing this basic requirement revealed how difficult it would be for countries such as the Republic of Sudan, which inherited an infrastructure built for the imperial economy to find a place for themselves in a world system of national economies competing with one another for advantage in international markets. Sudanese officials soon discovered that there was little room for them within a British trading system that was orienting itself toward the United States and the European economy at the expense of its former colonial possessions. The new officials of the Republic of Sudan also came to view maintaining a currency relationship with Egypt as dangerous if not for the same political reasons that had worried their colonial predecessors. British colonial officials had fretted about the "Unity of the Nile Valley" under Egyptian hegemony, the creation of a geopolitical entity that could challenge British hegemony in the Middle East, a region they intended to dominate long into the future.[64] The officials of the independent Republic of Sudan worried about being economically subordinated to the industrializing campaigns of Egypt. Their preference was to be able to earn the dollars necessary to maintain economic independence; yet, when confronted with a US economy that was largely self-sufficient in terms of crops such as cotton, Sudan's primary

---

times of the year. These trades would then be cleared in a negotiated third currency. Sudan consistently ran a trade surplus with Egypt, and in practice Egypt was Sudan's only market for many of its exports other than cotton, such as camels, dates, and legumes. The main Egyptian export to Sudan was sugar, which was purchased by the Sudanese government in order to supply its monopoly. There was also a bilateral agreement with Saudi Arabia that attempted to fix a long-term exchange rate between the Saudi riyal and the Sudanese pound. This agreement was designed to protect pilgrims from currency fluctuations. Staff Report. Prepared by Staff Representatives for 1958 Consultations with Sudan, "Staff Report and Recommendations—1958 Consultations," June 24, 1958, IMF, p 13, Download Date: 4/27/2009.

[64] Alden Young, "The Anglo-Egyptian Rivalry, the Cold War and Economic Development in Sudan: 1954–1958," in *The Middle East and the Global Cold War*, ed. Massimiliano Trentin and Matteo Gerlini (Newcastle-upon-Tyne: Cambridge Scholars Press, April 2012), 29–53.

export, Sudanese officials were forced to fear being ignored. This ultimately was the danger and paradox at the heart of the era of decolonization and development, that countries could follow all of the expert recommendations of the period and still find that there was no place for their national economy in a competitive world economy that lacked a center that could be held accountable.

8

Development, Space, and Counterinsurgency in South Vietnam's Bến Tre Province, 1954–1960

Edward Miller

The history of counterinsurgency is deeply intertwined with the history of development. While the efforts of states and rulers to suppress insurrection date back to ancient times, counterinsurgency is a manifestly modern practice. It began as a colonial mode of warfare during a moment of crisis for European empires. In the wake of World War II, as national liberation movements gained strength across Asia and Africa, colonial officials sought to combine military power with expert ideas about promoting and guiding social change in the Global South. The result was counterinsurgency, which has been defined as "the functional integration of destruction and development, of military and civil forces for the lasting transformation of societies." This formula proved more durable than the colonial empires that invented it. Since the 1950s, postcolonial states and western powers – most notably the United States – have repeatedly embraced counterinsurgency as a way to wage war and development at the same time.[1]

Recent scholarship highlights two ideological currents that shaped the emergence and evolution of counterinsurgency after 1945. First, intellectual historians have excavated the participation of European and American social scientists in counterinsurgency wars and in the devising of counterinsurgency strategies and doctrines. From this perspective, counterinsurgency emerged from the larger and longer history of the

---

[1] Moritz Feichtinger and Stephan Malinowski, "Transformative Invasions: Western Post-9/11 Counterinsurgency and the Lessons of Colonialism." *Humanity: An International Journal of Human Rights, Humanitarianism, and Development* 3:1 (2012): 35–63. http s://muse.jhu.edu/ (accessed February 19, 2017).

interplay between scientific expertise and empire.[2] Second, work by military historians shows that counterinsurgency ideas and practices were formulated explicitly as a response to contemporary theories about insurgency and "revolutionary warfare." British, French, and American strategists were fascinated by the writings of Mao Zedong on "People's War" – especially after the 1949 triumph of Mao and the Chinese Communist Party in their long-running civil war against the Chinese Nationalists. During the 1950s and 1960s, these strategists embraced militarized development as the best formula for undermining communist-led insurgencies across the Third World.[3]

Understanding the ideological and geopolitical origins of counterinsurgency helps explain some of its key features. Unlike conventional military tacticians, counterinsurgency theorists and experts professed intense interest in the ordinary people who lived in the countries and territories in which counterinsurgency wars took place. The counterinsurgents were especially concerned about the defense, control, and mobilization of "the population" – a category that they almost always depicted as singular and homogenous. In part, this practice of homogenizing the population reflected the outsized influence of Mao, who famously described revolutionary insurgents as fish swimming in the water of "the people." But it also grew out of contemporary social scientific ideas about the use of development aid to transform Third World societies. In this regard, the representation of "the population" by counterinsurgency theorists was strikingly similar to the treatment of "the economy" by economic experts, as described in Alden Young's chapter in this book. Both concepts were constructed as unitary objects that could be targeted, controlled, engineered, and developed.

The homogenization of people and populations went hand-in-hand with another feature of counterinsurgency theory: the abstraction of

---

[2] Ron Robin, *The Making of the Cold War Enemy: Culture and Politics in the Military-Industrial Complex* (Princeton: Princeton University Press, 2001), 185–205; Jefferson Marquis, "The Other Warriors: American Social Science and Nation Building in Vietnam," *Diplomatic History* 24:1 (2000): 79–105; Nicole Sackley, "The Village as Cold War Site: Experts, Development and the History of Rural Reconstruction," *Journal of Global History* 6 (2011): 481–504; and Daniel Immerwahr, *Thinking Small: The United States and the Lure of Community Development* (Cambridge, MA: Harvard University Press, 2015), 101–131.

[3] Douglas Porch, *Counterinsurgency: Exposing the Myths of the New Way of War* (Cambridge: Cambridge University Press, 2013), esp. 156–161; David French, *The British Way in Counterinsurgency, 1945–1967* (Oxford: Oxford University Press, 2011); Andrew Birtle, *U.S. Army Counterinsurgency and Contingency Operations Doctrine, 1942–1976* (Washington, D.C.: Center of Military History, 2006).

space. Counterinsurgency discourse was replete with references to explicitly militarized spaces such as Tactical Areas of Responsibility, Operational Environments, and Free Fire Zones. Yet it also relied on spatialized notions about Third World social and cultural landscapes. One spatial category with particular currency in the mid-twentieth century was "the village," which many social scientists and counterinsurgency theorists treated as a "homogenous and replicable unit" susceptible to development aid and transformation.[4]

The rendering of Third World populations and spaces as unitary and malleable helps explain the particular strategies and policies that experts designed for particular counterinsurgency wars. However, the experts' abstract ideas are insufficient by themselves to explain what actually happened on the battlefields and in the villages where counterinsurgency was waged. All too frequently, the behavior of farmers and the other people living in war zones did not match the theoretical formulas crafted in Paris, Nairobi, Santa Monica, or Saigon. Moreover, the construction of "the population" as a homogenous category clashed with the inconvenient reality that many counterinsurgency wars were often civil wars (or became civil wars).[5] In such situations, local military commanders and aid officials improvised their own strategies and tactics for creating, manipulating, and controlling populations and spaces. Meanwhile, insurgents had their own ideas about how communities and spaces could be constructed and configured – ideas that they frequently altered in response to what the counterinsurgents were doing, with varying degrees of success. Thus, the history of counterinsurgency is much more than just a series of top-down coercive development schemes. Instead, counterinsurgency was a violent form of politics in which development and state-building agendas interacted and collided with various local social and spatial practices.

This chapter is an attempt to examine some of the spatial dimensions of counterinsurgency in a particular historical context: the Mekong Delta of South Vietnam during the Vietnam War. The Vietnam War looms large in debates about counterinsurgency. Some historians have debated the counterinsurgency doctrines and tactics invoked by senior US commanders and strategists in Vietnam (often with an eye toward

---

[4] Sackley, "The Village as Cold War Site."
[5] Daniel Branch, *Defeating Mau Mau, Creating Kenya: Counterinsurgency, Civil War, and Decolonization* (New York: Cambridge University Press, 2009).

making arguments about the doctrines or tactics that US forces *should* have employed).[6] These authors have usually paid scant attention to South Vietnam's physical or human geography. In contrast, specialists in modern Vietnamese history and politics have been more interested in how the war unfolded in particular places in Vietnam. Several scholars in the latter group have produced studies of the war focused on specific South Vietnamese provinces or districts. Their accounts, unlike those of the first group of authors, are based at least in part on Vietnamese documentary sources and testimony and are well-grounded in the history of the local places they are investigating.[7] But attention to *place* does not always imply examination of *space*, or investigation of the myriad ways in which humans produce, represent, and experience spaces. During the Vietnam War, both insurgents and counterinsurgents – Americans, Vietnamese, and others – devoted enormous resources to building, occupying, controlling, transforming, and destroying different kinds of spaces in South Vietnam. Yet the spatial history of the war remains largely unexplored.[8]

My focus here is on the Mekong Delta province of Bến Tre, in the years following the Geneva Conference of 1954.[9] Outside of Vietnam, Bến Tre became famous in the late 1960s as the site of some of the war's most controversial and most destructive episodes.[10] In Vietnam, however, the commemorations of the war in Bến Tre focus not on the carnage of the latter years of the war, but on an event that took place during the war's

---

[6] See, for example, Andrew Krepinevich, *The Army and Vietnam* (Baltimore, MD: Johns Hopkins University Press, 1986); Lewis Sorley, *Westmoreland: The General Who Lost Vietnam* (Boston: Houghton Mifflin Harcourt, 2011); John Nagl, *Learning to Eat Soup with a Knife: Counterinsurgency Lessons from Malaya and Vietnam* (Chicago: University of Chicago Press, 2005).

[7] David Elliott, *The Vietnamese War: Revolution and Social Change in the Mekong Delta*, 2 vols. (Armonk, NY: M. E. Sharpe, 2003); David Hunt, *Vietnam's Southern Revolution: From Peasant Insurrection to Total War* (Amherst: UMass Press, 2008); James W. Trullinger, *Village at War: An Account of Revolution in Vietnam* (New York: Longman, 1980); Jeffrey Race, *War Comes to Long An: Revolutionary Conflict in a Vietnamese Province* (Berkeley: University of California Press, 1972).

[8] An important exception is David Biggs, *Quagmire: Nation-Building and Nature in the Mekong Delta* (Seattle: University of Washington Press, 2011).

[9] In 1956, the South Vietnamese government officially changed the name of Bến Tre province to Kiên Hòa, a practice that endured until the end of the war in 1975, when the province reverted to its traditional name. To avoid confusion, I use the traditional name in this chapter.

[10] In 1968–1969, the US Army likely killed thousands of rural residents of Bến Tre and two adjacent provinces during a campaign known as Operation Speedy Express. Elliott, *The Vietnamese War* 2:1161–1164.

early stages. In January 1960, a small team of communist cadres organized an uprising in one district of the province and briefly seized control of three villages. Although the insurrection was small in scale and short-lived, it was the first of what communist propagandists later dubbed the "Concerted Uprisings" – a series of anti-government rebellions in the delta that combined small-unit military attacks with demonstrations and the mass mobilization of local residents. Because the Bến Tre Concerted Uprising was the first in the series, Communist Party historians celebrate it as a key event in the origins of the "Việt Cộng" insurgency against the South Vietnamese government.[11]

This chapter seeks to understand the 1960 uprising in light of events in Bến Tre in the years leading up to the rebellion. I am particularly interested in the counterinsurgency policies and practices of the South Vietnamese state, known officially as the Republic of Vietnam (RVN). During these years, the RVN was ruled by its founding president, the anti-communist leader Ngô Đình Diệm. Both the RVN and Diệm have long been portrayed as mere creatures of American power who had no independent counterinsurgency strategy of their own. But South Vietnamese government records show that RVN officials in Bến Tre were intensely concerned about communist subversion after 1954, even though there was no active rebellion in the province. These officials therefore set out to pacify Bến Tre through a combination of internal security operations, mass mobilization activities, and development measures.

Analyzed as spatial practices, RVN counterinsurgency operations in Bến Tre between 1954 and 1960 yielded mixed results. Internal records show RVN leaders had a fairly clear grasp of the strengths and weaknesses of the communist movement in the province, and that they devoted considerable effort and resources to preventing the re-emergence of the communists as a revolutionary force in the area. For a time in the late 1950s, they appeared to have succeeded. But by 1959, the communists were laying the groundwork for a new insurgency, even as the government ramped up the scale and intensity of its counterinsurgency operations. A spatial history approach helps explain this

---

[11] The term "Việt Cộng" was adopted in the mid-1950s by the South Vietnamese government as an epithet. It was used to disparage members and sympathizers of the communist movement as national traitors. Since it was not a value-neutral term and was never used by the communists to refer to themselves, I mostly avoid using it here, except where it appears in South Vietnamese government sources.

remarkable turn of events. It also underscores the centrality of development in Vietnam War counterinsurgency – even during the earliest days of the conflict, years before the first American combat troops arrived in the Mekong Delta.

"COURTING THE HEARTS OF THE PEOPLE"

Bến Tre is a province of rivers and islands. Although it lies almost due south of Saigon, it is located within what Vietnamese call "the west," meaning the western region of southern Vietnam (*Miền Tây Nam Bộ*). This is the lower Mekong Delta, where Southeast Asia's largest river fans out into its eponymous "nine dragons" – the nine major branches of the system that flow into the South China Sea. Because four of these large river branches flow through and around Bến Tre, the province's land territory is made up entirely of riverine islands (Figure 8.1). The bulk of this territory

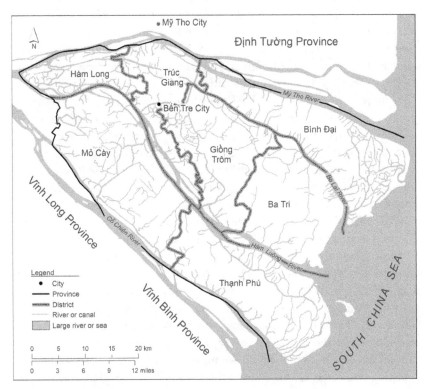

FIGURE 8.1. Bến Tre Province in 1956. Map by Jonathan Chipman, Citrin GIS/ Applied Spatial Analysis Laboratory, Dartmouth College.

is contained in three large islands (Cù Lao An Hóa, Cù Lao Bảo, and Cù Lao Minh), each of which stretches from the northwest to the southeast, parallel to the main flow of the river. Since all three islands are crisscrossed by numerous streams, canals, and smaller rivers, movement across and between various watery and land environments has long been a central feature of life in the province. Bến Tre is also a maritime province, and its rivers have long served as transport, trade, and communication avenues between the "Eastern Sea" (as Vietnamese call the South China Sea) and the interior of the Mekong Delta.

Bến Tre's modern history has been deeply shaped by insurgent movements and the counterinsurgency campaigns waged to suppress them. In 1867, the Nguyễn dynasty ceded Bến Tre and the rest of the Mekong Delta to France, which was then in the early stages of its imperial conquest of Indochina. Many local Vietnamese officials refused to serve the French colonial state; the Vietnamese governor of the region committed suicide, and two of his sons raised an army of rebels that fought in Bến Tre and adjacent districts for a few years before submitting to colonial troops. Another wave of rebellion and repression crested in the 1930s, when the newly formed Vietnamese Communist Party launched a campaign of demonstrations and agitprop activities. In November 1940, communist cadres in Bến Tre participated in the "Southern Uprising" (*Nam Kỳ Khởi Nghĩa*), an attempt to overthrow French rule in the delta. Colonial forces crushed the uprising in a few weeks and most party leaders in the area were killed, imprisoned, or forced to go into hiding. The Communist Party did not reemerge as a political and military force in Bến Tre until the "August Revolution" of 1945, when surviving cadres helped seize control of the province on behalf of Hồ Chí Minh's new state, the Democratic Republic of Vietnam (DRV). Bến Tre remained under DRV control for five months until colonial troops reentered the province in early 1946.

Most existing accounts of the history of Bến Tre have viewed the colonial-era cycle of rebellions and crackdowns in the province through a nationalist lens. In these accounts, the recurrent insurgencies in the province reflected the widespread desire of "the people" for national liberation. The counterinsurgents, in contrast, are treated as antinationalist collaborators. However, recent scholarship by Vietnamese Studies experts has challenged assumptions about the binary nature of rebellion and collaboration during the colonial era. In regions such as the Mekong Delta, where state sovereignty had long been tenuous and partial, rebellions often had less to do with the nationalist sentiments of "the people" than with contests among local elites.[12]

The limitations of the nationalist interpretation are especially evident in the case of Bến Tre's history during the First Indochina War (1945–1954). For much of the war, Bến Tre was the site of an elaborate counterinsurgency campaign designed and executed by its province chief, Jean Leroy. Because Leroy was a French citizen who held a commission in the French army, he has often been portrayed as a puppet or "lackey" of the colonial regime. But Leroy was far from the stereotypical French henchman. He was a Eurasian native of Bến Tre, the son of a wealthy French father and a Vietnamese mother. Moreover, he ruled not on behalf of France, but under the auspices of the Saigon-based State of Vietnam (SVN), which had been created by French officials in the late 1940s as an anti-communist Vietnamese alternative to Hồ's DRV.[13]

One historian aptly describes the State of Vietnam as a "work of bricolage" – that is, a state assembled from a motley collection of pre-existing elites, communities, and institutions.[14] Both Leroy and his counterinsurgency strategy in Bến Tre were part of this bricolage. His power in the province rested on a network of anti-communist militias. Although these militias were ostensibly recruited from Bến Tre's Catholic minority, many of the units were actually comprised mostly or entirely of non-Catholics. Leroy's rule in Bến Tre was thus based less on loyalty to France than on a blend of patronage, development aid, and divide-and-conquer military tactics. As province chief, Leroy claimed to have opened dozens of schools and clinics and to have implemented a far-reaching rent-reform program on behalf of tenant farmers. But he also blanketed Bến Tre with armed outposts and reportedly gave his troops license to slaughter and pillage – actions that led eventually to his removal from the province by SVN leaders in 1953. In the wake of Leroy's recall, DRV forces regained much of the territory they had previously lost. By the time the Geneva Agreements ended the Indochina War in mid-1954, SVN control over Bến Tre had been

---

[12] Christopher Goscha, *Vietnam: A New History* (New York: Basic Books, 2016), especially chapters 4 and 5; Keith Taylor, *A History of the Vietnamese* (New York: Cambridge University Press, 2013).

[13] Jean Leroy, *Fils de la rizière* (Paris: Robert Laffont, 1977), 94–230.

[14] Brett Reilly, "The Sovereign States of Vietnam, 1945–1955," *Journal of Vietnamese Studies* 11:3–4 (2016): 103–139.

reduced to the provincial capital and a few other scattered pockets of territory.[15]

The terms of the Geneva armistice required DRV partisans to surrender control of Bến Tre and all other Vietnamese territory south of the 17th parallel. By early 1955, the province was officially in SVN hands once again. Initially, however, the authority of Ngô Đình Diệm, the new SVN prime minister, was too tenuous to permit him to wield effective power over the Mekong Delta. It was only after Diệm's military victory over rival anti-communist groups in the Battle of Saigon in May 1955 that the situation turned in his favor. In October 1955, Diệm announced that the State of Vietnam had been superseded by a new entity, the Republic of Vietnam (RVN). A few months later, he replaced the officials in charge of most of the delta provinces. The new chief of Bến Tre province was Phạm Đăng Tấn, a young Army of the Republic of Vietnam (ARVN) captain who had backed Diệm during his shaky first months in power.

Communist Party historians have typically depicted the first years of RVN rule in Bến Tre as a continuation of pre-1954 patterns. In these accounts, Captain Tấn and other RVN officials were corrupt brutes who alienated local residents through their rapaciousness. Party cadres, in contrast, appear as resourceful, clever, determined, and heroic in the face of the RVN crackdown. Such representations neatly buttress the portrayal of the 1960 Bến Tre Concerted Uprising as a natural and all-but-inevitable event in which the cadres channeled and transformed the people's anger into a popular insurrection. Perhaps the most effective telling of this narrative appears in the memoir of Nguyễn Thị Định, a female Communist Party cadre who helped organize the uprising. Dinh's memoir depicts the rebellion as a straight-up morality tale in which dauntless cadres led ordinary villagers to victory over blood-thirsty local officials.[16]

Such narratives are problematic not because they are unfair to RVN officials but because they discount the important historical fact that the South Vietnamese regime was a postcolonial state. Like the elites in other newly independent countries in the Global South during the 1950s and

---

[15] Charles Keith, *Catholic Vietnam: A Church from Empire to Nation* (Berkeley: University of California Press, 2012), 232. For the harsh nature of Leroy's rule, see Lê Văn Dương et al., *Quân Lực Việt Nam Công Hòa Trong Giai Đoạn Hình Thành, 1946–1955* [The Armed Forces of the Republic of Vietnam in the formative stage, 1946–1955] (Saigon: Trung-tâm Ấn-loát Ấn-phẩm Quân-đội, 1972), 274–276.

[16] Nguyễn Thị Định, *No Other Road to Take: Memoir of Mrs. Nguyễn Thị Định*, Mai Van Elliott, trans. (Ithaca: SEAP, 1976).

1960s, RVN leaders were anxious to establish the state's sovereignty and legitimacy. They believed, moreover, that success in these efforts would depend at least in part on their ability to mobilize rural residents under the banner of development and positive social transformation. The central importance of development was also implicitly acknowledged by communist leaders, who recognized that the government's state-building programs – though coercive and heavy-handed – threatened the survival of their movement in Bến Tre. Thus, the 1960 Concerted Uprising was not an inevitable backlash against official corruption and exploitation. Instead, the rebellion emerged from the clash between RVN development efforts and the communists' calculated attempts to undermine those efforts.

At the time of Captain Tấn's arrival in Bến Tre in 1956, the central government in Saigon had not yet worked out a detailed set of policy prescriptions for state building and development in the countryside. For the moment, Diệm agrarian policies were focused mainly on undermining the power of a small group of wealthy landowners who had backed his rivals during 1954–1955.[17] In Bến Tre, however, Jean Leroy and the other anti-Diệm landowners had already been removed from positions of power and mostly lost their dominance in the province. Captain Tấn thus seems to have had considerable latitude to craft his own security policies as he saw fit.

In late May 1956, less than two weeks after his installation as province chief, Tấn drafted a plan for a "Provincial Pacification Campaign." Tấn's use of the term "pacification" (*bình định*) reflected prior French and SVN practice; it also anticipated later American language. However, the pacification he envisioned did not require the quelling of a violent insurgency, as there was currently no active rebellion in Bến Tre. In the entire province, Tấn estimated, communist operatives "had no more than five rifles" among them.[18]

In retrospect, the "campaign" that Tấn designed appears to have been less of a comprehensive plan than a cobbled-together patchwork of military and social welfare actions. In his draft proposal to Saigon, Tấn identified a total of 28 villages (out of 116 in the province) that remained "under communist influence." To eradicate this influence, he proclaimed

---

[17] Edward Miller, *Misalliance: Ngo Dinh Diem, the United States, and the Fate of South Vietnam* (Cambridge, MA: Harvard University Press, 2013), 160–161, 369n5.

[18] Phạm Đặng Tấn, "Dự-án Kê-Hoạch Áp-dụng trong Chiên-Dịch Bình-Định Bến Tre" [Implementation Plan for the Bến Tre Pacification Campaign], 31 May 1956, Folder 4170, Phủ Tổng Thống Đệ Nhất Cộng Hòa (hereafter PTTDNCH), Vietnam National Archives No. 2, Ho Chi Minh City (hereafter VNA2).

that his administration would "court the hearts of the people" (*thanh thủ nhân tâm*); this meant a focus on improving living standards, in tandem with security operations targeting individual enemy cadres. In this way, he hoped to "pull the masses toward us while dealing a deadly blow to the gang of V.C. cadres who are covertly acting against the republic."[19] At the rhetorical level, therefore, Tấn appeared to endorse what some British and American experts already called a "hearts and minds" approach to counterinsurgency. In its actual implementation, however, Tấn's campaign was considerably more eclectic and haphazard.

In his initial assessment of the security situation in Bến Tre, Tấn zeroed in on two districts that had a disproportionately high number of "VC villages." One of these was the coastal district of Ba Tri, on the eastern side of the province, adjacent to the South China Sea. Tấn considered Ba Tri a priority because it had been a center of communist armed resistance since the 1930s, as well as a gathering point for local communist cadres who regrouped to North Vietnam following the Geneva Agreements in 1954. To begin the work of pacification in the district, Tấn deployed a team of RVN government operatives known as Civic Action cadres. Diệm had founded the Special Commissariat for Civic Action in 1955 with the expectation that it would play a key role in state building and development in the Vietnamese countryside. In addition to indoctrinating the residents of the villages and hamlets in which they operated, Civic Action cadres were supposed to enlist local people in "welfare improvement" projects; these projects included the construction of roads, wells, and schools, as well as educational and public health initiatives.[20]

The steps that Tấn took in Ba Tri stood in contrast to his actions in Mỏ Cày, the other district deemed a communist stronghold. Tấn's anxieties about Mỏ Cày were heightened in July 1956, when communist cadres organized two anti-government demonstrations on the anniversary of the Geneva Agreements – the date that French and DRV negotiators had specified as the deadline for nationwide elections to reunify Vietnam under a single government. Because the demonstrators had criticized

---

[19] Ibid.; Phạm Đăng Tấn, "Phúc trình hàng tháng về tháng 5 năm 1956" [Monthly report for May 1956], Folder 37, PTTDNCH, VNA2.

[20] Phạm Đăng Tấn to Mai Lạc, June 23, 1956, Folder 4393, PTTDNCH, VNA2. See also, Geoffrey C. Stewart, "Hearts, Minds and Công Dân Vũ: The Special Commissariat for Civic Action and Nation-Building in Ngô Đình Diệm's Vietnam, 1955–1957," *Journal of Vietnamese Studies* 6 (Fall 2011): 44–100.

Diệm for his refusal to participate in those elections, Captain Tấn decided that the protests required a forceful response. In August, provincial and district authorities launched "Operation Nguyễn Chí Thiện," a pacification campaign named for an RVN policeman who had been assassinated in Bến Tre a few months earlier.

In the first stage of the Mỏ Cày operation, teams comprised of police officers, Civil Guard troops, intelligence operatives, and other local security forces were deployed across the 17 villages located in the southern half of the district. According to Tấn, these teams spent a week focused mainly on propaganda activities. The activities included rallies and public "congresses" held under the auspices of the "Denounce Communists" campaign, a major RVN government mass mobilization initiative that Diệm had launched a year earlier.[21]

After a week of propaganda activities carried out exclusively in the southern half of Mỏ Cày, the operation took a more coercive turn. On the afternoon of August 19, provincial Civil Guard units set up a series of roadblocks and fortified positions along large segments of the district's northern land and water borders. These deployments created a perimeter surrounding all twelve of the Mỏ Cày villages that had not been targeted in the first stage of the campaign. Having sealed those villages off, police and other security forces began to move systematically through them. As they did so, they conducted more rallies and other propaganda activities similar to those organized during the first stage of the campaign. At the same time, however, commandos were carrying out a separate mission: "exploiting intelligence and hunting down Việt Cộng cadres."[22] Tấn hoped to detain or kill at least some of the cadres responsible for the recent anti-government demonstrations. In the end, the dragnet's results were meager: just ten "VC cadres" and five "suspects" captured. But Tấn assured his superiors in Saigon that RVN police and intelligence officers would maintain a presence throughout the district in the months to follow, and that they would expose and arrest any more enemy cadres who might seek to resume clandestine resistance activities.[23]

Beyond these activities focused on communist stronghold districts, Captain Tấn also took steps to assert the sovereign claims of the RVN

---

[21] Phạm Đăng Tấn, "Phúc trình về cuộc hành quận cảnh sát 'Nguyễn chí Thiện'" [Report on Police Operation "Nguyễn Chí Thiện"], Sept. 4, 1956, Folder 4172, PTTDNCH, VNA2; Miller, *Misalliance*, 132–134.

[22] Ibid.; Phạm Đặng Tấn, Lịnh Hành Quân [Operational Orders], August 18, 1956, Sept. 4, 1956, Folder 4172, PTTDNCH, VNA2.

[23] Tấn, "Phúc trình về cuộc hành quận cảnh sát 'Nguyễn chí Thiện'."

government over every community – and indeed every household – in the entire province. In October, the provincial government began overhauling the membership of its 116 village administrative committees. While Vietnamese villages had traditionally elected their own leaders, Diệm had decided to abolish the elections in favor of appointed officials. Around the same time, the government began to implement a new "inter-family group" (*liên gia*) system. In Bến Tre, more than 18,000 households were categorized according to their loyalty to the government, and then placed into local groups. Each local group was under the watchful eye of a warden deemed loyal to the government.[24]

By late 1956, after less than a year on the job, Tấn seemed to be presiding over a pacified province. During his first summer in Bến Tre, the province's security forces arrested dozens of "Việt Cộng" suspects every month. But by year's end, the monthly rate of detentions had fallen to single digits, and growing numbers of communists were defecting to the government. Communist agitprop activities also declined, presumably because the enemy increasingly lacked the manpower to conduct such operations.

The apparent success of Tấn's policies in Bến Tre lasted for the rest of his two-year tenure as province chief. In mid-1958, Tấn was replaced by ARVN Major Lê Minh. Under Minh's direction, provincial security forces continued to investigate and arrest suspected communists, and to carry out the "Denounce Communists" campaign and other mass mobilization programs. Minh believed that these activities had taken a toll on the party. "In the face of our offensive," Minh told his superiors in May 1959, "the enemy has been forced into a 'cave,' and is focused more on hiding and protecting his bases than on active opposition."[25] One marker of Minh's confidence was his emphasis on reviewing the cases of individuals arrested for political crimes, with the goal of identifying those who could be safely released. Of the more than 750 people who were being held in provincial detention facilities at the time Minh took over, nearly 400 were freed after investigation by the province's "security committee."[26]

In some respects, Major Minh's optimism about the state of affairs in Bến Tre was justified. Later communist accounts would describe the

[24] Phạm Đăn Tấn, "Phúc-trình Tháng 10–1956" [Monthly Report for October 1956], Nov. 7, 1956, Folder 37, PTTDNCH, VNA2.
[25] Lê Minh, "Phúc-trình Tháng 5–1959" [Monthly Report for May 1959], May 28, 1959, Folder 212, PTTDNCH, VNA2.
[26] Lê Minh, "Phúc-trình Tháng 06–1958" [Monthly Report for June 1958], July 5, 1958; and Lê Minh, "Phúc-trình Tháng 07–1958" [Monthly Report for July 1958], August 1958; both in Folder 213, PTTDNCH, VNA2.

period from 1957 to 1959 as a particularly dark time in the party's fortunes in South Vietnam. Across the Mekong Delta, thousands of cadres were arrested or killed, or rallied to the government. In Bến Tre, according to party historians, the dwindling numbers of cadres who remained at large were often on the run or in hiding from government security forces.

Still, RVN leaders were reluctant to declare victory. Prior to his reassignment, Captain Tấn noted that the communists retained influence in some parts of the province, and that they were counseling their supporters to have "one face, two hearts" – that is, to pretend to be supportive of the RVN, while continuing covert resistance. He advised that more and better development measures were needed, especially with regard to the Civic Action program and the interfamily system.[27] Bến Tre remained at peace for the moment, but the contests over development and control in the villages were far from ended.

DENSE AND PROSPEROUS AREAS

By early 1959, Ngô Đình Diệm had become convinced that the senior leaders of North Vietnam had embarked on a new covert campaign to destabilize his government. Declaring that South Vietnam is "now in a state of war," he outlined a series of new counterinsurgency programs and policies. These included Law 10/59, a measure that created special military tribunals with the power to investigate, prosecute, and sentence anyone accused of an "offense to national security." To increase their visibility, these tribunals functioned as itinerant organizations that moved among provinces, dispensing justice on the spot – sometimes with a portable guillotine brought along to administer death sentences. Communist propagandists quickly seized on the law as obvious proof that the Diệm government was a brutal dictatorship ruling South Vietnam by pure coercion. But while the draconian qualities of the tribunals were evident, the available evidence suggests that the number of executions carried out by the tribunals was considerably smaller than what the communists claimed.[28] For Diệm, the centerpiece of the new campaign was actually not the 10/59 law, but an ambitious population regroupment initiative known as the Agroville Program.

Announced by Diệm in July 1959, the Agroville Program aimed to create new rural settlements at government-selected sites across the Mekong Delta. Unlike some of Diệm's earlier agrarian development schemes, this

---

[27] Ibid.   [28] Elliott, *The Vietnamese War*, 1: 195–203; Miller, *Misalliance*, 200–202.

program was not a reworked version of older colonial-era development plans. Previously, RVN rural development strategy had followed the pre-1945 French emphasis on trying to reduce population pressure in the countryside by moving rural residents – sometimes forcibly – from crowded coastal villages and districts to new "land development centers" in lightly settled interior and highland areas of the country.[29] In contrast, the Agroville Program was predicated on the assumption that the population of the Mekong Delta was already too thinly dispersed. The solution, according to the designers of the agrovilles, was to have all of the farming households in a given area relocate their homes onto small plots in a townlike core settlement. Although they would henceforth be living inside the agroville, residents would continue to farm their fields outside the settlement. The transformative aspirations of the program were neatly summed up in the Vietnamese term that the government coined for the new settlements: *khu trú mật*, which can be rendered as "dense and prosperous area."

Diệm rhapsodized about the material benefits that he expected the Agroville Program to produce. Every agroville household, Diệm told his cabinet, would receive a sixty-by-eighty-meter plot of land in the residential core of the settlement; on this land, a family could build a house of "a Vietnamese traditional type" that would be "tidy" and feature "separate rooms for men, women, and children." Residents would enjoy access to government offices, a market, shops, well-maintained roads, and communication services. Hydraulic systems would furnish fresh water during the delta's long dry season, and generators would supply electricity. For all of these reasons, Diệm expected rural residents to embrace participation in the system. At the same time, however, he made it clear that such participation was not voluntary, and that residents could be compelled to build and live in the agrovilles.[30]

Diệm selected Bến Tre as one of the provinces that would host some of the first agrovilles. To implement this task, he appointed a new province chief: Lê Văn Ba, a military officer who had previously served in the province as the official in charge of Mỏ Cày district. Mỏ Cày was one of

---

[29] Miller, *Misalliance*, 160–165.
[30] "Bản Tóm Lược các vấn-đề thảo-luận tại phiên họp Hội Đồng Nội-Các ngày 8.10.1959," [Summary of issues discussed at the Cabinet Meeting of Oct. 8, 1959], Folder 11485, Bộ Công Chánh và Giao Thông [hereafter BCCGT]. VNA2. For a discussion of the Agroville Program and its objectives, see Miller, *Misalliance*, 177–183.

the two districts that had been flagged as "communist influenced" back in 1956. Diệm was apparently impressed with Ba's energetic security measures in the district, such as an early 1959 raid that resulted in the capture of a radio transmitter and a member of the Communist Party's provincial leadership committee.[31] After Ba took over as Bến Tre chief in June 1959, the arrests of "VC suspects" in the province rose sharply, to over 150 a month.[32] Ba also implemented a new "security plan" for the province that involved the creation of mobile "special police squads" and companies of Civil Guard rangers, as well as the local expansion of the Republican Youth, a state-sponsored paramilitary organization with a mass membership.[33] These measures provided the backdrop against which Ba began the construction of Bến Tre's first three agrovilles in the fall of 1959.

The high modernist qualities of the Agroville Program in Bến Tre were reflected in the ways in which the government proposed to configure the built environments of the new settlements.[34] A blueprint for Bến Tre's flagship agroville in Thành Thới village depicted a gridded array of streets and housing plots (Figure 8.2). A central business and administrative section – featuring a school, government offices, a market, a clinic, a park with an artificial lake and island, and places of worship – was flanked on either side by a pair of residential neighborhoods. The three sections of the settlement were connected by wide, urban-style boulevards and the settlement was linked by road to adjacent communities.

In addition to fostering material prosperity, the pattern of residential density within the agrovilles was also intended to enhance the RVN state's ability to administer, protect, and control the population. In its public descriptions of the program, the government stressed that the concentration of the population into a compact area would make it easier to repel a communist attack. But the actual location of the agrovilles within Bến Tre province suggested that officials were not simply concerned about

[31] Lê Minh, "Phúc-trình Tháng 03–1959," [Monthly Report for March 1959], Folder 318, PTTDNCH, VNA2.

[32] Lê Văn Ba, "Phúc-trình Tháng 07–1959," [Monthly Report for July 1959]; Lê Văn Ba, "Phúc-trình Tháng 08–1959," [Monthly Report for August 1959] both in Folder 318, PTTDNCH, VNA2.

[33] Lê Văn Ba, "Phúc-trình Tháng 09–19," [Monthly Report for September 1959]; "Biên-Bản Phiên Họp Thường Nguyệt Tháng 10–1959" [Minutes of the October 1959 monthly meeting], Nov. 6, 1959; both in Folder 365, PTTDNCH, VNA2.

[34] The now-classic work on high modernism is James Scott, *Seeing Like a State: How Certain Schemes to Improve the Human Condition Have Failed* (New Haven: Yale University Press, 1998).

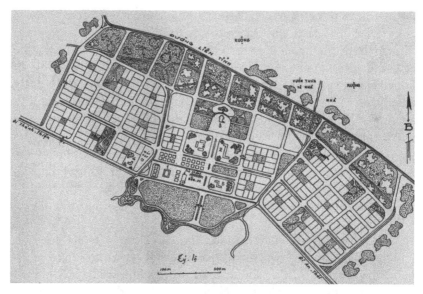

FIGURE 8.2. A Diagram Depicting the Agroville Constructed in Thành Thới
Village in Bến Tre Province during 1959–1960. General Sciences Library, HCMC.

defending against external assaults. All of the villages selected as sites for
Bến Tre's first three agrovilles were among those that had been identified
as "communist controlled" three years earlier. This included the flagship
settlement at Thành Thới village in Mỏ Cày district. By situating the new
settlements in what they deemed to be hostile territory, RVN officials were
targeting the areas and groups that had resisted previous pacification
efforts.

The compulsory nature of participation in the Agroville Program
quickly became evident to the residents of the target villages. During
the fall of 1959, large numbers of men at all three sites were dragooned
into teams and forced to clear land, move earth, and dig canals. Some
Bến Tre officials, worried about a popular backlash, suggested that the
government should compensate the workers. But Province Chief Ba
dismissed the proposal, saying that the funds were unavailable.[35]
In doing so, Ba was following the line laid down by Diệm, who repeatedly rejected entreaties from US officials and others for payments to

---

[35] "Biên-Bản Phiên Họp Thường Nguyệt Tháng 10–1959" [Minutes of the October 1959
monthly meeting], Nov . 6, 1959, Folder 365, PTTDNCH, VNA2.

workers, on the grounds that "all [residents] now see the many advantages of agroville life."[36]

Unsurprisingly, communist cadres in Bến Tre did not fail to notice the feelings of resentment that the Agroville Program generated. Nguyễn Thị Đình, one of the organizers of the 1960 uprising, later identified popular anger over the agrovilles as a key factor that aided the revolutionaries. According to Đình, of the thousands of people who were forced to live and work at the site of the Thành Thới Agroville, most were selected specifically because they had prior ties to the communists. "Calling them agrovilles was just a way to disguise the fact that they were prisons," she declared.[37]

In fact, Đình was half right: the agrovilles functioned not only as spaces of incarceration and surveillance but also as spaces for development. At first glance, the combination of these aspects of the Agroville Program might seem antithetical or contradictory. But to understand them in this way is to miss a key feature of postcolonial counterinsurgency: the configuration of coercion and social transformation as interdependent processes. In defending his decision to use forced labor to build the agrovilles, Diệm acknowledged the coercive qualities of the program but defended them as necessary to convert rural residents to "agroville life." US government officials, although they disagreed with Diệm on the question of compensation for labor, concurred on the importance of compulsion. One US analyst concluded that "There is little doubt that the fortress-like quality of the agrovilles, as well as the improved roads and the [regroupment] of the population, could provide greater physical security," and hence improve the RVN state's prospects for defeating the communists.[38] For US counterinsurgents, no less than for their RVN counterparts, the spatial sequestration and confinement of the rural population was an essential tactic – one that would be applied repeatedly in South Vietnam during the long years of war that lay ahead.

THE 1960 UPRISING

Although the implementation of the Agroville Program in 1959 provoked strong feelings of resentment in many parts of Bến Tre, the ability of the

---

[36] Diệm, quoted in Miller, *Misalliance*, 184.
[37] Nguyễn Thị Đình, "Bến Tre Đồng Khởi Năm 1960" [The Bến Tre Concerted Uprising of 1960], in *Huyền Thoại Quê Hương Đồng Khởi*, 50.
[38] Quoted in Miller, *Misalliance*, 183.

Communist Party to turn these feelings to its advantage was far from
a foregone conclusion. Because of the government's intensifying crackdown, the number of active party members in the province had declined
from around two thousand in the mid-1950s to just 162 by late 1959.
In a province that contained 116 villages, the party had a total of only 18
functioning cells, most of which comprised just a handful of operatives.
According to Nguyễn Thị Định, the party's ranks had been depleted not
only by killings and arrests at the hands of security forces, but also by
feelings of "despondency, defeat, and worries about survival" among
those who remained at large.[39] Viewed from this perspective, the 1960
Concerted Uprising appears not as an inevitable explosion that was bound
to take place sooner or later, but as an act of desperation carried out by an
organization on the verge of annihilation.

   In planning and executing the uprising, communist cadres had little
margin for error. Senior party leaders in Hanoi placed strict limits on the
kinds of revolutionary activities that they deemed acceptable in the south.
Although a January 1959 party directive had expanded the range of
permissible "armed struggle" operations in the south, the leadership still
expected any violent uprisings to remain small and localized. The primary
focus would continue to be on political struggle, Hanoi declared, not on
armed resistance.[40]

   The Bến Tre cadres also had to work within certain material and
geographical constraints. The main reason that the cadres decided to
launch the rebellion in Mỏ Cây district was that it was the only district
in the entire province in which the Communist Party still had
a functioning district committee. But even in Mỏ Cây, the party was still
too weak to mount direct attacks on the main symbols of RVN power in
the province. An assault on the Thành Thới Agroville was out of the
question, simply because of the number of government security forces
stationed in or near the site.

   The cadres eventually decided to launch the uprising in a small cluster
of just three villages located on the northeastern edge of the province
(Figure 8.3). These settlements contained a total of around 7,000 residents – less than 2 percent of the province's population. The villages,

---

[39] Nguyễn Thị Định, "Bến Tre Đồng Khởi Năm 1960," October 1969, printed in Huỳnh
    Văn Be et al., *Huyền Thoại Quê Hương Đồng Khởi* [The Legendary Homeland of the
    Concerted Uprising] (Hanoi: Nhà Xuất Bản Quận Đội Nhân Dân, 2008), 56.
[40] Pierre Asselin, *Hanoi's Road to the Vietnam War, 1954–1965* (Berkeley: University of
    California Press, 2013), 53–66.

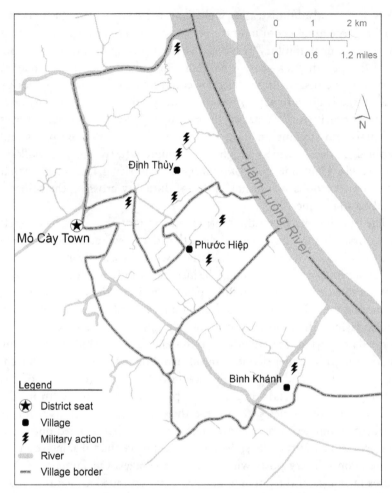

FIGURE 8.3. The Bến Tre Concerted Uprising of 1960. Map by Jonathan Chipman, Citrin GIS/Applied Spatial Analysis Laboratory, Dartmouth College.

known as Bình Khánh, Phước Hiệp, and Định Thủy, were selected in part because of their "revolutionary traditions" and because local residents had previously sheltered Việt Minh fighters during the First Indochina War. However, the organizers also chose the villages based on environmental considerations. Viewed as a single space, the three settlements formed a rectilinear area surrounded by rivers and canals on all sides. The northeastern edge of the rectangle was bounded by the Hàm Luông River, a branch of the Mekong more than 2 kilometers wide. Since the

RVN provincial administration lacked motorized boats capable of transporting large numbers of military personnel, the communists knew that any government military response to the uprising would come from the Mỏ Cây district seat, which lay inland of the three villages. However, the district town was not connected to the three villages by roads large enough to support large military vehicles; instead, any government security forces entering the area would have to negotiate a series of canals and streams on foot, using a network of narrow paths and footbridges barely wide enough to accommodate two people walking abreast. Hải Thủy, one of the organizers of the uprising, later recalled that "the puppet troops would have a lot of difficulty crossing the bridges, canals, and marshes."[41]

The uprising began on the morning of January 17, 1960. The rebels struck first in Định Thủy village, where they overpowered the local militia force with the aid of a village police officer who was secretly in league with the revolutionaries. That evening, the insurgents and some local sympathizers surrounded the main militia post in nearby Phước Hiệp village, prompting the soldiers inside to flee. Bính Khanh village was captured in similar fashion the following morning. To this point, the rebels had not suffered any casualties in their own ranks, and had only killed one enemy soldier, the commander of one of the local militia in the first village seized. But the rebels' good fortune did not last. On the second day of the uprising, RVN officials began to deploy security forces from the nearby Mỏ Cây district seat into the three villages, as well as to other nearby communities where communist operatives had carried out sabotage operations. Within days, the government forces had regained control of the main military posts within all three villages. On January 26, the cadres in charge of the uprising realized that continued armed resistance would be suicidal. They therefore ordered their followers to cease fighting and resume political struggle activities.[42]

As a challenge to RVN military power in Bến Tre, the January 1960 uprising was an insignificant event. But as a challenge to RVN claims of sovereignty over rural spaces in the South Vietnamese countryside, the uprising proved far more consequential. Although the rebels held the three

---

[41] Hai Thủy & Chí Nhân, "Trung Tâm Đồng Khởi Đợt Một" [The Center of the First Wave of the Concerted Uprising], in Huỳnh Văn Be et al., *Huyền Thoại Quê Hương Đồng Khởi* [The Legendary Homeland of the Concerted Uprising] (Hanoi: Nhà Xuất Bản Quận Đội Nhân Dân, 2008), 93–94.

[42] Ibid., 94–102.

villages for only a few days, their ability to seize those communities generated considerable disorder and fear in the ranks of government forces throughout the district and across the entire province. At a meeting with his subordinates on January 29, Province Chief Ba noted ruefully that the "recent upheavals" had "agitated the leaders and residents of a number of villages" in districts beyond Mỏ Cây. In some parts of the province, skittish village officials abandoned their posts immediately upon hearing the news of the uprising.[43] The officials may have been influenced by communist disinformation efforts, such as the use of noisemakers to simulate the sound of gunfire, and the circulation of rumors that North Vietnam had dispatched weapons and detachments of soldiers to the province.[44] These actions reinforce the findings of David Elliott, who concluded that a primary objective of the Concerted Uprisings of 1960 was to change the "balance of fear" in the countryside in favor of the revolutionaries.[45] By manipulating the anxieties of local officials and ordinary rural residents, the communists aimed to erode enemy morale and facilitate future recruitment efforts over a wide area stretching far beyond the three villages in which the initial attacks took place. Over the course of the next several months, the communists would seek to capitalize on the psychological fallout from the uprising, brief though it may have been.

CONCLUSION

Virtually all accounts of South Vietnamese counterinsurgency efforts in the Mekong Delta during 1954–1960 have depicted those efforts as a failure. In the months following the January 1960 uprising in Bến Tre, similar rebellions took place in several other provinces across the region. In addition, anti-government fighters carried out a wave of ambushes and military attacks on army bases and other South Vietnamese security installations. In December 1960, North Vietnamese radio announced the formation of a new insurgent organization: the South Vietnamese National Liberation Front (NLF). By that point, it was clear that the RVN state was facing the very thing that its leaders had aimed to prevent:

---

[43] Lê Văn Ba, Biên-Bản Phiên Họp Thường Nguyệt Tháng Giêng Năm 1960 [Minutes of the Monthly Meeting for January 1960], January 29, 1960, Folder 413, Folder 365, PTTDNCH, VNA2.

[44] Nguyễn Thị Định, "Bến Tre Đồng Khởi Năm 1960," 66–67.

[45] Elliott, *The Vietnamese War*, 1:258–265.

a widespread rural insurgency, organized and led by the leaders and cadres of the Vietnamese Communist Party.

Nevertheless, the account presented in this chapter is not *simply* a chronicle of state failure. In his now-classic study of development in Lesotho, the anthropologist James Ferguson observed that most of the development projects he studied did not meet the objectives set by their designers. Still, Ferguson warned that "it would be a mistake to make too much of the 'failure'" of these projects. Even when development projects failed, Ferguson noted, they could still produce lasting environmental or social changes; in addition, they often helped to entrench or consolidate the power of state bureaucratic actors. In such cases, Ferguson suggested, state leaders and their allies almost never opted to abandon development. Instead, they invariably sought to devise new development projects – projects designed specifically to remedy the perceived shortcomings of the earlier ones.[46]

In South Vietnam, the emergence of the communist-led insurgency during 1960–1961 marked not an abandonment of counterinsurgency but the beginning of a shift toward ever more ambitious forms of militarized development. In the years after the demise of the Agroville Program, the Diệm government would embark on a new counterinsurgency initiative, known as the Strategic Hamlet Program, which aimed to fortify and transform every hamlet in every village in South Vietnam. That program, in turn, would give way to a welter of US–RVN programs during the middle and late 1960s, ranging from the American-sponsored Civil Operations and Revolutionary Development Support (CORDS) to Nguyễn Văn Thiệu's "Land to the Tiller" land reform initiative and the CIA's infamous Phoenix Program. In the long run, these measures were not sufficient to build broad popular support for the Saigon government, or to ensure its ultimate survival in its contest with North Vietnam. Nevertheless, they massively affected the communist insurgency and hampered its ability to wage "people's war," especially after the 1968 Tet Offensive. They also profoundly impacted the people, land, and environments of the Mekong Delta. Down until the end of the Vietnam War in 1975 and beyond, counterinsurgency and development remained deeply intertwined in South Vietnam's rural spaces, and in the fates of the people who lived, worked, and fought in them.

---

[46] James Ferguson, *The Anti-Politics Machine: "Development," Depoliticization, and Bureaucratic Power in Lesotho* (New York: Cambridge University Press, 1990), 254–256, 267–277.

Decolonization and the Gendered Politics of Developmental Labor in Southeastern Africa

Priya Lal

Development was never a single project, as the term *developmentalism* suggests. It is not reducible to a discrete set of ideas authored by Western thinkers, nor can it be understood solely as a distinct group of policies imposed by Western actors and their secondary proxies scattered around the rest of the world. In fact, the global repertoire of developmental thought and practice was far more pluralistic and included a far more diverse set of primary agents than many scholarly accounts in the West recognize, as Paul Adler's chapter in this book shows. All global history is narrated from a specific vantage point, and much of the contemporary literature on development in the North American and European academies has been intellectually imprisoned within the geographic confines of its own position of inquiry. Accordingly, the story of development that has ascended in recent years[1] has often confused a particular range of Western approaches to the sprawling, enormous question of development – subsumed under the category of *developmentalism* – with the entire range of human attitudes and efforts manifesting a "will to improve" across the twentieth-century world.[2]

Shifting our vantage point on the history of development to one embedded in "the poorer nations"[3] of Latin America, Asia, and Africa

[1] As summarized in a recent two-part historiographical essay: Joseph Hodge, "Writing the History of Development," *Humanity* 6:3 and 7:1 (2015 and 2016): 429–463 and 125–174.

[2] Tania Li, *The Will to Improve: Governmentality, Development, and the Practice of Politics* (Durham: Duke University Press, 2007).

[3] Vijay Prashad, *The Poorer Nations: A Possible History of the Global South* (New York: Verso, 2014).

(in the spirit of Alden Young's chapter in this book) helps correct this distortion by substantively transforming the content of the discussion rather than merely modifying its geographic contours. One conceptual consequence of this move is to widen our understanding of the developmental spectrum to the extent that we are forced to discard, or at least particularize, the descriptive category of *developmentalism* that has mistakenly claimed universal representativeness. Writing postcolonial national development projects into the global history of development, for instance, challenges prevalent, if implicit, conceptions of development as a modular form[4] that originated in the West and was transplanted onto other sites.[5] Examining such efforts according to their own internal logic – through an emic lens – highlights the imaginative agency of postcolonial leaders and punctures unspoken assumptions of a Western monopoly on developmental thought.[6] Similarly, looking carefully at the concrete engagement of subaltern developmental targets with such policies as implemented in these same settings mandates a reconceptualization of common tropes of *developmentalist* power as a unilateral force imposed from above.[7]

In support of this analytical agenda, this chapter explores one underexamined dimension of national development efforts in Tanzania and Zambia during the early postcolonial period: their approach to the matter of what I call developmental labor. During the 1960s and early 1970s, after their respective transitions to political independence in 1961 and 1964, these neighboring countries adopted the loose ideology of African socialism in service of national development programs referred to as *ujamaa* in Tanzania and "humanism" in Zambia. African socialism, as I have suggested elsewhere, was a loose continental formation that was distinctly hybrid in composition, blending discursive, symbolic, and institutional elements of modernization theory, Marxism, Maoism, late colonial policy, and various Third World or nonaligned experiments with

---

[4] Benedict Anderson, *Imagined Communities: Reflections on the Origins and Spread of Nationalism* (New York: Verso, 1983).

[5] Manu Goswami, "Rethinking the Modular Nation Form: Toward a Sociohistorical Conception of Nationalism," *Comparative Studies in Society and History* 44:4 (2002): 770–799. I am referencing an extensive debate in the literature on nationalism here.

[6] In thinking about the imaginative agency of postcolonial thinkers, I am drawing on Partha Chatterjee, *Nationalist Thought and the Colonial World: A Derivative Discourse* (Minneapolis: University of Minnesota Press, 1993).

[7] On spatial metaphors of power and the state, see Akhil Gupta and James Ferguson, "Beyond Culture: Space, Identity and the Politics of Difference," *Cultural Anthropology* 7:1 (1992): 6–23 and James Ferguson, *Global Shadows: Africa in the Neoliberal World Order* (Durham: Duke University Press, 2006).

FIGURE 9.1. Map of Southeastern Africa. Drawn by David Cox.

development.[8] In the early postcolonial era, left-leaning governments in sub-Saharan Africa – among them Guinea, Ghana, and Mali – mobilized African socialism to substantively or more superficially underpin or organize ambitious nation-building projects. Such programs were not monolithic, consistent, or always sincere – but neither were most projects that scholars readily recognize under the label of *development*. This is equally true of Tanzanian *ujamaa* and Zambian humanism, which perhaps because of their African location have been dismissed by many scholars as incoherent and thus unworthy of serious consideration on their own terms. Yet it is precisely the internal contradictions of these projects that make them especially illuminating sites of inquiry into the complex character of national development in the postcolonial world.

[8] Priya Lal, *African Socialism in Postcolonial Tanzania: Between the Village and the World* (New York: Cambridge University Press, 2015).

A key theme of African socialism was its immediate emphasis on meeting what later came to be termed the "basic needs" of average people rather than achieving aggregate economic growth. By adopting African socialist agendas for national development in the 1960s, both the Tanzanian and Zambian political leadership prioritized the construction of robust welfare states that would materially and meaningfully improve the quality of life of their largely impoverished citizens. A central component of each welfare state apparatus was the labor force that would carry out the distribution of essential social services such as education and health care. The flimsy or negligible nature of state institutions for more advanced schooling and medicine that both regimes inherited from their colonial predecessors, combined with an extreme shortage of Africans who were sufficiently educated and adequately trained to staff schools or universities and hospitals, posed a seemingly intractable obstacle to national development at the moment of independence. The problem was a circular one: the same circumstances that rendered the work of educational and medical professionals so urgent had drastically constrained the production of such professional human resources. A logical solution to this impasse would be to import teachers, professors, doctors, and nurses to temporarily fill each country's skill gap so as to train a generation of domestic educational and medical professionals that could reproduce itself.

However, depending on foreign labor was antithetical to another key precept of African socialist ideology: self-reliance. In both iterations of African socialism, the political imperative of self-reliance was woven together with a seemingly contrary emphasis on an ethos of community and reciprocity (often metaphorically rendered as "familyhood," most explicitly in the case of *ujamaa*).[9] All of these principles were multivalent, but self-reliance took on slightly different meanings in each setting. At the macro level, both nonaligned countries configured self-reliance as a broad national goal with strategic value in a polarized Cold War world and particularly tense regional contexts. In Tanzania, official discourses of self-reliance reflected the marked influence of Maoism, while in Zambia, the cause of national self-reliance took on heightened geopolitical stakes given the country's position as a "frontline state" surrounded by hostile colonial or apartheid regimes. The precept of self-reliance held additional connotations for development policy within national borders in both sites. At the micro level, it exhorted citizens to not depend on their governments for their own development – an ideological impulse that existed in tension

[9] Translated from Swahili, *ujamaa* means "familyhood."

with the basic redistributive purpose of the welfare state itself. This contradictory interpretation of self-reliance directly and indirectly reflected the constraints of both countries' welfarist capacities, given their dearth of material resources for investment in such developmental activities.

To enforce or comply with the internal mandate of self-reliance, both postcolonial regimes partially delegated the task of providing average citizens with social security to what some would call the "private sphere" but what we might more precisely term the realm of unwaged work. The radical socialist aspirations embedded within certain strands of Tanzanian and Zambian policy sought to socialize the reproductive labor so critical to a population's overall quality of life – including the often intensive work of parenting, cooking, and cleaning or otherwise maintaining households and homes. Thus, government officials, official women's organizations, and other Tanzanian and Zambian voices called for the protection of women's position in the formal waged workforce and the establishment of day care centers and other "institutions and services" that could "free women from the drudgery of domestic life," as one correspondent for Tanzania's state-run newspaper put it.[10] However, a different thread of developmental ideology braided into *ujamaa* and humanism simultaneously reinscribed such labor into the space of the home. Moreover, both regimes often naturalized domestic reproductive labor as a female responsibility, an axiom that drew on colonial precedent and was reinforced by mainstream international development norms in the postcolonial era. In this sense, given the public benefit of such seemingly private work, all Tanzanian and Zambian women automatically became members of their country's developmental workforce. Although they were not compensated for their efforts, female homemakers – like their paid counterparts in the space of the university and hospital – had to be trained in order to perform this welfarist work or developmental labor efficiently and effectively in each regime's eyes. Accordingly, institutes for home economics training sprung up around Tanzania and Zambia in the early postcolonial period, alongside new universities, teacher training centers, and medical schools.

Both types of welfarist workers I have just described – educational and medical professionals, on the one hand, and average wives and mothers, on the other hand – were simultaneously developmental subjects and

---

[10] Amina Karrim, "A Look at Ten Years of African Women's Organisation: Big Role for UWT," *Daily News*, July 24, 1972. The *Daily News* was Tanzania's state-run newspaper, established in 1972 after the press was nationalized.

objects. Their assigned role was to develop their country's human resources, but in order to perform this work, they themselves had to be developed through interventions involving skills transmission. Thus, looking more closely at this aspect of southeastern African history unsettles easy distinctions between the agents and targets, or the subjects and objects, of development. A whole host of historical actors – many of them complicated, interstitial figures – were implicated in the labor of development in early postcolonial Africa, and national development indeed took *work*. In introducing the concept of "developmental labor" here, I put an extensive sociological literature on "care work"[11] into conversation with scholarship on labor history to add a missing layer to standard treatments of agency in the development story. The second theoretical contribution of my inquiry is to both illuminate the centrality of issues of gender to the history of national development in the postcolonial world, on the one hand, and demonstrate the utility of bringing gender as an analytical category into scholarship on development in general, on the other. Many historians of development treat gender as an incidental afterthought – a secondary theme embellishing a more fundamental, primary historical plot. For them, gender is a discrete topic that analysts must go searching for, usually in the particular site of women's bodies. Yet all developmental visions have gendered aspects, and the implementation of all development projects is always a gendered process. By including reproductive work as a key element of my analysis of developmental labor, I demonstrate how we might write gender into the mainstream narrative of development history.

***

As the deadlines of decolonization approached in the early 1960s British territories of Tanganyika and Northern Rhodesia, city dwellers, rural peasants, and local political elites – including officials of the leading political parties of TANU (the Tanganyika African National Union) and UNIP (Zambia's United National Independence Party) – had many concerns on their minds.[12] Such hopes and fears often centered on the overarching question of development. As a goal, development had individual and collective – micropolitical and macropolitical – meanings and

---

[11] Paula England, "Emerging Theories of Care Work," *Annual Review of Sociology* 31 (2005): 381–399.
[12] In 1964, Tanganyika merged with the British territory of Zanzibar, which gained independence in 1963, to form the United Republic of Tanzania.

dimensions. On the one hand, development signified *progress* – economic growth, the attainment of substantive political sovereignty, and an improvement of the material conditions of everyday life for all members of new national communities. On the other hand, development entailed achieving new forms of *stability* or social *security* – the creation of new mechanisms to maintain basic standards of living rather than solely enhancing them. These dual objectives informed the ways in which a range of southeastern Africans discursively and practically approached the impending transition to independence that would launch a new era of national development.

Yet the obstacles to achieving these aims were multiple, varied, and acutely perceived. In the realm of welfare state formation, an extreme shortage of domestic skilled labor threatened to negate the promise of substantive independence held out by decolonization. At the moment of independence, only approximately one hundred Zambians held university degrees;[13] Tanganyika had only twelve registered African doctors.[14] Neither territory had its own university. Secondary schools and hospitals were few and far between; they were staffed primarily by white expatriates, settlers, or missionaries.[15] This was a serious challenge, particularly given the pressing need for African educational and medical professionals to enact postcolonial regimes' promises to provide social services that would simultaneously *improve* and *secure* their citizens' standard of living. In the lead-up to and aftermath of independence in both Tanzania and Zambia, the Africanization of each country's developmental workforce became a rallying demand, but the material realization of this goal seemed close to impossible. In response, Tanzanian and Zambian leaders adopted a strategy of improvisation and flexibility, borrowing from and combining elements of a wide variety of developmental models with an eye toward preserving African Socialist principles while accounting for each country's limited resources and geopolitical concerns. Neither country's resultant policies surrounding the problem

---

[13] Zambia National Archives (ZNA), ED 1/11/63 University of Zambia Policy (1966–67). The University of Zambia: "University Manpower Planning," April 1, 1967. (Paper approved by the University Senate and the University Provisional Council, presented on February 9, 1967.)

[14] John Iliffe, *East African Doctors: A History of the Modern Profession* (Cambridge: Cambridge University Press, 1998), 113.

[15] Both countries also had a substantial number of Asian (South Asian) medical workers who occupied an ambiguous interstitial space in burgeoning, sometimes racialized, national imaginaries.

of skilled labor can be adequately explained by or understood under the category of a generic *developmentalism.*

The most immediate task at hand in the region involved the building of national universities that would begin producing developmental professionals. This situation was not unique to southeastern Africa. Between 1950 and 1962, the number of universities in Africa nearly tripled (from 16 to 41), while the total number of students enrolled in higher education institutions grew over sixfold, from 2,270 to 16,580.[16] The University College of Dar es Salaam was established as a constituent college of the University of London in 1961 (later to become part of a regional University of East Africa in 1963 and then the autonomous University of Dar es Salaam, or UDSM, in 1970). Meanwhile, the University of Zambia (UNZA) opened its doors as an independent institution in 1965. Both the Tanzanian and Zambian governments implicitly modeled these institutions after Western examples but explicitly configured them as "developmental universities."[17] Shortly after his announcement of the country's new program of *ujamaa* socialism in 1967, Tanzanian President Julius Nyerere pronounced, "a university in a developing society must put the emphasis of its work on subjects of immediate moment to the nation in which it exists," therefore calling for "its research, and the energies of its staff in particular" to "be relevant."[18] In discussions about the function of UNZA, Zambian President Kenneth Kaunda and his party similarly emphasized the precept of developmental relevance. Referring to the proposed university in 1963, just before independence, one UNIP official noted, "With the advent of self-government controlled by elected Africans, we envisage a massive expansion of our service (health, education, welfare, agriculture, etc.) and consequently an increased demand for the professional men and women who have the full training and qualifications to support and extend the services. The economic development of any part of Africa is closely linked with the availability of the 'expertise' to promote the

---

[16] UNESCO and United Nations Economic Commission for Africa 1963, cited in Joel Samoff and Bidemi Carrol, "The Promise of Partnership and Continuities of Dependence: External Support to Higher Education in Africa," *African Studies Review* 47:1 (2004): 77.

[17] James Coleman, "The Idea of the Developmental University," in *Universities and National Development*, ed. Atle Hetland (Stockholm: Almqvist & Wiksell, 1984), 85–104.

[18] Julius Nyerere, "The University's Role in the Development of the New Countries," in *Freedom and Socialism*, ed. Nyerere (Dar es Salaam: Oxford University Press, 1968), 183.

development schemes."[19] A 1970 report declared, "It is the University's task ... to relate the supply of University graduates to the manpower demands of the nation." Moreover, it insisted, "once graduates emerge from the University, it is important to ensure that their skills are used to maximum benefit."[20]

As factories for the production of a domestic developmental workforce, UDSM and UNZA had to fulfill their function within a compressed time frame. The first Tanzanian Minister of Education stated, "It is the policy of the Tanzania Government to achieve essential self-sufficiency in manpower at all skilled levels by 1980." Accordingly, he continued, "it is the policy of Tanzania to invest in education almost exclusively in relation to its contribution towards providing the skills needed for Tanzania's programme of economic and social development. Education for education's sake, whatever the value argued for it, must wait upon the 'take off.' This is particularly true of secondary and higher education."[21] In Zambia, too, 1980 was set as a target date for self-sufficiency in skilled labor. In a 1972 speech at UNZA, the Secretary General to the Government reminded his audience that "the Government set 1980 as the year of self-sufficiency in manpower."[22] The category of skilled manpower included numerous types of "experts" whose work was essential for national development, such as administrators for various sectors of the civil service bureaucracy, agricultural extension workers, and engineers (the latter were especially important for Zambia, given its dominant mining industry). Educators and medical workers were unique priorities, however, since their work would directly serve the fundamental priorities of African Socialist national development programs.

In a sense, until the projected "take off" of 1980, true decolonization would not be complete, because neither country would have a solid foundation of human resources for sustainable national development. The year 1980 was both an ambitious deadline and a disheartening one for the

---

[19] ZNA, ED 1/11/54 University of Zambia (1963–5). United National Independence Party, Northern Rhodesia: untitled. By J. M. Mwanakatwe, M.L.C. October 2, 1963.

[20] ZNA, ED 1/11/63 University of Zambia Policy (1966–67). The University of Zambia: "University Manpower Planning," April 1, 1967. (Paper approved by the University Senate and the University Provisional Council, presented on February 9, 1967.)

[21] Quoted in Solomon Eliufoo, "The Aims and Purposes of Tanzanian Education since Independence," in *Tanzania: Revolution by Education*, ed. Idrian Resnick (Arusha: Longmans, 1968), 42–43.

[22] U.K. National Archives (UKNA), Foreign and Commonwealth Office (FCO) 45–1133. Political situation in Zambia: Internal Security in Zambia, 1972. CSR 1/12 "Zambia: In Brief."

establishment of such a foundation. Throughout the 1960s and 1970s, popular politics in Tanzania and Zambia featured an intense preoccupation with the matters of Africanization and Zambianization, respectively – discussions that took on different racial connotations in both settings. Students, professors, and government officials across the region debated how and at what pace the Africanization or localization of labor should unfold at institutions of higher learning and in the broader developmental sector. The political principle of self-reliance seemed difficult to reconcile with the impossibility of attaining self-sufficiency in human resources in the short term. In a speech at UDSM in 1967, Nyerere offered a curt response to more radical demands for immediate Africanization, clarifying that self-reliance should be a guiding ethos rather than a literal imperative. "Few things make me more angry than a refusal to accept and to work with people from other countries," he explained, implicitly addressing a contingent of the university community that was calling for a more militant interpretation of Tanzania's socialist principles. "It is not being self-reliant to refuse to carry out the directions of a foreign engineer, a foreign doctor, or a foreign manager; it is just stupid," he continued. "We must look at this question of employing expatriates scientifically and without prejudice."[23]

Accordingly, both UDSM and UNZA recruited numerous faculty members from abroad to educate their expanding student bodies. These individuals ranged from Soviet engineers and Canadian political scientists to Indian biologists; they included representation from across the various "worlds" of the Cold War era. Similarly, in the field of medicine, the other critical staple of welfare state programs, a variety of foreign doctors, nurses, and medical assistants – along with linguistic interpreters when necessary – filled the desperate shortages facing Zambia and Tanzania in the early postcolonial era. Zanzibar's regime welcomed East German doctors, who replaced Arab-descended doctors who were killed during the 1964 revolution's political violence or fled in its wake.[24] Mainland Tanzania saw the arrival of, most notably, a series of visiting medical teams from China, which included among their ranks acupuncturists and practitioners of traditional Chinese medicine. In Zambia, doctors

---

[23] UKNA, FCO 31/155 Arusha Declaration. Speech by Nyerere on the "Arusha Declaration Teach-In" at the University College on August 5, 1967.
[24] The Zanzibar Revolution in early 1964 was a leftist movement to overthrow the largely Arab-descended ruling class. It involved massacres of large portions of the island territory's Arab and Asian-descended elites.

arrived from everywhere from Yugoslavia to Cuba, while the government recruited young, single female nurses from Britain. These women
became known as "Sunshine Girls," reflecting a recruitment slogan that
sought to attract them to southern Africa by emphasizing the region's
pleasant, sunny climate.[25] Their title also alluded to the gendered division of labor implicit in the professional developmental sphere. In both
Tanzania and Zambia, married women and mothers were poorly represented in university student bodies and faculties. Meanwhile, due to both
overtly exclusionary policies and social norms, younger unmarried
women mostly populated the fields of nursing and primary or secondary
teaching; men of varied ages tended to dominate fields that required
an MD or PhD. Among other things, the relative absence of
a substantial portion of the population – wives and mothers – from the
tertiary-level educational and medical sectors meant a further constraint
on workforce numbers.

Not every member of the diverse cohort of foreigners who arrived in
southeastern Africa fared well in their new settings, and not all of them
were received with open arms by the populations they were to serve. Some
Tanzanians and Zambians were suspicious of the paternalistic or potentially more insidious agendas of outsiders. During the 1960s, what I have
elsewhere called a *Cold War political culture* took root in Tanzania and
Zambia.[26] The hallmarks of this phenomenon were a preoccupation with
national security and autonomy, an emphasis on cultural policing to
preserve an idealized set of putatively indigenous norms, an impulse
toward "containing" potentially subversive social forces in the "sphere
of influence" of the home (or the realm of gender relations),[27] and an
overall tendency toward xenophobia and vigilance against people or ideas
deemed foreign. The source of this political culture was the same volatile,
decolonizing Cold War world that produced parallel attitudes in many
Western countries, although the particular inflection of global dynamics
within the specific regional context of southeastern Africa lent these
anxieties a uniquely local character. Tanzania and Zambia were both left-
leaning countries that had taken up socialist ideologies but practiced
a foreign policy of nonalignment. They both served as frontline states in

[25] UKNA, Overseas Dominion (OD) 8–2140. Recruitment of medical staff. Qualified
medical nurses for Zambia, 63–67.
[26] Lal, *African Socialism in Postcolonial Tanzania*, chs. 1 and 2.
[27] Here I draw on Elaine Tyler May, *Homeward Bound: American Families in the Cold War
Era* (New York: Basic Books, 1990).

the ongoing struggle against colonial and apartheid rule in southern Africa; this activism entailed all sorts of covert trafficking in arms, soldiers, and information by liberation armies, their champions from across the socialist world, and their opponents from the colonial and capitalist worlds. Both countries also practiced pan-Africanist solidarity by receiving often unregulated rivers of refugees from neighboring territories wracked by civil wars or anti-colonial wars, including Angola, Mozambique, Rhodesia (Zimbabwe), South Africa, South West Africa (Namibia), the Congo, Rwanda, and Burundi. Such refugees strained already meager Tanzanian and Zambian welfare state capacities, threatening to render national self-reliance an even more distant goal. As one UNIP official commented in a discussion on Zambia's medical system, "The political situation in Southern Africa is such that Zambia is full of refugees from the racist countries. These refugees have swollen the numbers of patients who need treatment."[28]

These complex geopolitical coordinates generated a heightened sense of concern about the fragility of African national sovereignty and paradoxically produced a sentiment of nativism alongside that of pan-Africanist, Third Worldist, and nonaligned cosmopolitanism. Accordingly, even foreign aid in the apparently innocuous realms of education and medicine could be perceived as a threat to national autonomy or security. This was particularly apparent in both countries' reception of foreign voluntary labor. The 1960s marked the emergence of a new international volunteer economy that sent large numbers of predominantly Western young people to predominantly Third World countries to participate in local developmental activities. These volunteers mythologized themselves as apolitical humanitarian actors; many African socialist countries viewed them simultaneously as a threat and a potential boon, given domestic resource shortages. In 1972, the Zambian Ministry of Foreign Affairs instructed its UN delegate that "Zambia actively pursues a policy of nonalignment and therefore would like to diversify offers from foreign countries as much as possible." The Ministry urged the delegate "to be extra-critical in determining whom Zambia may accept as its volunteers, what their nationality is, what proportion of these to other nationalities, etc."[29] In another correspondence around the same

---

[28] United National Independence Party (UNIP) Archives at the British Library, EAP 121-2-6-6-18. The Social and Cultural Committee, "Ad Hoc Meeting on Health."

[29] ZNA, FA 1/11/322 International Secretariat for Volunteer Service, 1969–72. From the Permanent Secretary, Ministry of Foreign Affairs to the Permanent Representative,

time, the Ministry explained that its "investigations into the activities of the United Nations Volunteer Programme" revealed that "basically, all volunteer organizations engage in espionage activities one way or the other and that the volunteers are a potential danger to any recipient country whether they come from Sweden, Canada, the USSR or the USA." Accordingly, the Ministry urged the exercise of "extreme caution and scrutiny of each batch of these volunteers."[30] For such reasons, Zambia did not host the US Peace Corps, which officials considered "another arm of the invisible government,"[31] and Tanzania expelled the Peace Corps in 1969. This latter action followed shortly after Nyerere professed that the "Peace Corps has become a problem" and "gets infiltrated by people whose motives are no good."[32]

Such moves did not simply reflect a paranoid posturing. Foreign aid – especially in human form, whether skilled or unskilled (as in the case of most volunteers) labor – did represent potential security risks, given tense regional dynamics. More to the point, however, accepting foreign volunteers or recruiting foreign labor posed a threat to the integrity of each country's respective nation-building program. The difficulty of maintaining a coherent domestic developmental agenda when relying on outside workers and training and aid was undeniable; professors, teachers, and medical workers from across the world brought with them diverse professional and political assumptions and aims. In this way, the obligatory recruitment of foreign developmental labor until the "take-off" entailed the unavoidable importation of a wide range of sometimes opposing ideologies. In the sphere of medicine alone, these could include "Chinese pride in indigenous medicine, Russian eagerness to display Soviet technology, Scandinavian earnestness about primary health care, or the World Bank's obsession with cost-sharing."[33] When combined, these professional agendas sometimes clashed. Thus, the process of building a self-reliant developmental workforce in southeastern Africa could be marked by intense friction and

---

Mission of the Republic of Zambia to the UN, May 16, 1972. "United Nations Volunteers Programme."

[30] ZNA, FA 1/11/322 International Secretariat for Volunteer Service, 1969–72. From the Permanent Secretary, Ministry of Foreign Affairs to the Permanent Secretary, Personnel Division, Lusaka, October 13, 1972. "United Nations Volunteer Programme."

[31] ZNA, FA 1/11/322 International Secretariat for Volunteer Service, 1969–72. November 8, 1971 (unknown Ministry).

[32] US National Archives and Records Administration (NARA), General Records of the Department of State, Record Group (RG) 59, Central Foreign Policy Files, 1967–69, Box 493. US Embassy Dar es Salaam to Secretary of State, March 5, 1967.

[33] Iliffe, *East African Doctors*, 120.

inconsistency. Such considerations partly informed the decision of many African countries to construct mandatory National Service units that would mobilize unskilled developmental labor from within domestic borders rather than relying on external armies of Western volunteers to complete the same tasks. (Tanzania developed a National Service program in 1964, while Zambia did the same in 1971.) Yet a similarly neat internal solution was impossible when it came to the skilled developmental labor that both countries so desperately needed.

***

Although the construction of robust welfare state services was a national priority under African socialism, many Tanzanian and Zambian officials were painfully aware of the limitations of this endeavor. The widespread and multifaceted poverty that pervaded southeastern Africa mandated that welfarist efforts be extended to the space of intimate – moving from what some might call the "public sphere" to the "private sphere." Advanced schooling and health care would be rendered irrelevant where average citizens – whether children or adults – were unfed, unclothed, and uncared for by their social networks or within their local communities. Moreover, when advanced schooling and health care were simply not available, the Tanzanian and Zambian regimes implicitly calculated, welfarist interventions should be concentrated at lower levels. Both countries accordingly devoted considerable national energy to augmenting the reproductive labor that was an essential prerequisite for or complement to the cultivation of a more skilled developmental workforce. In this campaign, Tanzania and Zambia featured a mixed tendency toward the socialization of reproductive labor, on the one hand, and the reinscription of such work into the space of the home and the hands of women, on the other. That is, there was considerable debate about the extent to which less highly skilled forms of developmental labor should be migrated from the "private" to the "public" sphere – that is, from the unwaged to the waged sector, moving from the independent responsibility of individual families (tended to by wives and mothers) to the collective undertaking of the state and its employees. Certain socialist elements of and influences within the developmental imaginaries of *ujamaa* and humanism encouraged such a shift, but colonial legacies and international developmental norms – along with aspects of both countries' Cold War political culture – worked against it.

Reproductive labor – the work of supplying nourishing food, maintaining clean and conducive living environments, attentively raising children, and providing intimate forms of care essential to human welfare – is often overlooked by historians of development, despite the obvious importance of this activity to many historical actors undertaking development projects. This analytical neglect may be due to the overwhelming propensity of such projects to inscribe reproductive labor into the space of the home, outside of the boundaries of the formal waged economy. Such a move renders this critical type of work invisible to scholars who have not absorbed the insights of a large Marxist and feminist literature on the topic and hence confine their inquiry to more easily identifiable developmental activities in more supposedly public settings. Yet unpaid care work represents a very real investment of time and energy into the development of human resources, as some scholars in other fields have noted. This labor has concrete "social benefits" that "create public goods" – it "contributes to the intellectual, physical, and emotional capabilities of recipients" that in turn "contribute to recipients' own and others' development."[34] The early postcolonial Tanzanian and Zambian governments certainly recognized unpaid, relatively less skilled care work as developmental labor. In doing so, however, they adhered not to one single *developmentalist* approach to improving the conditions and content of this labor, but to multiple and sometimes conflicting developmental models. Thus, both regimes' agendas in this realm took on a fundamentally hybrid and sometimes contradictory character, mirroring the pluralistic and multivalent nature of the broader nation-building programs in which they were embedded.

Even before independence, the deficiencies of standard welfare state services as a sufficient means of providing social security to and generating social improvement among average Tanzanian and Zambian men and women were well understood by many future postcolonial officials at various levels of government. During the final days of colonial rule in one secondary school in Ndola, Zambia, the chairman of the regional education authority observed, "Many pupils live several miles from the school. They left their homes at 5:30 am without breakfast, walked to the school, remained there until the afternoon's activities were over and did not reach their homes again until early evening when they had their only meal of the day. For a large part of the day pupils were hungry and this adversely affected their rate of learning." Others echoed this complaint,

[34] England, "Emerging Theories of Care Work," 384.

pointing out that teachers in many schools lamented, "the pupils were too tired and hungry to absorb the teaching." Given that "a great deal of the cost and effort put into the secondary schools would be wasted if the pupils were too hungry to learn properly," the authority implemented "a feeding system whereby each pupil received half a pint of milk and some bread rolls every morning" that had "proved extremely beneficial."[35] In this case, the government assumed the responsibility of feeding children along with educating them, a task that would otherwise be a domestic or private duty. In other words, the state would assume some of the burden of raising children in order to be able to more effectively use them as developmental resources in the future. This paradigm persisted into the early post-colonial period.

In many other cases, however, such responsibilities were delegated to average urban and rural women, who were exhorted to intensify their efforts to care for their families because, as mothers and wives, they were effectively producing and reproducing human resources for their country's development. Rather than taking on the task of feeding children themselves, for instance, some Tanzanian and Zambian officials devoted substantial resources and energy to teaching women "how to improve diets based on locally available foods, to introduce more efficient and nutritious ways of preparing foods, to learn proper meal planning and food preservation methods" as well as to "find possible solutions to the nutritional problems of different areas in the country within the economic and cultural framework in which the family lives."[36] Home economics training became a conspicuous component of both countries' postcolonial agendas, as manifested by the work of institutions such as the Buhare Home Economics Training Centre in Musoma, Tanzania. Buhare was established in 1964 after the Tanzanian government requested support from the UN's Food and Agricultural Organization (FAO) for such an institute.[37] Supervised by the Swedish International Development

---

[35] UNIP Archives at the British Library, EAP 121-2-4-7-17-3 pt.1. Western Province Education Authority, Minutes of the 20th meeting held at Ndola on June 5, 1964.

[36] Tanzania National Archives (TNA), Prime Minister's Office (PMO) Records, Dodoma, RD/E6/1 FAO Home Economics. Report to the Government of Tanzania (Swedish Funds in Trust, FAO/SWE/TF 44): "The Home Economics Training Centre, Buhare, Musoma, Tanzania." Food and Agriculture Organization of the United Nations, Rome, 1971.

[37] TNA, PMO Dodoma, RD/ED 6/1 FAO Home Economics General #113. Request to UN/FAO Assistance to Establish a Diploma Course at Buhare H.E. Training Centre. From J. M. Rutashobya, Commissioner for Rural Development, to Treasury, Dar es Salaam and Maendeleo, Dar es Salaam. December 10, 1971.

Corporation until 1971, staffed by foreign "experts" and Tanzanian teachers (many of whom had been trained abroad in areas as disparate as Canada and the Philippines), and funded in part by UNICEF, Buhare trained hundreds of female rural development workers in home economics techniques that were supposedly crucial for "raising living standards" and "making the development programme a success."[38] In courses such as "Home Management," women would learn methods of "planning for better use of time, energy and family resources, both human and material, and the protection of human resources" that could "contribute considerably to the country's development." The subjects studied ranged from "the cleaning of houses, both local and modern" to "how to make starch from cassava and how to make soap." Other courses focused on issues such as "Child Care and Child Development," since one report noted that "child care and hygiene, together with nutrition, are among the most important subjects being taught in relation to national well-being."[39]

Such forms of development training configured average women as guardians of their homes and families, first and foremost. This notion flew in the face of the fact that across southeastern Africa, rural women often performed the majority of agricultural work (especially given the tendency of men to periodically leave their homes as waged migrant workers) and urban women were active participants in the money economy as "productive" workers (albeit usually in the informal sector, often as petty traders). Moreover, actual family structures – especially in rural areas – tended to be far more complicated than home economics programs allowed for. The myth of a bounded nuclear family unit that women would tend was profoundly at odds with the reality of "unstable marriages and frequent temporary migration" in many areas, which meant that, in fact, "the household form [was] constantly shifting."[40] Such relational flexibility among men and women was often a practical

---

[38] TNA, PMO Dodoma, RD/E6/1 FAO Home Economics. Report to the Government of Tanzania (Swedish Funds in Trust, FAO/SWE/TF 44): "The Home Economics Training Centre, Buhare, Musoma, Tanzania." Food and Agriculture Organization of the United Nations, Rome, 1971.

[39] Ibid.

[40] Elizabeth Harrison, "Men, Women and Work in Rural Zambia," in *Men at Work: Labour, Masculinities, Development*, ed. Cecile Jackson (London: Frank Cass, 2001), 57. See also, Priya Lal, "Militants, Mothers, and the National Family: Ujamaa, Gender, and Rural Development in Postcolonial Tanzania," *Journal of African History* 51:1 (2010): 1–20.

response to extreme poverty, which could render home economics ineffectual when there was simply no food to cook or no money to spend on sewing materials.

At times, government policy and public conversations in both Tanzania and Zambia acknowledged the inconsistency of actual domestic economies and gender relations with the naturalized order assumed by many developmental training programs. Discussing appropriate developmental curricula at the secondary school level, a number of educational authorities in one corner of Tanzania noted that rural women "actually do more than their fair share of the agricultural work in the country," and that "women do, in fact, very often surpass men as 'bread winners.'" Accordingly, they proposed that "as much of the agricultural training as possible now given to the boys should also be undertaken by the girls, girls and boys working side by side in practical work," and "some facets of Home Economics could appropriately be taught to the boys."[41] Women's advocacy organizations argued that women were "beasts of burden" who "work[ed] harder than men,"[42] and contended that "men must be taught" to more "fully [participate] in productive work."[43] As mentioned above, although men dominated most skilled developmental labor in both countries, many urban women sought employment as paid care workers in positions ranging from teachers to nurses. Yet in this sector, too, they encountered challenges from those who assumed that their primary contribution to national development should occur within the space of their homes. However, popular and official attitudes on this subject were often remarkably ambivalent. For instance, even while the Zambia National Union of Teachers asserted on the one hand that "Home Science is a vital subject in both our Primary and Secondary Schools for preparing the young girls as future mothers of this country," they criticized the fact that female teachers occupied a lower rung on the educational hierarchy than "males [who] advance[d] rather rapidly to administrative positions within the system." The Union decried "societal expectations regarding [women's] home responsibilities, marriage role and the lack of career opportunity and mobility" and demanded that "more chances for promotions should be open to female teachers who put in an equal amount of

[41] TNA, PMO Dodoma CD/CD/T.3/5 (2) Homecraft Centres Policy #109. "Record of a Meeting Held to Discuss Proposal for a Girls' Training Department at Mahiwa on 1st July, 1968 at Pamba House."

[42] "Focus on Tanzanian women." *Nationalist*, October 9, 1967. The *Nationalist* was a national Tanzanian newspaper published by TANU, the ruling political party.

[43] Editorial: "Stop this Practice." *Nationalist*, September 9, 1967.

work and time as men do."[44] This simultaneous insistence on assigning women the job of unpaid reproductive labor and asserting that women should be treated as equals to men in the paid developmental sector captured some of the fundamental contradictions underpinning official policy across the region.

As part of a contrary push to relieve women of domestic duties, some groups called for the establishment of day care centers throughout their countries. Even Buhare trained day care center assistants in an official course,[45] and the Tanzanian women's union "realised the need for making child-care a social responsibility rather than just a task for women, by taking active part in establishing Child Day-care Centres. Here, the children can be looked after during the day by paid workers while their mothers are engaged in productive work outside the home."[46] Other efforts to protect the position of women in the paid developmental workforce included calls for mandatory maternity leave in the civil service, while more oblique measures to combat the burdening of women with reproductive labor included campaigns to make family planning mechanisms such as contraception more widely available. In 1967, Tanzania's TANU-run newspaper criticized the conditions of civil service "guiding expectant mothers either on the application of maternity leave and expectant unmarried mothers on their dismissal from service." Unpaid maternity leave in particular, the piece insisted, was "blatantly out of place in a socialist country like ours."[47] Paid maternity leave was implemented in the Tanzanian civil service two years later, with the Vice President explaining, "expectant mothers [are] entrusted with a big national responsibility."[48] In Zambia, too, after considerable agitation by the national teachers' union, maternity leave was regularized and many female employees achieved "a fixed salary scale" and "permanent and pensionable establishment" by 1971.[49]

---

[44] UNIP Archives at the British Library, EAP 121-2-10-1-48. Zambia National Union of Teachers: The 9th Annual General Council Resolutions: January 3–4, 1976.

[45] TNA, PMO Dodoma, RD/E6/1 FAO Home Economics. Report to the Government of Tanzania (Swedish Funds in Trust, FAO/SWE/TF 44): "The Home Economics Training Centre, Buhare, Musoma, Tanzania." Food and Agriculture Organization of the United Nations, Rome, 1971.

[46] Scholastica Mushi, "UWT's Ten Years of Existence: A Survey." *Daily News,* November 2, 1972.

[47] "Tanzania Women Workers and Their Conditions of Service." *Nationalist,* June 10, 1968.

[48] "New deal for maternity women from July 1." *Nationalist,* June 6, 1969.

[49] UNIP Archives at the British Library, EAP 121-2-10-1-56 pt.1. Zambia National Union of Teachers to the Minister of Education and Culture, April 16, 1973.

While such policies were widely supported in both countries, the promotion of family planning technologies was more controversial. The early postcolonial era in southeastern Africa coincided with the rise of international concerns about an impending demographic explosion in the Third World; many conversations about development accordingly began to feature a fixation with managing population growth. In 1967, the FAO's Home Economics Branch, ostensibly concerned with "raising levels of nutrition and family living and the development of human resources," insisted that "the effective mobilization of human resources so that sound national development can take place necessarily requires planning."[50] The organization's new Planning for Better Family Living Programme – active in Tanzania, among other places – aimed to help governments "foster among their people awareness of the relation between rapid population growth and hunger, malnutrition, ill health, and low levels of living."[51] Some Tanzanian activists established a Family Planning Association in 1966, and although the government hesitated to formulate a "national family planning policy," medical officers in state hospitals were granted permission to set up family planning clinics,[52] and rural development officers began to acknowledge that "planning is essential in the development and mobilization of human resources at both family and national levels." However, they acknowledged that "in an agricultural country like Tanzania, the large family [was] a sign of wealth."[53] International family planning activists also noted the sensitivity of many Zambians to any discussion of population control, given "a preponderant Zambian view that this nation needs more population and a persistent belief, reinforced by observations of governments to the south, that population control is a white supremacist conspiracy to avoid African ascendancy."[54] Yet in Zambia, too, health clinics made family planning information available, and a Family Planning and Welfare Association had been founded by 1971 in order to "see that contraceptive knowledge can be obtained by those

---

[50] TNA, PMO Dodoma, RD/E6 1 – FAO Home Economics General. "The Planning for Better Family Living Programme," Undated (1970/71).
[51] Ibid.   [52] Ibid.
[53] TNA, PMO Dodoma, RD/E6/1 FAO Home Economics General #114. "Report on the Seminar on 'Planning for Better Family Living' Held in Rome between 22nd and 31st July 1971. Prepared by Mrs. A. Abdallah and Mrs. C. Tarimo, Senior Rural Development Officers."
[54] NARA, General Records of the Department of State, RG 59, Central Foreign Policy Files 1964–66, Social. Box 3115. "Lusaka TOAID A-148."

who want it."[55] Such endorsement of reproductive technologies hinted that the ability to scientifically regulate the size of families – and, by extension, the burden of caregivers – could align with the imperative of systematically planning national development, in addition to or instead of posing a simple demographic threat to national growth.

***

All of the proposals, efforts, and debates surveyed in the section above directly or indirectly addressed the place of reproductive labor in national development. Like the conversations and contestation over the work of skilled educational and medical professionals addressed earlier in this chapter, they also reflected varying interpretations of African socialism itself, exposing the lack of easy consensus among citizens and governments regarding how to best manage difficult developmental problems. Tanzanian *ujamaa* and Zambian humanism were not meaningless projects, however; such varied prescriptions for producing, regulating, and enhancing developmental labor reflected the knotty composition of these political imaginaries, not their hollow character. Divergent proposals and methods for maintaining and improving social welfare also revealed the impact and influence of a broad range of developmental ideologies and models circulating in the 1960s and 1970s world. Forced by material deficiencies to turn to outside aid and assistance, southeastern African nation-building projects took on a fundamentally hybrid quality mirroring the plurality of developmental approaches available across the globe. Reducing the story of these projects to a neat tale of hegemonic *developmentalism* at work obscures the distinctive logic of African socialism and the uneven, complex nature of the early postcolonial world in which it was embedded. By contrast, paying careful attention to the internal tensions of Tanzanian and Zambian visions and strategies for coordinating developmental labor helps illuminate heretofore unrecognized layers and dimensions of the global history of development.

---

[55] Professor Maurice King, Social Medicine, "It's a time for quality, not quantity." *Times of Zambia*, October 30, 1971.

PART III

INTERNATIONAL DEVELOPMENT IN COLD WAR POLITICS

I O

De-Stalinizing Growth: Decolonization and the Development of Development Economics in the Soviet Union

Alessandro Iandolo

In her chapter in this book, Amanda McVety shows how thinking about international relations and about development were intrinsically linked in the Western world since Adam Smith's days. This entanglement produced a plethora of understandings of and perspectives on development, as both an idea and a policy to pursue. The socialist tradition, while about one century younger than its liberal counterpart, is no less complex and equally intertwined with global politics. Few among the variety of socialist approaches to development left a more profound mark on the contemporary world than the Soviet Union's attempt to create a new model of development. This model was rooted in the Marxist tradition, but influenced at the same time by traditionally capitalist attitudes to production and economic growth. This chapter focuses on the shift in Soviet thinking about development that took place in the second half of the 1950s, which transformed the USSR's class-based understanding of human evolution and societal progress into a body of thought closer to contemporary development economics than classical Marxism. It argues that this change occurred in reaction to the process of decolonization, which forced the Soviet leadership to reinterpret their understanding of economic relations. In the socialist as in the Western world, development emerges as a multifaceted concept that is impossible to separate from international politics, and that is necessarily global in nature – two of the key themes of this volume.

FROM CLASSICAL MARXISM TO "SOCIALISM IN ONE COUNTRY"

In December 1955, Nikita Sergeevich Khrushchev, First Secretary of the Central Committee of the Communist Party of the Soviet Union, described the trip to India he had taken the previous month to his colleagues in the Central Committee Presidium. He spoke at length about his meetings with Jawaharlal Nehru and with other members of the Indian government, during which they had discussed the state of the world. "It is evident," Khrushchev reported, "that they [the Indians] appreciate our steps." The meetings were presented as a success, and Nehru and the Indian people as sympathetic to the Soviet Union. To give his colleagues a sense of modern India using a parallel that they were certain to understand, Khrushchev explained that India was "something similar to a *kerenshchina*," a society that was still bourgeois in nature, but where the class struggle was destined to increase in the near future.[1] The choice of words was not casual. The name *kerenshchina* was a construction derived from Aleksandr Kerenskii, the leader of the Russian Provisional Government that was established following the February 1917 Revolution, and that was eventually overthrown by the Bolsheviks in the October Revolution. In official Soviet discourse, the experience of the Provisional Government was far from laudable. The second edition of the *Bol'shaia Sovetskaia Entsiklopediia* (the "Great Soviet Encyclopedia") defined the Provisional Government as an "organ of the bourgeois dictatorship" and Kerenskii as "a dangerous agent of the imperial bourgeoisie," citing Lenin.[2] Stalin's *Kratkii kurs* (the official history of the Bolshevik party) dismissed the Provisional Government as made up of "bourgeois and proto-bourgeois landowners."[3]

The bourgeois nature of Nehru's government in India, comparable to the much-maligned Provisional Government, was at the heart of the

---

[1] Doklad tt. Khrushcheva i Bulganina o poezdke v Indiiu, Birmu i Afganistan, December 22, 1955, in *Prezidium Tsk KPSS 1954–1964: Chernovye Protokolnye Zapisi Zasedanii Stenogrammy Postanovleniia*, vol. 1, ed. Aleksandr A. Fursenko (Moscow: Rosspen, 2004), 73–74.

[2] 'Vremenno Pravitel'stvo v Rossii v 1917' in *Bol'shaia Sovetskaia Entsiklopediia*, 2nd ed., vol. 9, ed. B. A. Vvedenskii (Moscow: Gosudarstvennoe Nauchnoe Izdatel'stvo "Bol'shaia Sovetskaia Entsiklopediia," 1951), 264; 'Kerenskii, Aleksandr Fedorovich' in *Bol'shaia Sovetskaia Entsiklopediia*, 2nd ed., vol. 20 (Moscow: Gosudarstvennoe Nauchnoe Izdatel'stvo "Bol'shaia Sovetskaia Entsiklopediia," 1953), 553.

[3] TsK VKP (b), *Istoriia Vsesoiuznoi Kommunisticheskoi Partii (Bol'shevikov): Kratkii Kurs* (Moscow: Izdatel'stvo TsK VKP (b) "Pravda," 1938), 171.

FIGURE 10.1. From right: First Secretary of the Soviet Communist Party's Central Committee Nikita Khrushchev (1894–1971) and Soviet statesman and Marshal of the Soviet Union Nikolai Bulganin (1895–1975) at a meeting in Jaipur, India.

discussion in the Presidium. In theory the USSR, which presented itself as the representative of the workers and peasants of the world in their struggle against capital, should have had no desire to associate itself with a *kerenshchina*-type of government, where the wrong class still held power. Yet, Khrushchev presented his tour of India in enthusiastic terms, and complained that the USSR knew and understood little about countries like India. "Perhaps we should think through the issue of aid," he exhorted his colleagues.[4] In fact, Moscow had already pledged to build a large steel plant in Bhilai, which the Delhi government regarded as a landmark development project and which signaled the beginning of large-scale Soviet-Indian economic cooperation. Moreover, India was by no means unique. Between 1955 and 1960, the Soviet Union established formal relations and signed economic and technical cooperation agreements with countries as diverse as Afghanistan, Burma, Egypt, Ghana, Guinea, India, Indonesia, Iraq, Mali, Syria, and eventually Cuba. None

---

[4] Doklad tt. Khrushcheva in Fursenko, *Prezidium TsK KPSS*, 74.

of them qualified as a communist state. In fact, most became members of the Non-Aligned Movement, a grouping of Third World countries born out of the 1955 Bandung Conference, which had the explicit aim of seeking distance from either Cold War bloc, while prioritizing economic modernization at home and the fight against colonialism abroad.[5] All were run by elites that the USSR regarded as bourgeois. Third World states like Gamal Abdel Nasser's Egypt, Sukarno's Indonesia, and Kwame Krumah's Ghana, all major recipients of Soviet development and/or military aid, could be described as *kerenshchiny* as easily as Nehru's India. Coming to terms with this specific kind of bourgeoisie and understanding what the effect of Soviet economic aid would be on these societies was one of the big intellectual challenges of the Khrushchev era. It involved policymakers and academics, party members and state officials and, as this chapter argues, changed radically the way the Soviet Union approached two of the key themes of the twentieth century: decolonization and development. Spurred by the opportunities offered by the end of empire in Africa and Asia, the Soviet leadership – intellectual as well as political – was forced to question some long-established beliefs of the communist tradition, abandoning the last Stalinist legacies and coming closer to a Western approach to "development economics," which was being formulated at the same time. Capital, and the bourgeoisie that controlled capital in the Third World, could no longer be only an enemy for the Soviet Union.

This was a momentous change that broke with several long-standing assumptions in the communist tradition. Karl Marx sketched a vision of societal evolution based on the attainment of progressive stages of development, from "primitive" to full socialism. He maintained that any society must first reach a fully developed capitalist stage before transitioning to socialism. According to Marx, colonial societies such as British India, about which he wrote, were far from this stage and therefore still unable to develop a proletarian revolutionary movement. Economic development, which only bourgeois capitalism produced, was a prerequisite for the revolution. Marx famously argued that British colonialism in India, however violent and exploitative, was a necessary

---

[5] For more context on Bandung, see Mark Philip Bradley, "Decolonization, the Global South, and the Cold War, 1919–1962" in *The Cambridge History of the Cold War*, Volume 1: Origins, ed. M. Leffler and O. A. Westad (New York: Cambridge University Press, 2010), 464–485.

step toward economic development first, and then the possibility of revolution in the subcontinent.[6]

The early Soviet leaders were caught in the tension between Marx's logic and the temptation of exporting the revolution abroad. Russia itself, where the first socialist revolution had somewhat unexpectedly taken place, was different from the kind of advanced capitalist society Marx had indicated as the only one that could produce a true postcapitalist society. Could there be a way to build socialism from a lower stage of economic development? Lenin certainly thought so, as long as there was a vanguard party to direct the transition and the global circumstances were favorable. Lenin famously believed that imperialism was "the highest stage of capitalism," and that therefore the destruction of the great European empires would accelerate the end of the capitalist order.[7] In practical terms, this meant opening up the Comintern, the Communist International, to revolutionaries from the Third World. However, the Soviet government was still skeptical as to the prospect of a socialist revolution in the extra-European world, since the economic conditions in the colonial world seemed utterly unfavorable. At the Second Congress of the Comintern in 1920, Lenin's views clashed with those of the Indian communist M. N. Roy, who argued that certain regions of the Third World had already obtained a sufficient level of economic development to be ready for the emergence of a real communist movement.[8] At the heart of the debate was the fact that Roy and Lenin disagreed on their understanding of economic development. Lenin saw the world as an integrated economic system, where the core determined the level of development of the periphery. Roy, on the contrary, allowed for the possibility of a rapid "catch-up" with the more advanced economies due to technological change. These two positions, and the attempts to synthesize them in a single theory of development, constituted the basis of

---

[6] Karl Marx, "The British Rule in India," *New-York Daily Tribune*, June 25, 1853; "The Future of the British Rule in India," *New-York Daily Tribune*, August 8, 1853. For a critical view, see Edward W. Said, *Orientalism* (London: Routledge, 1978), 125.

[7] Vladimir I. Lenin, *Imperializm, kak Vysshaia Stadia Kapitalizma* (Petrograd: Zhizn' i Znanie, 1917).

[8] Vladimir I. Lenin, "Pervonachal'nyi Nabrosok Tezisov po Natsional'nomu i Kolonial'nomu Voprosam" (1920), in Institut Marksizma-Leninizma pri TsK KPSS, *V.I. Lenin, Polnoe Sobranie Sochinenii*, Tom 41 (Moscow: Izdatel'stvo Politicheskoi Literatury, 1981), 166; M. N. Roy, "Supplementary Report on the National and Colonial Questions" (1920) in *Workers of the World and Oppressed Peoples, Unite! Proceedings and Documents of the Second Congress, 1920*, vol. 1, ed. John Riddell (New York: Pathfinder, 1991), 223.

Soviet intellectual efforts to analyze and understand economic growth and its relationship with national liberation.

In the short term, however, Stalin's rise to power cut short any possibility for the intellectual debate to sharpen or for Soviet policy to become more active in supporting liberation movements in the Third World. The reason for this was once again primarily economic. Stalin was no sophisticated economic theorist, but he had clear ideas. Similarly to other Marxist thinkers, he linked success in the revolutionary struggle with economic development. In his view, economic development at home guaranteed the Soviet Union's survival against a hostile capitalist world. This meant measuring the USSR's success against the standards set by the advanced economies of the West: the large-scale production of those good and commodities usually associated with industrial development – steel, machines, trains. By the end of the first Soviet five-year plan in 1933, Stalin could boast about the Soviet Union's rapid ascension to modern industrial power. By the end of the second five-year plan in 1938, he could claim that "socialism in one country" had been achieved.[9]

Socialism in other countries, however, had to wait. Convinced that the capitalist world remained strong and hostile, Stalin saw no possibility for the birth of socialist societies abroad. His approach to economic development was different from both Lenin's and Roy's. First, Stalin separated technological change – the engine of economic development – from the capitalist system. "The basic law of modern capitalism," Stalin wrote in 1951, is "the necessity of obtaining the maximum profit. Capitalism is in favor of new techniques when they promise it the highest profit. Capitalism is against new techniques, and for resorting to manual labour, when the new techniques do not promise the highest profit."[10] The adoption of new techniques in a still-capitalist context was meaningless in terms of stages of development. If new technologies were applied to industrial production in India, this did not imply an increased level of economic development, and therefore the possibility of a proletarian revolution, as Roy had argued. It simply signaled that these techniques guaranteed maximum profit to the British capitalists and their local supporters, who were however ready to revert to more primitive production methods if they saw fit.

[9] Itogi pervoi piatiletki: Doklad na ob"edinennom plenume TsK i TsKK VKP(b) (1933) in I. V. Stalin, *Sochineniia*, Tom 13 (Moscow: Gosudarstvennoe Izdatel'stvo Politicheskoi Literatury, 1951), 161–215; Otvet tovarishchu Ivanovu, Ivanu Filippovichu (1938) in I. V. Stalin, *Sochineniia*, Tom 14 (Moscow: Izdatel'stvo "Pisatel'," 1997), 244–248.

[10] Ekonomicheskie problemy sotsializma v SSSR (1951) in I. V. Stalin, *Sochineniia, Tom 16* (Moscow: Izdatel'stvo "Pisatel'," 1997), 181.

The economic development of the Soviet Union was instead different, because this was a society that had done away with profit and private property altogether, and was now in a position to outperform the capitalist world in terms of factory building, steel production, kilometers of railways, and so on.

Stalin's political understanding of development left the communist movement in an inescapable catch-22: real economic development could happen only in the context of a socialist society, which however required preexisting economic development to be born. This framework left no space for cultivating the socialist revolution in the Third World and very little space for the Soviet Union to engage in the development of other countries. It was therefore not surprising that Soviet assessments of early decolonization were unreservedly negative. Following India's independence, *Novoe Vremia* (New Times), the Soviet political magazine published in several languages and destined to a foreign audience, called Nehru a "nimble servant" of the British and his government a "bourgeois pseudo-democracy."[11] The Soviet government ignored repeated Indian requests to establish closer relations and to talk about economic cooperation, in spite of the very obvious interest in the Soviet approach to economic planning that Nehru and the Indian government had manifested on multiple occasions.[12] The issue was the usual one: planning was simply a technique. In the context of a bourgeois democracy (as Stalin considered India at the time), economic planning by itself had no connection to socialism.[13]

Not much changed when Moscow confronted countries that considered themselves socialist. Stalin's skepticism on the Chinese Communist Party (CCP) and his doubts about Mao Zedong's approach to Marxism-Leninism are well known.[14] The Soviet approach to the Democratic

[11] A. D'iakov, "The Indian National Congress in Power," *New Times* (Moscow), January 12, 1949; T. Ershov, "Indian Version of Bourgeois Pseudo-Democracy," *New Times* (Moscow), March 15, 1950; both cited in David C. Engerman, "Learning from the East. Soviet Experts and India in the Era of Competitive Coexistence," *Comparative Studies of South Asia, Africa and the Middle East* 33:2 (2013): 227.

[12] Andreas Hilger, "The Soviet Union and India: The Years of Late Stalinism," in *Indo-Soviet Relations: New Russian and German Evidence*, ed. Andreas Hilger et al. (Zurich: Parallel History Project on Cooperative Security, 2009), http://www.php.isn.ethz.ch/collections/coll_india/intro_stalin.cfm?navinfo=56154#F8.

[13] Ekonomicheskie problemy sotsializma v SSSR (1951) in Stalin, *Sochineniia*, Tom 16, 182–183.

[14] Jeremy Friedman, *Shadow Cold War: The Sino-Soviet Competition for the Third World* (Chapel Hill: University of North Carolina Press, 2015), 1–24; Nlu Jun, "The Origins of the Sino-Soviet Alliance," in *Brothers in Arms: The Rise and Fall of the Sino-Soviet*

People's Republic of Korea was very similar. According to Arne Westad,
"it was pessimism and not optimism about the future of the Korean
revolution that led Stalin to accept [North Korean Leader] Kim's plan
for reunification [of the Korean peninsula] by military force" for Stalin
believed that "even under the best of geographical and political circumstances – such as in North Korea – the primary objective of Third World
Communism should be to serve Soviet purposes in the global Cold War,
because the defined circumstances under which they themselves could
carry out a successful social transformation were so narrow as to be
almost nonexistent."[15]

During the Stalin era, most economic research in the Soviet Union was
conducted at the *Institut Mirovogo Khoziaistva i Mirovoi Politiki*
(Institute of World Economy and World Politics, IMKh), created in the
mid-1920s. The fortunes of the Institute were tightly related to the political and personal vicissitudes of Eugen Jenö Varga, the Hungarian-born
economist who directed it from 1927 until 1947. Varga's main contribution to Soviet economic theory was stressing the differences that existed
between capitalist countries, which contradicted the assumption that
a single worldwide crisis would wipe out the whole capitalist system.
The Institute of World Economy and World Politics focused mostly on
the core Western countries, and paid relatively less attention to the problems of empire and development in the Third World. Nevertheless,
Varga's theories broadly conformed with Stalin's views on the matter:
by allowing for a longer survival of the world capitalist system, including
its imperial appendixes, Varga de facto confirmed that the Soviet Union
had limited room for maneuver in the Third World. In 1947, the Institute
was closed down following the "anti-cosmopolitanism" campaign and
Varga lost part of his political influence.[16]

Following Stalin's death in 1953, it did not take long for the attitude in
the Kremlin to change. Even before Khrushchev and Bulganin set off for
their visits in Asia, there were signs that Stalin's restrictive ideas on

Alliance, 1945–1963, ed. Odd Arne Westad, Cold War International History Project
Series (Washington, D.C.: Woodrow Wilson Center Press, 1998), 49.

[15] Odd Arne Westad, *The Global Cold War: Third World Interventions and the Making of
Our Times* (Cambridge: Cambridge University Press, 2005), 66.

[16] Eugen S. Varga, *Izmeneniia v ekonomike kapitalizma v itoge vtoroi mirovoi voiny*
(Moscow: Gospolitizdat, 1946); for more context, see André Mommen, *Stalin's
Economist. The Economic Contributions of Jenö Varga* (London: Routledge, 2011);
Kyung Deok Roh, "Rethinking the Varga Controversy, 1941–1953," *Europe-Asia
Studies* 63:5: 833–855.

economic development in the Third World could be overcome. Already in February 1955, Viacheslav Molotov, usually a staunch Stalinist, argued that the "correlation of forces" between the USSR and the USA was slowly but steadily changing in Moscow's favor, citing the new support that the Soviet Union enjoyed in Asia and the possibility of entering cooperative relations with countries in Africa and Latin America, once they freed themselves from colonialism and economic imperialism.[17] This was a line the Soviet leadership was more than happy to adopt. A few days before Khrushchev and Bulganin returned to Moscow from their tour of Asia, the Presidium discussed Afghanistan's request for economic and military aid. Molotov and Lazar Kaganovich, among the most conservative figures in the Kremlin, judged the Afghan request of a $120 million aid package excessive, and worried that conceding it may constitute a precedent that other countries would exploit to ask for more aid. Both, however, agreed that it was in the Soviet Union's interests to provide at least a generous loan to Afghanistan, as did Georgii Malenkov, Maksim Saburov, and Mikhail Suslov. As Kaganovich put it, "we must make sacrifices" (*dolzhny poiti na zhertvy*).[18]

Anastas Mikoian, traditionally less conservative, went much further.

There is already a precedent. Aid to Afghanistan strengthens the precedent. We have to help a few countries if we want to engage in a more serious competition with the USA. From the point of view of state interests, it is necessary to provide aid. Burma too may ask for aid. As for Afghanistan – this money will pay off.[19]

A couple of days later, Khrushchev signed the agreement with Afghanistan in Kabul.[20] This was only one among several. As Mikoian reminded his colleagues in the Presidium there were precedents already, such as the 1954 extensive aid package granted to China or the cooperation agreement with India signed a few months earlier.[21] Many more

---

[17] Reports on and statements of Soviet foreign policy: notes on USSR, Communism and the Cold War, February 1955 in The National Archives of the United Kingdom (henceafter, TNA), FO371/116650, file NS1021/12.

[18] Telegramma tt. Khrushcheva i Bulganina o voprosakh okazaniia pomoshchi Afganistanu, in Fursemko, *Presidium TsK KPSS*, vol. 1, 71.

[19] Ibid., 72.

[20] Timothy Nunan, *Humanitarian Invasion: Global Development in Cold War Afghanistan* (New York: Cambridge University Press, 2016), 61.

[21] For context, see Shu Guang Zhang, "Sino-Soviet Economic Cooperation," in *Brothers in Arms: The Rise and Fall of the Sino-Soviet Alliance, 1945–1963*, ed. Odd Arne Westad (Washington, D.C.: Woodrow Wilson Center Press, 1998), 117–140; Vojtech Mastny,

would follow soon.[22] By the end of 1955, two years after Stalin's death, the Soviet Union was ready to launch itself into the global competition for development assistance. As Mikoian explained, this was not a matter of choice. Development cooperation in the Third World had become a core dimension of Cold War competition. The new Soviet strategy was simple, but ambitious: "'when the revolutionary process in the Western countries was frozen,' Khrushchev's leadership expected 'to use postcolonialist momentum, break into the 'soft under-belly of imperialism' and win sympathies of the millions of people who woke up to the new life.'"[23]

Soviet theory changed accordingly. The Soviet conception of economic development was still officially what it had been under Stalin. At the Twentieth Congress of the Communist Party of the Soviet Union (CPSU) in 1956, Khrushchev delivered his famous "secret speech" that initiated the process of de-Stalinization in the Soviet Union. The same applied to the Soviet theory of economic development, which starting in 1956 began to be reformulated to take into account the new direction that Soviet policy had taken.

Khrushchev's own understanding of economic development was very traditional, not unlike Stalin's. At the Twentieth Congress, he boasted that

The high rates of development of industrial production are the guarantee of the new successes of socialism in its economic competition with capitalism. At the present time, the USSR already occupies the second place in the world for total volume of industrial production. In terms of production of cast iron, steel, aluminum, copper, machines, electrical energy, cement, and coal the Soviet Union has long surpassed France, West Germany, and Britain and is steadily catching up with the USA.[24]

However, Khrushchev's idea of development was rooted in material welfare rather than revolutionary fervor. When Richard Nixon during the famous 1959 "kitchen debate" at the opening of the US National

"The Soviet Union's Partnership with India," *Journal of Cold War Studies* 12:3 (2010): 50–90.

[22] For an approximate idea of the geographic range and figures involved, see Central Intelligence Agency, *Communist Aid Activities in Non-Communist Less Developed Countries, 1979 and 1954–79* (Washington, D.C.: CIA, 1980).

[23] Georgii Mirskii quoted in Vladislav M. Zubok, *A Failed Empire: The Soviet Union in the Cold War from Stalin to Gorbachev* (Chapel Hill: The University of North Carolina Press, 2007), 139.

[24] N. S. Khrushchev, "Otchetnyi doklad tsentral'nogo komiteta kommunisticheskoi partii Sovetskogo Soiuza XX s''ezdu partii," February 14, 1956 in TsK KPSS, *XX S''ezd Kommunisticheskoi Partii Sovetskogo Soiuza. Stenograficheskii otchet*, Tom I (Moscow: Gosudarstvennoe Izdatel'stvo Politicheskoi Literatury, 1956), 12.

Exhibition in Moscow proudly showed Khrushchev a dishwasher, a symbol of American wealth, a piqued Khrushchev replied (lying) "we have such things!"[25] Indeed, compared to Stalin's days, during the Khrushchev era the Soviet state paid significantly more attention to increasing consumption and improving everyday life. As Khrushchev himself put it: "it is not bad if in improving the theory of Marxism one throws in also a piece of bacon and a piece of butter."[26]

Khrushchev added a crucial global dimension to his simplistic vision of economic development. He showed himself to be fully aware of what was happening in the Third World. "The attainment of political freedom by the peoples of the former colonies and semi-colonies is a first and important step towards their full independence, that is to say the achievement of economic independence (*ekonomicheskaia samostoiatel'nost'*)."[27] The socialist world was to play a key role in the economic emancipation of Asia, Africa, and Latin America.

To create an independent national economy and increase the standard of living of their peoples, these countries, even though they do not belong to the world socialist system, can rely on its achievements. Today they no longer need to go begging [*na poklon*, literally 'kneeling down'] their former oppressors to obtain modern equipment. They can receive such equipment from the socialist countries, without contracting for this any kind of obligation of a political or military character.[28]

In a nutshell, Khrushchev had already outlined the foreign economic policy that would characterize his era. The Soviet Union presented itself as a provider of capital and expertise to the newly independent countries of the Third World, expecting nothing in exchange other than the possibility of separating the former colonies from the former colonial masters. At no point in his 1956 speech did Khrushchev mention the question of the transition to socialism of the Third World countries. In Khrushchev's vision, there was no space for stages of development or for a political

[25] Harrison E. Salisbury, "Nixon and Khrushchev Argue in Public as U.S. Exhibit Opens; Accuse Each Other of Threats," *New York Times*, July 25, 1959.

[26] Khrushchev quoted in Susan E. Reid, "Cold War in the Kitchen: Gender and the De-Stalinization of Consumer Taste in the Soviet Union under Khrushchev," *Slavic Review* 61:2 (2002): 221. For more context on the US exhibition in Moscow, see also, Susan E. Reid, "Who will beat whom? Soviet Popular Reception of the American National Exhibition in Moscow, 1959," *Kritika: Explorations in Russian and Eurasian History* 9:4 (2008): 855–904.

[27] Khrushchev, "Otchetnyi doklad tsentral'nogo komiteta kommunisticheskoi partii Sovetskogo Soiuza XX s"ezdu partii," 25.

[28] Ibid.

understanding of economic development based on class. Development was reduced to mere economic growth and better living standards, which were attainable through the use of those productive and organizational techniques the Soviet Union had mastered, and therefore easily exportable abroad. The USSR was no longer preoccupied with the class balance of the Third World elites it intended to assist. It was content to pull them away from the imperialist bloc, offering an alternative system of aid and trade, and in the process gaining new allies and denying the capitalists access to the markets and resources they used to control.

This was a crucial component of Khrushchev's concept of "peaceful coexistence" (*mirnoe sosushchestvovanie*), which did not mean abandoning competition with the West, but rather shifting it from the military to the economic sphere. It was in India in 1955 that Khrushchev outlined it for the first time. Addressing both his hosts and an imaginary Western audience, he declared: "Let us verify in practice whose system is better. We say to the leaders of the capitalist states: let us compete without war."[29] The Third World was to be the theater of this competition to establish who could provide better development assistance.

IMEMO AND THE "NONCAPITALIST PATH OF DEVELOPMENT"

The new policy required new institutional structures. Following the Twentieth Congress, a number of Party and State agencies were created or reorganized to manage relations with the Third World. In addition, several academic research institutes were either created from scratch or revived after having been heavily purged during Stalin's years. Most focused on a specific region of the world with the aim of providing the political leadership with knowledge on previously overlooked areas, and at the same time training a new generation of "area studies" specialists. However, the institute that most closely worked on issues of economic theory applied to a global context was the Institute of World Economy and International Relations (*Institut Mirovoi Ekonomiki i Mezhdunarodnykh Otnoshenii*, IMEMO), the heir of what had been Varga's institute during the 1930s. A larger institute than its area studies cousins, IMEMO was composed of separate divisions that looked at

---

[29] Excerpt of Khrushchev, November 26 speech, at Bangalore, in W. Park Armstrong to Secretary of State, "Recent Communist Statements," December 13, 1955, cited in Aleksandr A. Fursenko and Timothy Naftali, *Khrushchev's Cold War: The Inside Story of an American Adversary* (New York: W.W. Norton, 2006), 57.

regions of the world or at thematic issues, always from the point of view of international relations and political economy.[30]

IMEMO was instrumental in the introduction and refinement of development economics in the USSR. Khrushchev's vague formulations needed to be translated into an official Party line that would guide policy in the following decades. IMEMO immediately set to work on the question of economic development in the Third World and its implications for Soviet policy. As Anushavan Arzumanian, the institute director, put it in one of the first meetings of his staff, "we are faced with the problem of solving theoretical questions relating to colonial countries and countries that have escaped from under the domination of imperialism."[31] One of the key tasks for IMEMO would be to "solve" the question of the political and economic development of the Third World. According to Arzumanian, to address it Third World states should resort to central planning, and through central planning create a "state sector" that dominated the economy.[32] This would become the key concept of Soviet development thinking.

A little over a year later, the CPSU Central Committee commission for "Questions of Ideology, Culture and International Party Contacts" enshrined IMEMO's vision in its official policy for the USSR. As the pace of decolonization was destined to quicken, numerous problems would emerge for the newly independent states, which the commission related to "underdevelopment" – from illiteracy to poor sanitation, and from malnutrition to lack of local industry. According to the report,

not one of these problems can be solved with the path of capitalist development. The peoples of the countries of Asia and Africa will therefore step by step turn to the socialist side and, after finding a complete understanding of their interests from the socialist camp, will all be more and more convinced that that their future is to be linked not with capitalism, but with socialism.[33]

The struggle against global imperialism needed Moscow's active support for progressive postcolonial leaders, who could become important allies for the USSR. Soviet policy should begin with highlighting the positive role that the USSR could play for economic and social

---

[30] Petr Cherkasov, *IMEMO. Portret na fone epokhi* (Moscow: Ves' Mir, 2004), 81–200.

[31] "Zasedaniia Direktsii Instituta Mirovoi Ekonomiki i Mezhdunarodnykh Otnoshenii ot 20 dekabria 1956 goda", in Arkhiv Rossiiskoi Akademii Nauk (henceforth, ARAN), fond 1978, opis' 1, delo 2, list 30.

[32] Ibid., l. 32.

[33] "Spravka", October 28, 1958, in Rossiiskii Gosudarstvenyi Arkhiv Noveishii Istorii (henceforth, RGANI), fond 5, opis' 30, delo 273, lista 40.

development in the Third World. Given the existing interest in the Soviet Union among Third World countries, the commission thought that this goal "can and must be reached."[34]

In particular, the experience of economic development and social transformation in the Soviet Republics of Central Asia and the Caucasus would play a key role in guiding Soviet policy toward Asia, Africa, and Latin America. In the Soviet discourse that the Ideology commission espoused, those territories had been conquered by tsarist Russia, a colonial power, and later set free by Soviet rule. Thanks to central planning and Moscow's policy of large investments in infrastructure, modernization in the southern fringes of the USSR was by the late 1950s a reality. This was one of the most important foundational myths of the Soviet Union. The grand narrative of the state's successful battle against "backwardness" (*otstalost'*) had long been a key preoccupation of Soviet official discourse. Both Lenin and Stalin had preached the necessity to overcome political, economic, and – above all – "cultural" backwardness among certain "nationalities" (which in Russian indicated a people, or an "ethnic" or religious minority).[35]

The Khrushchev leadership considered the task of defeating backwardness at home largely accomplished and, crucially, assumed that the same tools could be used abroad to solve similar problems. Like Stalin, the kind of modernity in which Khrushchev and the others believed was concrete and easily measurable, based on advancements in technology, production, and the availability of goods and services to both the state and individuals. Unlike Stalin, the Khrushchev leadership considered this modernity replicable abroad. The assumption was that economic growth would make more and less advanced (or "backward") economies converge toward the same version of modernity, in spite of their different sociopolitical systems. This had more in common with Alexandre Kojève's contemporary thinking on the "end of history" than with the recent Marxist

---

[34] Ibid., l. 67.

[35] For context on the Soviet approach to "nationalities," in particular in Central Asia and the Caucasus, and the notion of "cultural backwardness," see Douglas Northrop, *Veiled Empire: Gender and Power in Stalinist Central Asia* (Ithaca: Cornell University Press, 2003); Terry Martin, *The Affirmative Action Empire: Nations and Nationalism in the Soviet Union, 1923–1939* (Ithaca: Cornell University Press, 2001); for more discussion of Central Asia as a development model in the USSR, see Artemy M. Kalinovsky, "Not Some British Colony in Africa: The Politics of Decolonization and Modernization in Soviet Central Asia, 1955–1964," *Ab Imperio* 2 (2013): 191–222; Masha Kirasirova, "'Sons of Muslims' in Moscow: Soviet Central Asian Mediators to the Foreign East, 1955–1962," *Ab Imperio* 4 (2011): 106–132.

tradition in the USSR. On the surface, Stalin's "catch up and overtake" and Khrushchev's "we will bury you" had the same meaning – the Soviet Union would beat the capitalists at their own game of economic development. However, the Khrushchev leadership maintained that Asian, African, and Latin American countries could obtain the same result, despite their bourgeois nature, if only they adopted the approach to development that came from the USSR.[36]

Thus, the Soviet Union was ready to offer assistance to Third World countries looking for rapid modernization after independence. Socialist aid was presented as disinterested and fraternal. It aimed to foster an economic "brotherhood" among countries, founded on principles of mutual help and friendly relations, the exact opposite of Western "economic imperialism." The fact that the Third World elites that showed interest in the Soviet model were nationalist and "bourgeois," but definitely not communists (in fact, they were more likely to imprison communists than to collaborate with them), was not a problem. The general consensus in the CPSU was that an alliance between the USSR and the national bourgeoisie could be a useful "tactical compromise" motivated by "strategic considerations." Academician Evgenii M. Zhukov, a respected historian of Japan who also taught at the CPSU school for cadres, thus summarized the official take: "Lenin indicated that when the national bourgeoisie fights with imperialism, we are firmly and resolutely for it. But only as long as [it fights imperialism]." The most important task for the Soviet Union and the other socialist countries was to show that socialism was the only way to achieve economic development. Development would eventually "unleash the revolutionary energy of the masses."[37]

Indeed, economic development was already changing the class structure of Third World countries, as Roy had argued nearly forty years earlier. In 1960, Rostislav Ul'ianovskii, the deputy head of the Institute of Oriental Studies, published a pamphlet on "the struggle for economic

---

[36] On Kojève and convergence, see James H. Nichols, *Alexandre Kojève: Wisdom at the End of History* (Lanham, MD: Rowman & Littlefield, 2007), 89–90 and Alexandre Kojève, *Introduction to the Reading of Hegel: Lectures on the "Phenomenology of Spirit"* (Ithaca: Cornell University Press, 1980); on the intertwined Soviet and American view of development at the time, see David C. Engerman, *Modernization from the Other Shore: American Intellectuals and the Romance of Russian Development* (Cambridge, MA: Harvard University Press, 2003).

[37] RGANI, f. 5, op. 30, d. 273, l. 44–46, 112–5, 121–6, 177–84; RGANI, f. 5, op. 35, d. 79, l. 1, l. 137, 139.

independence in the non-socialist countries." His argument was that the national bourgeoisie in the Third World was succeeding in staving off Western economic imperialism through the creation of a large state sector in the economy that oversaw agricultural modernization and industrialization. However, the class struggle remained important. Thanks to rapid economic development, and industrialization in particular, the workers were growing in numbers and acquiring class consciousness. "State capitalism," as described by Ul'ianovskii, was indeed the first step on the way to socialism. This made it theoretically possible for the Soviet Union to assist Third World countries in their push for modernization.[38] Boris Ponomarev, the head of the CPSU's International Department, elaborated the same concepts in an article in *Kommunist*, the USSR's top ideology journal, clarifying a few important points.

The position of the national democratic state is a Marxist-Leninist theoretical position. The point is not to pigeonhole all liberated states and then to declare: these belong to one category, and these other ones to a second or a third. Such approach would be schematic and detrimental. It is important to highlight a different aspect: the national democratic state opens the way towards the strengthening of political and economic independence, towards social progress. In the real world, there exist already some newly-independent countries that have made a series of significant steps of social progress: they introduced limitations for the development of capitalism, drove the imperialist monopolies out of the economy, created and strengthened a state sector in the economy, conducted an agrarian reform in the interests of the peasantry, granted democratic freedoms to all strata of population, created the necessary conditions for the creation of a national democratic state. The peoples themselves decide which countries proceed on the way of the national democracy.[39]

For countries like Cuba, Ghana, Guinea, and Mali, which Ponomarev praised for their reforms and progressive agendas, the USSR was an obvious inspiration. "The Soviet Union's world-famous historical successes in the development of industry and of the whole economy, in the raising of the prosperity and culture of its people, produce a revolution in the minds of the people of the national democratic countries." Thanks to the successes of the USSR, they understood that socialism was a superior economic system and were ready to adopt it, at their own pace. "Marxism-Leninism teaches that all countries proceed towards

---

[38] Rostislav A. Ul'ianovskii, *Nekotorye voprosy za ekonomicheskuyu nezavisimost' v nesotsialisticheskikh stranakh* (Moscow: Akademiya Nauk SSSR, 1960).

[39] Boris N. Ponomarev, "O gosudarstve natsionalnoi demokratii," *Kommunist* 8 (1960): 43.

socialism. However, each choose their own path of transition."[40] According to Ul'ianovskii and Ponomarev, it did not matter whether Third World elites were communist or nationalist, as long as they were willing to subscribe to state capitalism. Stalin was dead and buried. Economic growth had been "freed" from class and made into a tool of Soviet policy.

The ball was back into IMEMO's court to refine the concepts that the CPSU had elaborated and sanctioned. The model that led from an "underdeveloped" society to one with a large state sector that could steer the economy toward industrialization was called "noncapitalist path of development" – a concept that dominated Soviet thinking on development in the Third World almost until the USSR's collapse. Arzumanian was among the first to use the term noncapitalist path of development in the context of development in the Third World.[41] In a later article in the institute's journal, *Mirovaia Ekonomika i Mezhdunarodnye Otnosheniia* (MEiMO), Arzumanian argued that economic growth in the Third World contributed to the crisis of capitalism worldwide, because it broke the links between capitalist world and national bourgeoisie in the former colonies.[42]

In practical terms, the noncapitalist path of development targeted dependency. Anatolii El'ianov, a young doctoral student at IMEMO, believed that there was "not a single recipe" to create "a developed diversified economy, taking into account the features and capabilities of each country, the size of the territory, availability of human and natural resources." Nevertheless, there were policies that a newly independent state on a noncapitalist path to development should adopt to oust foreign capital – namely the establishment of import quotas, control over prices, and the nationalization of key productive sectors. In line with Arzumanian, El'ianov argued that a strong state sector would allow Third World countries to do away with the "intermediation" of foreign businesses, and thus "receive all revenues from foreign trade" so to "liquidate dependency."[43]

---

[40] Ibid., 47.
[41] Doklad i otchet o rabote Instituta Mirovoi ekonomiki i mezhdunarodnykh otnoshenii Akademii Nauk SSSR v 1956–1960 gg, August 31, 1969, in ARAN, f. 1556, op. 1, d. 135, l. 31–2; cited in Cherkasov, *IMEMO*, 163–164.
[42] Anushavan A. Arzumanian, "Noviy etap obshchego krizisa kapitalizma." *Mirovaia Ekonomika i Mezhdunarodnye Otnosheniia* 2 (1961): 12.
[43] Stenogramma zasedaniia sektsii "Sovremennaia epokha i puti razvitiia osvobodivshikhsia stran" i nauchnoi sessii Instituta mirovoi ekonomiki i mezhdunarodnykh otnoshenii

Together with control over international trade, two other elements made up the backbone of the noncapitalist path of development: agricultural modernization and industrialization. Agriculture was considered in many cases the most immediate priority for newly independent countries. Light industry would follow. This was necessary to address the most immediate needs of a Third World country – "that is to say disgusting food, no clothes, health insecurity, illiteracy," as an IMEMO staff member put it rather patronizingly.[44] Counterintuitively, heavy industry was not an absolute priority. Ul'ianovski, who often acted as a bridge between the CPSU and IMEMO, argued that "not all underdeveloped countries need to develop all or even just the main branches of mechanical and heavy industry. Many cannot do it and have no objective need for it (Ceylon is not India, Laos is not Indonesia)."[45] "Only hopeless critics from the reactionary bourgeois economic school," Ul'ianovskii continued, "can ascribe to Soviet economists and Marxists in general that they require from all less developed countries the compulsory and universal development of heavy industry at all costs."[46] The goal was not the establishment of a Soviet-style command economy, but rather of a "mixed economy" (*smeshannaia ekonomika*) in which state and private sector could temporarily coexist. The key to a transition toward socialism was the willingness of the ruling elites to prioritize the state sector and reduce the space for private capital.[47]

The culmination of the work of the International Department of the CPSU in conjunction with IMEMO was the production of the "Theses of the Central Committee of the CPSU on the Problems of the National Liberation Movement," a document that summarized the official Soviet take on questions of imperialism, decolonization, and economic development. Leaving behind the idea of a totalizing system that looked at economic development as the engine of human history, the theses moved to a less ambitious framework, losing in analytical sophistication but gaining in political flexibility. The new Soviet approach to development,

---

(IMEMO) "XXII s"ezdu KPSS o krizise mirovogo kapitalizma" na temu "Raspad kolonial'noi sistemy imperializma," February 5, 1962, in ARAN, f. 1978, op. 1, d. 112, l. 73–76.

[44] Ibid., 21.

[45] Stenogramma diskussii "Bor'ba dvukh sistem i osobennosti sotsial'no-ekonomicheskoogo razvitiia osvobodivshikhsia stran," prevedennoi redaktsiei zhurnala "Mirovaia ekonomika i mezhdunarodnye otnosheniia," May 13, 1963, in ARAN, f. 1978, op. 1, d. 134, l. 21.

[46] Ibid., l. 22.   [47] Ibid., l. 40–48.

which focused on factors driving economic growth and on the division between agricultural and industrial sectors in a developing economy, was not too far from the contemporary Western tradition. Indeed, Soviet economists were shown to be familiar with ideas that came from their colleagues in the United States and Western Europe. Khrushchev's "Thaw" at home made it easier to access academic literature that came from the West. Furthermore, Soviet and other Eastern bloc economists were now able to attend international conferences and workshops with their Western colleagues. Wassily Leontief, the Soviet-born American macroeconomist, organized a number of meetings aimed precisely at fostering the exchange of ideas between professional economists from the two blocs. The International Economic Association, funded by UNESCO, offered more such occasions. As Johanna Bockman has written, "[o]nce they came into direct contact, many economists found that they, in fact, shared similar professional tools and methods."[48]

While the official Soviet position remained a rejection of "bourgeois economics," the work of Soviet economists at IMEMO was not incompatible with the work of some pioneers of macroeconomics and development economics in the West. Some of these ideas were influential in the USSR too. Leontief's early work on how changes in individual productive branches impacted the growth of the whole economic system was cautiously praised at IMEMO.[49] Moreover, W. Arthur Lewis's pioneering "dual-sector" model of development was much more sophisticated than anything produced by Soviet economists at the time, but its basic assumptions – treating agriculture and industry as separate sectors of an economy, in which industrialization happens once the agricultural sector has reached full productive capacity – were similar to the idea of a Third World economy that existed at IMEMO. "On some questions, the bourgeois economists have achieved something," the author of a Soviet monograph on Western economics had to admit.[50] The intellectual foundations

---

[48] Johanna Bockman, *Markets in the Name of Socialism: The Left-Wing Origins of Neoliberalism* (Stanford: Stanford University Press, 2011), 64–67.

[49] Stenogramma zasedaniia direktsii Instituta mirovoi ekonomiki i mezhdunarodnykh otnoshenii (IMEMO) po obsuzhdeniu monografii Bliumina I.G. "Krizis sovremennoi burzhuaznoi politicheskoi ekonomiki," June 17, 1958, in ARAN, f. 1978, op. 1, d. 39, l. 8; Wassily Leontief, "Input-Output Economics," *Scientific American* 185:4 (1951): 15–21. Leontief received the Nobel Prize in 1973.

[50] Stenogramma zasedaniia, June 17, 1958, in ARAN, f. 1978, op. 1, d. 39, l. 13; W. Arthur Lewis, "Economic Development with Unlimited Supplies of Labour," *The Manchester School* 22 (1954): 139–191. Lewis later won the Nobel Prize for his work on development economics (1979).

of the global Cold War as a conflict between competing but related models of development were thus laid precisely at this time.

***

The theses on the national liberation movement never saw the light of day. In 1964, the Central Committee decided not to publish them, signaling that the political atmosphere in the Kremlin had changed. Shortly thereafter, in October of the same year, Khrushchev was ousted from First Secretary of the CPSU in a coup led by Leonid Brezhnev and Aleksei Kosygin, who replaced him as top Soviet leaders. In his former colleagues' indictment of Khrushchev, it is easy to see an implicit, but harsh, criticism of his "adventurism" in the Third World – "subjectivism and drift in Communist construction, hare-brained scheming, half-baked conclusions and hasty decisions and actions divorced from reality."[51] The new Soviet leadership reined in support for Third World countries and cut economic aid and technical cooperation. IMEMO adapted itself to the new climate, concluding that the national bourgeoisie had demonstrated its inability to find a quick solution to the main problems of development. In the future, more "progressive" forces – closer to "pure" Marxism-Leninism – would need to be the Soviet partners in the Third World.[52]

The Brezhnev era, however, was not the end of the noncapitalist path of development. The concept remained the compass that guided Soviet understanding of the Third World and its political and economic evolution. Once the Kremlin leadership was once again prepared to invest resources into the Third World, the noncapitalist path of development was readily resurrected in a streamlined form that gave priority to aiding Marxist-Leninists governments.[53] In the second half of the 1970s, following the Soviet interventions in Angola, Ethiopia, and Afghanistan, development aid and technical cooperation became once again part of Moscow's approach to the Third World.[54] It was only shortly before the

---

[51] *Pravda*, October 16, 1964, cited in William Taubman, *Khrushchev: The Man and His Era* (London: Free Press, 2003), 620.

[52] Otchet o nauchnoi deiatel'nosti Instituta mirovoi ekonomiki i mezhdunarodnykh otnoshenii (IMEMO) za 1964 g., in ARAN, f. 1978, op. 1, d. 152, l. 11–12.

[53] On the evolution of Soviet foreign policy during the Brezhnev era, see Zubok, *A Failed Empire*, 192–264.

[54] Artemy M. Kalinovsky, *A Long Goodbye: The Soviet Withdrawal from Afghanistan* (Cambridge, MA: Harvard University Press, 2011), 206–228; Timothy Nunan, *Humanitarian Intervention*, 150–180.

collapse of the USSR itself that the Soviet leadership abandoned its particular vision of progress in the Third World based on state capitalism and the noncapitalist path of development. As a consequence of Mikhail Gorbachev's refocusing on the Western world, the Soviet Union withdrew from the Third World both politically and intellectually just before disintegrating in 1991.[55]

Moreover, the legacy of Soviet thinking on international development and engagement in developing countries left a deep mark on the evolution of development as idea and policy. The end of the Khrushchev era did not spell the end of the transnational networks that involved Soviet economists. In fact, the onset of détente multiplied the opportunities to exchange ideas with foreign colleagues, and to participate in new initiatives. Besides academic exchanges, the United Nations system proved a fruitful platform to think about development. The birth of new dedicated UN agencies, such as the United Nations Conference on Trade and Development (UNCTAD) in 1964 and the United Nations Industrial Development Organization (UNIDO) in 1966, allowed Soviet specialists to be involved in a new wave of reflection and intellectual innovation on the themes of development, global trade reform, and foreign aid.

In this context, the intellectual debates that had taken place in the Soviet Union during the 1950s and 1960s, and the experiments with state capitalism that Soviet allies in the Third World had conducted at the same time, echoed the debates and policies that dominated the theory and practice of development in later decades. Concepts such as dependency theory and the policy of import-substitution industrialization shared the same goals and many of the same techniques with the theory of economic development that took shape in the USSR during the Khrushchev era. They focused on structural inequalities between groups of countries and aimed to engineer economic growth through state investment while controlling foreign trade. After all, Soviet support at the United Nations was instrumental in the creation of UNCTAD, which was born precisely as an attempt by radical Third World countries to address issues of global development and inequality in the terms of international trade. Raúl Prebisch himself, UNCTAD Secretary-General until 1969 and one of the "founding fathers" of dependency theory, was keen to have the USSR and the socialist world on board in the organization he directed.[56] Other radical economists were directly influenced by the Soviet experience at home and abroad. For example, Andre Gunder Frank began his career as a student of Soviet agriculture, and Samir Amir was a junior economic advisor in postindependence Mali, a major recipient of Soviet aid and ideas in the 1960s.[57] In more recent years, the idea of "state capitalism" has had a spectacular comeback thanks to the economic successes (and failures) of countries such as Brazil, Russia, India, China, and South Africa – the "BRICS."[58] The terms of the debate – whether or not the state is a better provider of economic development than the market – are the same ones that Soviet policymakers and scholars faced from the 1950s onward.

In conclusion, this chapter demonstrates that the Soviet approach to development was in dialogue with the global evolution of the idea and policy of development, rather than a separate tradition altogether. The classical socialist view of development was based on class and centered on the role of capital in a historically determined transition to communism. Breaking with this tradition, since the mid-1950s Soviet scholars and policymakers focused instead on the role of the state, which they opposed to the market as the main engine of development. The new Soviet theory of development championed the state regardless of its potentially bourgeois nature in the Third World. As other chapters in this book show, this tension between state and nonstate actors in the pursuit of development was at the core of the global Cold War.[59] Even

---

[56] John Toye, *UNCTAD at 50: A Short History* (Geneva: United Nations, 2014), 1–14. See also, Johanna Bockman, "Socialist Globalization against Capitalist Neocolonialism: The Economic Ideas behind the New International Economic Order," *Humanity* 6:1 (Spring 2015): 109–128.

[57] Andre Gunder Frank, "General Productivity in Soviet Agriculture and Industry: The Ukraine, 1928–55," *Journal of Political Economy* 66:6 (December 1958): 498–515; Samir Amin, *Trois Expériences Africaines de Développement: le Mali, la Guinée et le Ghana* (Paris: Presses Universitaires de France, 1965).

[58] See, for example, Joshua Kurlantzick, *State Capitalism: How the Return of Statism Is Transforming the World* (New York: Oxford University Press, 2016).

[59] Nathan J. Citino, "Nasser, Hammarskjöld, and Middle East Development in Different Scales of Space and Time"; Priya Lal, "Decolonization and the Gendered Politics of Developmental Labor in Southeastern Africa"; Timothy Nunan, "Graveyard of Development? Afghanistan's Cold War Encounters with International Development and Humanitarianism"; Alden Young, "A Currency for Sudan: The Sudanese National Economy and Postcolonial Development."

after the end of the Cold War, the state-focused approach to development pioneered by the Soviet Union inspired a number of experiments with state capitalism, some of which continue in the present day. Accordingly, a history of development cannot be truly global without taking into consideration the Soviet, and more generally socialist, experience.

Graveyard of Development? Afghanistan's Cold War Encounters with International Development and Humanitarianism

Timothy Nunan

Early on the morning of May 16, 2016, residents of the Afghan capital woke up to find government helicopters circling the sky and many streets in central Kabul blocked off by double-stacked shipping containers. The reason? Thousands of Afghans, many among them from the country's Shi'a Hazara minority (who reside at the bottom of the social and economic totem pole in Afghanistan), had organized protests against the proposed route for a power transmission line connecting energy-rich Turkmenistan with energy-poor Afghanistan and Pakistan. The project, funded by the Asian Development Bank, had been planned to pass through the Hazaras' home provinces in central Afghanistan. However, last-minute revelations showed that the Afghan government had opted to reroute the line through the snowier Salang Pass, thus depriving the Hazara of electrical power.[1] Protestors marching through the streets unfurled a large banner declaring that "the principle of social justice and equitable development mandate that some of the energy from such a big energy transfer line should pass through the central areas."[2]

---

[1] For more on the background of how Hazaras relate to a lack of electricity, see Melissa Skye Chiovenda, "The Illumination of Marginality: How Ethnic Hazaras in Bamyan, Afghanistan Perceive the Lack of Electricity as Discrimination," *Central Asian Survey* 33:4 (December 2014): 449–462.

[2] In Persian, "'*Asl-i 'adālat-i ajtamā'i va ankashāf-i motawāzan hukum mikonad ki az chenin lin-i bozorg-i intiqāl-i anarzhi, yeki az ānhā bāyad az manātaq-i markazi 'abur konad.*" Thanks to Rustam Seerat and Melissa Skye Chiovenda for obtaining the picture of the poster as well as the full Persian text. Other posters – here one thinks of Stephen Macekura's work – called for "equitable development, sustainable Afghanistan."

The episode demonstrates how far the rhetoric of development has traveled. The thought that an Afghan government with microscopic state capacity can, or should, be in the business of leveraging complex multilateral institutions to "develop" remote regions populated by ethno-confessional minorities is not one that would have occurred to many Afghans only a few decades prior. But it also demonstrates the impact of Afghanistan's Cold War engagements with the Soviet Union as a vector of development. The streets that the demonstrators marched upon were first paved by Soviet road graders in the 1950s, while the Salang Pass first emerged as a north-south connector within the country when Soviet engineers built what was then the world's highest tunnel through it.[3] The reverb of the Soviets in Afghanistan – who developed the country only to wreck it, prompting an almost four-decade cycle of war and "reconstruction" – thus echoes *sotto voce* in debates about the country's future.

What is true for Afghanistan is true for much of the rest of the world, at least when it comes to the history of development. Bringing what used to be called the "Second World" into histories of development matters not only as an additional case study or perspective, but also because it offers valuable theoretical insights into the field as a whole.[4] Beyond the sheer geographical spread of Soviet models of development (one-sixth of the planet's surface, plus China for a time and a bestiary of dictatorships ranging from Havana to Kabul), for many, "development" revolved around the democratization of the means of production, not just a rise in living standards. What David Engerman calls "development politics," namely the structure that governed the politics of internal development for many countries from the mid-1950s to the late 1960s, depended on the intersection of the American-Soviet rivalry with decolonization.[5] Likewise, scholars like Joseph Hodge and Tom Robertson are right when they argue for a greater focus on gender and the environment as dimensions of development. But future scholars who follow their call

---

[3] The Salang Pass saw modest north-south trade flows before the construction of the tunnel by Soviet engineers, but anthropological accounts written in the first half of the twentieth century emphasize that the Khawok Pass (passing through the Panjshir Valley) or the route through Bamiyan (which the protestors in 2016 would prefer) were preferred over the Salang as transit routes in the first half of the twentieth century.

[4] David Engerman, "The Second World's Third World," *Kritika* 12:1 (Winter 2011): 183–211.

[5] David Engerman, "Development Politics and the Cold War," *Diplomatic History* 41:1 (January 2017): 1–19.

would do well to remember that the Soviet Union and socialist states championed themselves as the world's most progressive countries when it came to "the women question," since they not only offered women full employment, abortion on demand, and exhaustive childcare services, but had also championed deveiling in "the socialist East."[6] Not only that, but the intersection of development and the environment looks very different when seen from a state that exported oil and gas infrastructure and expertise more frequently than did its American counterpart.

Keeping Soviet and socialist development at the center of any global history of development matters for getting our timelines right, too. Satellites like Mongolia received the Soviet development package starting in the 1920s, while the idea that "development politics" petered out in the mid-1970s would come as news to most Cubans, Afghans, and Angolans. Finally, while we are indebted to new histories of transnational nongovernmental organizations (NGOs) like *Médecins sans Frontières* (MSF) that examine their roots in domestic contexts, it is also crucial to remember that the crucial theaters where so many of them burst onto the global scene of the 1980s pitted them against socialist dictatorships like those in Cuban-backed Addis Ababa, Soviet-occupied Kabul, or Vietnamese-occupied Phnom Penh.[7]

The global history of development remains, in short, ripe for reassessment from the vantage point of the socialist world. This chapter uses the experience of Afghanistan during the Cold War to do so, making the argument that Afghanistan, far from some remote mountain kingdom (as it was viewed by many a traveler on the Hippie Trail) or "the graveyard of empires," belongs at the center of the global history of development. That's because there are few other countries whose twentieth-century histories mirror the major trends in the history of development practice – and where so many actors, from American hydrologists to Soviet gas engineers, from West German foresters to French "doctors without borders," passed through the same piece of real estate. If in the 1960s, Afghanistan numbered among the largest recipients of foreign aid per capita, then by the late 1980s, Peshawar, hub of the jihad in neighboring Pakistan, hosted more

---

[6] Celia Donert, "Women's Rights in Cold War Europe: Disentangling Feminist Histories," *Past and Present* 218 (2013): 180–202.

[7] Anne Vallaeys, *Médecins sans Frontières. La biographie* (Paris: Fayard, 2004); Eleanor Davey, *Idealism beyond Borders: The French Revolutionary Left and the Rise of Humanitarianism* (Cambridge: Cambridge University Press, 2015); *Human Rights and Humanitarian Intervention: Legitimizing the Use of Force since the 1970s*, ed. Norbert Frei, Daniel Stahl, and Annette Weinke (Göttingen: Wallstein Verlag, 2017).

transnational NGOs[8] than any other place in the world. Studying the history of development in Afghanistan therefore helps to illuminate this global turn "from empires to NGOs," while also contributing to an ongoing turn in the historiography of Afghanistan that understands the country neither solely nor primarily through the lens of ethnic politics, political Islam, or war.[9] Let us visit, then, several locales and moments in the history of global development in Cold War Afghanistan. What emerges from such a tour is the outline of a new global history of development, albeit one centered less on states, the United States, and the 1960s than our present literature.

"ECONOMIC KOREA"

Our journey begins in Afghanistan in the late 1950s, a time and place sometimes defined more through sepia photographs of Kabul University students in miniskirts than through the historical record. But first, a primer for the uninitiated: Although nominally independent since the collapse of the eastern half of the Afsharid Empire in 1747, the territory we know today as "Afghanistan" was only gradually seen as a single polity over the course of the nineteenth century. After losing choice territory in Kashmir, the Punjab, and what is today Khyber-Pakhtunkhwa to Sikh armies in the 1810s and 1820s, the rulers of Afghanistan were reduced to ruling over marginal lands west of Ranjit Singh's domains. Following two British wars (1839–1842 and 1878–1880) prompted by fears of Russian incursion into India, the Afghan ruler 'Abdurrahman Khan (r. 1880–1901) was bought off with an annual British subsidy and arms shipments in exchange for forfeiting control of foreign relations. In 1893, British diplomat Mortimer Durand agreed with 'Abdurrahman Khan on the so-called Durand Line, fixing the Emirate of Afghanistan's border along a 1,400-mile-long line

---

[8] A word on terminology: in this chapter, I use the term "transnational NGO" to describe private nongovernmental organizations like MSF, Médecins du Monde, and the Swedish Committee for Afghanistan. These are distinct from *international* humanitarian organizations like the International Committee of the Red Cross, the United Nations High Commissioner for Refugees (UNHCR), and the United Nations Children's Emergency Fund (UNICEF) that were the original subjects of international humanitarian law. Distinguishing between the two kinds of organizations is important because both are subject to different rights and responsibilities in international humanitarian law.

[9] Gregory Mann, *From Empires to NGOs in the West African Sahel* (Cambridge: Cambridge University Press, 2016). For one recent useful statement on the state of the field, see the introduction to *Afghan History through Afghan Eyes*, ed. Nile Green (Oxford: Oxford University Press, 2016).

along the Indo-Afghan frontier. As a result, however, the Pashtun people living between Kabul, Qandahar, Quetta, and Peshawar were divided between the Raj and the Emirate. Twice as many Pashtuns ended up in the British Empire as in Afghanistan. (Pashtuns, who speak an Indo-Iranian language related to Persian, represent the world's largest patriarchal lineage group, as well as one of the world's largest stateless nations.)[10]

When 'Abdurrahman died in 1901, his son, Habibullah Khan (r. 1901–1919), attempted to modernize the country. True, already under 'Abdurrahman Khan, there had been exchanges of letters and small numbers of advisers with the Ottoman Empire. But under Habibullah, many Urdu-speaking Indian Muslims in particular were recruited to this "free Muslim nation" to man schools, presses, mints, and bureaucracy.[11] As Nile Green puts it, even as Afghanistan's rulers also attracted American engineers to Kabul, more important was how "a multiplicity of ideological investors regarded Afghanistan as a unique space for the grand Muslim experiment of *tajaddud*, or 'renewal.'"[12] The stakes invested in Afghanistan as an outpost of Muslim experimentation grew greater after World War I, when the Ottoman Empire (and caliphate) collapsed and Habibullah's son, Amanullah (r. 1919–1929), declared Afghanistan independent and defeated the British in the Third Anglo-Afghan War (1919). This, however, meant the end to subsidies and the return of great power maneuvering for influence in Kabul. Hence, as Afghan intellectuals continued to debate the merits of an "Iranian" reform trajectory, the project of Muslim modernism, or transforming Afghanistan into a Pashtun nation-state – the latter the choice endorsed by the government – Afghan volitions intersected with the funding available from the Germans, Soviets, Japanese, Turks, and Italians.[13] All of this underscores that as important as the shift from

---

[10] For a broad introduction to these issues, see Thomas Barfield, *Afghanistan: A Cultural and Political History* (Princeton: Princeton University Press, 2012); on state formation during this period, see Shah Mahmoud Hanifi, *Connecting Histories in Afghanistan: Market Relations and State Formation on a Colonial Fronter* (Stanford: Stanford University Press, 2011).

[11] Hakeem Naim, "Conscripted Modernity: Rethinking State Formation and the Politicization of Islam in Afghanistan and the Ottoman Empire," "Afghanistan in the Modern World" Workshop, May 6, 2016; Nile Green, "The Trans-Border Traffic of Afghan Modernism: Afghanistan and the Indian 'Urdusphere'," *Comparative Studies in Society and History* 53:3 (2011): 479–508.

[12] Dietrich Reetz, *Hijrat: The Flight of the Faithful: A British File on the Exodus of Muslim Peasants from North India to Afghanistan in 1920* (Berlin: Das Arabische Buch, 1995).

[13] On Iranian trajectories, see Jawan Shir Rasekh, "Contesting Histories: The Persian/Iranian Discourse of Contemporary 'Afghan' History and Politics," "Afghanistan in the Modern World" Workshop, May 6, 2016. On Pashtun nation building, see

colonial development to postcolonial development politics is for, say, Africa, many "crypto-colonial" regions of the world have their own distinct path histories.[14] Following the suggestion of Corinna Unger, future scholarship would do well to understand how the rise and fall of a Muslim *taraqi* ("progress") project, which reached its *apogee* in socialist Afghanistan, intersected with, but was distinct from, the ideological investments made by the anti-colonial Germans and Soviets.[15] This means changing professionalization patterns (think languages), but it is essential to avoid falling into the trap of narrative patterns that affirm "donor" countries (those with agency) and "recipient" countries (those without it).

This raises the question of how the global Cold War intersected with Afghan national projects. Soviet Russia had been the first country in the world to recognize Afghan independence, but Afghanistan had been irrelevant to American foreign policy, and John Foster Dulles rebuked Afghan petitions to join the Central Treaty Organization (CENTO). But in December 1955, Soviet First Secretary Nikita Khrushchëv and Premier Nikolai Bulganin made a surprise visit to the Kabul "airport" en route back from a passage to India (and Burma). There, they announced a surprise low-interest loan of approximately $100 million to fund Afghan infrastructure and training for Afghanistan's officer corps (themselves still wearing gear donated from the Nazis). Most spectacularly, at a dinner reception, Bulganin appeared to endorse Afghan claims for "Pashtunistan," a proposed ethnic Pashtun nation-state to be carved out of western Pakistan. Building on the discourses of Pashtun nationalism first developed in the 1930s, Afghanistan's leaders challenged the territorial settlement of the Durand Line that Indian Partition had unwittingly reaffirmed. Over time, Pakistan's military and intelligence establishment would make the disabling of a sovereign and independent Afghanistan (at least one that endorsed Pashtun irredentism and could ally with India) a core national security interest.

Shah Mahmoud Hanifi, "Quandaries of the Afghan Nation," in *Under the Drones: Modern Lives in the Afghanistan-Pakistan Borderlands*, ed. Shahzad Bashir and Robert D. Crews (Cambridge, MA: Harvard University Press, 2012), 83–101. On Pashtun nationalism, see James M. Caron, "Cultural Histories of Pashtun Nationalism, Public Participation, and Social Inequality in Monarchic Afghanistan, 1905–1960" (PhD diss., University of Pennsylvania, 2009).

[14] Michael Herzfeld, "The Absent Presence: Discourses of Crypto-Colonialism," *The South Atlantic Quarterly* 101:4 (2002): 899–926.

[15] Corinna Unger, "Comment on Joseph Hodge, on the Historiography of Development (Parts I and II)," *Humanity* Forum, April 28, 2016, available online at: http://humanity journal.org/blog/comment-on-joseph-hodge-on-the-historiography-of-development-part-i-and-ii/

The Americans, as well as key allies like the West Germans, feared a Soviet "aid offensive" in Kabul in partnership with Afghan nationalist Prime Minister Mohammad Daoud Khan (r. 1953–1963), whom American media dubbed "the Red Prince." Existing American corporate projects in the Helmand River watershed were taken over by the United States Agency for International Development (USAID), and the West Germans sponsored a forest development project in the Himalayan cedar groves of eastern Afghanistan.[16] Just as the Americans bought into the idea of turning southern Afghanistan into the agricultural base for a definitively *Pashtun* Afghan nation, the West Germans sought to redirect the illegal wood trade (which fed mills and workshops in Pakistan) toward "natural" national markets in Kabul.[17] Observers like Louis Dupree, the United States' foremost authority on Afghanistan during the Cold War, aptly called the country an "economic Korea" seeing how "peaceful coexistence" played out in the Afghan countryside. (Afghanistan in the 1960s saw investment from a variety of actors, but the three biggest were the Soviets by a large margin, then the Americans, and West Germans. Future research should focus on the role of China, Czechoslovakia, India, and Japan, not to mention the World Bank, the Asian Development Bank, and the United Nations Development Programme [UNDP].)

However, these developmental projects encountered problems. Inattention to fertilizer use and drainage in the Helmand Basin, not to mention the wanton resettlement of nomads from eastern Afghanistan to the south, deteriorated soil quality and made small-scale farming uneconomical, given population growth and inheritance patterns. In eastern Afghanistan, West German efforts to implement "scientific" forest management techniques did little to halt the flourishing transborder traffic in cedar. By the late 1960s, many parts of the once-verdant east had turned to desert.

This makes Cold War Afghanistan seem like a case of James C. Scott-style "high modernism" run amok – which it is. Less obvious, however, are the ways in which "development politics" and decolonization made the territorial nation-state the only lingua franca that donors and recipients could speak during the high developmental moment of the 1960s. Afghan élites were often most concerned with creating

---

[16] Nick Cullather, "Damming Afghanistan: Modernization in a Buffer State," *The Journal of American History* 89:2 (September 2002): 512–537.

[17] Timothy Nunan, *Humanitarian Invasion: Global Development in Cold War Afghanistan* (Cambridge: Cambridge University Press, 2016), 82–92, 106–116.

Piedmonts of Pashtun modernity that would compare favorably to the Pashtun areas of western Pakistan. But when they had to sell projects like the forest management scheme to the Germans, they explained the grave threat of a "hunger march" of wild Pashtun tribesmen upon Kabul were measures not taken. Western Cold Warriors seldom probed at the contradiction: how could Afghanistan *both* be a Pashtun nation-state and simultaneously under threat from Pashtun invasion?[18]

Afghan nationalist had élites leveraged the idealized form of the developmental nation-state to forward projects aimed at anything but – in this case, the avatar of "Pashtunistan." In doing so, they aped from preexisting discourses of nationalism to legitimize themselves in the eyes of foreigners as "real" Pashtuns invested in crypto-colonial devices like the *loya jirgah*. Along these lines, future work on the global history of development might investigate how the funding streams associated with Cold War geopolitics empowered entrepreneurial élites to push forward nationalist agendas (think the modern culture of adoration of the Thai king) with often disastrous consequences for ethnic minorities (think the Shi'a Hazara in Afghanistan, the Chinese in much of Southeast Asia, or Bengalis in pre-1971 Pakistan). Even as development politics advanced some elements of indigenous modernization projects (although Indian Muslims and Turks were now replaced by Russians and Americans), it also precluded the possibility of non-nation-state based forms of political organization. Visions of Afghanistan as an incubator for pan-Islamic renewal or some Persianate sphere were occluded by the language of the nation-state.[19]

Like the Americans and West Germans, the Soviets were conned by Afghan élites' appeals to help them modernize. As noted, Soviet engineers paved the roads of the Afghan capital, erected Soviet-style five-story apartment buildings (the most desirable housing stock in Kabul), built state farms near the Khyber Pass, and, last but not least, built the Bagram Air Base that since 2001 has served as the hub of the Western military presence in Afghanistan (and an international penal colony). By the mid-1960s, however, Soviet economists admitted that they had no idea how Afghanistan could pay back its loans to Moscow. Kabul's irredentist position on "Pashtunistan" had alienated Pakistan and prompted border

---

[18] Hanifi, "Quandaries of the Afghan Nation," 99.
[19] For one example of recent work on notions of a Persianate sphere, see Mana Kia, "Indian Friends, Iranian Selves, Persianate Modern," *Comparative Studies of South Asia, Africa and the Middle East* 36:3 (2016): 398–417.

closings to a potential market for Afghan agricultural goods. Beyond this, the Indo-Pakistani cold war meant that Pakistan refused Afghan goods transit to traditional markets in India. Far from reaching its claws toward the Persian Gulf – a piece of geopolitical apocrypha – the Russian bear, or, more precisely, Soviet economists, were looking for a way to recoup their losses.

Mercifully, they found a solution. In the late 1960s, Soviet geologists found oil and gas deposits in northern Afghanistan that were connected to Soviet gas networks. These made Khrushchëv's diplomatic adventurism (one of the reasons for his 1964 "retirement") more fiscally sustainable. Less obvious is how Afghan and Iranian gas tapped during these years allowed the Soviets to supply Western European gas markets until Siberian fields came online in the 1970s. Yet the material and ideological bases for Soviet power in the world were shifting. The late 1960s marked a crucial turn in the USSR's claim to international leadership, namely as a time when the export of oil and weapons, and the memory of the Great Patriotic War (parades for which started in 1965), rather than the forward-looking timeline of communism and the export of international revolution, provided legitimacy for the world's first socialist state.[20]

When historians seek to explain the decline of development politics in the late 1960s, then, they might look not just to the election of Richard Nixon and a renewed American emphasis on realpolitik, but also shifts in how the Soviet Union "did" development around the Third World. Because we still lack for in-depth case studies of Soviet policies to many countries, one is hesitant to generalize. The broad picture, however, is one of Moscow making more economically efficient investments (read: oil and gas extraction) at the cost of enterprises that would supposedly generate a postcolonial working class.[21] Future work on the global history of development would contrast how the post–1973 American and Soviet

---

[20] At the CPSU Party Congress in 1961, Nikita Khrushchëv predicted that the USSR (officially a socialist society since 1934, but not yet *communist*) would reach communism within twenty years. Under Leonid Brezhnev (r. 1964–1982) and his successors, this transition was indefinitely delayed, with the official line being that the USSR exhibited characteristics of "developed socialism," although true communism was still emerging. For a brief history of Victory Day parades, see: "Eti dni pobedy," *Itogi*, May 10, 2005, available online at: http://www.itogi.ru/archive/2005/19/57588.html

[21] Ragna Boden, *Die Grenzen der Weltmacht. Sowjetische Indonesienpolitik von Stalin bis Brežnev* (Stuttgart: Franz Steiner Verlag, 2006); Alessandro Iandolo, "Soviet Policy in West Africa, 1957–64" (PhD diss., University of Oxford, 2011); Christopher Miller, "Decolonization and Soviet Theories of Economic Development," ASEEES Annual Convention, November 19, 2015.

empires of energy management, arms exports, and clients (Iran and Saudi Arabia for the United States; Syria and Iraq for Moscow) mutually reinforced one another and laid the material foundation for contemporary "pipeline politics."[22] While the Communist Party political archives remain only half-open, the economic and technical archives are wide open. Future scholarship would connect the Soviet and American turns toward energy security and weapons, exports to the indigenous visions of "progress" discussed earlier, albeit with Ba'athism or late Pahlavi anti-Westernism standing in for the Indo-Afghan Muslim modernism discussed earlier.

SOCIALISM WITH AFGHAN CHARACTERISTICS

As in many other locales around the planet, development politics in Afghanistan failed to achieve its stated aims of "takeoff" or the construction of a proletariat. But the Afghan monarchy had raised expectations throughout the 1960s, and when a drought and famine flattened the countryside in the early 1970s, the Afghan King's cousin, Daoud (the "Red Prince" of the 1950s), saw an opening for a coup d'état. He did so in 1973 with implicit Soviet backing and the support of Afghan communists (themselves established in Kabul since the mid-1960s and the latest iteration of the Indo-Afghan "progress" story) while the King, Zahir (r. 1933–1973), was in Italy.

There were no grand Soviet geopolitical designs behind the coup. Soviet diplomats viewed Afghanistan as a Central Asian Finland; Party and KGB leaders had their focus on Europe, not the Third World, and Moscow had, in any event, shown itself ready to sell domestic communists down the river in favor of tyrants like Saddam Hussein and Hafez al-Assad.[23] Soon, however, Daoud began jailing not only Afghan Islamists but also members of both "wings" (really parties unto themselves) of the People's Democratic Party of Afghanistan (PDPA). The first of these was *Khalq* ("masses"), a violent Pashtun chauvinist organization committed to overthrowing what it viewed as a Punjabi dictatorship over disenfranchised Pashtuns in Pakistan next door; the other was *Parcham* ("flag"), an

---

[22] Andrew Scott Cooper, *The Oil Kings: How the U.S., Iran, and Saudi Arabia Changed the Balance of Power in the Middle East* (New York: Simon & Schuster, 2012); Victor McFarland, "Living in Never-Never Lands: The United States, Saudi Arabia, and Oil in the 1970s" (PhD diss., Yale University, 2015).

[23] Vladimir Snegirëv and Valeriĭ Samunin, *Virus "A": Kak my zaboleli vtorzheniiem v Afganistan*, 19, available online at: http://nsarchive.gwu.edu/rus/VirusA.html

ethnically mixed organization in favor of socialist revolution and align-
ment with the USSR, but without bestriding the ocean of blood necessary
to forge a Pashtun nation-state. No wonder Zahir was content to live out
his days playing golf in the Roman countryside rather than attempt
a countercoup.

Once developmental projects failed to deliver either as bedrocks of
a "national economy" or irredentist piedmonts, fantasies of ethnic purity
plus the rise of the nation-state as the only form of political organization
created disastrous consequences around the Third World. Once Third
World intellectuals discovered "the social consequence of joining the
global market as a pavement beggar," many rejected the prospect of
a tariff-walled world of the General Agreement on Tariffs and Trade
(GATT) and détente for the fantasy of the ethnically pure socialist nation-
state as their ticket to international society.[24] The most destructive
instances of this were in societies like Afghanistan or Somalia, where
crypto-colonial regimes first touted ideas of "Greater Afghanistan" or
"Greater Somalia" in lieu of robust nationalisms, only to find parvenu
intellectuals take these ideas seriously as a political program to be realized
with the backing of the superpowers. The stakes were particularly dire in
an era of decolonization when nationalists viewed the purified postcolonial nation-state as the only legitimate vehicle for the nation. Future
research would do well not only to produce rise-and-fall "modernization
comes to town" narratives of dashed hopes, but also how the breakdown
of nation building created a political vacuum ready to be filled by new
visions of this or that nation's place in the sun.[25]

Worried that Daoud was another Saddam Hussein type, Moscow
demanded that the two PDPA wings unify posthaste, which they did.
The Kremlin also instructed the two wings to postpone any coup attempts
against Daoud, which they did not. Following crackdowns in April 1978,
Khalqists inside the Afghan military assassinated Daoud and declared
Afghanistan a Democratic Republic. A mix of parades by day and mass
shootings at night followed. But Afghanistan also became party to an
intellectual traffic with other "People's Democratic Republics" across the
Third World throughout the late 1970s. In October 1978, for example, the

---

[24] Pankaj Mishra, *Butter Chicken in Ludhiana: Travels in Small Town India* (New Delhi:
Penguin Books India, 1995), 179. Jeffrey Byrne gestures in this direction in *Mecca of
Revolution: Algeria, Decolonization and the Third World Order* (Oxford: Oxford
University Press, 2016).

[25] Daniel Immerwahr, *Thinking Small: The United States and the Lure of Community
Development* (Cambridge, MA: Harvard University Press, 2015).

Afghan communists hosted a Vietnamese delegation to the Soviet-built state farms in eastern Afghanistan, where they celebrated both nations' victories against imperialism.[26] Afghan socialists, like their counterparts Zulfiqar 'Ali Bhutto (r. 1971–1977) in Pakistan and Indira Gandhi (r. 1966–1977 and 1980–1984) in India, spoke of the need to promote "food, housing, and clothes" (*roti, kapra aur makan* in Urdu, *khāneh va kālā va nān* in Persian).[27] They participated, too, in the 1979 Non-Aligned Movement Conference in Havana. But the regime's efforts at land reform alienated many. The PDPA's calls to annex one-third of Pakistan according to some Pashtun *megali idea* prompted Islamabad to intensify aid to Afghan Islamist rebels. And when Hafizullah Amin, a thuggish type within the Khalq wing of the PDPA, assassinated General Secretary Nur Muhammad Taraki after the latter's return from the Havana conference, the Soviets thought they were seeing a sequel to Anwar Sadat's Egyptian betrayal. Having invested huge sums in Afghanistan to maintain its Finland-like status and facing the *fait accompli* of NATO's Double-Track Decision, a Special Commission of the Politburo decided to invade Afghanistan without informing the bureaucracy, much less the citizenry.[28]

To stress: the Soviet occupation of Afghanistan was not the "Soviet Union's Vietnam." Still less did it have anything to do with the Soviet collapse. The United States had 550,000 troops in Vietnam by 1969, whereas the Soviets had no more than 120,000 at their peak in Afghanistan (itself a territory five times the size of South Vietnam). Soviet deployments to Afghanistan represented 2 percent of total Soviet military forces, and total combat deaths numbered one-fourth of those the Americans suffered in Indochina. True, KGB analysts noted that the number of soldiers removed from combat due to squalid sanitary conditions was extraordinary (400,000 from 1979 to 1989).[29] But hepatitis and typhoid outbreaks do not a Soviet Vietnam make.

The better question, rather than whether the Soviet-Afghan war constituted a strategic disaster for the USSR, was why a model of socialist

[26] Robert Crews, *Afghan Modern: The History of a Global Nation* (Cambridge, MA: Harvard University Press, 2015), 237.

[27] Sulaiman Layeq, National Anthem of the Democratic Republic of Afghanistan, sung in "Red Flag" (1979), available online at: https://pad.ma/BSI/player/00:07:01.841

[28] For more detailed accounts, see Odd Arne Westad, *The Global Cold War* (Cambridge: Cambridge University Press, 2005), 288–330; Artemy Kalinovsky, *A Long Goodbye: The Soviet Withdrawal from Afghanistan* (Cambridge, MA: Harvard University Press, 2011).

[29] Nikolaï Leonov, *Likholet'e* (Moscow: Mezhdunarodnye Otnosheniia, 1995), 229.

economic policy and despotism that had functioned serviceably well both inside the Soviet Union as well as in allies like South Yemen (the world's first Marxist-Leninist Muslim-majority state) broke down so dramatically in Afghanistan in the 1980s. Any sufficient answer to this question must also address both the Soviets in Afghanistan themselves (the focus of this section) as well as the shifts in the politics of pan-Islamism and left-wing solidarity, which, together, facilitated a "humanitarian invasion" of the country during the 1980s.

Shortly following the Christmas Day invasion and the liquidation of Hafizullah Amin in favor of the Parchamist quisling Babrak Karmal, thousands of Soviet Party and civilian advisers joined the hundreds already present in Kabul since April 1978. Much of the material in Soviet archives remains closed, but through the memoirs of CPSU advisers to the PDPA, the archives of Communist Youth League advisers, and the files of Soviet women's organizations, one can begin to discern the meaning of the Soviet-Afghan experience of the 1980s from the inside out. Youth advisers deployed to the countryside met enthusiastic Afghan socialists eager to build Pashtun socialism on their side of the Durand Line with a keen eye to its transborder ripples. (Lest this sound fanciful, recall that democratic socialist Pashtun parties thrived in Pakistan until Bhutto and his successor Zia ul-Haq jailed their leadership and promoted Islamist parties against them.)

However, Soviet advisers and their Afghan partners encountered serious obstacles. The Soviet system of cadre management and mass politics was optimized for the Soviet rust belt, cotton farms, and labor-intensive forms of energy extraction that had peaked in the mid-1970s. But Soviet economists had already urged shifting Soviet aid away from these forms of development a decade ago. Even where advisers did possess the security backing from Soviet and Afghan armed forces to leave the cities for the countryside, there were precious few industrial enterprises or large farms around which to organize workers or peasants. The Soviet project, so geared toward the possibilities presented by bordered industrial space, struggled to adapt to a space in which "we have workers, but no working class," and where the Afghan government did not even recognize the Durand Line as its legitimate border (still true today).[30]

---

[30] "Zapis' besedy s sekretarem pervichnoĭ partorganizatsii 10-go raĭona g. Kabula, sostoiavsheĭsia 28 sentiabria 1987g," in Vladimir Plastun and Vladimir Andrianov, *Nadzhibulla: Afganistan v tiskakh geopolitiki* (Moscow: Russkiĭ biograficheskiĭ institut, 1998), 182.

The sense of indigenous Afghan and Soviet visions of "progress" passing one another in the night was especially visible when it came to what was called "the woman question." Mid-century Kabul was home to a variety of women's movements, most sponsored by the government, but with underground movements growing out of the small number of female university graduates enthralled by issues of *Soviet Women* or, alternatively, radical visions of women's equality common to urban guerrilla, Maoist, and Trotskyist movements. Once the Soviets arrived, however, these alternative visions of women's liberation were driven into exile. Within Afghanistan, the Soviets and Afghans produced the largest female professional class in the history of Kabul – think tens of thousands of secretaries, teachers, and translators. But Soviet women's activists remained fixated on a very specific vision of women's liberation that was anything but intersectional. Any "women's movement," Soviet activists insisted, had to be subjugated to proletarian internationalism. As for Muslim women in the Afghan countryside, the Soviets browbeat their Afghan colleagues about the urgency of deveiling, even as Afghan socialist women explained to them that it was, in fact, possible to be for "progress" without abandoning the veil that allowed women to leave their home in the first place.[31]

Soviet socialism and development held a powerful attraction for many well into the 1970s, it turned out, but Moscow's was a project with a shelf life. Soviet-style institutions were optimized for places like Bohemia or Silesia with sooty industrial bases that served as the bedrock for social constituencies, trade unions, and the Communist Party itself. The USSR of the mid-1980s had around 70 percent of its economy in industry, transportation, and construction (the highest share of any country in world history!). So committed was Moscow to this vision that its Siberian and Far Eastern hinterlands were fifteen times more densely populated with factories and defense installations than equivalent latitudes in Alaska or the Yukon.[32] Effective though it was in upholding a social order, this Fordist economy grew obsolete vis-à-vis the Western "empire of consumption" that emerged out of the earlier "empire of production" that the Soviets thought they were competing with.[33] And the Soviets'

[31] Nunan, *Humanitarian Invasion*, ch. 5.
[32] Stephen Kotkin, *Armageddon Averted: The Soviet Collapse, 1970–2000* (Oxford: Oxford University Press, 2001), 17; Clifford G. Gaddy and Barry W. Ickes, "Caught in the Bear Trap," Legatum Institute *Prosperity in Depth* Report (2013), 5.
[33] Charles S. Maier, *Among Empires: American Ascendancy and Its Predecessors* (Cambridge, MA: Harvard University Press, 2006).

imaginary of white Russian male factory workers as the historical actor *par excellence* made it difficult to address a world composed increasingly of yellow revolutionaries, brown and black peasants, and a pink-collar Western precariat.[34] In short, the restructuring of the global economy, combined with decolonization and the Maoist challenge, undermined the raison d'être of Soviet socialism.

True, future histories of the Soviet project in the world should not overstate the disjuncture between Soviet and indigenous Third World visions of progress. Intellectuals and authors like the Pakistani poet Faiẓ Ahmed Faiẓ (winner of the Lenin Peace Prize in 1962) or the Iranian poet Siavash Kasraie (who lived in Kabul, then Moscow, from 1983 to 1995) still commanded respect in their home societies. "For boys like me, in North Indian railway towns in the '70s and '80s, where nothing much happened apart from the arrival and departure of trains from big cities," wrote one Indian intellectual, "the Soviet Union alone appeared to promise an escape from our limited dusty world. [...] Self-consciously, I'd prepared myself for adult life in the Soviet Union."[35] But the gap between these echoes of a progressive Indo-Afghan tradition and "real existing socialism" was growing wider and wider.[36]

Making things worse, even as the Soviet occupation turned five out of fifteen million Afghans into refugees (most in Pakistan, but many in Iran), both Moscow and Kabul remained insistent that the refugees were terrorists or had forfeited the right to return to the authentic nation housed within the nation-state. But this itself was out of step with shifting global trends, which saw the emergence of so-called "transnations" that "retained a special ideological link to a putative place of origin, but [were] otherwise a thoroughly diasporic collectivity."[37] The Soviet Union had been entangled with such "transnations" from its very

---

[34] Jeremy Friedman, *Shadow Cold War: The Sino-Soviet Competition for the Third World* (Chapel Hill: University of North Carolina Press, 2015).

[35] Pankaj Mishra, "First Love," *n+1* 3 (Fall 2005): 60.

[36] The same was true for the Soviet claim to justice vis-à-vis the New Left in the West, as well. So, too, was the distance between Soviet visions of workers' solidarity as the most primal expression of left-wing politics, as opposed to visions of social justice that placed women, racial minorities, homosexuals, or children in intersectional juxtaposition or even opposition to (white, male) trade unionists. For more on these shifts, see Daniel Rodgers, *Age of Fracture* (Cambridge, MA: Harvard University Press, 2011), ch. 5.

[37] Arjun Appadurai, "The Heart of Whiteness," *Callaloo* 16:4 (Autumn 1993): 804. See also, Arjun Appadurai, *Modernity At Large: Cultural Dimensions of Globalization* (Minneapolis: University of Minnesota Press, 1996).

inception – consider the White Russians, the Armenians, or the internal Georgian diaspora.[38] During the Cold War, Moscow threw itself into the championing of Palestinian "transnationality" in the 1970s.

And yet, Soviet intuitions about the relationship between development and the nation remained fixated around Soviet Republics' "titular nation" at home and the postcolonial territorial nation abroad. Development was conceived in terms of energy inputs or steel outputs within the borders of territory identified with a primordial nation, rather than, say, remissions from abroad. Future histories of development might think transnationally where the Soviets did not, investigating how donor states and NGOs adapted their practices to the diasporic and refugee communities that became ever more visible in the 1980s, like the Palestinians, Vietnamese, Tamils, and Afghans, the latter the focus of this chapter's final section.

THE KHYBER PASS TO NONGOVERNMENTALITY

The outflow of three million Afghan refugees into Pakistani territory created an opening for transnational actors to challenge the Soviet model of development in Afghanistan. Much attention has been devoted to the Afghan *mujāhidin* and the Arab jihadist internationale that gathered in Peshawar to roll back the Soviets from occupied Muslim lands (note, though, that most Afghans are either ethnic Pashtuns or Tajiks, not Arabs, and speak languages like Pashto or Persian unrelated to Arabic). The Afghan Islamists interested in establishing an Islamic Republic tolerated the Arab brigades that had rejected Palestine Liberation Organization (PLO) or Algerian-style secularism and national liberation in favor of global *jihad*.[39]

Instrumental to the success of the Afghan national liberation *jihad*, however, were its ties with Arab and European transnational humanitarian organizations that created a web of clinics, schools, and postal and financial services spanning from Peshawar to western Afghanistan. The real question, then, is not why Sunni Arab Islamists came to Peshawar. Rather, we need to ask why Western humanitarian actors

---

[38] For recent work on the Georgian diaspora, see Erik R. Scott, *Familiar Strangers: The Georgian Diaspora and the Evolution of Soviet Empire* (Oxford: University of Oxford Press, 2016).

[39] Lawrence Wright, *The Looming Tower: Al Qaeda and the Road to 9/11* (New York: Knopf, 2006).

sympathetic to Third World movements, Maoism, and Trotskyism in the mid-1970s allied with the *jihad* against a "progressive" government.[40] This might seem like a question for intellectual history. However, insofar as intellectual shifts brought European NGOs to run schools, hospitals, and veterinary programs on the ground everywhere from Asadabad to Zabul, it also must be of relevance to global histories of development.

The crucial shift, at least for the NGOs to be most active in occupied Afghanistan, had to do with a reprioritization of precarious human lives (not "human rights") over Third World socialism. Many of the European organizers who went on to lead the largest NGOs to operate in Afghanistan – namely, France's *Médecins sans Frontières* (MSF) and the Swedish Committee for Afghanistan (SCA) – had opposed the American war in Vietnam, and they celebrated the Viet Cong's sack of Saigon in 1975. Some (not all) regarded the Soviet Union as a necessary evil in a world otherwise threatened by American imperialism. Within European domestic contexts, however, the publication of *The Gulag Archipelago* destroyed the myths of a humanist socialism, while an emerging consciousness of the Holocaust encouraged Europeans to avoid its repeating in Kabul or Phnom Penh. And once Vietnamese communists' brutality created the "boat people" crisis, where hundreds of thousands of Vietnamese and ethnic Chinese fled the country on dinghies, many activists, especially in France, reevaluated the legitimacy of socialist utopianism.

Without abandoning their sympathy for other Third Worldist causes (the PLO, the African National Congress [ANC], and southern African liberation movements), humanitarian groups found themselves on the anti-communist side of conflicts in Cambodia, Ethiopia, and Afghanistan. In effect, humanitarian actors came to view Afghan lives as equivalent to those of black South Africans, Mozambicans, or Palestinians; the Afghan socialist regime, as equivalent to apartheid, Portuguese colonial, or Zionist domination. Conceived of in this way, Third World socialist regimes lost the privileges of sovereignty that South Africa, Portugal, and Israel had seen challenged earlier in the 1970s.[41]

---

[40] On the globalization of Islam, see Ayesha Jalal, "An Uncertain Trajectory: Islam's Contemporary Globalization, 1971–1979," in *The Shock of the Global: The 1970s in Perspective*, ed. Niall Ferguson, Charles S. Maier, Erez Manela, and Daniel Sargent (Cambridge, MA: Harvard University Press, 2010).

[41] Timothy Nunan, "The Anti-Colonial Origins of Humanitarian Intervention: NGOs, Human Rights," *Jadaliyya*, September 15, 2016; Eleanor Davey, *Idealism beyond*

The global spread of "real existing socialism" – itself a powerful force of development in Angola, Ethiopia, Cambodia, and Afghanistan – was thus instrumental in the formation of transnational humanitarianism. If a global moment of Western state-centric development did end in the mid-1970s, future global histories of development must take seriously the transition from that world to the NGO-centric order that replaced it. Future works could examine how the interplay between NGOs and socialist development generated the condition described as postcolonial. They should also contrast the post-Leftist trajectory of organizations like MSF or SCA with that of confessional groups like Caritas International or Muslim Aid. Finally, future work on the global history of development might delve more deeply into the refugee camps *qua* infrastructure, or on cross-national comparisons between such installations on the Thai-Cambodian and Afghan-Pakistani frontiers.

As the American-, Pakistani-, and Saudi-backed Afghan *jihād* ground down the Soviet 40th Army and the Afghan socialist government, transnational humanitarian organizations – backed by both private donors and European governments' aid agencies – doubled down on their work in the refugee camps and the *mujāhidin*-controlled Afghan countryside. New Soviet General Secretary Mikhaïl Gorbachëv described the conflict as "a bleeding wound" for the Soviet Union, and top advisers urged him to dissociate socialism from the likes of Muammar Gaddafi and Saddam Hussein. Gorbachev responded by internationalizing many of the Soviet Union's Third World quagmires, agreeing to a UN-overseen withdrawal from Afghanistan (the agreement did not include the *mujāhidin* as a party). Moscow also removed an effective Security Council veto on peacekeeping operations that dated to the Congo Crisis. This allowed the United Nations to take a much more proactive role in regulating conflict zones like Afghanistan, southern Africa, and Cambodia. Active to the bitter end, Soviet aid institutions liaised with UN emergency relief programs for Afghanistan (the latter dubbed "Operation Salam"). But the politics were complicated, as the United Nations had to deal both with the Kabul government and the NGO-*mujahidin* bricolage based out of Peshawar. And it was the latter kinds of partnerships that formed the basis for UN aid to the country during the Afghan Civil War (1992–1997)

Borders: The French Revolutionary Left and the Rise of Humanitarianism (Cambridge: Cambridge University Press, 2015). On Sweden, see Tor Sellström, *Sweden and National Liberation in Southern Africa* (Uppsala: Nordiska Afrika Institutet, 1999).

and Taliban rule (1997–2001), when UN food aid programs and NGOs kept the country from total involution.

While sometimes in the background of global histories of development, the United Nations and its developmental institutions, like UNDP, UNICEF, and the United Nations Development Fund for Women (UNIFEM), matter, not least because the "new world order" of the late 1980s allowed them to spread to conflict zones once made off-limits by the Cold War. Beyond writing tight empirical histories of these institutions, future histories of global development should examine how issues like child labor, domestic abuse, equal pay, or women's "empowerment" (a term coined in 1981) entered the lifeblood of international politics, as veterans of NGOs and domestic women's and children's rights campaigns made the long march through the UN institutions of Geneva and New York.[42] More Afghan girls were educated under the Taliban in the 1990s than under Zahir Shah in the 1960s, and yet the former regime aroused outrage from women's activists in a way that the latter did not. But as the Afghan case reminds us, future histories will have to take account not only of the United Nations on its own terms, but also how it interacted with groups on the ground – NGOs, *mujāhidin*, and the communist government in Afghanistan; or NGOs, the Khmer Rouge, and the former Kampuchean People's Revolutionary Armed Forces, in the case of Cambodia. In doing so, they will also contribute to discussions about the entangled postsocialist and postcolonial conditions that define so many of the places where the United Nations intervened, like Cambodia, if also the locales where it did not, like Srebrenica.

***

Reviewing his earlier enthusiasm for the Soviets' attempts to "modernize a backward and feudal country" from a squalid hotel room in Mazar-i Sharif, Afghanistan, in 2005, the aforementioned Indian intellectual had only one thought: "What the hell had I been thinking?"[43] Yet as this chapter has shown, late-century adherents to a South Asian progressive tradition were not the only ones left reconsidering their priors after embarking on the quest to develop Afghanistan. During the twentieth

---

[42] For one example of new works that properly focus on the relationship between development and sovereignty, see Eva-Maria Muschik, "Building States through International Development Assistance: The United Nations between Trusteeship and Self-Determination, 1945 to 1965" (PhD diss., New York University, 2017).

[43] Mishra, "First Love," 59.

century, Afghanistan had gone from "the country of all Muslims" to an "Emirate" hosting Islamist castoffs from around the world.[44] But the story of the rise and fall of Afghan-Muslim modernism itself framed a story of global development in which actors from the United States to the Soviet Union to NGOs were all active across many decades, drawing on state budgets, private donors, and religious endowments to realize visions of postcolonial sovereignty within the borders drawn up by Mortimer Durand and 'Abdurrahman Khan. Afghanistan's is also a story of development that continues to the present moment, since after 1997 and 2001, NGOs and the United Nations have been joined by institutions like the Department for International Development (DFID), ECHO, and the Japan International Cooperation Agency (JICA), not to mention the US military. In Afghanistan, at least, development "isn't history" – it's present.[45]

Perhaps there was something special about the period of high "development politics" that peaked in the 1960s, but the Afghan case reminds historians of the need to adopt longer-term perspectives and the vantage points of non-Western and nonstate actors as we seek to understand the place of development in global history. Afghan actors today may speak in the postmodern language of "equitable development" or a "sustainable Afghanistan," but as this chapter has shown, the history of development in Afghanistan goes back to at least the early twentieth century – a timeline on which the "development politics" of the 1960s appears as but one episode among many. One cannot but imagine that the timeline looks different seen from Cairo, Khartoum, or Bogotá. Here, future research would do well to capture how long, or short, later moments of NGO-ification and the insertion of the United Nations into other national contexts were. It is by blending these perspectives from the periphery with the imaginaries of development in Washington, Moscow, and other centers that we can appreciate the collective story of when development happened and when – if? – it will ever end.

---

[44] Sayyid Sulaymān Nadwī, *Sayr-e Afghānistān* (Lahore: Sang-e Mīl, 2008), 41, cited in Green, "The Trans- Border Traffic of Afghan Modernism," 508.
[45] Nick Cullather, "Development? It's History," *Diplomatic History* 24:4 (Fall 2000): 641–653.

Postwar European Development Aid: Defined by Decolonization, the Cold War, and European Integration?

Corinna R. Unger*

INTRODUCTION

In a book on the global history of development, which position should Europe take? Some would argue that for two interrelated reasons Europe should not figure very prominently in such an account. For one, Europeans, in the eyes of many contemporaries from the so-called Global South, after the end of colonialism lacked the moral legitimacy to provide any kind of guidance in terms of development. Europe was associated with the legacy of colonialism and imperialism, specifically with exploitation, violence, racism, and degradation. Hence, while many governments of the newly independent nations cooperated with their European counterparts on the level of trade and development agreements, the public perception of Europe in the former European colonies was characterized by distrust and aversion. It was therefore no coincidence that the Soviet Union and the socialist countries of Central and Eastern Europe, the United States, the People's Republic of China, but also new international organizations and private actors often received a warmer welcome as potential providers of development assistance than the Western European countries, not the least because the quantities of support and the conditions under which they granted it were sometimes more attractive. Secondly, many scholars of development see the danger of reproducing exactly those Eurocentric notions for which colonial and postcolonial development projects have long been criticized.

* For helpful comments on earlier drafts of this chapter, I would like to thank Muriam Haleh Davis, Heike Wieters, and two anonymous reviewers.

Emphasizing the role of Europe in the global history of development might then be understood as an indirect affirmation of the idea that Europe did, in fact, have an advantage over the so-called less developed countries, which in turn might serve to reinforce essentialist notions of cultural difference that, in the eyes of the critics, should have been discarded long ago.

Yet with all the justified criticism of Eurocentrism in mind, it is impossible to overlook the fact that Europe – whether as an imagined or real entity – for a long time served as a model or inspiration for development to many societies in many parts of the world. Furthermore, there can be no doubt that European expertise, technology, capital, and power influenced the discourses about the possibilities, conditions, and directions of development as well as the ways in which development took place, even if for political, philosophical, or ideological reasons many people would have preferred to see this influence reduced. In other words, as important as it is to provincialize Europe, it would be ahistorical to marginalize its role in the global history of development due to political concerns. Yet instead of celebrating European contributions to global development we should analyze them critically in order to arrive at a differentiated understanding of Europe's place in the global history of development. This is what this chapter aims to contribute to.

Specifically, the chapter probes the question of where to position European development assistance in the triangle of decolonization, European integration, and the Cold War. By asking this question, the chapter joins in the book's effort to broaden and complement our understanding of development history in a twofold way. For one, it highlights the importance of development approaches and traditions that coexisted with but differed from those that dominated American development policies. In doing so, it also points toward the need to refine the predominant periodization with its emphasis on 1945 as the beginning of international development history. To understand the particularities of European development policies and practices, it is inevitable to include colonial experiences in the analysis, which reach back at least to the interwar period. Secondly, the chapter contributes to refining our understanding of the relevance of the Cold War by studying development policies and practices through the lens of countries that were part of the Cold War conflict but not its central players, and for whom the processes of decolonization and European integration might have been more important in shaping their development aid policies.

Since Europe is too large and vague a category to study, it is necessary to select actors who represent the complexity of European development interests. The countries included here are France, Great Britain, Switzerland, and the Federal Republic of Germany (FRG). All of them were part of the Cold War's Western alliance, but they had very different positions in and abilities to shape the conflict. Also, their relation to colonialism differed markedly. France and Great Britain both were imperial powers but diverged in their approaches to colonial rule and decolonization. Switzerland was one of the so-called small nations without an imperial past but with ambitions to participate in international politics. Similarly, the FRG was not considered to be one of the traditional colonial powers but became very active in development aid as well as in the European Economic Community (EEC), as did France. The use of countries as reference points should not suggest that development happened only within the confines of the nation-state. Nongovernmental actors were numerous and active in the development arena, and many development projects took place in a highly international or transnational environment. Referring to countries therefore only serves as a heuristic tool to frame the analysis.

EARLY DEVELOPMENT APPROACHES AND EXPERIENCES

The roots of European development policies and practices reach back at least to the period after World War I.[1] We can distinguish broadly between two forms of development-related activities in the interwar period: Development efforts in Europe by European governments and international actors in the 1920s and 1930s, and colonial development policies abroad in the 1930s and 1940s. In the first field, the League of Nations played an important role. The League promoted international cooperation and economic reconstruction, particularly in the new nation-states in Southern, Southeastern, and Central Eastern Europe that had emerged out of the former empires. Against the background of the Russian Revolution in 1917, the League's representatives believed that the stability of the new states and their ability to neutralize socialist tendencies depended not only on the establishment of sound political structures but also on an increase in living standards and economic productivity, which in turn required

---

[1] For a more extensive discussion of the early history of development, see Corinna R. Unger, *International Development: A Postwar History* (London: Bloomsbury, 2018), ch. 3.

a stable financial situation.[2] Thus, efforts to improve and standardize structures in the fields of finance, infrastructure, education, health care, and labor conditions (for which the International Labor Organization [ILO] took responsibility) became entangled with broader political and ideological goals.[3]

Nongovernmental actors, including a large number of experts from different national, political, and disciplinary backgrounds, took on a very active role in the newly emerging field of activity. Not everyone involved in early humanitarian and development efforts was primarily driven by a liberal political conviction. Many experts saw modernization and development projects as a chance to try out new ideas and approaches in an international setting and with government support.[4] Also, private organizations contributed expertise and funding for the establishment of clinics and research and educational institutes, hoping to improve the living situation and the productivity of war-torn or seemingly underdeveloped regions while simultaneously anchoring liberal structures in Europe's new nation-states.[5]

The internationalist mission of the League did not stop at Europe's borders, of course. Many of the actors involved were believed to be recognizing similar problems and opportunities outside of Europe,

---

[2] Cf. Patricia Clavin, *Securing the World Economy: The Reinvention of the League of Nations, 1920–1946* (Oxford: Oxford University Press, 2013), 25–33; Zara Steiner, *The Lights That Failed: European International History, 1919–1933* (Oxford: Oxford University Press, 2007), 349–386.

[3] See, for example, Vincent Lagendijk, "'To Consolidate Peace'? The International Electrotechnical Community and the Grid for the United States of Europe," *Journal of Contemporary European History* 47:2 (2012): 402–426. Also see Sönke Kunkel and Christoph Meyer, "Fortschritt nach Plan? Der globale Entwicklungsdiskurs des Völkerbundes und die Anfänge des systemischen Denkens," in *Aufbruch ins koloniale Zeitalter: Globalisierung und die außereuropäische Welt in den 1920er und 1930er Jahren*, ed. Kunkel and Meyer (Frankfurt am Main: Campus, 2012), 123–141. On ILO, see Sandrine Kott and Joëlle Droux, eds., *Globalizing Social Rights: The International Labor Organization and Beyond* (Basingstoke: Palgrave Macmillan, 2013); Daniel Maul, *Human Rights, Development and Decolonization: The International Labour Organization, 1940–70* (Basingstoke: Palgrave Macmillan, 2012).

[4] See Margherita Zanasi, "Exporting Development: The League of Nations and Republican China," *Comparative Studies in Society and History* 49:1 (2007): 143–169.

[5] See, for example, Davide Rodogno, Francesca Piana, and Shaloma Gautier, "Shaping Poland: Relief and Rehabilitation Programmes Undertaken by Foreign Organizations, 1918–1922," in *Shaping the Transnational Sphere: Experts, Networks, and Issues from the 1840s to the 1930s*, ed. Davide Rodogno, Jakob Vogel, and Bernhard Struck (New York: Berghahn Books, 2014), 259–278.

ranging from China to Latin America.[6] At the same time, various European governments and authorities conducted development programs in those parts of their countries – especially in rural regions – they considered backward or wanted to turn into showcases of modern and efficient socioeconomic life, not the least to prevent a rural exodus.[7] These efforts, while often considered progressive in nature, were not limited to democratic countries. The Italian and German fascist projects of rural improvement, land reclamation, anti-malaria campaigns, and infrastructure development mirrored the authoritarian fascination with a particular kind of modernity as well as the need of the regimes to secure popular support at home and make themselves visible internationally.[8]

Colonial development, while similar in its focus on infrastructure, agriculture, public health, and basic education, followed a different logic, not the least because the colonial powers did not envisage the colonies becoming independent anytime soon. The driving force behind colonial development was the idea of making the colonies more productive (*mise en valeur*) in order to increase the revenue the colonial powers could extract from them. This seemed particularly important because of the economic problems many European countries were experiencing in the postwar period. Importantly, the colonial populations, not the colonial powers, were supposed to cover the costs for those development efforts.[9]

In addition to the economic interest driving colonial development, political concerns played an important role, too: Colonial politicians

---

[6] See Zanasi, "Exporting Development"; Marcus Cueto, ed., *Missionaries of Science: The Rockefeller Foundation and Latin America* (Bloomington: Indiana University Press, 2004); Iris Borowy, *Coming to Terms with World Health: The League of Nations Health Organization, 1921–1946* (Frankfurt am Main: Peter Lang, 2009).

[7] See the contributions in the theme issue on "Experimental Spaces: Planning in High Modernity," *Journal of Modern European History* 13:4 (2015).

[8] On Italy, see among others, Federico Caprotti, "Destructive Creation: Fascist Urban Planning, Architecture and New Towns in the Pontine Marshes," *Journal of Historical Geography* 33 (2007): 651–679. More generally, see the contributions to the roundtable on Italian Fascism in *Contemporary European History* 24:2 (2015). On Germany, see among others, Willi Oberkrome, "National Socialist Blueprints for Rural Communities and Their Resonance in Agrarian Society," in *Visions of Community in Nazi Germany: Social Engineering and Private Lives*, ed. Martina Steber and Bernhard Gotto (Oxford: Oxford University Press, 2014), 270–280; Thomas Zeller, *Driving Germany: The Landscape of the German Autobahn, 1930–1970* (New York: Berghahn, 2007), chs. 4 to 6.

[9] Cf. Herward Sieberg, *Colonial Development: Die Grundlegung moderner Entwicklungspolitik durch Großbritannien, 1919–1949* (Stuttgart: Steiner, 1985), 1–8.

argued that investing a limited amount of resources into the colonies would help to counter the growing anti-colonial sentiment both in the colonies and internationally. For a long time the colonial powers had argued that they had a moral obligation to uplift the supposedly less civilized societies in Africa and Asia, and that therefore foreign rule was inevitable. Similarly, the abolition of slavery in Africa had often been cited as a reason for European colonialism.[10] However, after World War I, the concept of the so-called civilizing mission was no longer sufficient to publicly legitimize colonialism. The colonies had served as reservoirs of resources to the European powers during the war, and the colonial elites demanded that this service be honored by granting them a larger degree of freedom and support. To counter their demands for self-determination along the lines advocated by US President Woodrow Wilson, and to prevent radical political ideas from taking root in the colonies, the British made political concessions in India in 1919, and in 1929 passed the Colonial Development Act, which was to provide one million pounds annually to improve the colonial infrastructure in order to increase the colonies' revenue and create employment in Great Britain.[11]

In Africa most colonial governments tried to avoid far-reaching political changes. In doing so, they emphasized the need to protect the colonial subjects from the effects of global change and to maintain their traditional ways of living, especially the tribal structure considered characteristic of and crucial to rule over African societies.[12] However, the socioeconomic reality in many African colonies was changing rapidly as a result of labor migration and urbanization, with many strikes and protests taking place in the second half of the 1930s.[13] By promising the colonies to improve their economies and infrastructures and to provide

---

[10] See, among others, Amalia Ribi Forclaz, *Humanitarian Imperialism: The Politics of Anti-Slavery Activism, 1880–1940* (Oxford: Oxford University Press, 2015). On the concept of the civilizing mission, see Harald Fischer-Tiné and Michael Mann, eds., *Colonialism as Civilizing Mission: Cultural Ideology in British India* (London: Anthem Press, 2004); Miguel Bandeira Jerónimo, *The "Civilising Mission" of Portuguese Colonialism, 1870–1930* (Basingstoke: Palgrave Macmillan, 2015).

[11] Cf. Sieberg, *Colonial Development*, 56.

[12] Cf. Frederick Cooper, "Writing the History of Development," *Journal of Modern European History* 8:1 (2010): 5–23, 9. Also, see the contributions to the special issue on late colonial development experiences in Africa in the *Journal of African History* 41:1 (2000).

[13] Cf. Frederick Cooper, *Decolonization and African Society: The Labor Question in French and British Africa* (Cambridge: Cambridge University Press, 1994); Samuël Coghe, "Reordering Colonial Society: Model Villages and Social Planning in Rural Angola, 1920–45," *Journal of Contemporary History* 52:1 (2017): 16–44.

knowledge and technology needed for the elevation of colonial living standards, the colonial powers tried to counter anti-colonial protests (or what they understood as such) and to gain support for the colonial project at home and abroad.[14] Frederick Cooper has called this effort, which went hand in hand with attempts to rationalize the colonial administration, "the modernization of colonialism."[15]

Initial suggestions of colonial officials and lobby groups to increase colonial development funds met with much resistance among European politicians in the 1920s and early 1930s, when the idea of using public money to stimulate growth was not yet established as broadly as it would be in later years. However, the intellectual and political climate changed toward the end of the 1930s and early 1940s, when several European governments began to plan the establishment of welfare systems at home. At least on a minimal level the colonies had to be given similar services, reaching from hospitals to basic education centers to rural credit schemes.[16] Consequently, the British passed the Colonial Development and Welfare Act in 1940 (which was renewed and expanded in 1945), and the French followed in 1946 with the *Fonds d'Investissement et de Développement Économique et Sociale* (FIDES).[17]

What added to the perceived urgency of providing development support to the colonies was the experience of World War II, in which the European powers drew on the colonies' resources to an even larger extent than in World War I. The perception on the part of the colonial societies that they were fighting a war for a colonial power that was not interested in their well-being gave power to anti-colonial voices. Numerous protests, strikes, and underground activities in the colonies reflected the increasingly challenged status of imperial rule.[18] In this situation, the promise of

---

[14] Cf. Sieberg, *Colonial Development*; Dirk van Laak, *Imperiale Infrastruktur: Deutsche Planungen für eine Erschließung Afrikas 1880 bis 1960* (Paderborn: Schöningh, 2004), 211–213.

[15] Frederick Cooper, "Development, Modernization, and the Social Sciences in the Era of Decolonization: The Examples of British and French Africa," [2004] in *The Ends of European Colonial Empires: Cases and Comparisons*, ed. Miguel Bandeira Jerónimo and António Costa Pinta (Basingstoke: Palgrave Macmillan, 2015), 15–50, 21.

[16] Cf. Marc Frey, "Control, Legitimacy, and the Securing of Interests: European Development Policy in South-east Asia from the Late Colonial Period to the Early 1960s," *Contemporary European History* 12:4 (2003): 395–412, 397.

[17] Cf. Ibid, 397–398; Cooper, "Development, Modernization, and the Social Sciences in the Era of Decolonization," 22–23; van Laak, *Imperiale Infrastruktur*, 342–343.

[18] See Martin Shipway, *Decolonization and Its Impact: A Comparative Approach to the End of Colonial Empires* (Malden: Blackwell, 2008), chs. 2 and 3; Yasmin Khan, *India at*

development and future progress through technical aid and financial support was meant to reign in the most radical anti-colonial voices and to stabilize the imperial order.

EUROPEAN DEVELOPMENT POLICIES AND APPROACHES AFTER 1945: ACTORS, INTERESTS, CHALLENGES

The term second colonial occupation has been used to characterize the efforts of the European powers after World War II to counter the disintegration of empire by strengthening colonial rule. While this often implied the use of violence and force, development became a popular tool to tighten the grip on colonial societies.[19] Officially, the colonies were supposed to receive support in order to prepare for their eventual independence. Late colonial development schemes were designed to introduce colonial populations to more efficient technologies, particularly in the field of agriculture, and to form behavior considered in line with modern forms of living. Imperialism as such was not supposed to end, but its proponents wanted to adapt it to the postwar situation by replacing outright physical force with developmental measures of different kinds, from infrastructure projects to literacy campaigns to rural improvement schemes.[20]

One of the most dramatic expressions of the late colonial development approach was the French *Plan de Constantine* for Algeria, which President Charles De Gaulle announced in October 1958, at a time when Algerian resistance to French rule was intensifying rapidly. The plan was supposed "to raise Algeria's national revenue by seven and a half percent, educate one and a half million children, and lodge a million inhabitants in what would come to be known as the *campagne de mille villages* [thousand

---

War: *The Subcontinent and the Second World War* (New York: Oxford University Press, 2015), 51–61, 132–141.

[19] Of course, not all colonial administrators were using development as a tool of control. Some were actively trying to improve the living situation of the local population and criticized development approaches for being too narrowly focused on the European powers' interests. Cf. Monica van Beusekom, *Negotiating Development: African Farmers and Colonial Experts at the Office du Niger, 1920–1960* (Oxford: Oxford University Press, 2002); Joseph Morgan Hodge, *Triumph of the Expert: Agrarian Doctrines of Development and the Legacies of British Colonialism* (Athens: Ohio University Press, 2007).

[20] Cf. Cooper, "Development, Modernization, and the Social Sciences in the Era of Decolonization," 25.

villages campaign]."[21] Those villages were resettlement camps that the French military had established a few years earlier as part of its counter-insurgency strategy against the *Front de Libération Nationale* (FLN), the Algerian liberation movement. Now, in the late 1950s, some of those camps, in which Algerians were forcefully interned, were supposed to be turned into villages to make the inhabitants familiar with the modern ways of living of French civilization. At the same time, the villages had the purpose of monitoring the inhabitants and preventing them from support-ing the FLN.[22] Furthermore, according to the *Plan de Constantine*, hun-dreds of thousands of new jobs would be created, massive amounts of land redistributed, and 350 million francs spent on the development of agri-culture, forestry, and hydraulics. "France hoped to convince Algerians that prosperity would be found under the umbrella of French Algeria rather than with the FLN."[23] Following the imperial logic, development programs were not meant to free the colonies from their dependence on the colonial powers but to maintain and stabilize foreign rule.

Apart from the political expectations tied to colonial development, imperial powers hoped to benefit from the modernization efforts economically.[24] The British groundnut scheme in Tanganyika can serve as an illustration. Britain's economy had suffered much during World War II, and food rationing in the United Kingdom continued into the early 1950s. Vegetable fats and oils were particularly scarce. Against this back-ground, the managing director of the United Africa Company, a subsidiary of the Dutch-British company Unilever, which produced margarine and soap, in 1946 visited the British colonies in East Africa in search of land where new oil-producing plantations could be set up. Tanganyika, which Great Britain had taken over from Germany as a mandate territory after 1918, seemed to have much land available, and

---

[21] Muriam Haleh Davis, "Restaging Mise en Valeur: 'Postwar Imperialism' and the Plan de Constantine," *Review of Middle East Studies* 44:2 (2010): 176–186, 176.

[22] See Moritz Feichtinger and Stephan Malinowski, "'Eine Million Algerier lernen im 20. Jahrhundert zu leben': Umsiedlungslager und Zwangsmodernisierung im Algerienkrieg 1954–1962," *Journal of Modern European History* 8:1 (2010): 107–135, 114–120; Moritz Feichtinger, "'A Great Reformatory': Social Planning and Strategic Resettlement in Late Colonial Kenya and Algeria, 1952–63," *Journal of Contemporary History* 52:1 (2017): 45–72.

[23] Davis, "Restaging *Mise en Valeur*," 177.

[24] See, for example, Dorothy L. Hodgson, "Taking Stock: State Control, Ethnic Identity and Pastoralist Development in Tanganyika, 1948–1958," *The Journal of African History* 41:1 (2000): 55–78; James L. Brain, "The Uluguru Land Usage Scheme: Success and Failure," *The Journal of Developing Areas* 14:2 (1980): 175–190.

the British government agreed to the company's suggestion to set up a fully mechanized production of groundnuts on 3,210,000 acres of land, with an estimated cost of £24 million and expected savings on British food imports of £10 million.[25]

Although the project did have the effect of stimulating the local economy, its general outcome was dramatically different from the expectations: "When it was finally shut down in 1951, over £36 million of British public money had been spent on a scheme that imported more groundnuts as seed than it actually harvested."[26] Looking back, the reasons for these problems seem easy to identify: The planners had surveyed the region very superficially and had not taken much interest in the geographical, climatic, ecological, and socioeconomic conditions of the region. Lack of rain, plant diseases, lack of machinery, and an inadequate labor supply proved to be insurmountable problems that resulted in the project's premature end.[27] Apart from the technical problems, the groundnut scheme reflects many of the inherent problems of colonial development thinking: The idea that a colony was a source of profit the imperial power could tap on with the help of so-called development; the belief in the universal value and applicability of European scientific expertise; and the assumption that Western technology was superior to African agricultural practices. When employing development schemes to maintain control over the colonies, many European administrators strongly trusted in the power of social engineering. Yet development projects that included forced labor or resettlement schemes, limited access to land, or imposed new taxes often led to resistance, sabotage, and protest on the part of the population affected by the projects, which presented grave interventions in and interruptions of their lives.[28] Arguing that colonial rule came to an end in most parts of Africa in the late 1950s and early 1960s because of colonial development

[25] Cf. Matteo Rizzo, "What Was Left of the Groundnut Scheme? Development Disaster and Labour Market in Southern Tanganyika 1946–1952," *Journal of Agrarian Change* 6:2 (2006): 205–238, 207–208.

[26] Ibid., 208. [27] Cf. ibid., 208–210.

[28] See, for example, Dorothy L. Hodgson, *Once Intrepid Warriors: Gender, Ethnicity, and the Cultural Politics of Maasai Development* (Bloomington: Indiana University Press, 2001), 106–122; Julia Tischler, *Light and Power for a Multiracial Nation: The Kariba Dam Scheme in the Central African Federation* (Basingstoke: Palgrave Macmillan, 2013), 184–213; Helen Tilley, *Africa as a Living Laboratory: Empire, Development, and the Problem of Scientific Knowledge, 1870–1950* (Chicago: The University of Chicago Press, 2011), ch. 2; Rohland Schuknecht, *British Colonial Development Policy after the Second World War: The Case of Sukumaland, Tanganyika* (Berlin: LIT, 2010).

strategies creating and intensifying anti-colonial protest would be too strong of an argument, but there can be no doubt that late colonial development schemes did not live up to the expectations of the European planners in terms of their material and symbolic effects with regard to stabilizing colonial rule.

This observation leads to the question to which degree development approaches changed in the context of decolonization and in which ways they presented a continuation of colonial practices. Notably, many of the imperial powers after the end of formal colonial rule tried to use development aid to secure economic, political, and cultural influence in their former colonies. For one they did so by providing investments and credits on favorable terms to the new nations, offering educational and training opportunities for students, and building infrastructure in the form of streets, bridges, housing, ports, and railroads. Secondly, they often reserved the right to intervene, directly or indirectly, in the affairs of their former colonies. This is not to say that all development assistance from the former colonial powers was a neocolonial tool, or a prolongation of colonialism under a different heading. At least formally, the former colonies had become independent, sovereign nation-states. As independent countries, they now had the freedom to ask governments and organizations for support, to accept it or reject it. Also, and importantly, development aid was no longer based on colonial taxation but came from the donors' domestic budgets and, at least in later years, from national contributions to multilateral funds like the consortia organized by the World Bank.[29]

What added to the changing nature of development was that the range of development actors became much more diverse. Politicians in many Western European countries understood that decolonization and the emergence of development as an international field of activity provided opportunities to gain visibility, especially if they felt their countries suffered from a lack of strategic, political, and symbolic importance.[30] Swiss politicians, for example, in the early postwar years identified the provision of development assistance as a way in which their country could improve its reputation, which had suffered from Switzerland's cooperation with the Fascist regimes during the war, and overcome its internationally

---

[29] Cf. Frey, "Control, Legitimacy, and the Securing of Interests," 408; Amit Das Gupta, "Development by Consortia: International Donors and the Development of India, Pakistan, Indonesia and Turkey in the 1960s," *Comparativ* 4:19 (2009): 96–111.

[30] On the Scandinavian countries' involvement in and contributions to development aid, see Helge Pharo and Monika Pohle Fraser, eds., *The Aid Rush: Aid Regimes in Northern Europe during the Cold War*, 2 vols. (Oslo: Unipub, 2008).

marginal position by gaining respect for its technical skills and generosity.[31] Since the Swiss principle of neutrality seemed to make it impossible for Switzerland to join the United Nations Organization (UNO), being an active member in the seemingly technical field of development was considered the second-best option in building relations with the new nations, which were considered economically promising.[32]

When UNO asked Switzerland in the late 1940s to contribute to its Expanded Cooperative Program of Technical Assistance for Economic Development (EPTA), the Swiss government forwarded the task to a newly established committee under the leadership of the prestigious Swiss Federal Institute of Technology. Following a request by the Nepalese ambassador, the committee formulated a development plan for Nepal and sent an exploratory mission to the country in 1950. The members of the mission were aware of the advantage they had compared to other Western visitors to Nepal because of Switzerland's lack of a colonial past, and they cultivated an image as modest and hardworking experts.[33] Apparently Cold War considerations did not play a prominent role in the discussions of the Nepal project. This can be explained, for one, with Switzerland's neutrality. Secondly, if the image of Swiss generosity and expertise was to improve the country's position in the international arena, the country's political reasons for providing aid had to be kept in the background.

Compared to government representatives, nongovernmental actors could afford to be more outspoken about their interests in development. This was especially true of those whose primary focus was not on development *per se*. Company representatives understood very clearly that decolonization and the need for development opened up new business

---

[31] Cf. Sara Elmer, "Postkoloniale Erschließung ferner Länder? Die erste Schweizer Nepalmission und die Anfänge der, technischen Hilfe an unterentwickelte Länder,'" in *Postkoloniale Schweiz: Formen und Folgen eines Kolonialismus ohne Kolonien*, ed. Patricia Purtschert, Barbara Lüthi, and Francesca Falk (Bielefeld: transcript, 2nd ed., 2013), 245–266, 248.

[32] Cf. ibid., 249 and 251; Daniel Speich Chassé, "Verflechtung durch Neutralität: Wirkung einer Schweizer Maxime im Zeitalter der Dekolonisation," in *Postkoloniale Schweiz*, ed. Purtschert, Lüthi and Falk, 225–244, 232–235. Also, see Lukas Zürcher, "'So fanden wir auf der Karte diesen kleinen Staat': Globale Positionierung und lokale Entwicklungsfantasien der Schweiz in Rwanda in den 1960er Jahren," in *Entwicklungswelten: Globalgeschichte der Entwicklungszusammenarbeit*, ed. Hubertus Büschel and Daniel Speich (Frankfurt am Main: Campus, 2009), 275–273; Patricia Purtschert and Harald Fischer-Tiné, eds., *Colonial Switzerland: Rethinking Colonialism from the Margins* (Basingstoke: Palgrave Macmillan, 2015).

[33] Cf. Elmer, "Postkoloniale Erschließung ferner Länder?", 257.

opportunities. Most of the new nations had predominantly rural economies, with the large majority of the population depending on agriculture.
Many anti-colonial leaders believed that if their countries were to gain true
independence and political respect they had to industrialize, for which they
needed capital, technology, and machinery. International companies selling
these goods saw a unique opportunity arising, especially since the demand
for heavy industry goods was steadily decreasing in the industrialized
countries. Other entrepreneurs expected that as the new nations were
industrializing a large number of potential buyers of consumer products
would emerge, and new markets for consumer goods would open up.[34]

However, investing in industrialization schemes in so-called developing
countries involved a high-financial risk for private companies, whose
representatives therefore demanded public guarantees. Western
European governments were usually eager to lend this support to companies that were willing to do business abroad, both in the interest of the
domestic economy and because of the political capital they saw attached
to international economic relations. For instance, the Federal Republic of
Germany gave guarantees to West German companies investing in or
selling products to Latin American, African, and Asian countries. At the
same time, it offered credits to the governments of the so-called developing
countries to enable them to buy the goods needed for industrialization
from West German producers. Granting development-related credits or
loans turned the FRG into a provider of development assistance –
a position that, at least theoretically, implied the possibility to exercise
political influence over the recipients, which was considered particularly
valuable in the context of the Cold War. In fact, it was the main reason
why, in the 1950s and early 1960s, the FRG gave foreign aid to so-called
developing countries.[35]

---

[34] See, among others, Timothy Burke, *Lifebuoy Men, Lux Women: Commodification,
Consumption, and Cleanliness in Modern Zimbabwe* (Durham: Duke University Press,
1996), ch. 4; Corinna R. Unger, "Export und Entwicklung: Westliche
Wirtschaftsinteressen in Indien im Kontext der Dekolonisation und des Kalten
Krieges," *Jahrbuch für Wirtschaftsgeschichte/Economic History Yearbook* 1 (2012):
69–86, 69–74.

[35] "Export promotion [. . .] led Germany into the foreign aid business." Carol Anderson,
Foreign Aid: Diplomacy, Development, Domestic Politics (Chicago: The University of
Chicago Press, 2007), 29–30. For overviews of West German development aid,
seeHendrik Grote, "Von der Entwicklungshilfe zur Entwicklungspolitik:
Voraussetzungen, Strukturen und Mentalitäten der bundesdeutschen Entwicklungshilfe
1949–1961," *Vorgänge* 43:2 (2004): 24–35; Bastian Hein, *Die Westdeutschen und die
Dritte Welt: Entwicklungspolitik und Entwicklungsdienste zwischen Reform und
Revolte* (München: Oldenbourg, 2005), ch. 1; Heide-Irene Schmidt, "Pushed to the

West Germany used development assistance as a diplomatic tool to ensure that the newly created nations in Asia and Africa would not recognize the German Democratic Republic (GDR), and to increase the likelihood that they supported the West German claim to be the sole legitimate representative of Germany (*Alleinvertretungsanspruch*).[36] The FRG gave money and technical aid to those who accepted its demand and threatened to take it away from those who did not. For example, when Ceylon signed an agreement with the GDR to turn the East German trade mission into a consulate general in 1964, the FRG decided to end its economic support for Ceylon, hoping that this step would prevent other countries from following Ceylon's example.[37]

Eastern bloc development aid to African countries, ranging from financial to military to technical assistance, increased from the late 1950s onward and was considered more successful in terms of publicity than Western assistance.[38] Whereas many Western experts were accused of harboring racist prejudices, Eastern European specialists were praised for being unpretentious and for behaving collegially vis-à-vis their African counterparts.[39] Also, the Marxist interpretation of African history, according to which Africa's underdevelopment was a result of European imperialist exploitation, helped the representatives of the Eastern European countries to gain sympathy among African elites.[40] Against this background, West German politicians were afraid that the

Front: The Foreign Assistance Policy of the Federal Republic of Germany, 1958–1971," *Contemporary European History* 12:4 (2003): 473–507.

[36] See Amit Das Gupta, *Handel, Hilfe, Hallstein-Doktrin: Die bundesdeutsche Südasienpolitik unter Adenauer und Erhard 1949 bis 1966* (Husum: Matthiesen, 2004); Christian Jetzlsperger, "Die Emanzipation der Entwicklungspolitik von der Hallstein-Doktrin: Die Krise der deutschen Nahostpolitik von 1965, die Entwicklungspolitik und der Ost-West-Konflikt," *Historisches Jahrbuch* 121 (2001): 320–366, 321–325.

[37] Cf. Foreign Office, I B 5, to the West German embassies, February 19, 1964. Politisches Archiv des Auswärtigen Amtes, Berlin (PA), B 34/557.

[38] See, among others, Sara Lorenzini, "Comecon and the South in the Years of Détente: A Study on East-South Economic Relations," *European Review of History: Revue européenne d'histoire* 21:2 (2014): 183–199; Alessandro Iandolo, "The Rise and Fall of the 'Soviet Model of Development' in West Africa, 1957–64," *Cold War History* 12:4 (2012): 683–704.

[39] Cf. Foreign Office, Referat 408, November 23, 1959. PA, B 12/356; West German Consulate General Léopoldville to the Foreign Office, August 29, 1959. PA, B 12/357.

[40] Cf. Foreign Office, Referat 702, May 5, 1960. PA, B 12/339; West German Embassy Pretoria to the Foreign Office, August 11, 1959. PA, B 12/357. Also, see Steffi Marung, "A 'Leninian Moment'? Soviet Africanists and the Interpretation of the October Revolution, 1950s–1970s," *Journal für Entwicklungspolitik* 33:3 (2017): 21–48.

Soviet Union could succeed in reducing Western European influence in Africa, and that this would lead to the integration of the African countries into the "Eastern system of rule, which aims for world revolution."[41] In the eyes of West German strategists it was necessary to counter these efforts by providing economic and military support to the African nations to counter-balance the support from the GDR, the Soviet Union, or other countries from the Eastern bloc. For example, the FRG donated a mobile clinic to Ghana upon Ghanaian independence in 1957, hoping that this would create political goodwill before the GDR or another Eastern bloc country arrived on the scene.[42] When, in 1959, it became clear that several African colonies would soon become independent, the Foreign Office decided to give a mobile clinic worth DM 150.000 to each of them. Interestingly, two of the four recipients (Togo and Cameroon) were former German colonies to which the Federal Republic was believed to have a special affiliation or responsibility.[43]

The latter example suggests that development aid practices were not entirely defined by the Cold War and decolonization but were also shaped by older historical ties and cultural assumptions. Yet the diplomatic relevance of development assistance in the context of the Cold War for a long time determined West German governmental aid policies and practices.[44] At least until the second half of the 1960s, the FRG did not formulate any kind of systematic development program based on the countries' needs but provided support whenever and wherever it was deemed necessary or useful for political reasons. Critics called this the watering can principle – sprinkling aid everywhere without aiming at a specific region or development problem.[45]

The fact that development aid was supposed to serve political and economic interests does not mean, of course, that it did not have any

---

[41] West German Embassy Conakry to the Foreign Office, December 11, 1959, PA, B 12/357. Also see, among others, Foreign Office, Referat 702, October 1 and 22, 1959. PA, B 12/340.

[42] Cf. Foreign Office, Referat 400, February 2, 1957. PA, B 58-407/35.

[43] Cf. Foreign Office, Referat 307, September 2, 1959. PA, B 34/123. On the legacy of German colonialism and its afterlife in West German development aid, see van Laak, *Imperiale Infrastruktur*, 344–353, 366–372.

[44] On nongovernmental aid from West Germany, which initially was largely conducted by church organizations, see, among others, Hein, *Die Westdeutschen und die Dritte Welt*, 60–77. On public private partnerships, see ibid., 77–92.

[45] See, for example, Kurt Simon, "Entwicklungshilfe in der Krise: Nach dem ‚häßlichen Amerikaner' ‚nun der ‚häßliche Deutsche'? Das Gießkannenprinzip hat sich nicht bewährt," *Die Zeit*, March 5, 1965.

notable effects or that the recipients were reduced to a passive role. Many countries benefited from the fact that capital and technology was relatively easily available and received generous funding for development projects. What made "shopping around for patrons"[46] possible was, to a large degree, an effect of the Cold War. If a Western European government, company, or nongovernmental organization was not willing to offer the type of aid demanded, the country in question could easily turn to an Eastern European government and ask for support, thereby playing with the Western fear that the communists would be able to gain a strategic advantage.[47] The same was true of the United States or any other country in the Western alliance, of course.[48] What was characteristic of European actors was that many of them felt that they had a disadvantage because they were being associated with the legacy of colonialism, aggression, and exploitation. For example, the West German government was concerned about the communist press in India, which, in a 1958 article titled "German Herrenvolk Refuse to Work with Indian Men," portrayed technicians and engineers from the FRG involved in the construction of a steel mill in Rourkela as racist neocolonialists enjoying luxury while "ignoring Indian talents."[49] West German domestic reporting about development projects was critical, too. A report on Rourkela by the investigative journal *Der Spiegel* in 1960 emphasized the fact that the engineer Hans Heinrich, who was in charge of the steel mill's construction, had enjoyed a brilliant career in the steel industry during the Nazi period, and suggested that he now applied his questionable expertise to India in neo-imperial fashion.[50]

On the other hand, colonial experiences and connections could be very valuable in securing a niche in the postcolonial development arena. For example, the *Handelsvereeniging Amsterdam* (HVA), a Dutch company that had been active in the plantation economy in the Dutch East Indies,

---

[46] Cooper, "Writing the History of Development," 15.
[47] See Tony Smith, "New Bottles for New Wine: A Pericentric Framework for the Study of the Cold War," *Diplomatic History* 24:4 (2000): 567–591.
[48] Consider, for example, the case of nonaligned Egypt, which played out the USSR and the USA against each other. Cf. Guy Laron, *Origins of the Suez Crisis: Postwar Development Diplomacy and the Struggle over Third World Industrialization, 1945–1956* (Washington, D.C.: Woodrow Wilson Center Press; Baltimore, MD: Johns Hopkins University Press, 2013), 94–97 and ch. 4.
[49] See the newspaper clipping in Bundesarchiv Koblenz, B 102/58481.
[50] "Rourkela: Russen auf dem Dach," *Der Spiegel*, March 30, 1960. Also, see Corinna R. Unger, *Entwicklungspfade in Indien: Eine internationale Geschichte, 1947–1980* (Göttingen: Wallstein, 2015), 207.

after the end of Dutch colonial rule became an international provider of agrotechnology and know-how. Starting out in Ethiopia in
the late 1940s, its activities became increasingly widespread over the
years; by the 1970s, the HVA was active in at least thirty so-called
developing countries across the globe.[51] Likewise, the British Royal
Mint, which had been responsible for producing colonial currencies,
after the formal end of colonialism offered its services to African
governments looking for newly designed currencies, stamps, and
commemorative medals. The Mint did face competition from other
companies and had to adapt to the new nations' expectations but
generally benefited from the status it had established in the colonial
context.[52]

Something similar was true of the educational and administrative
organizations that had been associated with the colonial apparatus in
one way or another. For example, the training courses for British colonial
administrators offered by the universities in London, Cambridge, and
Oxford in the 1950s and 1960s began to cater to participants from the
(former) colonies who came to Great Britain to acquire the knowledge
needed to establish and run the bureaucracies of the new nations. Initially,
the content and political orientation of the courses remained modeled on
late colonial policies; only in the late 1960s and 1970s were they revised or
replaced by development studies programs.[53] Similarly, colonial development ideas and experiences made their way into postcolonial settings
through individuals. Many former colonial administrators took up positions as development experts in the newly created ministries of development of the European countries, in the new international organizations, or
as private consultants.[54] Their knowledge proved to be valuable in what
was quickly becoming a professional field of expertise and policy-making,
but at the same time it had to be adapted to changing political conditions.

---

[51] Cf. Donna C. Mehos and Suzanne M. Moon, "The Uses of Portability: Circulating
Experts in the Technopolitics of Cold War and Decolonization," in *Entangled
Geographies: Empire and Technopolitics in the Global Cold War*, ed. Gabrielle Hecht
(Cambridge, MA: MIT Press, 2011), 43–74, 45–56. On Dutch interests in Indonesia, see
Frey, "European Development Policy in South-east Asia," 404–406.

[52] Cf. Sarah Stockwell, "Exporting Britishness: Decolonization in Africa, the British State
and Its Clients," in *The Ends of European Colonial Empires* ed. Bandeira Jerónimo and
Costa Pinta, 148–177, 164–166.

[53] Cf. Stockwell, "Exporting Britishness," 156–157.

[54] See Joseph M. Hodge, "British Colonial Expertise, Post-Colonial Careering and the Early
History of International Development," *Journal of Modern European History* 8: 1
(2010): 24–46.

The development policies and practices of the European Economic Community, which was established in March 1957 as the successor of the European Coal and Steel Community, can serve to illustrate this phenomenon.

The responsibility for development aid within the EEC lay with the Directorate Generale (DG) VIII. The large majority of DG VIII officials were former French colonial administrators, and French concepts and practices very much shaped the Directorate's conduct in the early years. This was especially true of the so-called European Development Fund, which was modeled on FIDES, the French colonial development fund. The French authorities hoped that the new European structures would provide additional funding for France's late colonial and postcolonial projects, and they tried to influence European decision-making vis-à-vis the (former) colonies along French interests.[55]

The French-Senegalese groundnut scheme is a case in point. Senegal, a former French colony, became independent in 1960. Originally Senegalese politicians expected that the colonial trade agreements with France would continue beyond independence, and France lobbied the EEC to pay for the subsidies it had given to the Senegalese economy in colonial times. Yet the other EEC members, especially West Germany and the Netherlands, were strictly against using EEC funds to support French national economic and political interests. As much as the DG VIII represented French concerns, it was part of a genuinely European administration, and its French members were aware of the risk of being accused of favoring France and thereby undermining their country's position in the EEC. In the end the French representatives gave in to European pressure, and Senegal did not receive trade privileges from the European Community. Instead the country was expected to rapidly modernize its peanut economy so that it could compete on the world market, and the French agreed to support this endeavor with bilateral aid. However, the outcome of the French-Senegalese project was highly disappointing. The reasons cited were a lack of infrastructure and personnel and an unwillingness or inability on the part of the French

---

[55] Cf. Véronique Dimier, *The Invention of a European Development Bureaucracy: Recycling Empire* (Basingstoke: Palgrave Macmillan, 2014); idem, "Bringing the Neo-Patrimonial State Back to Europe: French Decolonization and the Making of the European Development Aid Policy," *Archiv für Sozialgeschichte* 48 (2008): 433–457.

development agency to pay attention to the local and national interests of Senegal.[56] Meanwhile, the DG VIII went to great length to establish its own, supranational quality standards and evaluation processes to assess development aid project applications. Also, once the older generation of experts retired, a new form of development thinking began to replace older, more clientelistic practices within the Directorate. In this sense, the legacy of French colonialism was slowly but continuously overshadowed by the new realities of decolonization and European integration.[57]

CONCLUSION

The aim of this chapter has been to assess the extent to which the Cold War, decolonization, and European integration shaped the development policies and approaches of Western European actors. What the examples suggest is that there was no single or coherent European model that could be contrasted with other models, and that Western European development strategies were far from being defined by American (development) hegemony. Although US organizations were highly influential in shaping Western international development assistance structures and practices, there was much room left for other actors (governmental as well as nongovernmental) to follow their own, particular development-related interests. The degree to which decolonization and the Cold War shaped Western European development approaches varied greatly. While West Germany's development aid policies were heavily influenced by Cold War-related strategic concerns vis-à-vis the German Democratic Republic, for France the colonial legacy and the process of European integration were clearly more important than Cold War logics.

Yet of course neither the Cold War nor decolonization nor European integration was static category. Their content and meaning changed continuously, as did their impact on the formulation of development

---

[56] Cf. Martin Rempe, "Fit für den Weltmarkt in fünf Jahren? Die Modernisierung der senegalesischen Erdnusswirtschaft in den 1960er Jahren," in *Entwicklungswelten*, ed. Büschel and Speich, 241–273, 247-252-267.

[57] Cf. Martin Rempe, *Entwicklung im Konflikt: Die EWG und der Senegal, 1957–1975* (Köln: Böhlau, 2012), 73–82. Also, see idem, "Decolonization by Europeanization? The early EEC and the Transformation of French-African Relations," *KFG Working Paper Series* 27 (May 2011), http://www.polsoz.fu-berlin.de/en/v/transformeurope/pub lications/working_paper/WP_27_Rempe.pdf.

policies. For example, once the West German government, in the context of détente, gave up the principle of *Alleinvertretung*, the use of development aid as a diplomatic tool vis-à-vis the GDR lost much of its meaning. Similarly, European integration did allow France to use European resources to promote its interest vis-à-vis its former colonies, but the relations with those countries had to be adapted to the new situation produced by decolonization and the political decisions and demands of the new nations' governments. Although Great Britain was not a member of the EEC and initially did not have access to European development funds, British relations with the former colonies remained strong because the different actors involved – individual experts, non-governmental organizations, government officers – proved able to adapt to the new political setting. This was particularly true of business representatives, not only in the case of Great Britain but in all of Western Europe. Entrepreneurs were acutely aware of the new opportunities contained in the continuously changing conglomerate of decolonization, the Cold War, and European integration. In fact, the importance of companies as agents of development seems strong enough to consider transforming the triadic framework into a quadrangular one, with economic interests and strategies as a key factor in determining the ways in which European development policies and practices were formulated and realized.

With regard to the question about the importance of 1945, there is no universal answer either. For countries like Switzerland and West Germany the global situation after World War II presented new challenges and opportunities, which they, like the Scandinavian countries, tried to embrace by becoming active in the field of development. For imperial powers like France and Great Britain 1945 was much less of a caesura, seeing that they in many ways continued and intensified their colonial development policies initiated in the interwar period. But even in those European countries that were not traditional imperial powers did the colonial legacy leave an imprint on public and expert perceptions of underdevelopment and development and thus on the formulation of development policies.

To better understand the specificities of this legacy, a comparison with other development approaches would be useful. The insight gained from such a comparison could also help us to learn more about the ways in which Western European countries influenced the development policies and practices of other actors in the field and *vice versa*, not only of international organizations and nongovernmental groups but also of the socialist countries. Finally, what future research will have to incorporate much more systematically is the behavior of the recipients of European development assistance and the ways in which they made sense of, contributed to, or challenged the structures and interests that defined the plurality of European development policies and practices.

PART IV

DEVELOPMENT AND INTERNATIONAL SOCIETY

13

"Mexico Has the Theories": Latin America and the Interwar Origins of Development

Christy Thornton

Even with renewed scholarly attention to the history of development in recent years, the conventional wisdom around its origins remains stubbornly tenacious: we still labor to displace received narratives that locate "the invention" of development in Harry Truman's 1949 Point Four Program, or "the birth" of development in the creation of new international institutions like the World Bank at the end of World War II.[1] In this origin story, longer histories of Western enlightenment thought and European imperial practice were combined at mid-century to produce a worldview in which development was now something to be *done to* the rest of the world, and therefore a rising United States created agenda for economic hegemony and a set of powerful international institutions for its realization.[2] But how did the US planners who "birthed" development at mid-century come to their ideas when they did, and why did they think they might work? Taking up Amanda McVety's insistence elsewhere

---

[1] Gilbert Rist, *The History of Development: From Western Origins to Global Faith* (New York: Zed Books, 2002), 69–79; Amy Staples, *The Birth of Development: How the World Bank, Food and Agriculture Organization, and World Health Organization Changed the World, 1945–1965* (Kent: Kent State University Press, 2006). This is, of course, the story of what Gillian Hart calls "big-D Development"; that is, development as a concerted international project, which she also understands with the conventional postwar narrative. Gillian Hart, "Development Critiques in the 1990s: Culs de Sac and Promising Paths," *Progress in Human Geography* 25:4 (December 2001): 649–658. An important corrective to this narrative is Eric Helleiner, *The Forgotten Foundations of Bretton Woods* (Ithaca: Cornell University Press, 2014).

[2] In the 1990s, scholars began to identify important origins for the development project in the colonial practices of European powers such as France and Great Britain. See, for example, Michael Cowen and Robert W. Shenton, *Doctrines of Development* (London: Taylor & Francis, 1996) and Frederick Cooper, *Decolonization and African Society: The Labor Question in French and British Africa* (New York: Cambridge University Press, 1996).

in this book that, in fact, "The world asked for development, and the Allies ... built an international machinery for it," this chapter argues that one crucial way that development emerged as an international project was through an iterative process of conceding to, deflecting, and coopting longstanding and repeated demands emanating from Latin America – and in particular, from postrevolutionary Mexico.[3]

The military phase of Mexico's fractious social revolution lasted until roughly 1920, after which, various experts – lawyers, diplomats, and the first generation of Mexicans to receive formal economics training – were tasked with rebuilding the country's economy, which had been devastated by a decade of war. That task was necessarily international, not least because Mexico owed large sums to foreigners whose property and business interests had been destroyed or expropriated during the revolution. The postrevolutionary government needed to find a way to meet these obligations, but also to fulfill the promises of the revolution, which had kicked out a venal dictator who had made too many concessions to foreign capital. Mexican experts recognized that many of Latin America's economic troubles could be traced to the subordinate position of the region within the global economic system, but they also insisted on the importance of Latin American markets, commodities, and labor to that system. For postrevolutionary Mexican leaders, then, it was clear that the path to national development required real changes in the international financial system – it required an international development project, and institutions that would ensure its fairness.

Similar to the Middle Eastern context examined in the chapter by Cyrus Schayegh, then, in the Mexican imaginary, development was not an outside imposition, but a necessary international program for overcoming the dislocations that unfettered capitalism had brought to their region. It is true that development, in fact, "emerged and traveled in complex, multidirectional pathways," as the editors argue and as the chapters by Priya Lal and Alden Young also demonstrate. This chapter will argue that a crucial one of those pathways originated in postrevolutionary Mexico, and therefore that one of those directions was from South to North – in this case, from Mexico City to Washington.[4] By pushing our histories

---

[3] McVety, "Wealth and Nations: The Origins of International Development Assistance," 21.

[4] Stephen Macekura and Erez Manela, "Introduction," 1; Priya Lal, "Decolonization and the Gendered Politics of Developmental Labor in Southeastern Africa," 173; Alden Young, "A Currency for Sudan: The Sudanese National Economy and Postcolonial Development," 130.

back, into the interwar period, and beyond the United States, into Latin America, we can begin to see broader origins for development as an international project. From the 1920s to the 1940s, Mexican and other Latin American economists, politicians, and diplomats imagined and advocated for a coordinated program of redistributive multilateralism. In the process, Latin Americans not only fashioned new international institutions for economic development, but demonstrated their potential uses – and their limitations – to the planners in Washington so often credited with their creation.[5]

***

In the context of the massive capital flight that followed the 1929 stock market crash and the onset of the Great Depression, Latin Americans began to formulate new ideas about the cooperative management of global finance, and in the process, laid the groundwork for new institutions of international development. At a moment when spiraling economic nationalism was contributing to the deepening global recession, it is perhaps surprising that a nationalist, revolutionary government such as Mexico's began to develop and advocate plans for international economic cooperation. But diplomats from Mexico and other Latin American countries recognized that the Great Depression revealed the extent of international economic interdependence – and they therefore actively sought collective, international solutions.

In Mexico, one impetus for these proposals was the pressure that the country faced from international bankers, landowners, and oil companies. These foreign interests wanted not only compensation for their lost property, but repeatedly leaned on their contacts in Congress to demand that Mexico sign a treaty specifying exactly what Article 27 of the new constitution – which stated that property rights were vested not in individuals, but in the nation – would mean for their existing and future investments. Land reform and the management of subsoil resources, however, were central tenets of the revolution, and despite the howls of protest in New York and London, successive Mexican presidents continued their efforts to redistribute unproductive agricultural land and to manage the investments of foreign petroleum companies, in order to ensure that the wealth derived from Mexico's natural resources

---

[5] "Redistributive multilateralism" is a phrase used by Jens Steffek, *Embedded Liberalism and Its Critics: Justifying Global Governance in the American Century* (New York: Palgrave Macmillan, 2006).

stayed in the country.[6] Throughout the 1920s and 1930s, tense international negotiations over oil, land, and debt contributed to continued domestic turmoil, and Mexican experts hoped that by combining forces with other Latin American countries, they might exert more leverage on the creditor countries.

One early locus of this activism was the Inter-American High Commission, a Washington-based body created in 1915 under the auspices of the Pan-American Union, with a mandate to "bring about the uniformity of laws" relating to commerce and finance.[7] During the 1920s and early 1930s, the High Commission had been considering an idea that had been advocated in fits and starts in the region for decades, and had been concretely proposed to the Commission by representatives of Venezuela in 1922: the creation of a multilateral banking institution for the Americas.[8] When Mexico's existing problems with international creditors were mirrored elsewhere in Latin America, as speculative capital fled the region after the stock market crash, members of the Mexican national section of the High Commission undertook a 1931 study that examined the Venezuelan and other antecedent proposals for such a bank in light of the new problems of the world economy.[9] The Mexican representatives looked especially to the recently created Bank for International Settlements as a model, as they were particularly interested in the changes made to the level of German reparations under the 1929 Young Plan, which mandated consideration of the debtor's ability to pay. "The Committee of Experts of the Young Plan," the Mexican Section wrote, "has inspired the principle that, before accepting that a people should restrict consumption to pay a debt, the base should be *the*

---

[6] There is a vast literature on this period. See, for example, Linda B. Hall, *Oil, Banks, and Politics: The United States and Postrevolutionary Mexico, 1917–1924* (Austin: University of Texas Press, 1995) and Robert Freeman Smith, *The United States and Revolutionary Nationalism in Mexico, 1916–1932* (Chicago: University of Chicago Press, 1972).

[7] John B. Moore, "The Pan American Financial Conferences and the Inter-American High Commission," *The American Journal of International Law* 14 (1920), 344.

[8] Various Latin American representatives had been calling for the creation of a hemisphere-wide lending institution since the creation of the Pan-American Union in 1889. After the Federal Reserve Act of 1913 allowed US banks to open branches overseas, the proposal was put on the back burner, until the speculative financing boom of the 1920s began to make Latin American experts reconsider its utility.

[9] See Carlos Marichal, *A Century of Debt Crises in Latin America: From Independence to the Great Depression, 1820–1930* (Princeton: Princeton University Press, 1989).

development of production."[10] Countries had already been seeking international loans aimed at "fomenting national economic progress" and "establishing industrial exploits of diverse orders," they wrote, so there should be established an institution that would not only make fulfilling loan commitments less contentious, but would actually aim to increase the resources of the borrowing country, thereby easing the conditions for loan fulfillment. The Mexican experts, joining colleagues from other countries, envisioned that what they called an International American Bank should make loans that would stabilize currencies, facilitate payments, and, most importantly, increase the productive capacity of borrowing countries.[11]

In the early 1930s, in fact, Mexico and the other Latin American countries made a range of interventions advocating for international economic cooperation.[12] At the World Economic Conference in London in 1933, Mexico's Finance Secretary Alberto J. Pani made clear his country's interest in fostering international economic cooperation. Pani had been the Mexican representative in a number of international debt negotiations already, and was therefore known to many financial officials in the United States and Great Britain. At London, Pani argued that Mexico's intentions were broadly congruent with those of the United States, and declared that Mexico had already

[10] Sección Nacional Mexicana, Alta Comisión Inter-Americana, "Memorandum sobre la fundación de un Banco Internacional Americano," June 15, 1931, in Archivo Histórico de la Secretaria de Relaciones Exteriores de México (AHSREM), L-E 210 (I), f. 548–557. Of course, as Adam Tooze points out, the Young Plan was conceived at least in part to make sure that state-to-state reparations payments didn't "crowd out Germany's private debts to Wall Street." Adam Tooze, *The Deluge: The Great War, America and the Remaking of the Global Order, 1916–1931* (New York: Viking, 2014), 488. And, of course, the Mexicans' admiration for the Young Plan took no note of the nationalist reaction it was engendering in Germany.

[11] Sección Nacional Mexicana, Alta Comisión Inter-Americana, "Memorandum," June 15, 1931.

[12] This was stressed at the Pan American Commercial Conference of 1931, as well, where the creation of a "Pan American Economic Committee" to address the hemisphere's economic problems was proposed by Cuban and other representatives. See Pan American Union, *Fourth Pan American Commercial Conference: Final Act with Annexes and a Summary of the Work of the Conference* (Washington, D.C.: Pan American Union, 1931), 117–118. For the Mexican evaluation of this plan by Daniel Cosío Villegas, see "Study on the Establishment of an Inter-American Economic and Financial Organization," in Inter-American Conference (7th: 1933: Montevideo, Uruguay), *Plenary Sessions: Minutes and Antecedents, Fourth and Ninth Committees: Economic and Financial Problems* (Montevideo, 1933).

undertaken many of the countercyclical measures that would come to define a Keynesian agenda in the following years. When Roosevelt disavowed any international economic cooperation in his "bombshell message" that July, however, the Mexicans prepared to bring their fight for cooperation back to the Western Hemisphere. The convening of the Seventh Inter-American Conference in Montevideo, Uruguay later that year offered Mexico another chance to assert its vision for the world economy, and Mexico's attempts at leadership did not go unnoticed. In London, Paul Mason of the Foreign Office, having observed Pani in London, reported that it was likely that the Montevideo conference was to bring a contest "between Argentina and Mexico for the theoretical leadership of Latin America." Mason continued, "Argentina has the resources, Mexico the theories."[13]

Back in Mexico City, the government had already created a special commission to prepare for the Montevideo conference, composed of the Finance Minister Pani, the former President, Plutarco Elías Calles, and the Foreign Minister, José Manuel Puig Casauranc, a close confidant of Calles, who had recently been named Foreign Minister after serving in a number of crucial domestic economic positions, such as the Secretary of Industry, Commerce, and Labor.[14] For Calles, the dominant figure in Mexican politics at the time, the central issue was the protection of debtor countries – there had been a wave of defaults on sovereign debt throughout the region in 1931 and 1932 – and he released a number of statements calling for a world in which "rich and strong countries will cease being exploiters of the weak countries."[15] Most importantly, he called for a moratorium on the payment of foreign debts, which would allow time for a system of "moral and prudent credit" to be created. With this mandate, Foreign Minister Puig then concretized Calles' vision into a series of proposals for the radical revision of the economic agenda of the Montevideo meeting, which he circulated to representatives from throughout the Americas. They included not just a debt moratorium, but the explicit recognition of the Drago Doctrine, mandating nonintervention over debt; the creation of systems of arbitration for commercial disputes;

---

[13] Cover attachment to Thompson to Foreign Office, Oct. 4, 1933, The British National Archives (TNA): Foreign Office Files (FO) 371/16530.

[14] Calles was considered the "Jefe máximo" in Mexico at the time, representing the real power behind a series of figurehead presidents; the period is known as the "Maximato."

[15] Memo "IV. Circunstancias Políticas internacionales características del momento actual," n.d., in AHSREM, L-E-245, f. 378–379.

questions of trade and tariffs; and the creation of a "continental central bank."[16]

Once in Montevideo, Puig gave an address to the innocuously named Committee on Initiatives, which met in the first days of the conference to discuss the changes that Mexico proposed to the economic sections of the agenda. In a surprisingly rousing speech, Puig defended Mexico's proposals by arguing for a radical change to the very meaning of international credit: it should be understood, he argued, not as a technical economic science, but as "a 'social function' the same as property." Much as Mexico's revolutionary constitution of 1917 redefined property rights as vested not in the individual, but in the nation, Puig's proposal sought to reveal the *social* character of international finance, and to create institutions that would serve its social function. He called for "a new legal and philosophic conception of credit" that recognized that "credit is not an act of charity." Just as borrowers needed capital for their industrialization and development efforts, he noted, lenders needed to make productive use of their surplus capital. Therefore, he argued, "exactly the same service is rendered by the party who grants the loan as by the party that takes it." The Mexican proposals, including the creation of a new multilateral lending institution, would therefore embody "something logically, decidedly, systematically and firmly on behalf of 'the many' as against the unjust privileges and interests of the few."[17]

The United States had come to Montevideo hoping to put off any discussion of the Mexican economic proposals; they were already facing the radical redefinition of US political and military prerogatives in the region with Latin American proposals to formally codify nonintervention.[18] Against the best efforts of Secretary of State Cordell Hull, however, Puig's ideas became a central preoccupation of the conference over the following days, and proposals for an Inter-American

---

[16] See México, Secretaria de Relaciones Exteriores, *Temario Económico Financiero Sometido Por México a La Septima Conferencia Internacional Americana* (México: Imprenta de la Secretaría de Relaciones Exteriores, 1934).

[17] José Manuel Puig Casauranc, *Remarks on the Position Taken by Mexico at Montevideo* (Mexico: Ministry of Foreign Affairs, 1934), 23. This English translation was published and distributed by the Mexican government after the conclusion of the conference.

[18] At Montevideo, the United States acceded to the Charter of Right and Duties of States, which forbade intervention in the internal affairs of another state. On this, see Greg Grandin, "The Liberal Traditions in the Americas: Rights, Sovereignty, and the Origins of Liberal Multilateralism," *The American Historical Review* 117:1 (February 1, 2012) and Arnulf Becker Lorca, *Mestizo International Law* (Cambridge: Cambridge University Press, 2014).

economic organization and a multilateral bank were put forward by representatives of Mexico, Peru, and Uruguay.[19] After days of deliberation, the
subcommittees considering the various proposals produced a joint report,
which recommended the creation of an Inter-American Economic and
Financial Institute (which would replace the High Commission in
Washington), under which would be created an Inter-American Bank.
The Bank, the delegates argued, would be a "cooperative and associated
instrument" of the central banks and "a regulator of credit and currency,"
and thereby would rectify what they saw as massive imbalances in an
"unhinged" international financial system, and thereby would "improve
the onerous conditions in which many of the Latin American countries
negotiate their foreign loans."[20] Argentina's Carlos Saavedra Lamas – who
disagreed with Mexico's debt proposals, as his country was one of the few
that had not defaulted, and called Puig's plan "a sort of continental
bankruptcy"[21] – argued that the proposals should be considered at a later
date, rather than by the Montevideo delegates. Puig insisted that they be
placed on the agenda of the forthcoming, but as yet unplanned, Third Pan
American Financial Conference, to take place in Santiago, Chile.[22]

Mexico's interventions, however, did not end with the referral of Puig's
proposals to a future conference. After finally securing support from
a reluctant White House to do so, US Secretary of State Cordell Hull
gave a speech to the conference railing against economic nationalism, and
laying forth his free-trade vision for the hemisphere. Though some
US historians recall the proposal as a diplomatic triumph for Hull, contemporary observers noted that his proposal "met with a mixed
reception."[23] Puig led the criticism of the Hull proposal. Every nation,
Puig noted, wanted an increase in trade among the member nations, but,
he continued, "economic recovery, both national and international,

---

[19] These proposals can be found in Inter-American Conference (7th: 1933: Montevideo,
Uruguay), *Plenary Sessions: Minutes and Antecedents, Fourth and Ninth Committees:
Economic and Financial Problems* (Montevideo, 1933), 30.

[20] "Statement of motives concerning the establishment of an Inter-American Economic and
Financial Organization," in Inter-American Conference (7th: 1933: Montevideo,
Uruguay), *Plenary Sessions*, 48–49.

[21] Inter-American Conference (7th: 1933: Montevideo, Uruguay), *Plenary Sessions*, 166.

[22] United States Department of State, "Seventh International Conference of American States
Held at Montevideo, December 3–26, 1933," *FRUS* IV (1933): 159–171.

[23] "Reciprocity Pacts Proposed by Hull," *New York Times*, December 13, 1933. For the
view of the Hull intervention at Montevideo as a diplomatic triumph, see Michael
Anthony Butler, *Cautious Visionary: Cordell Hull and Trade Reform, 1933–1937*
(Kent: Kent State University Press, 1998).

demands a revision of tenets and systems."[24] Prefiguring in some ways the terms-of-trade thesis that would come to define the theories of Raúl Prebisch and his Economic Commission for Latin America in the decades to come, Puig argued that Latin America consisted of "countries whose economy is of the colonial type, countries exporting raw products and necessarily importing manufactured products." This imbalance created deleterious effects on reserves and currency values, and, quite frequently, led countries to contract further debt to cover balance-of-payment problems – all of which had especially adverse impacts on the *workers* in the primary exporting countries. In such a situation, he argued, it was natural that countries should resort to tariffs, exchange controls, and import restrictions, precisely the instruments that Hull railed against. (In this criticism, Puig signaled toward the import substitution industrialization that was to define the Mexican economy in the postwar years.) Criticisms such as those leveled by Puig persisted as Hull moved forward with his reciprocal trade agenda in the United States. While the United States tried to assuage its critics with the creation of the Export-Import Bank in 1934, Mexico and other Latin American countries would continue to push for deeper cooperation through the creation of new international instruments and institutions.[25]

At around the same time as the creation of the Export-Import Bank, the United States also created the Exchange Stabilization Fund (ESF), a \$200 million pool of dollars used to buy and sell foreign currencies in order to prop up their values.[26] Congress authorized the creation of the ESF in 1934 with the profits from Roosevelt's devaluation of gold, allowed it to work in relative secrecy, and gave the Treasury Secretary full discretion over its use. The ESF is best remembered for being the instrument of the Tripartite Agreement with Great Britain and France in 1936, but this was not the Fund's first stabilization loan: in fact, the first transfer of dollars to stabilize a foreign currency was made in January of 1936, to none other than Mexico, with another agreement coming five years later, in 1941.

---

[24] "Statements made by Dr. J.M. Puig Casauranc on the subject of tariffs, in connection with the Hull Motion," December 12, 1933, in *Remarks on the Position Taken by Mexico at Montevideo*, 63.

[25] The *New York Times* reported, "When it appeared that the smaller nations might precipitate a deluge of denunciation on the United States tariff policy, Señor Saavedra Lamas adjourned the discussion until tomorrow without definite committee action on the proposal." "Reciprocity Pacts Proposed by Hull," *New York Times*, December 13, 1933.

[26] Anna J. Schwartz, "From Obscurity to Notoriety: A Biography of the Exchange Stabilization Fund," *Journal of Money, Credit and Banking* 29:2 (May 1997): 135–153.

Indeed, Mexican experts approached the negotiations around the second ESF agreement with the explicit goal of using the fund to promote Mexico's economic development. In February of 1941, US Treasury officials Harry Dexter White and Edward Foley traveled to Mexico. Though the documentary record of the trip is thin, it is clear that White traveled to Acapulco for a bankers' conference accompanied by his good friend Antonio Espinosa de los Monteros, who had been a Harvard classmate of his in the late 1920s and was then the head of Mexico's national development bank, Nacional Financiera.[27] White and Foley met with Mexican government officials as well as private bankers and businessmen, and came away with a clear understanding of the Mexican government's position on long-term development finance.[28] The US relationship with Mexico was, at the time, a quite complicated one: Mexico had in 1938 nationalized its petroleum industry, and there were difficult ongoing negotiations between oil companies and the Mexican government around compensation. The State Department, which was overseeing the negotiations, sought Treasury's help in determining how the United States might meet Mexico's demands: "It is State's idea that the time has come," wrote Frank Coe, assistant to White, "to discuss with Mexico what we may give to her so that the discussions concerning what we want from Mexico can be expedited."[29] What the United States wanted at that particular moment was the ability to transit planes protecting the Panama Canal through Mexican airfields, as well as access to strategic materials that would aid US support of the allies. State suggested that a Mexican negotiator be called to Washington to work out a deal, and so, in July of 1941, just a few months after White's return from Mexico, his old friend

---

[27] The two were so close, in fact, that Mexican economist Víctor Urquidi would later remember that White referred to Espinosa as "Tony" during the Bretton Woods conference a few years later. Víctor L. Urquidi, "Reconstruction vs. Development: The IMF and the World Bank," in *The Bretton Woods-GATT System: Retrospect and Prospect after Fifty Years*, ed. Orin Kirshner and Edward M. Bernstein (Armonk, NY: M. E. Sharpe, 1996), 50. Espinosa received his master's degree from Harvard in 1927; White was there beginning in 1925 and finished his PhD in 1930. Daniel Cosío Villegas was also at Harvard in 1925. See James W. Wilkie and Edna Monzón Wilkie, *Daniel Cosío Villegas: Un Protagonista de La Etapa Constructiva de La Revolución Mexicana* (Mexico, DF: El Colegio de Mexico, 2013) and Sarah Babb, *Managing Mexico: Economists from Nationalism to Neoliberalism* (Princeton: Princeton University Press, 2001), 30.

[28] White to Espinosa de los Monteros, Feb. 27, 1941, in National Archives and Records Adminstration (NARA) RG 56, Division of Monetary Research (hereafter TDMR) Box 51, Folder MEX/o/70 Records of Special Missions.

[29] Coe to Morgenthau, May 21, 1941 in NARA RG 56, Harry Dexter White Chronological File, Entry 360-P (hereafter HDWC), Box 4.

Antonio Espinosa de los Monteros arrived for negotiations. The resulting agreement between the old friends contained not just a new Exchange Stabilization Fund agreement, but also the resumption of the US silver purchase program, a promise of a reciprocal trade agreement, and the announcement of an Export-Import Bank loan as precursor to "other requests for credit for development in Mexico."[30] The Mexican government had successfully argued that currency stabilization alone would be insufficient: instead, they had secured a comprehensive development package that would come to serve as a model for future efforts.[31]

Even as these bilateral negotiations were underway, however, Mexican experts were still pushing for the creation of a permanent multilateral institution that would perform many of these functions: an Inter-American Bank. After the recommendations made at Montevideo, the idea of the creation of a bank was discussed again at meetings in 1936 in Buenos Aires and 1938 in Lima, but it was not until 1939 that the proposals began to take a more concrete shape.[32] In the context of the growing war in Europe, many Latin American delegates arrived at a September 1939 emergency meeting of Foreign Ministers in Panama demanding a plan to counter the economic dislocations that the war was causing throughout the hemisphere. US Under Secretary of State Sumner Welles presented a resolution on economic cooperation, but the Latin Americans expressed their dissatisfaction with what they saw as vague promises that relied only on Export-Import Bank loans and private finance.[33] The Mexican delegation, headed by Foreign Minister Eduardo Hay, responded by proposing the creation of "an inter-American financial institution of a permanent character," and the meeting agreed to create an Inter-American Financial and Economic Advisory

---

[30] Department of State Bulletin November 22, 1941; followed up on April 11, 1942 with "additional agreements for collaboration with Mexico."

[31] The 1941 stabilization agreement was so comprehensive, in fact, that a former International Monetary Fund official would later argue that it "contained the germ of the idea of combining regulatory and financial provisions that is so prominent a feature of the IMF." Joseph Gold, "Mexico and the Development of the Practice of the International Monetary Fund," *World Development* 16:10 (October 1988): 1127–1142.

[32] Eduardo Villaseñor, "Memorandum sobre el Banco-Interamericano," n.d., Archivo Histórico del Colegio de México (AHCM), Fondo Eduardo Villaseñor (FEV), Caja 32.

[33] Speech reproduced in US Department of State Publication 1983, *Peace and War: United States Foreign Policy, 1931–1941* (Washington, D.C.: U.S. Government Printing Office, 1943), 488–494.

Committee (IFEAC).[34] Then, less than a month later, at another Inter-American gathering – this one of Finance Ministers, in Guatemala – Mexico's Eduardo Villaseñor submitted a detailed proposal for the creation of an Inter-American Bank, and made explicit the role that such an institution would play in development finance: it should, he proposed, "act as a channeling agent for investment of capital intended to foment the economic development of the different countries of the Americas," while "avoiding in all cases the aspect of hegemony or privilege that [foreign] investment could represent in the internal econom[ies]" of the borrowing countries.[35]

After the Panama and Guatemala meetings, it was clear that the Latin Americans were not going let their proposals for a permanent, multilateral financial institution continue to be put off, so US officials decided that they needed to take an active role in its creation, to ensure US interests were protected. The US Treasury Department's Harry Dexter White, who had already been arguing for increased aid to both China and Latin America as a crucial component of US economic leadership in the world, stewarded the project via the IFEAC, which held its first consultations in Washington in December of 1939. He set about convincing his superiors of the utility of the Bank, arguing to Treasury Secretary Morgenthau that a multilateral institution would not only reduce the risk of default on the part of borrower countries, but also that with such a bank, "the charge of dollar diplomacy would be absent."[36] In this formulation, it was clear that US officials had learned from the criticisms that had been leveled against them over the preceding decades. They sought to take these lessons beyond the hemisphere. Assistant Secretary of State Adolf Berle, for example, came to argue that the Inter-American Bank might serve as a "laboratory study," in which the United States might develop techniques

---

[34] Quoted in David Green, *The Containment of Latin America: A History of the Myths and Realities of the Good Neighbor Policy* (Chicago: Quadrangle Books, 1971), 61. See also, *Diario de la reunión de consulta entre los ministros de relaciones exteriores de las repúblicas americanas* (Panamá: Talleres gráficos Panamá, 1939).

[35] "Iniciativa de México Que Fue Bien Recibida," *Excelsior* (Mexico City), November 16, 1939, in AHCM, FEV Caja 32 Exp 9. Pan American Union, "Inauguration of the Inter-American Financial and Economic Advisory Committee," *Bulletin of the Pan American Union* LXXIV:1 (January 1940): 1–7, and "First Meeting of Finance Ministers of the American Republics," *Bulletin of the Pan American Union* LXXIV:2 (February 1940): 61–70. Villaseñor would later call his work at this meeting "the most important public manifestation" of his career. Eduardo Villaseñor, *Memorias-Testimonio* (México: Fondo de Cultura Económica, 1974), 127–133, 257–281.

[36] White to Morgenthau, "Proposed Inter-American Bank," November 28, 1939, in NARA RG 56, HDWC Box 3, File 14.

that could later be used in Europe and elsewhere.[37] In other words, it was through the repeated demands of Mexican and other Latin American representatives that the US planners had come to see how a multilateral development institution might serve their emerging visions for a postwar world economy.

Over the next few months, a complicated negotiation among the various US planners involved in the IFEAC and the representatives of the Latin American countries came to a surprisingly quick resolution: in February of 1940, the IFEAC submitted to the member states a convention establishing the Inter-American Bank, along with a charter and bylaws for the new institution.[38] As conceived, the Mexican vision for an institution that would provide long-term development financing was fully integrated into the design of the Bank, and was, as one scholar has argued, one of the institution's most innovative features.[39] But while a handful of the Latin American countries signed on right away, there was fierce opposition to the new bank from Wall Street interests. The New York bankers made their stance clear to the Senate Banking and Currency Committee, which insisted on reviewing the charter before ratification. Despite multiple hearings, and the assurances of officials like Nelson Rockefeller and even President Roosevelt himself, Wall Street was not assuaged, and the charter was left to languish, abandoned by the Senate by 1942. Despite the US intransigence, however, Mexico's Eduardo Villaseñor continued to argue for the creation of the Bank in every available venue over the coming years, even as US planners began to take the lessons they had learned through the Inter-American Bank negotiations to the global stage.[40]

Soon after shepherding the charter for the Inter-American Bank through the IFEAC and overseeing the comprehensive Exchange Stabilization agreement with Mexico, Harry Dexter White began to consider much bigger plans for the postwar economy – just as Berle had predicted. Now, the United States would take these lessons in economic leadership to the global stage, as officials began to plan for an allied monetary conference, which would come to take place in the tiny hamlet

---

[37] Memorandum of Conversation re: Proposed Inter-American Bank, January 23, 1940, in FDR Presidential Library (FDR), Morgenthau Diaries, vol. 237, part 2, f. 266.

[38] See Green, *The Containment of Latin America*, 60–75, and Helleiner, *Forgotten Foundations*, 52–79, for a detailed accounting of the US negotiations involved.

[39] Helleiner, *Forgotten Foundations of Bretton Woods*, 63–66.

[40] Eduardo Villaseñor, "El Banco Interamericano," *El Trimestre Económico* 15:58(2) (1948): 177–193.

of Bretton Woods, New Hampshire. The extensive contact with Mexican economic planners over the course of the preceding years meant that the ideas that Mexico had championed were a crucial part of White's vision, and he sought the input of Mexican officials early in the process of his planning for Bretton Woods. During the wartime meeting of Foreign Ministers in Rio in January of 1942, White had signaled to the Latin Americans that he was working on a global stabilization fund, and began to lobby for their adherence to his plans. A few months later, in April of 1942, the Treasury Department went so far as to draw up an early agenda for their planned meeting, at which White envisioned that representatives from both Brazil and Mexico would prominently outline the benefits to their economies of the Bank and the Fund.[41]

In July of 1942, the IFEAC convened a conference in Washington to deal with the business interests of Axis countries in Latin America, and Mexico sent a delegation that included the young economist Víctor Urquidi. Urquidi spoke fluent English and was among the first generation of Mexicans to receive formal economics training, having studied at the London School of Economics. At a dinner banquet during the conference, Urquidi found himself sitting next to Harry Dexter White, who invited the young Mexican economist to meet with him in his office the following day.[42] There are no records of what was said during that meeting, but Urquidi departed with a copy of White's April 1942 draft of the plan for an International Stabilization Fund, with instructions to read it carefully and to convey it to central bank and finance ministry officials in Mexico. Urquidi returned to Mexico City and immediately did so. Urquidi was part of a group within the Office of Economic Studies at the Banco de México, which had been convened to address postwar plans for the Mexican economy, and they began to carefully follow proposals from both the United States and Great Britain for the postwar international economic institutions.[43] When the next draft of White's plan was officially circulated for comment in April of 1943, the Mexicans delegated a small

---

[41] Treasury even went so far as to draw up draft speeches for officials from Mexico, Brazil, and Great Britain in support of White's plans. "Conference on Agencies for International Monetary and Financial Cooperation," April 1942, NARA RG 56, Entry 360-O, Records of the Bretton Woods Agreements, 1938–46, Box 47.

[42] Urquidi, "Reconstruction vs. Development," 32.

[43] Eduardo Turrent y Diaz, *México en Bretton Woods* (México, DF: Banco de México, 2009), 26.

team, including Urquidi and Daniel Cosío Villegas, to draft a formal study of the plan.[44] It was on the basis of this study that a larger group of Mexican officials began to meet to consider the postwar plans, including Rodrigo Gómez of the Banco de México, who became a constant presence at meetings in Washington on the matter. Beginning in 1943, officials from the US Treasury, the Federal Reserve Board, and the New York Fed paid visits to Mexico for meetings on the topic, as did as the famed Argentine economist Raúl Prebish.[45]

Conventional histories of Bretton Woods write off Latin American participation in the conference as little more than a multilateral fig leaf covering US pretensions to power, and therefore assume that the many Latin American participants merely acquiesced to US plans.[46] This view was widespread at the time, as well: one British Treasury official objected to too much Latin American participation at the conference, arguing that "their function is to sign in the place for the signature."[47] But a study of Mexico's analysis of the US drafts reveals a much more contentious history, and demonstrates that the fight for development that Mexico had been waging for over a decade continued forcefully at Bretton Woods. One of the main objections raised in the Mexican study was regarding the institutionalization of US power in the new organization: it was not the selfless international project that some in the press had declared, the Mexican analysts wrote, but "rather, North American interests, prejudices, fears, and ideas have presided over it at a rather close distance."[48] With each subsequent draft release, the Mexican experts worried that the proposals were "turning away each time more from the possibility of resolving, or helping to resolve, the fundamental economic problem of the next few years: the profound disturbance that the excessive wealth of the United

---

[44] Banco de México, Departamento de Estudios Económicos, "El Proyecto Norteamericano de Establización Monetaria Internacional," Junio 1943, in Archivo General de la Nación Mexico (AGN), Fondo Particular García Robles, Caja 43, Exp 21. See also, "Comparación de los dos Proyectos Norteamericanas de Establización," AGN, Fondo García Robles, Caja 43, Exp 18, and related files in the AHCM, Fondo Víctor Urquidi (FVU).

[45] Urquidi, "Reconstruction vs. Development," 34.

[46] Eric Helleiner's recent revision of this history in *Forgotten Foundations* is a notable exception, as he makes clear the importance of the various Latin American interlocutors to White's planning.

[47] Sir Wilfred Eady to Padmore, January 12, 1944, TNA: Treasury Files, Papers of Lord Keynes, T247/27.

[48] Banco de México, "El Proyecto Norteamaericano," 6.

States represents in the world."[49] Mexico would stake its interventions at the Bretton Woods conference on counteracting that disturbance. While much attention was being devoted to the new Monetary Fund, the Mexican experts reiterated that the Fund would only be useful as part of a larger set of institutions that would address the particular problems of the less-industrialized world, especially primary commodity producers. Mexico should "consider not just the advantages and drawbacks of the Fund," but also champion the creation of "the other institutions whose organization and functions are already set down: the Bank of Reconstruction and Development, and, at least, an organization whose field of work will be the production, distribution and pricing of primary products."

Even as these preparatory documents were being drawn up, Antonio Espinosa de los Monteros and his colleague Rodrigo Gómez were in Washington for negotiations with Treasury officials for the bilateral Stabilization Fund agreement. During the last week of May 1943, Espinosa and Gómez met four times with White and his team. During those meetings, Espinosa again emphasized the need not just for currency stabilization, but for "long-term capital," as he had been advocating for years. White indicated to the Mexican team that his postwar plans would include the "other agencies for long-term capital" that Espinosa thought so vital.[50] These negotiations, which had been taking place over the course of the previous years, meant that while White was considering technical aspects of an international proposal, he was working out precisely how such agreements would be implemented in practice through negotiations *with Mexico*. And it had become clear to White, given this history, that Mexico was an important interlocutor for the forthcoming conference: by June of 1943, White argued to the State Department, "If we get agreement by the US, UK, Russia, and China on the main points in the draft, we shall probably want to get an indication from Minister Suarez as to his reaction."[51]

---

[49] Banco de México, SA, Conferencia Monetaria Internacional, Memorandum No. 3, "Orientación General para la Delegación Mexicana," n.d., folder marked July 10, 1943, AHCM, FVU Caja 9, Expediente 5.

[50] "Memorandum of a Meeting on the International Stabilization Fund," May 25, 1943, NARA RG 56, Memoranda of Conferences held in Harry Dexter White's Office, 1940–1945, (HDWO) Box 20.

[51] White to Messersmith, June 26, 1943, NARA RG 56, Entry UDUP/734A1, Division of Monetary Research – Latin America, Box 51, MEX/o/oo General Vol 1. White even told Morgenthau that he should meet with Suárez in Washington just before the meeting: "His representatives here are very helpful and are likely to prove invaluable at Bretton Woods in winning support for our views young the Latin American States." White to

And so the Mexican delegation arrived at Bretton Woods already unwavering advocates for the rights of what were variously called the small, poor, weak, or debtor states. A headline in Mexico City put it clearly before the conference began: "Mexico Will Seek Voice and Vote for the Weaker Nations at the Monetary Meeting."[52] This was especially important to Antonio Espinosa de los Monteros – Harry Dexter White's old Harvard friend Tony – and White passed on this emphasis to Morgenthau: "The Mexicans feel that many matters to be considered by the Fund involve questions of sovereignty," he wrote in a memo, "and that small countries have interests and responsibilities no less than the large countries."[53] At the conference, the Mexican delegation made this quite clear. On a proposal that gave the power to determine gold parities of currencies only to the most powerful nations – thereby, in the Mexican view, effectively removing the sovereignty over currency valuation from all but a few countries – Espinosa submitted a strenuous objection. He argued that the proposal was exactly the kind of relinquishment of sovereignty that the rich countries would never accede to, and they should not expect the poorer ones to have to do so. As such, he concluded, "the Mexican delegation will vote against the original formula because it shows a great disrespect for the problems of the smaller nations …. It presupposes that small countries will change their laws and perhaps even their constitutions at a minute's notice, regardless of political, social or economic difficulties."[54]

Of course, in arguing for the rights of the poorer countries – and the duties of the rich ones – the Mexican delegation was making an explicit argument about economic development, drawing on the experiences outlined above. As Víctor Urquidi would later remember, after the Inter-American Bank negotiations, the bilateral agreements with the United States, and their long study of US plans, "the Mexican delegation thus arrived at Bretton Woods ready to inject some interest

Morgenthau, Memorandum for the Secretary, June 24, 1944, in NARA RG 56, (BWA), Box 1.

[52] "Mexico Pedirá Voz y Voto para los Países Débiles en la Junta Monetaria," *Excelsior* (Mexico City), June 14, 1944.

[53] White to Morgenthau, June 23, 1944, NARA RG 56, BWA, Box 1.

[54] *Proceedings and Documents, United Nations Monetary and Financial Conference (1944: Bretton Woods, NH)* (Washington, D.C.: U.S. Government Printing Office, 1948), vol. II, 1179. The final provision included a clause for countries "large and small" to opt out of the provision with notice.

in economic development issues into the debate."[55] In an early session, Urquidi stood before Lord Keynes to read into the record a lengthy revision of a section of an article of the charter for the International Bank, arguing for the mobilization of resources equally for reconstruction *and* development. The statement echoed many of the sentiments previously expressed in negotiations over the Inter-American Bank: as the idea was to make an institution of permanent, and not temporary, character, development considerations would prove crucial once reconstruction of Europe had been accomplished. "In the very short run," Urquidi argued, "perhaps reconstruction will be more urgent for the world as a whole, but in the long run, Mr. Chairman – before we are all *too* dead, if I may say so – development must prevail if we are to sustain and increase real income everywhere. Without denying the initial importance of reconstruction, we ask you not to relegate or postpone development."[56] After this, Urquidi remembered, "there followed a silence. Keynes at one point shoved his eyeglasses to the tip of his nose, shuffled some papers ... and said something like this: 'With regard to the amendment submitted by Mexico, I think it can be made shorter and can be adopted by substituting equitable consideration for equal consideration.'"[57] With that, the fight that Mexico had been waging for a multilateral development institution over the preceding decade was, it seemed, won.

But the question of whether these new institutions would function as the Mexican experts hoped was still an open one – and skepticism emerged quickly. In 1945, Víctor Urquidi published an analysis of the new institutions in which he noted that, as they were constituted, they "didn't attack the root of the problem of investments for world economic development."[58] To address this shortcoming, Mexican experts like Eduardo Villaseñor continued to advocate for the creation of an Inter-American Bank, lobbying to resurrect the institution after its stall in the US Senate.[59] One crucial aspect that Mexican economists continued to emphasize was the need for a comprehensive trading

[55] Urquidi, "Reconstruction vs. Development," 40.
[56] *Proceedings and Documents, United Nations Monetary and Financial Conference*, vol. II, 1176.
[57] Urquidi, "Reconstruction vs. Development," 42.
[58] Víctor L. Urquidi, "Elasticidad y Rigidez de Bretton Woods," *El Trimestre Económico* 11:44(4) (January 1945): 595–616.
[59] Eduardo Villaseñor, "El Banco Interamericano."

framework, to complement the credit and stabilization that the Bretton Woods institutions were supposed to offer. So experts in Mexico began to look to the proposed International Trade Organization (ITO), and developed detailed proposals for the Havana Charter in 1948, including trade regulations that would help stimulate industrialization and support primary commodity prices, as well the creation of development and employment programs within the ITO itself.[60] Mexico's long fight for development – and for international institutions and agreements that would secure and regulate it – would continue.

***

Histories of development that locate its origins in the genius of US experts – whether beneficent or avaricious – ignore the sustained history of demands for development emanating from Latin America, and the struggles they waged to create institutions for it. When Franklin Delano Roosevelt looked to Latin America in 1940 and famously decided it was time for the United States to "give them a share," it was not because he spontaneously reconsidered the history of his country's financial penetration of the region. It was because of the repeated, forceful demands made on him by Latin Americans. Often forgotten is the second part of Roosevelt's formulation: "They think they're just as good as we are," he told reporters, "and many of them are."[61] Condensed in that admission was a grappling with not only the place of the United States in the global economy, but the importance of Latin America to how that economy would be governed.

In overlooking Latin America, then, we obscure how US planners came to understand and create many of the tools they would use to manage the United States' new global power. As Mark Mazower has recently argued, "What really demands explanation is why first the British, at the height of their world power, then the Americans should have invested time and political capital in building up international institutions at all."[62] Just how

---

[60] Jill M. Jensen, "Negotiating a World Trade and Employment Charter: The United States, the ILO and the Collapse of the ITO Ideal," in *The ILO from Geneva to the Pacific Rim*, ed. Jill M. Jensen and Nelson Lichtenstein (London: Palgrave Macmillan, 2016), 83–109. For the Mexican proposals at Havana, see United Conference on Trade and Employment, "Draft Charter, Mexico: Proposed Amendments," E/CONF.2/11/Add.3, 3 December 1947.

[61] Press Conference of January 12, 1940, No. 614-A, FDR President's Personal File No. 1P.

[62] Mazower acknowledges that "much more will certainly be written from the vantage point of what was once known as the Third World to reframe the version of history told here,"

did the United States come to see international development via multi-lateral organizations as in their interest? In recovering the history outlined above, we can decenter the origins of development, and see that in countries like Mexico in the 1930s, development was not understood as something to be *done to* them – it was, rather, a central principle of their vision for a more equitable international economic order. This is a difficult history to tell with our existing theoretical frameworks: in theories of both diffusionist modernization and dependent development, powerful states act, weak ones react; powerful countries and capitalist imperatives shape the parameters within which weak countries operate, but the actions of the weak countries never penetrate those parameters. In attempting to explain why states like Mexico lack political and economic power, these theories actually naturalize this lack: the United States is always already powerful, and always already understands and deploys the mechanisms for the projection of its power. But by examining the history of development from the perspective of a country like Mexico, we can begin to understand the exchange between center and periphery – of activists, diplomats, and intellectuals; the ideas with which they analyzed their world; and the policies they put in place to shape it – not as a one-way diffusion from West to rest, but a multidirectional and reciprocal process unevenly structured by power. We can come to see that it was, in fact, through the process of responding to the demands made by Mexican and Latin American experts that US planners learned how development might be a useful idiom for global economic power, and shaped the institutions that would govern it. If we shift our perspective, we can see that Mexico did, indeed, have the theories – and that development was, just as Berle put it so presciently, learned in the laboratory of Latin America.

but his intention is to focus on European and American actors "who were primarily responsible for originating the institutional and conceptual apparatus." Mark Mazower, *Governing the World: The History of an Idea* (New York: Penguin Press, 2012), xv–xviii.

I4

Nasser, Hammarskjöld, and Middle East Development in Different Scales of Space and Time

Nathan J. Citino

"I do not aim at a complicated philosophical discussion of 'time and place,' but there is no doubt that the world, and not our country only, is the result of the action of time and place."
–Gamal 'Abd al-Nasser, *The Philosophy of the Revolution* (1955)

Narrative has proven to be both a useful analytical concept and a vexing problem in the history of development. On one hand, historians who study development as a twentieth-century discourse of power have zeroed in on the narrative techniques employed by elites to legitimize their attempts at engineering social and economic change. Much of the early scholarship, observes Joseph Hodge, focused on "the metaphorical language of development, on viewing development as a form of writing or 'text', with narrative qualities, story plot lines, and various actors." Jonathan Crush similarly notes that development texts are written in "a language of metaphor, image, allusion, fantasy, and rhetoric."[1] Recognizing these techniques has given scholars an external position from which to criticize development as a political tool, a useful collection of stories promising future societal improvements in exchange for elite authority over the present. On the other hand, historians are themselves in the business of constructing narratives, of describing how change unfolds within strategically defined horizons of space and time. Historians of development face the particular challenge of writing about future-oriented narratives. In framing inherited conceptualizations of change

---

[1] Joseph Morgan Hodge, "Writing the History of Development (Part 1: The First Wave)," *Humanity*, February 10, 2016, http://humanityjournal.org/issue6-3/writing-the-history-of-development-part-1-the-first-wave/ (accessed January 17, 2017); *The Power of Development*, ed. Jonathan Crush (New York: Routledge, 1995), 4.

both spatially and temporally, scholars risk internalizing the world views of the elites whom they study. These problems confront a critical history of development especially given that available primary sources tend to record elites' prescriptive visions rather than the experiences of the ordinary men and women such as peasants, workers, and refugees who were the focus of development schemes. Writing a critical history therefore requires not only recognizing the narrative elements present within development discourses but also analyzing the ways that elites themselves employed time and space, both in conflicts with one another and as strategies for sustaining their authority during a revolutionary age.

This chapter grapples with the problems of writing development history by examining two development schemes for the postcolonial Middle East defined according to different scales of space and time. It juxtaposes Gamal 'Abd al-Nasser's vision for Egyptian national development and Arab leadership with a scheme promoted by the UN Secretary-General Dag Hammarskjöld for regional development of the Arab world. Both men subscribed to a postwar consensus that favored elite planning, economic growth, and "balanced development." But they differed in their regard for the nation-state as a sufficient unit for pursuing development; in their perspective on the Arab region and its oil-producing periphery; and in imagining a timetable for progress. For Nasser, the burdens of national leadership focused his attention on developing Egypt within the horizon of five-year plans and led him to perceive the Middle East as a contested space in which Egypt vied for influence with other Arab states and Israel. Hammarskjöld, by contrast, sought to apply the universal postwar concept of "balanced development" regionally to the Arab Middle East, which was divided sharply between haves and have-nots, as well as to a global economy partitioned by the Cold War. Drawn into managing successive crises, the UN Secretary-General nonetheless sought to lay the foundations for long-term regional development in the intervals between crises. But the crosscurrents of the Arab-Israeli conflict, Nasser's rivalries with other Arab leaders, and the interests of the United States, Britain, and major oil companies prevented Nasser and Hammarskjöld from realizing an important opportunity for investing oil wealth and establishing a redistributive mechanism that could contribute to greater equality across the Arab region. Although this account focuses on the Arab Middle East, it demonstrates the usefulness of situating development within alternative geographic scales. It shifts among global, regional, and national frames, and even considers the local implications of development from the perspective of Palestinians living in the Gaza Strip, where the United Nations and Egypt ambiguously shared authority following the 1956 Suez War. My approach therefore carves out analytical space between the partially overlapping visions of Nasser and Hammarskjöld, playing on their discrepancies as well as similarities to understand their agendas without adopting the parameters of either man's developmental vision.

As the young colonel who led the Free Officers' coup in July 1952, Nasser came to embody the hopes of many Egyptians for revolution against a corrupt party system, colonial occupation, the British-aligned monarchy, an extreme concentration of landownership, and staggering inequality. While consolidating political power and negotiating the withdrawal of British forces from the Suez military base, however, Nasser simultaneously confronted the dilemmas inherent in postcolonial economic development. These included reconciling the redistribution of land with increasing agricultural productivity, and pursuing state-administered industrialization without alienating foreign and domestic sources of capital. Accumulating capital posed a serious challenge to promoting industrial-sector growth in Egypt, and Nasser's shifts in policy can be explained in large part as attempts at addressing it. As Robert Vitalis has shown, the Free Officers pursued a strategy of state administration and ownership of industry earlier than previously thought. This strategy was apparent in the regime's 1955 anti-monopoly measures that broke up "the pattern of centrally controlled, cross-sectoral holdings and interlocking directorates" on which entrepreneurial families had based their control of the economy following its Egyptianization a generation earlier. This "nationalization by degree" of domestic capital advanced from the mid-1950s, when the regime pressured financial firms to accept officially approved board members and expropriated certain properties of the leading oligarch Muhammad 'Abbud, through the nationalization decrees of summer 1961 and the establishment of Arab Socialism. Nasser also courted foreign sources of capital, such as Anglo-American and World Bank funding for the Aswan High Dam. When the United States rescinded its offer, Nasser nationalized the Suez Canal as an alternative source of funds and sequestered British and French assets in response to the military invasion that those countries launched together with Israel. He also turned to the Soviet Union as a source of low-interest credit that could be repaid with Egyptian cotton.[2]

[2] Robert Vitalis, *When Capitalists Collide: Business Conflict and the End of Empire in Egypt* (Berkeley: University of California Press, 1995), 204, 215. See also, Guy Laron,

Although Nasser is remembered for his charisma, displayed most vividly during his dramatic July 1956 speech nationalizing the canal, he also promoted technocratic management of the economy and proved adept at constructing politically useful development narratives.[3] For instance, at a time when his regime was pursuing land reform, Nasser portrayed Egypt's nineteenth-century Ottoman governor, Muhammad 'Ali Pasha, as a foreigner who burned cultivators' titles and expropriated Egyptian land for his Turco-Circassian retinue; yet the 1962 National Charter inaugurating Arab Socialism lionized Muhammad 'Ali as the father of modern Egypt who demonstrated the sort of leadership needed for carrying out sweeping reforms.[4] In *The Philosophy of the Revolution,* Nasser famously alluded to Luigi Pirandello's play "Six Characters in Search of an Author" and situated Egypt's national revolution spatially within the "three circles" of the Arab world, the Islamic community, and Africa. The Arab circle he described as the most important, in part because of petroleum, the "vital nerve of civilization" and an "element of power" in Arab relations with the rest of the world.[5] Such narrative elements helped to bridge a divide between the bureaucratic planning that characterized Egyptian development policies and the popular support for Egypt's revolution that made Nasser into a hero of Arab nationalism and anti-colonialism.

To understand the regime's economic development policies during the 1950s, historians have looked to Rashid al-Barrawi, the economist who designed Egypt's land reform and served on the Permanent Council for the Development of National Production. According to historian Roel Meijer, al-Barrawi conceived of a "revolution from above, technocratic rationalization of the economy through planning, and politics as 'administration.'" A nonrevolutionary socialist who had studied at the London School of Economics, al-Barrawi was influenced by both the Fabianism of Beatrice and Sidney Webb and the democratic socialism of Harold Laski.

Origins of the Suez Crisis: Postwar Development Diplomacy and the Struggle over Third World Industrialization, 1945–1956 (Baltimore, MD: Johns Hopkins University Press, 2013).

[3] For the nationalization speech, see "*Khitab al-ra'is Gamal 'Abd al-Nasser fi 'id al-thawra al-rabi' min al-Iskandariya 'al-khitab ta'mim al-qanat al-suways'*," http://nasser.org/Speeches/browser.aspx?SID=495&lang=ar, accessed January 17, 2017.

[4] See Rashid al-Barrawi, *Al-Falsafah al-iqtisadiyah lil-thawrah: min al-nahiyatayni al-nazariyah wa-al-'ilmiyah* (Cairo: Maktabat al-Nahdah al-Misriyah, 1955), 2; and United Arab Republic, *Draft of the Charter,* May 21, 1962 (Cairo: Information Department, 1962).

[5] Gamal Abdel Nasser, *The Philosophy of the Revolution* (Buffalo: Economica Books, 1959), 61, 72, 74.

Al-Barrawi "rejected the argument that the contradiction between the forces of production and the relations of production must necessarily find a new equilibrium through violent revolution."[6] In *The Economic Philosophy of the Revolution*, al-Barrawi's own manifesto written to complement Nasser's, the economist emphasized that in addition to agricultural reforms, the state would have to undertake industrial planning to achieve the economic growth necessary to keep pace with the population. It would have to assume unprecedented functions to foster a "balanced economic system [*nizam iqtisadi mutawazin*]." Al-Barrawi wrote that the state would also need to mobilize all sources of capital for industrialization, including gold reserves and foreign aid, while creating "the environment for investment [*al-biy'a al-istithmariyya*]" and "incentives [*hawafiz*] that could motivate private capital large and small, domestic and foreign." He concluded by citing the American economic historian George Henry Soule, advocate of a "mixed" economy, whose study of great economists al-Barrawi had personally translated into Arabic.[7] Al-Barrawi's agenda therefore applied the universal postwar values of planning, growth, and "balance" in a mixed economy to the task of developing the Egypt state.

In January 1957, Nasser's government created an Economic Organization to administer sequestered Anglo-French properties and set up a National Planning Council and National Planning Committee. The government then announced a five-year industrial plan in April.[8] Nasser's speech delivered at Cairo University later that year defined the country's post-Suez economic goals. The speech added the recent tripartite aggression against Egypt to the long record of imperial oppression under the British, French, and Ottomans. Nasser repeated the commitment made in *Philosophy of the Revolution* to promoting "side-by-side" political and social revolutions in Egypt. But he also presented a compressed timetable for Egypt's industrial development, promising that the five-year industrial plan would begin showing results after only three years. It would employ a million workers, speeding up Egypt's industrialization to compensate for a century of underdevelopment while providing work, food, and output for the 350,000 new Egyptians born every year. Emphasizing the state's need to work with private capital in the interest of industrialization, Nasser vowed to use state authority to

---

[6] Roel Meijer, *The Quest for Modernity: Secular Liberal and Left-Wing Thought in Egypt, 1945–1958* (New York: RoutledgeCurzon, 2002), 67, 72.

[7] Al-Barrawi, *Al-Falsafah al-iqtisadiyah lil-thawrah*, 53, 55, 102, 166–168.

[8] Meijer, *The Quest for Modernity*, 198–199.

protect the interests of small capitalists and those with savings. In an approach consistent with al-Barrawi's Fabianism, Nasser rejected class conflict but advocated economic supervision by the state to lessen class divisions, a "balanced" policy that Nasser described as fostering a "well-ordered system [*nizam mutanasiq*]."[9] Looking toward the future, Nasser vowed to implement an equally ambitious, second five-year plan. Given Egypt's need to finance industrialization on the timetable he envisioned, Nasser urgently needed capital. He therefore proved receptive to Hammarskjöld's post-Suez plans for regional economic development of the Arab Middle East, particularly if it meant gaining access to a share of Gulf states' oil revenue as the Secretary-General's scheme appeared to promise.

In terms of personality, Dag Hammarskjöld could not have drawn a greater contrast with the military officer Nasser, veteran of the 1948 Arab-Israeli war. Son of a Swedish politician and diplomat, the urbane Hammarskjöld practiced a quiet religious faith borrowed from botanist Karl Linnaeus and wrote contemplative poetry in Swedish. A "confirmed bachelor" who maintained a small circle of friends, the introverted Hammarskjöld was capable of what one acquaintance described as a "crushing efficiency." Alluding to Hammarskjöld's sexuality, however, biographer Roger Lipsey writes that the reputedly "monastic" Swede possessed a "whole, broken heart" and "to this we owe some part of his breadth and humanity."[10] Following his elevation to Secretary-General as a compromise candidate among the permanent members of the Security Council, Hammarskjöld worked to strengthen an institution that had faced not only a Soviet boycott but also charges leveled by Senator Joseph McCarthy that it was riddled with subversives and Red spies. Through careful public statements, candid meetings, and personal letters, Hammarskjöld sought to create a role for the United Nations in a divided world. Unlike Nasser, who regarded regional conflict in terms of state policy and whose perspective on Third World anti-colonialism emerged from attending the 1955 Bandung Conference of Afro-Asian states, Hammarskjöld approached the Middle East as one area of the world where regional cooperation faced the greatest obstacles. It was in the

---

[9] "*Khitab al-ra'is Gamal 'Abd al-Nasir fi mu'tamar al-ta'awuni bi-jami'a al-Qahira*," December 5, 1957, http://nasser.org/Speeches/browser.aspx?SID=565&lang=en, accessed January 17, 2017.

[10] Brian Urquhart, *Hammarskjold* (New York: Knopf, 1972), 22; Roger Lipsey, *Hammarskjöld: A Life* (Ann Arbor: University of Michigan Press, 2013), 100, 112.

Middle East under his leadership that the United Nations largely defined its distinct peacekeeping, humanitarian, and development functions.[11]

Despite their opposing styles and career paths, Hammarskjöld shared with Nasser and other postwar leaders a faith that technocratic management could foster economic growth and transcend political and class conflicts. After earning his economics PhD from the University of Stockholm, Hammarskjöld served in the Swedish Finance Ministry under Fabian socialist economist Ernst Wigforss, whom he called his "second father."[12] Hammarskjöld's remarks to members of the UN Economic and Social Council, meeting in July 1957 to discuss the world economic situation, closely paralleled the language used by al-Barrawi in *The Economic Philosophy of the Revolution*. The leading question of the postwar decade, Hammarskjöld declared, had been "the question of achieving and maintaining economic balance while accelerating the rate of growth," and "[m]ost important in this respect is a proper balance between industrial and agricultural development." Countries "with high population densities," he noted, "are particularly dependent upon the expansion of industry for their economic development and the creation of adequate employment opportunities." From his perch as Secretary-General, however, Hammarskjöld believed that the shared problem of development could offer the basis for cooperation within regional groupings and even for gradual ideological convergence at the global level between "private-enterprise" and "centrally planned economies." With "similar problems of economic growth being faced by so many countries, and with regional arrangements for expanding markets being freely discussed," he declared, "the loosening of the bonds of doctrine in the field of economic policy presents us with an opportunity for serving the world economy." He concluded: "no more than individuals can countries 'live unto themselves.'"[13]

---

[11] See Andrew Gilmour, "The Role of the UN Secretary-General: A Historical Assessment," in *Land of Blue Helmets: The United Nations and the Arab World*, ed. Karim Makdisi and Vijay Prashad (Berkeley: University of California Press, 2016), 23–25.

[12] Urquhart, *Hammarskjold*, 22. See also, Hans Landberg, "The Road to the UN – The Emergence of the International Civil Servant," in *The Adventure of Peace: Dag Hammarskjöld and the Future of the UN*, ed. Sten Ask and Anna Mark-Jungkvist (New York: Palgrave Macmillan, 2005), 26–42.

[13] "Text of Statement by Secretary-General Dag Hammarskjold Opening Economic and Social Council Discussion of the World Economic Situation, Geneva, July 4, 1957," folder: Sec'y Gen Press Releases, Feb. 1–Dec. 19, 1957, S-0928–0001-05, Subject Files

FIGURE 14.1. Caption: Hammarskjöld and Nasser following the Suez War, Cairo, November 1956. Photo by Howard Sochurek/The LIFE Picture Collection/Getty Images.

Hammarskjöld personally confronted the challenges of Middle East diplomacy for the first time in April 1956, when the Security Council named him "agent-general" for the purpose of traveling to the region to

of the Secretary General Dag Hammarskjold, United Nations Archive [UNA], New York, New York.

shore up the beleaguered cease-fire agreements between Israel and the Arab states.[14] During that trip, Hammarskjöld met Nasser and established a particular *rapport* with the Egyptian foreign minister Mahmoud Fawzi. The Suez Crisis and War intervened, however, and Hammarskjöld was forced to focus his attention on establishing a United Nations Emergency Force (UNEF) for Gaza and Sinai and organizing the UN-led campaign to salvage ships that Egypt had scuttled to block the canal. These experiences fostered Hammarskjöld's sense that long-term regional development would have to be pushed forward aggressively in the relative calm between crises. In March 1957, his assistant Andrew Cordier explained to New York City planning czar Robert Moses:

Ever since last October we have been working seven days and seven nights a week on problems relating to the cease-fire, the withdrawal of troops, the operations of the United Nations Emergency Force, the clearance of the Suez Canal, interim arrangements for its operation, negotiations for permanent operation, and a whole host of other problems which, if properly handled, would lay the foundation for the handling of the large, long-range problems of the area.[15]

That same month, just prior to launching his five-year industrialization plan, Nasser told Hammarskjöld that while he was not interested in negotiating any final agreement with Israel, Egypt desired "peaceful conditions without a settlement."[16] As the Secretary-General explained to US Under Secretary of State Christian Herter, if "we manage to maintain the present degree of quiet around Israel, there may be a chance to approach the bigger problems of the area" before another crisis throws "the region back into an acute period of fever." For Hammarskjöld, "any approach to the Palestine situation must take the refugee question as its starting point."[17] He believed that addressing the plight of the 750,000 refugees driven from their homes by the establishment of Israel represented an initial step toward resolving the conflict and that it could

---

[14] See Urquhart, *Hammarskjold*, 138–149.
[15] Cordier to Moses, March 4, 1957, folder: AWC Middle East File, box 193, Andrew Cordier Papers [ACP], Rare Book and Manuscript Library, Butler Library, Columbia University, New York, New York.
[16] Quoted in Urquhart, *Hammarskjold*, 219.
[17] Hammarskjöld to Herter, June 17, 1957, folder: Middle East 17 June 57 Herter, Christian A. (Under-Secy of State USA), L179: 107, Dag Hammarskjöld Collection [DHC], National Library of Sweden, Stockholm.

proceed only on the basis of "co-responsibility" shared between Israel and the Arab states.[18]

A new crisis intruded before Hammarskjöld's efforts got off the ground, however, when the United States attempted to destabilize the Syrian government and Nasser landed 1,500 troops at Latakia in a move he described as protecting Syria from aggression by America's ally Turkey. The Soviet Union also came to Syria's defense at the United Nations.[19] Hammarskjöld told another US official that this "was not the time to take the initiative in solving the refugee problem."[20] Rather than confront the refugee crisis directly, Hammarskjöld decided that in the respite before the next crisis, he would pursue Arab economic cooperation that over the long term could potentially transform the region. The Secretary-General proposed utilizing capital from the Arab oil states to finance development projects in the resource-poor, more densely populated Arab countries. He would begin by gaining the support of Nasser, whom he would approach through Fawzi.

Hammarskjöld's plan drew inspiration from a variety of sources. In early 1957, staff from the World Bank drafted the charter for a regional development bank on behalf of the Arab League, which had proposed it four years earlier.[21] Per Jacobsson, managing director of the IMF, contacted Hammarskjöld in March to recommend promoting a community of interests between states lying east and west of the Suez Canal. This would be accomplished by encouraging oil-producing states to provide incentives to oil-transit countries including Egypt. After raising the idea at the Bilderberg Conference in February, Jacobsson claimed to have garnered support from CIA director Allen W. Dulles.[22] In June, Senator J. William Fulbright nominated David Rockefeller to lead an envisioned Middle East development

---

[18] See Aide-mémoire, August 16, 1957, folder: Middle East Refugees, 1957, L179: 107, DHC.

[19] See Salim Yaqub, *Containing Arab Nationalism: The Eisenhower Doctrine and the Middle East* (Chapel Hill: University of North Carolina Press, 2004), 147–180.

[20] Memorandum by Villard, September 19, 1957, folder: Refugees PCC 1950–1957 REF 1 General Policy & Plans, box 10, NEA Bureau, Office of the Country Director for Israel and Arab-Israel Affairs (NEA/IAI), Records Relating to Refugee Matters and Jordan Waters, 1957–1966 Lot 70 D 229, General Records of the Department of State, Record Group [RG] 59, National Archives and Records Administration [NARA], College Park, Maryland.

[21] Black to Hassouna, with attachments, January 15, 1957, folder: Middle East M.E. Development (Arab Dev. Bank, etc.) 1957–58, L179: 129: 2, DHC.

[22] Jacobsson to Hammarskjöld, March 19, 1957, folder: Middle East 1957–59 (Misc. Documents as put together by D.H.), L179: 116, DHC.

authority.[23] State Department official Herbert Hoover, Jr. proposed having oil-producing states and petroleum companies contribute a fixed percentage of their incomes to regional development; and Italian foreign minister Giuseppe Pella suggested that European countries repay their Marshall Plan loans into a Middle East development fund.[24] Another idea came from Lebanese minister Emile Bustani, who in December sent Hammarskjöld his article "Sharing Oil Benefits" published in *Middle East Forum*. Bustani proposed deducting 10 percent from the proceeds of Middle East oil operations annually before dividing royalties, taxes, and profits between oil companies and producing governments. This tithe "would form the capital for an Arab Development Bank which could finance development and industrial projects in the Arab World."[25] Hammarskjöld shared with all of these figures a sense that planning for the long-term economic development of the Middle East was essential to breaking the pattern of successive regional crises.

Hammarskjöld traveled to Cairo at the end of December 1957 to sell the idea of regional economic development to Nasser and Fawzi, who were then absorbed with Egypt's national development plans.[26] Nasser accepted the concept, but Hammarskjöld responded that "this was not enough" and "he wanted to know what the Egyptians could do to help bring the scheme to fruition." Nasser promised to sound out Saudi Arabia's foreign minister Prince Faysal, but the Egyptian leader believed that Iraq, the other major Arab oil producer besides Kuwait, would refuse to participate. The Iraqis were "interested only in their own development," Nasser reportedly said, "and would not be attracted by the idea of sharing" oil income.[27] Iraqi leader Nuri al-Sa'id was Nasser's rival for

[23] See Fulbright to Black, June 17, 1957, Papers of Eugene R. Black, World Bank Group Archives Holdings, http://pubdocs.worldbank.org/pubdocs/publicdoc/2015/4/2023014044 00312468/wbg-archives-1769156.pdf, p. 46. Accessed January 17, 2017. Thank you to Emily S. Abdow for locating this document.

[24] See minute by Morris, January 6, 1958, FO 371/133843, British National Archives [BNA], Kew, England. On the Pella Plan, see memorandum by Torbert, September 25, 1957, *Foreign Relations of the United States [FRUS], 1955–1957*, vol. 12, Near East Region; Iran; Iraq (Washington, D.C.: U.S. Government Printing Office, 1991), 584–585.

[25] Bustani to Hammarskjöld, December 30, 1957, and enclosed January 1958 issue of *Middle East Forum*, folder: Middle East 1957–59 (Misc. Documents as put together by D.H.), L179: 116, DHC.

[26] See Cordier to Lodge, December 3, 1957, folder: AWC: Middle East General File, box 193, ACP; and memo of talks in Cairo with Nasser and Fawzi, December 25–26, 1957, folder: Fawzi, Mahmoud/Dr., Minister for Foreign Affairs, Egypt/UAR 135 letters/memo./messages from D.H. 1956–61, L 179: 130, DHC.

[27] Minute by Dixon, December 30, 1957, FO 371/133843, BNA.

Arab leadership, and the pair waged a bitter propaganda war over Iraq's participation in the Anglo-American Baghdad Pact. Hammarskjöld nevertheless hoped that British officials and US banker John J. McCloy could help to bring the Iraqis along. McCloy had close ties with the oil companies, which shipped oil from the Gulf to Europe through the Suez Canal, and had quietly provided legal advice to Egypt about its post-nationalization Suez Canal Authority.[28] Hammarskjöld believed that McCloy's participation, together with that of World Bank president Eugene R. Black, could head off oil company opposition.[29] The Bank had fulfilled a similar role when it managed contributions on behalf of the United Nations for financing the canal salvaging operation.[30] Hammarskjöld had obviously anticipated objections to his plan, and he was right to expect opposition.

Having secured Nasser's support, Hammarskjöld sent a draft of his plan to British foreign secretary Selwyn Lloyd.[31] Citing other regional bodies such as a proposed Economic Commission for Africa and the Organization for European Economic Cooperation, Hammarskjöld argued that the Arab League had "too political a character to be a useful instrument" for coordinating regional development in the Middle East. The UN Secretariat should therefore take the initiative in proposing a Middle Eastern Economic Development Fund. It would be directed by a board consisting of finance ministers from the Arab states but be advised jointly by the Secretariat and World Bank. The Fund would negotiate credits for development projects initially from western governments and oil companies. Later, loans from oil-producing states within the region would provide a way for "the 'Haves' [to] channel part of their income to the 'Have-nots'." Potential sites for major projects included the Tigris Valley, Syrian plains, Jordan Valley, the Suez Canal, and irrigation in Egypt. The Fund's "guiding principle" would be to promote "balanced

---

[28] See memo for Fawzi from McCloy, with appendicies, April 1, 1957, folder: Fawzi, Mahmoud/Dr., Minister for Foreign Affairs, Egypt/UAR 135 letters/memo./messages from D.H. 1956–61, L179: 130, DHC; memos of Hammarskjöld conversations with Fawzi, March 24 and 26, 1957, Secretary – General – Suez Crisis – Meetings with Nasser & Fawzi in Cairo 21/3/1957–26/3/1957, S-370-0044-04, UNA.

[29] See de Seynes to Hammarskjöld, November 27, 1957, folder: Middle East Refugees, 1957, L179: 107, DHC; and Hammarskjöld to Fawzi, January 27, 1958, folder: Fawzi, Mahmoud/Dr., Minister for Foreign Affairs, Egypt/UAR 135 letters/memo./messages from D.H. 1956–61, L179: 130, DHC.

[30] See Hammarskjöld to Black, January 2, 1957, folder: Suez Canal Financing 1956–1958, L179: 129: 2, DHC.

[31] Hammarskjöld to Lloyd with attachment, January 6, 1958, FO 371/133843, BNA.

economic development" across the region in order to avoid "the dangers of a serious variation in economic progress as among the various Arab countries." Although not directly conceived as a plan for addressing the Palestinian refugee crisis, the Fund could help to foster the economic growth necessary for resettling refugees without adding to existing unemployment in the countries that accepted them. Hammarskjöld insisted that considerable resettlement would prove necessary even if a compromise were reached in which Israel agreed to take co-responsibility for repatriation. He informed the British that the Israeli prime minister David Ben-Gurion had reacted favorably when he broached the idea of regional development during a previous trip to Jerusalem.[32] The document concluded that sufficient "planning cannot be undertaken by any one Arab country," nor would any single Arab government "consider it possible on its own to take any initiative for resettlement." Although Hammarskjöld told Fawzi that the plan "must be detached completely from the refugee question," the Secretary-General confided in Swedish foreign minister Östen Undén that he intended it as an indirect approach to the refugee problem.[33]

Hammarskjöld appealed to Britain and the United States on Cold-War grounds, arguing that regional economic development would "check the present trend" in which have-not Arab countries such as Egypt and Syria sought aid from the Soviet Union.[34] But these arguments convinced neither Lloyd nor the US Secretary of State John Foster Dulles. Meeting on the sidelines of a Baghdad Pact conference in Ankara, the pair raised objections, with Lloyd in particular saying that the plan "played into Nasser's hands."[35] Officials at the Foreign Office worried that by "pumping into Egypt wealth generated in the oil-producing countries," the Fund would eliminate the political leverage over Nasser that the western powers exerted through offers of development assistance.[36] Revenues diverted from Iraq and Kuwait would also come at the expense of the sterling area, and rather than serving as a regional development authority the Fund

---

[32] See Dixon to Foreign Office, January 4, 1958, FO 371/133843, BNA.

[33] Hammarskjöld to Fawzi, January 27, 1958, cited above. See Hammarskjöld to Undén, January 27, 1958, folder: Middle East Conflict Economic Development (as put together by D.H. 1958), L179: 107, DHC.

[34] Dixon to Foreign Office, January 4, 1958, cited above.

[35] See Caccia to Foreign Office, January 5, 1958, FO 371/133843, BNA; and Memo of conversation by Reinhardt, January 30, 1958, *FRUS, 1958–1960*, 12: 35.

[36] See comments forwarded by Lord Hood to Foreign Office, January 10, 1958, FO 371/133843, BNA.

might simply become a means for the individual Arab states to "back each other's plans."[37] Representatives from Shell and British Petroleum told the Foreign Office that their companies and the major US firms opposed the scheme because the "'have' oil nations will not disgorge" and so "the oil companies are likely to be the victims."[38] McCloy initially expressed a willingness to support the plan in the face of such objections and argued that the World Bank and Secretariat could restrain Nasser, as they had done by providing behind-the-scenes counsel following his nationaliza-tion of the canal.[39] But Hammarskjöld correctly attributed a "lowering of McCloy's temperature" to Dulles' opposition.[40] Only Black remained "strongly in favor," predicting that oil-producing Arab countries might well generate $10 billion within a decade, thus accumulating more reserves than they could possibly spend on their own national development.[41]

The announcement by Nasser on February 1 that Egypt would join with Syria to form the United Arab Republic (UAR) forced Hammarskjöld to moderate his ambitions for a Middle Eastern Economic Development Fund. The Secretary-General had planned to travel to Baghdad to appeal directly to Nuri al-Saʿid. Hammarskjöld believed oil-rich Arab states that developed themselves in isolation did so at their peril. Responding to Nuri's objections, Hammarskjöld observed that "Iraq's unwillingness to share in any form its resources with other Arab countries" threatened "to isolate them in a way which certainly should worry Nuri." The Iraqi leader, wrote Hammarskjöld, "seems to underestimate badly the probable developments of oil revenues."[42] But Humphrey Trevelyan, the British ambassador to Iraq who joined Hammarskjöld's staff, thought that the Secretary-General should postpone his trip. In light of the UAR announce-ment, Trevelyan wrote, Nuri was likely to give Hammarskjöld a "flat refusal."[43] Trevelyan himself went to Iraq, where he found some support for the plan among finance minister Nadim Pachachi, diplomat Tawfiq al-

---

[37] Rickett to Thorold, January 24, 1958, FO 371/133844, BNA. On Kuwait and sterling, see Caccia to Foreign Office, January 5, 1958, cited above; and brief by Official Committee on the Middle East, January 14, 1958, FO 371/133843, BNA.

[38] Ayers to Gore-Booth, January 31, 1958, FO 371/133844, BNA.

[39] Dixon to Foreign Office, January 16, 1958, FO 371/133843, BNA.

[40] Hammarskjöld to Lloyd, January 27, 1958, folder: Middle East Conflict Economic Development (as put together by D.H. 1958), L179: 107, DHC.

[41] Ibid.; Minute by Morris, January 6, 1958, cited above.

[42] Hammarskjöld to Lloyd, February 11, 1958, folder: Middle East Conflict Economic Development (as put together by D.H. 1958), L:179: 107, DHC.

[43] Handwritten letter, Trevelyan to Lloyd, February 8, 1958, FO 371/133844, BNA.

Suwaydi, and former finance minister 'Ali Mumtaz al-Daftari, a longtime advocate of an Arab development bank. Nuri, however, proved to be "definitely hostile," on the stated grounds that the United States would be more likely to aid national development projects than those recommended by the proposed regional Fund. He also disliked the plan's redistributive intent, noting its resemblance in this respect to Bustani's proposal published in *Middle East Forum*. But Nuri opposed the idea most of all because Nasser was likely to gain personal control over the Fund, a concern that the UAR announcement increased dramatically.[44] Although Nuri conceded that Hammarskjöld's plan was not "simply a scheme for extracting money from the countries with oil for the benefit of those without," wrote a British diplomat, the Iraqi leader feared "that it might be turned in this way by an unscrupulous Nasser."[45] The Egyptian-Iraqi conflict intensified as the two Hashemite kingdoms of Iraq and Jordan negotiated an Arab Union to rival Nasser's UAR.[46] Hammarskjöld's hopes that regional economic development could promote cooperation among the Arab states and set the stage for addressing larger regional problems were therefore overtaken by Nasser's rivalry with Nuri. Both Egypt and Iraq began revising their national development plans to reflect their antagonistic conceptions of Arab unity.[47] Nasser, for his part, hoped that Syria would become a source of wheat for Egypt and a market for Egyptian industrial output.[48]

---

[44] A State Department official calculated that the UAR would control over a quarter of the "subscribed Arab capital" for a proposed Arab development bank that was similar in conception to Hammarskjöld's Fund. See Wiens to Bell, "Comments on Federation of Arab Development Bank," February 20, 1958, folder: General Subject – Economic Development Middle East Development Fund Proposals 1958 6., box 11, General Subject Files Relating to the Middle East, 1955–1958, Lot 61 D12, RG 59, NARA.

[45] Michael Wright to Denis Wright, February 25, 1958, FO 371/133844, BNA.

[46] See Yaqub, *Containing Arab Nationalism*, 193. On negotiations between Iraq and Jordan, see Tawfiq al-Suwaydi, *Mudhakkirati: nisf qarn min ta'rikh al-Iraq wa-l qadiya al-'Arabiya* (Beirut: Dar al-Katib al-'Arabi, 1969), 580. On Nuri's concerns about the economic costs of federation with Jordan, see Charles Tripp, *A History of Iraq*, rev. ed. (New York: Cambridge University Press, 2000), 145; and Phebe Marr, *The Modern History of Iraq*, 3rd ed. (Boulder, CO: Westview Press, 2012), 76–77.

[47] On Iraq's plans for economic development within the Arab Union with Jordan, see Dixon to Foreign Office, March 26, 1958; and Foreign Office to UK Mission to the United Nations, March 27, 1958, FO 371/133844, BNA.

[48] See Elie Podeh, *The Decline of Arab Unity: The Rise and Fall of the United Arab Republic* (Portland, OR: Sussex Academic Press, 1999), 68–84; and James P. Jankowski, *Nasser's Egypt, Arab Nationalism, and the United Arab Republic* (Boulder, CO: Lynne Rienner Publishers, 2002), 120–122.

In the wake of the UAR announcement, Hammarskjöld circulated a memo drafted by Trevelyan that offered a revised version of the plan. The revised plan defined the Fund in mostly negative terms:

> The scheme now under consideration is not one to 'Arabize' Iraqi or Saudi Arabian oil revenues. Its purpose is not to transfer revenues from the oil producing Arab countries to the other members of the organization. There is no suggestion of demands on the oil companies for the benefit of the institution. There is no intention that one part of the Arab world should be favoured at the expense of another. The scheme should not conflict in any way with other schemes now under consideration for the constitution of special funds for the development of under-developed countries.[49]

One British official pointed out that the revised document is "still very vague on the essential point of where the capital is to come from," while Dulles's subordinates at the State Department told Hammarskjöld that they could not offer "even acceptance in principle at the present time."[50] Although the United States declined to endorse the plan on the technical grounds that it would prejudice ongoing negotiations over compensation for the Suez nationalization, Washington's Ambassador to the United Nations, Henry Cabot Lodge, admitted that the United States opposed giving Nasser any opportunity to "play oil politics."[51] Oil company executives were reportedly "much relieved" that they would not be forced to contribute to the Fund, and McCloy openly voiced his opposition for the first time.[52] In any case, a major new regional crisis soon erupted involving a clash between Nasserists and their opponents in Lebanon. Hammarskjöld became directly involved through the establishment of a United Nations Observation Group in Lebanon (UNOGIL) charged with monitoring infiltration into Lebanon from the Syrian region of the UAR.[53] Civil war in Lebanon was quickly followed by a revolution in Iraq that overthrew the Hashemite monarchy and, in a grim validation of Hammarskjöld's earlier warnings, resulted in Nuri's murder. The United States landed marines in Lebanon, and the British dispatched troops to

---

[49] Memo by Trevelyan, March 12, 1958, FO 371/133844, BNA.
[50] Moore to Wright, March 14, 1958, FO 371/133844, BNA; Rountree to Dulles, April 5, 1958, folder: General Subject – Economic Development Middle East Development Fund Proposals 1958 6., Box 11, General Subject Files Relating to the Middle East, 1955–1958, Lot 61 D12, RG 59, NARA.
[51] Dixon telegram to Foreign Office, March 24, 1958, FO 371/133844, BNA. See also, printed transcript of talks with Hammarskjöld, April 1, 1958, ibid.
[52] Minute by Gore-Booth, April 10, 1958; Thorold to Gore-Booth, April 21, 1958, ibid.
[53] Regarding UNOGIL, including reports about infiltration, see documentation contained in L179: 104, DHC.

Jordan to support the government of King Husayn.[54] The crisis brought an abrupt end to the relative calm in which Hammarskjöld had tried to lay the groundwork for regional economic development.

Although Hammarskjöld's defeat appears inevitable given the opponents arrayed against him, a comparison between his plan and Nasser's policies can serve as the basis for historical criticism of development in the Arab Middle East during the late 1950s.[55] Such an analysis must consider not only elite politics but also how these development visions might have appeared to their intended beneficiaries "on the ground." A central consideration is the degree to which political legitimacy in the postcolonial era came to be associated with the sovereign national state. As Matthew Connelly has shown in his study on Algeria, the growth of the UN General Assembly, the diffusion of development as a universal value, and an increasingly transnational environment for intellectuals and the media served ultimately to reinforce state sovereignty as a global norm. In 1959, Hammarskjöld met French president Charles De Gaulle, who previewed his plan conceding the principle of self-determination to Algerian anti-colonialists. Later that year, a US abstention in a key UN vote seriously hampered De Gaulle's attempts at working out a compromise with the *Front de Libération Nationale* that amounted to something less than full Algerian independence.[56] As a military officer and nationalist hero, Nasser therefore found greater political support among Egyptians for his economic plans than Hammarskjöld did across the Arab Middle East, because the Secretary-General's scheme granted supranational bodies paternalistic authority over Arab governments. Plans to tap oil wealth for regional development also confronted nationalist rivalries among Arab states, such as between Egypt and Iraq. Finally, stateless Palestinians looked with suspicion on both Egypt and the United Nations, which subordinated Palestinians' political demands to visions for either national or regional economic development.

As previously mentioned, the pair subscribed to the postwar consensus in favor of economic planning, growth, and balanced development. But

---

[54] See Yaqub, *Containing Arab Nationalism*, 205–236; and Irene L. Gendzier, *Notes from the Minefield: United States Intervention in Lebanon and the Middle East, 1945–1958*, rev. ed. (New York: Columbia University Press, 2006), 229–337.

[55] For an important interpretation, see Cyrus Schayegh, "1958 Reconsidered: State Formation and the Cold War in the Early Postcolonial Arab Middle East," *International Journal of Middle East Studies* 45 (August 2013): 421–443.

[56] Matthew Connelly, *A Diplomatic Revolution: Algeria's Fight for Independence and the Origin of the Post-Cold War Era* (New York: Oxford University Press, 2002), 205, 211.

they also shared the high-modernist tendency to regard underdeveloped peoples in the aggregate and to represent them quantitatively as inter-changeable units within large-scale plans.[57] For Nasser, this tendency was apparent in his portrayal of Egypt's development as a race between the growth of the economy and that of the population. It was for this reason that he described the 1957 industrial plan as "speeding up" Egypt's development to make up for a century of supposed stasis and to provide for the hundreds of thousands of Egyptians born annually. Nasser later told a former American official: "I am haunted by the birth of nearly 800,000 new people each year."[58] His government therefore pursued population control policies alongside industrialization, but Nasser was personally skeptical that rural peoples would adopt contraception. "You know," Nasser explained later, "here in the cities we have the cinema and television to occupy us in the evenings, but in the villages making love is the only way that a man can find any pleasure."[59]Hammarskjöld exhibited a similar tendency in his descriptions of Palestinian refugees. He repeatedly referred to the capacity of development projects to employ given numbers of refugees as "manpower" without regard for differences in social class, occupation, or educational levels, let alone for the desires of Palestinians themselves.[60] Only rarely does the researcher encounter individual Palestinians or communities in the Secretary-General's papers, such as in the petitions of owners whose properties had been taken over by Israel.[61]

Judging from available sources, Palestinians living in the Gaza Strip during this period held deeply ambivalent attitudes toward the authority of both the United Nations and the Egyptian government. Gaza serves as a microcosm of Hammarskjöld's proposed regional economic

---

[57] See James C. Scott, *Seeing Like a State: How Certain Schemes to Improve the Human Condition Have Failed* (New Haven: Yale University Press, 1998).

[58] Polk to Battle, November 16, 1965, folder: POL 7 Visits. Meetings. UAR 1965., box 2, NEA Bureau, Office of the Country Director for the United Arab Republic (NEA/UAR) Records Relating to United Arab Republic Affairs, 1961–1966, RG 59, NARA.

[59] Memo by Polk, November 20, 1968, folder 13, box 26, Papers of the Adlai Stevenson Institute of International Affairs, Special Collections Research Center, Regenstein Library, University of Chicago, Chicago, IL.

[60] For "manpower," see Hammarskjöld to Lloyd, January 6, 1958, cited above, p. 5 of attachment.

[61] See Mohammad T. el Daoudi and Antoine F. Al bina, Moslem Christian Association of Property Owners – Jerusalem to Hammarskjöld, December 2, 1957; Mukhtar Ghannameh, Mukhtar Baggarah, and "The Land lords of the De militarized Zone" to Hammarskjöld, December 1, 1957, folder: Sec'y General's trips – Correspondence & Cables – Nov– Dec 1957, S-01590004–09, UNA.

cooperation with Nasser, because following the withdrawal by Israeli forces the territory came under *de facto* control of the UNEF at the same time that Nasser sought to restore Egyptian administration in Gaza. The United Nations Relief and Works Agency (UNRWA) provided for the daily needs of more than 200,000 refugees, or two-thirds of those living in the Strip.[62] Hammarskjöld would feature the UN's humanitarian role during his tour of Gaza in late 1957. The Secretary-General observed food distribution at the Jabaliya refugee camp, visited the Burayj tuberculosis hospital, toured refugee homes in the Nuseirat camp, and inspected the Rimal Girls' School.[63] But Palestinian communist Mu'in Basisu notes that Gazans profoundly mistrusted any UN development plans following a reported 1955 scheme to relocate refugees to a desolate site in the Sinai away from the Israeli-Egyptian armistice line.[64] As a student, 'Abd al-Qadir Yassin chanted, "No resettlement schemes, No housing plans; You Agents of the Americans!" during the March 1955 *intifada* that followed Israeli raids on the Gaza Strip. Yassin and other students opposed what were believed to be US-inspired plans to relocate Palestinians from Gaza to Northwest Sinai as a way of "liquidating the Palestinian cause."[65] Palestinians also demonstrated later in Gaza City during meetings between Nasser and Hammarskjöld's envoy Ralph Bunche. The demonstrators opposed what they saw as Bunche's promotion of Israeli-inspired plans to "internationalize" the strip under UN control, and they demanded the return of an Egyptian governor. As historian Husayn Abu al-Naml notes, the two UN resolutions during the Suez Crisis providing for Israeli withdrawal and then establishment of the UNEF created "ambiguity [*ghumud*]" around political authority in Gaza.[66] A similar ambiguity characterized Hammarskjöld's plans for an Arab development fund. The Secretary-General had sought to allay concerns among oil companies and the western powers by proposing

---

[62] Legal Counsel to Secretary-General, March 5, 1957, folder: Middle East/Suez Story – 27, March 5–8, 1957 Interoffice memoranda to D.H. from the U.N. Legal Counsel, L 179: 114, DHC.

[63] Telegram to Cordier, December 24, 1957, folder: SG Trip – Dec. 1957, box 119, ACP.

[64] Mu'in Basisu, *Descent into the Water: Palestinian Notes from Arab Exile*, trans. Saleh Omar (Wilmette, IL: The Medina Press, 1980), v, 22.

[65] 'Abd al-Qadir Yassin, *'Umr Fi al-Manfa, Mudhakirat 'Abd al-Qadr Yassin* (Damascus: al-Dar al-Wataniya al-Jadida, 2009), 39–43. Translated by *The Palestinian Revolution*, 2016. http://learnpalestine.politics.ox.ac.uk/ (accessed August 23, 2017).

[66] Husayn Abu al-Naml, *Qita Gaza, 1948–1967: Taṭawwurat iqtiṣadiyya wa-siyasiyya wa-ijtimā'iyya wa-'askariyya* (Beirut: Markaz al-Abhat, Munazzamat al-tahrir al-Filastiniyah, 1979), 158.

supervisory roles for the World Bank and UN Secretariat. These actors would have compromised the fund's administration by Egypt and other Arab states. Lacking clear lines of political authority, Hammarskjöld's plan could hardly have inspired confidence among Arab government officials, let alone among the stateless Palestinians who were supposed to benefit from regional economic development. Although Hammarskjöld believed that the national state was an insufficient unit for developing Arab societies given inequality between states, political sovereignty was essential to legitimizing development. Ground-level mistrust of the United Nations spread among Palestinian refugees in Gaza, in part because they believed Egypt's compromised sovereignty over the territory would benefit Israel following its withdrawal. They regarded the United Nations' development planning much less favorably than its humanitarian assistance.

Palestinians also had reasons to mistrust the Egyptian state, which had policed Gaza between 1948 and 1956, with security forces carrying out extensive arrests of Communist Party and Muslim Brotherhood members following the 1955 *intifada*.[67] *Fida'iyin* raids launched against Israel from Gaza, over which Nasser sought control, posed a challenge to his pursuit of "peaceful conditions without a settlement" in the interest of focusing on Egypt's economic development. Indeed, regional conflict presented Nasser with an ongoing and ultimately insoluble problem. Advancing revolution in the Arab world and addressing the threat posed by Israel increasingly consumed his attention and Egypt's resources. The Arab circle from *The Philosophy of the Revolution* grew in significance to the extent that Nasser justified the establishment of the UAR proclaiming: "every state influences the fate of every other state."[68] Later, following the breakup of the UAR, Nasser launched a ruinous intervention in Yemen by associating that country's liberation with the goals of Arab Socialism. Egypt backed the Yemeni republican government in a proxy war against forces supported by Saudi Arabia, which over the course of the conflict became the leading Arab oil producer.[69] With his order to evict the UNEF from Sinai in May 1967, Nasser sacrificed Egypt's development to his

---

[67] Ibid., 145; and Ilana Feldman, *Police Encounters: Security and Surveillance in Gaza under Egyptian Rule* (Stanford: Stanford University Press, 2015).

[68] "*Kalimat al-ra'is Gamal 'Abd al-Nasser min dar al-riy'asa bi-munasaba i'lan al-jumhuriya al-'Arabiya al-mutahida*," February 1, 1958, http://nasser.org/Speeches/brow ser.aspx?SID=577&lang=ar, accessed January 17, 2017.

[69] See Gamal Abdel Nasser, *Majmu'at khutab wa tasrihat wa bayanat al-Ra'is Gamal 'Abd al-Nasir* (Cairo: Maslahat al-Isti'lamat, n.d.), 4: 253–274. See also, Jesse Ferris, *Nasser's*

rivalry with the Syrian Ba'th and confrontation with Israel.[70] The historian is left to wonder whether the events leading to the Six Day War would have unfolded as they did, had Hammarskjöld lived to see them.

Comparing these two development visions, which occupied distinct but overlapping temporal and spatial registers, can help to transcend each man's perspective, especially given that both suffered early deaths. Hammarskjöld's plane crashed in Northern Rhodesia in September 1961, and Nasser died suddenly from a heart attack nine years later at the age of fifty-two. The passage of time has revealed the ways in which both of their perspectives were limited and far-sighted. The timetable that Nasser set for Egypt's industrialization proved to be unrealistic, but under his successor Anwar al-Sadat, who dismantled Arab Socialism and liberalized the economy, the country struggled with unemployment. In the absence of state-directed industrialization within Egypt, industrial growth stagnated and some four million Egyptians were forced to seek employment abroad, many as expatriate laborers in the oil-rich Gulf states.[71] Hammarskjöld's temporal distinction between crisis and normal times corresponded to the misconception that it was possible to pursue development apart from politics. As more than one critic observed, economic development alone could never resolve the fundamental political conflict over who should bear responsibility for Palestinian refugees.[72] The Secretary-General's concern about "the dangers of a serious variation in economic progress as among the various Arab countries" proved warranted, however, particularly after the 1973 oil embargo and price hike flooded the oil producers' treasuries with petrodollars. On one level, state sovereignty in the Arab world perpetuated economic inequality by permitting oil states to determine when and how much they would share their wealth with more populous, less wealthy Arab countries, including oil transit states such as Egypt. World Bank president Eugene R. Black proved to be the most prescient advocate of Hammarskjöld's plan. Black noted that while oil producers in 1958 may not have had much of a surplus to share, within a decade they would accumulate more than they

---

Gamble: How Intervention in Yemen Caused the Six-Day War and the Decline of Egyptian Power (Princeton: Princeton University Press, 2013).

[70] See Guy Laron, "Playing with Fire: The Soviet-Israeli-Syrian Triangle, 1965–1967," *Cold War History* 10 (May 2010): 163–184.

[71] Robert Bianchi, *Unruly Corporatism: Associational Life in Twentieth-Century Egypt* (New York: Oxford University Press, 1989), 46.

[72] See Caccia to Foreign Office, January 8, 1958, FO 371/133843, BNA.

could reasonably spend on their own development. This prediction later proved correct to a greater extent than Black anticipated, with Arab oil exporters earning some $421 billion during the period 1974–1982.[73] The investment of a significant proportion of these petrodollars in purchasing weapons and supporting military proxies continues, in the era of the Syrian civil war, to perpetuate the cycle of armed conflict that Hammarskjöld had faced. Whatever the flaws in his plan, sharp economic inequality within and between Arab states is one legacy of the Secretary-General's defeat.

Finally, the comparison between Nasser and Hammarskjöld helps to illustrate what purposes development narratives served during the twentieth century. Nasser created successive development narratives as a way of establishing his own authority in the face of revolution, decolonization, and contests over Arab leadership. His ability to depict Egypt's movement across compellingly defined historical *tableaux*, along with perceived foreign policy successes, enabled him to build political support for his regime's economic policies. Nasser also appealed to a wide swath of Egyptians by portraying development as a shared national struggle rather than as class conflict. Although Hammarskjöld faced criticism for pursuing economic solutions to the region's political problems, evidence from his papers suggests that he turned to development astutely as a way of starting "nonpolitical" conversations that would otherwise have been impossible. By promoting his Arab development plan, the Secretary-General drew Nasser, Nuri, and Ben-Gurion into the same discussion, even if they never negotiated directly with one another and no political solutions ultimately emerged. Both Nasser and Hammarskjöld confronted economic problems as well as the political challenge of garnering support among non-elites. At the moment when Nasser sought to raise capital for industrialization through means short of nationalizing the Egyptian economy and Hammarskjöld quietly pursued an economic path to stabilizing the post-Suez Middle East, the two men's agendas intersected. In the spaces between visions such as theirs, historians can find room to analyze the meaning of development.

---

[73] See Abbas Alnasrawi, "The Rise and Fall of Arab Oil Power," *Arab Studies Quarterly* 6 (Winter/Spring 1984): 3–4.

15

Creating "The NGO International": The Rise of Advocacy for Alternative Development, 1974–1994

Paul Adler

"Another World Is Possible." So declared twelve thousand activists convening in Porto Alegre, Brazil in late January 2001 for the first annual World Social Forum. Coming from nations across the globe and representing a wide swath of left-wing perspectives, those assembled at Porto Alegre agreed on the need to transform the workings of the world economy. According to them, "a process of globalisation commanded by the large multinational corporations and by the governments and international institutions at the service of those corporations" that intensified starting in the 1980s and 1990s had led to a world defined by "exclusion and social inequality."[1]

Most of those present in Porto Alegre represented various forms of civil society, ranging from unions to feminist groups to think tanks to professionalized advocacy nongovernmental organizations (NGOs).[2] The fact that few governmental representatives attended (or even received invitations) was no accident. The organizers of the World Social Forum wanted a space in which "only organisations and movements of civil society" could gather.[3]

The social movement organizations and NGOs present at Porto Alegre showcased a part of civil society that differs sharply from the groups that appear in most histories of development. For the most part, the first major

---

[1] "World Social Forum Charter of Principles," April 9, 2001, http://www.colorado.edu/A mStudies/lewis/ecology/wsfcharter.pdf

[2] See Janet M. Conway, *Edges of Global Justice: The World Social Forum and Its "Others,"* (London: Routledge, 2013).

[3] "World Social Forum Charter of Principles."

wave of development histories portrayed NGOs as creatures of the Global
North. These works tended to place NGOs within a taxonomy consisting
of three species: philanthropic foundations, think tanks, and humanitarian relief and development NGOs. By concentrating on these three, scholars situated NGOs as one more protagonist in what historian Daniel
Immerwahr dubs the "Modernization Comes to Town" story. As
Immerwahr explains, this narrative depicts "how a world that was once
rooted in local, heterogeneous, informal, flexible, pluralistic, and, above
all, small-scale institutions was lost. It was bureaucratized, mechanized,
quantified, commodified" by outside forces trying to induce
development.[4]

While governments occupy the leading role in this narrative, philan-
thropies like the Ford and Rockefeller foundations and think tanks such as
the Center for International Studies appear as significant supporting
actors. The Rockefeller Foundation receives recognition for its vital role
in promoting the Green Revolution. Think tanks like the Center for
International Studies are analyzed for their part in incubating much of
the intellectual work that forged modernization theory.[5] Focusing on
organizations such as these, it is easy to see why NGOs are perceived as
predominately Global North institutions who helped drive mainstream
development thought and practice.

The first wave of development histories had relatively little to say about
NGOs engaged in "on-the-ground" anti-poverty work. However, a separate scholarship does exist about them. According to historians like
Matthew Hilton and Kevin O'Sullivan, relief and development NGOs
underwent a three-stage evolutionary process during the twentieth century. In the first stage (covering the period up to roughly 1945), organizations like Save the Children or Oxfam focused on immediate
humanitarian responses to floods, droughts, and wars. In the second
stage, during the 1950s and 1960s, NGOs went beyond immediate crises
to aiding long-term development by sending money and people to assist in
small-scale projects, from irrigation to education. The third stage arrived

---

[4] Daniel Immerwahr, *Thinking Small: The United States and the Lure of Community Development* (Cambridge: Harvard University Press, 2015), 5.

[5] David Ekbladh, *The Great American Mission: Modernization and the Construction of an American World Order* (Princeton: Princeton University Press, 2010); Nils Gilman, *Mandarins of the Future: Modernization Theory in Cold War America* (Baltimore, MD: Johns Hopkins University Press, 2003); Nick Cullather, *The Hungry World: America's Cold War Battle Against Poverty in Asia* (Cambridge: Harvard University Press, 2010).

in the 1980s and 1990s, with the addition of policy advocacy to development NGOs' repertoires. According to this telling, Northern NGOs only recently began thinking about poverty and inequality as public policy challenges necessitating political engagement.[6]

There is much to commend in this scholarship, but it also elides an important subset of NGOs. While some nonprofit groups added policy advocacy to their work recently, others, from their very inception, foregrounded social change. While individual groups existed for decades, it was in the 1970s that a network of ideologically left-leaning groups began coalescing, which I term the "NGO International." These groups challenged development policies they saw as accelerating forms of capitalist development that further enriched the wealthy while immiserating the poor. While members of the NGO International partner with grassroots organizations, its core members consisted of small, professionalized advocacy groups and think tanks, both Northern and Southern.

Examining the NGO International challenges standard narratives about NGOs and development in three principal ways. First, rather than a story of Northern NGOs swooping in to "save" the South, this narrative tells a transnational tale of Northern and Southern actors forging partnerships, with Southern groups often taking prominent or leading roles. Second, examining the NGO International moves away from depictions of "professional" development thinkers and practitioners as treating "popular resistance to modernization, and all political problems, as technical difficulties."[7] Activists within the NGO International embraced the opposite perspective, frequently invoking the refrain that "problems of development… are fundamentally political."[8]

Third, highlighting the NGO International presents a more holistic portrait of late-twentieth-century development politics. While historians such as Matthew Hilton and Stephen Macekura have examined NGOs

---

[6] Matthew Hilton, "International Aid and Development NGOs in Britain and Human Rights Since 1945," *Humanity* 5:3 (Winter 2012): 449–472; Maggie Black, *A Cause for Our Times: Oxfam, the First 50 Years* (Oxford: Oxfam Publications, 1992); Kevin O'Sullivan, "A 'Global Nervous System': The Rise and Rise of European Humanitarian NGOs, 1945–1985," in *International Organizations and Development, 1945–1990*, ed. Marc Frey, Sönke Kunkel, and Corinna Unger (New York: Palgrave Macmillan, 2014), 196–220; Joshua Hideo Mather, "Citizens of Compassion: Relief, Development, and State-Private Cooperation in U.S. Foreign Relations, 1939–1973" (PhD diss., Saint Louis University, 2015).

[7] Nick Cullather, "Development? It's History," *Diplomatic History* 24:4 (Fall 2000): 645.

[8] Richard J. Barnet, *Can the United States Promote Foreign Development?* Development Paper 6 (Washington, D.C.: Overseas Development Council, 1971), 7.

tackling specific issues (namely consumer and ecological protection), exploring the NGO International shows the links among different issue-focused movements. The NGO International's story reveals a history of activists conceptualizing an alternative worldview about poverty and economic growth – and acting upon it.[9] That worldview, which I call "social justice development," expressed a deep skepticism of capitalism. However, social justice development did not embrace statist socialism as an answer. Building on lived experiences with the inadequacies and inequities produced by many state-led development programs, NGO activists looked to the politicized empowerment of communities as the most promising avenue for ushering in greater equity.

The NGO International began forming at the moment when much of the current development historiography ends: the 1970s. During the NGO International's first decade, think tanks bolstered efforts by Global South states to reform the global economy, while consumer groups confronted multinational corporations. In the 1980s, the NGO International shifted focus to engage with the sweeping changes wrought by the debt crisis and the neoliberal turn.[10] The 1980s saw new groups of activists join the NGO International, highlighting aspects of development long sidelined or ignored, like ecological sustainability. However, it was not until the early 1990s that the NGO International congealed. Spurred by the debates over the creation of the World Trade Organization, disparate actors solidified both their critique of a fast-changing global economy and their own networks.

THE DREAM OF A NEW ORDER IN THE 1970S

Addressing a gathering of development experts in Switzerland in 1976, Malaysian consumer activist Anwar Fazal laid out a vision for going "in

---

[9] See Matthew Hilton, *Prosperity for All: Consumer Activism in an Era of Globalization* (Ithaca: Cornell University Press, 2009) and Stephen Macekura, *Of Limits and Growth: The Rise of Global Sustainable Development in the Twentieth Century* (Cambridge: Cambridge University Press, 2015).

[10] I use the term neoliberalism to mean the push by corporations, multilateral institutions, and governments both Northern and Southern to liberalize and privatize national economies. For texts on global neoliberalism, see Quinn Slobodian, *Globalists: The End of Empire and the Birth of Neoliberalism* (Cambridge: Harvard University Press, 2018); Judith A. Teichman, The *Politics of Freeing Markets in Latin America: Chile Argentina, and Mexico* (Chapel Hill: The University of North Carolina Press, 2001); Sarah Babb, "The Washington Consensus as Transnational Policy Paradigm: Its Origins, Trajectory, and Likely Successor," *Review of International Political Economy* 20, no.2 (2013): 268–297.

search of social justice." He asserted that the Global South's best hope for overcoming "injustice" lay with "two broad movements" attacking inequality at distinct levels. The first movement emphasized a macro view, denouncing the "unequal economic relations between developing and developed nations." The second movement brought a "new appreciation that struggle for a better life... must be viewed from the 'bottom-up'" with approaches highlighting "grassroots development" and the "ingenuity and capability of the common man." He emphasized that grassroots movements and NGOs, "because they are people oriented... have a critical role to play" at both levels.[11]

Fazal's praise of nongovernmental actors and local activism reflected growing disillusionment throughout the Third World with technocratic solutions as the path to raising living standards. Accelerating with post–World War II decolonization and Cold War competition, during the 1950s and 1960s rich and poor nations undertook a myriad of development schemes, from community projects to massive industrial infrastructure-based nation building. Epitomizing the optimism of the time, in 1961 the United Nations proclaimed the 1960s the "Decade of Development."[12]

This optimism did not last. By 1968, most observers viewed the 1960s as "nothing more than a 'decade of frustration and disillusionment.'"[13] In response, many Global South intellectuals, activists, and leaders (as well as some from the Global North) searched for alternative perspectives to explain the continuation of underdevelopment. Increasingly, many working on development rejected explanations for inequality that blamed "backwards" or "traditional" cultural and economic systems. They pointed out that such explanations ignored how the dynamics of the world economy factored into development. Instead, some Third World intellectuals stressed that many of the "concepts of development... which were often externally induced" had proven "inappropriate."[14]

---

[11] Anwar Fazal, "In Search of Social Justice: The Population/Food/Environment Perspective," December 1976, http://www.anwarfazal.net/speech-SocialJustice.php

[12] See Olav Stokke, *The UN and Development: From Aid to Cooperation* (Bloomington: Indiana University Press, 2009), 131–157.

[13] "Summary of Statement made at the 57th plenary meeting by Mr. Gunjeswari Prasad Singh, Minister of Commerce and Industry of Nepal," February 13, 1968 in *Proceedings of the United Nations Conference on Trade and Development Second Session, New Delhi, 1 February–29 March 1968* (United Nations Publication, Sales Number E.68.II. D.14), vol. 1, 146.

[14] Third World Forum, "The Santiago Statement," undated, S-0446-0273-000, United Nations Archives (hereafter UNA.)

Disillusionment bred new thinking during the 1970s. Over the course of the decade, a raft of ideas entered the discourse of intellectuals, policy thinkers, and practitioners around confronting global poverty and inequality. At the World Bank, President Robert McNamara supported the idea of "redistribution with growth," steering (to an extent) funding toward smaller-scale projects, as well as health, education, and other areas the bank had rarely ventured in before.[15] Across the world, conversations turned to the idea of "basic needs," that development work should aim to improve people's lives through social and entrepreneurial programs now, rather than waiting for industrialization. Women, often sidelined or dismissed, received increasing attention from formal development institutions as powerful actors in their own right.[16]

Of the many heterodox development initiatives in the 1970s, one of the most radical took at least partial inspiration from dependency theory. This worldview's main voices came not from the North, but the Global South, especially Latin America. Building off Marxism and ideas of structuralism associated with the Argentine economist Raul Prebisch, dependency theory divided the world into "core" nations (the North) and "periphery" nations (the South). According to *dependentistas*, European and US colonialism and imperialism had converted Southern nations' economies into export engines, whose operations siphoned the wealth out of Africa, Asia, and Latin America and to Europe and the United States, facilitating the rich nations' industrial supremacy. To break this cycle, *dependentistas* urged Southern states to undertake a radical rupture with the world economy. Instead of relying on exports, the Third World needed to build an industrial base while simultaneously fighting for substantial wealth and power redistribution both within and among nations.[17]

Of course, making a critique is easy – turning it into a plausible political program offers the real challenge. What differentiated the mid-1970s from the decades before and since was that, for a moment, the Global South boasted a plausible strategy for enacting such change. The turning point arrived in December 1973, when the Organization of Petroleum Exporting Countries (OPEC) quadrupled world oil prices. Among the

---

[15] See Patrick Allan Sharma, *Robert McNamara's Other War: The World Bank and International Development* (Philadelphia: University of Pennsylvania Press, 2017).

[16] See, for example, Gina Koczberski, "Women in Development: A Critical Analysis," *Third World Quarterly* 19:3 (1998): 395–409.

[17] See Joseph L. Love, "The Origins of Dependency Analysis," *Journal of Latin American Studies* 22:1 (February 1990): 143–168.

countries leading this charge was Algeria, then also chairing the Non-Aligned Movement. Seeing an opportunity to use OPEC's sway as a battering ram to push a broader Third World agenda, the Algerians successfully lobbied for a Special Session of the United Nations General Assembly to convene in April 1974. After a monthlong set of meetings, a large coalition of Southern states passed a resolution committing the United Nations to support the creation of a New International Economic Order (NIEO).[18]

The NIEO outlined a plan for systematically reforming the global economy. Its provisions included programs to free Southern nations from the unpredictable roller coaster of commodity markets by stabilizing prices. Foreign aid would not only increase but also undergo reforms to prevent Northern nations from using assistance as a tool of control. Multilateral institutions like the World Bank, the IMF, and the United Nations would be democratized to give the South real power within these institutions.[19]

The launch of the NIEO lobbying drive in 1974 provided an intellectual and political foundation for left-leaning NGOs' organizing efforts, particularly policy-oriented think tanks. These organizations' influence stemmed from two factors: their ability to produce research respected by government and UN policy makers, and their staffs' connections to officials in those same institutions. Critically, much of the intellectual vibrancy of this incipient network of left-leaning think tanks emerged from the Global South, including organizations such as the Third World Forum and the African Institute for Economic Development. Global North think tanks such as the International Coalition for Development Action, the Dag Hammarskjöld Foundation, and the Institute for Policy Studies also focused on these issues and in so doing often employed individuals from the Global South in leadership positions.[20]

In practical terms, think tanks defined their goal as backing the pro-NIEO coalition of nations. They would do so by supplementing those

---

[18] On the NIEO, see, for example, Craig Murphy, *The Emergence of the NIEO Ideology* (Boulder, CO: Westview Press, 1984) and *Humanity* 6:1 (Spring 2015).

[19] UN General Assembly, Twenty-Ninth Session, *Charter of Economic Rights and Duties of States*, A/RES/29/3281, December 12, 1974. Available: http://www.un-documents.net/a29r3281.htm

[20] For a detailed examination of this part of the NGO International, see Victor V. Nemchenok, "A Dialogue of Power: Development, Global Civil Society, and the Third World Challenge to International Order, 1969–1981" (PhD diss., University of Virginia, 2013).

governments' capacity to analyze and formulate policy. While the NIEO declaration put forward broad recommendations, much work lay ahead in fleshing out the specifics. As the Third World Forum, which brought together leading Southern economists, proclaimed, the "main function" for NGOs backing the NIEO lay in stimulating "self-reliant thinking in the Third World and to generate ideas and proposals that may be useful to those governments, social groups, and individuals that agree with the FORUM's objectives."[21]

In the U.S. and Western Europe, think tanks interested in challenging development orthodoxy also aided the NIEO agenda. For instance, the Amsterdam-based left-wing think tank, the Transnational Institute (TNI), identified a crucial task as the "development and dissemination of an accurate and dynamic analysis of resource diplomacy." With Southern states trying to gain higher prices and greater control over their natural resources, TNI saw an opening in providing these nations as much information as possible on commodity markets. During the 1970s, TNI produced reports and started a monthly magazine, *The Elements*, that researched and reported on various multinational corporations and commodities shared its findings actively with Third World negotiators.[22]

The policy influences of think tanks on the NIEO were short lived, however, because the NIEO did not last long. Launching in May 1974, by December 1976 the coalition of pro-NIEO countries increasingly fractured. Many factors contributed to the coalition's decline, from the intransigence of certain Global North governments to internal divisions among Southern nations to the worldwide economic downturn of the second half of the 1970s.[23] This truncated time period meant that many of the NIEO's supporters had only started to mobilize by the time it ceased being a political possibility.

While think tanks dreamed of influencing the high diplomacy of the New International Economic Order, other NGOs attempted to advance one of the NIEO's main planks: the call for creating global mechanisms to "regulate and supervise the activities of transnational corporations."[24]

---

[21] "Third World Forum Newsletter," 1, no. 1 (December 1976), S-0446–0273-000, UNA.

[22] "Progress Report on Program of TNI for 1974–1975," September 1974, Box 106, Folder 42, Institute for Policy Studies Papers, Wisconsin Historical Society Library and Archive, Madison, WI (hereafter IPSP.)

[23] On the decline of the NIEO, see Vijay Prashad, *The Poorer Nations: A Possible History of the Global South* (London: Verso, 2014), 15–85.

[24] *Charter of Economic Rights and Duties of States.*

This activist segment of the NGO International initially arose from the international consumer movement. Frequently thought of as a middle-class movement concerned with depoliticized notions of "consumer safety," as historian Matthew Hilton has shown, the international consumer movement's history is much richer. While some consumer groups maintained a narrow focus on product safety, others used consumerism as an entry point to address broad issues of social, economic, and ecological injustice.[25]

Essential to the story of transnational consumer agitation – and to that of the NGO International – is the Malaysian consumer movement based in the state of Penang.[26] The organization that made Penang a global activist center, the Consumers Association of Penang (CAP), commenced operations in 1969. CAP identified its mission as fighting not only for safe consumer products, but against corporate power that was creating "a new economic imbalance that will be detrimental to the proper development of the nation."[27]

Although CAP initially concentrated on domestic issues, within a few years its founders sought transnational ties. The leader of this endeavor, Anwar Fazal, rose meteorically through the ranks of international consumer activism during the 1970s. In the late 1960s, he helped to found CAP. In the early 1970s, he became CAP's liaison to the International Organization of Consumer Unions (IOCU), a network of mostly Global North-based large consumer groups. In 1974, Fazal became the director of IOCU's Asia Regional Office, where he served until 1978. Then, Fazal achieved a rare feat. Few if any predominately Global North institutions in the 1970s had Global South-based presidents, but in 1978 Fazal won election to become head of IOCU. As president, Fazal found himself well positioned to act as a bridge between Northern and Southern advocates while promoting Third World concerns.[28]

Under Fazal, IOCU's regional office in Penang essentially became its global headquarters. From this perch Fazal used IOCU's resources to "Let

---

[25] Hilton, *Prosperity for All*.

[26] On Penang as a hub of civil society activism, see Edmund W. Cheng and Shu-yun Ma, "A City's Status and Its Civil Society," *Penang Monthly*, January 2015, http://penang monthly.com/a-citys-status-and-its-civil-society/.

[27] "Address by Enche S.M. Mohd Idris, J.P.," March 31, 1971, *Consumerism: The Penang Experience* (Penang: Consumers Association of Penang, 1973), 2. See also, Matthew Hilton, *Choice and Justice: Forty Years of the Malaysian Consumer Movement* (Pulau Penang, Malaysia: The Universiti Sains Malaysia Co-operative Bookshop, Ltd., 2009).

[28] Hilton, *Prosperity for All*, 84–86; 107–108.

a thousand coalitions for social justice bloom!"[29] One of his first opportunities came with the emergence of a campaign targeting breast milk substitutes marketing throughout the Global South. Sold by major multinationals like Nestlé, products such as infant formula promised to bring modern technology to child-rearing. Yet, as a growing number of individuals North and South began warning as early as the 1930s, breast milk substitutes posed severe risks to newborns. Used without clean water or refrigeration, these products increased rates of infant disease and death.[30]

In the Global North, activism around this controversy began in 1974, as activists from the United Kingdom, Switzerland, and the United States launched a series of national efforts targeting different corporations selling breast milk substitutes in the Global South. The most successful of these originated in the United States. After years of failed shareholder resolutions and a lawsuit, a coalition of activists committed to social justice development launched a boycott of the Swiss corporation Nestlé on July 4, 1977. Activists selected Nestlé because it was the world's largest purveyor of breast milk substitutes, as well as one of the largest corporations on Earth.[31]

Led by the Infant Formula Action Coalition (INFACT), US activists viewed the boycott as an experiment in challenging multinational corporations. Building on a mix of academic writing about multinationals (including by *dependentistas*) and reports on companies' intrusions into Third World societies, activists in the 1970s saw private enterprise as a major culprit in perpetuating global poverty.[32] Tackling multinational capital necessitated multinational activism and INFACT therefore endorsed a vigorous internationalism. They sought connections to Global South health providers, bringing several to testify at a US Senate hearing chaired by Ted Kennedy in 1978. They also allied with Western European activists who were organizing their own national boycotts.[33]

---

[29] Fazal, "In Search of Social Justice."

[30] See, for example, Penny Van Esterik, *Beyond the Breast-Bottle Controversy* (New Brunswick, NJ: Rutgers University Press, 1989).

[31] On the campaign's origins, see Rita Catherine Murphy, "The Facts of INFACT: How the Infant Formula Controversy Went from a Public Health Crisis to an International Consumer Activist Issue" (Master's thesis, University of Minnesota-Minneapolis, 2012).

[32] See Tagi Sagafi-Nejad in collaboration with John H. Dunning, *The UN and Transnational Corporations: From Code of Conduct to Global Compact* (Bloomington: Indiana University Press, 2008), 41–54.

[33] Leah Margulies, "Status Report: Infant Formula Education/Action Program," August 18, 1978, Box 3, Action for Corporate Accountability Records. Minnesota Historical Society (hereafter ACA); Doug Clement to War on Want, April 28, 1978, Box 36, ACA.

These international connections intensified beginning in the summer of 1978. Building on the momentum of the Kennedy hearing, the World Health Organization (WHO) and the United Nations International Children's Emergency Fund (UNICEF) announced a joint meeting in October 1979 to formulate a global code of conduct for breast milk substitutes advertising. The WHO-UNICEF meeting catalyzed the formation of the International Baby Food Action Network (IBFAN), an NGO that coordinated the growing number of Northern and Southern groups campaigning on the breast milk substitutes issue.[34] Activists' efforts produced a major success in May 1981, when the WHO and UNICEF implemented the International Code of Marketing of Breast-milk Substitutes, a policy supported by every nation except the United States.

In the wake of this win, a division of labor emerged between Northern and Southern IBFAN members. For those in the rich countries, their mission lay in maintaining and intensifying national boycotts of Nestlé, now aimed at pressuring the company to abide by the code. Meanwhile, Global South NGOs dealt with two main tasks: monitoring multinational companies' compliance with the code and fighting for the passage of laws in their home countries based on the code. This labor energized a diverse range of Southern groups, from professionalized nonprofits to grassroots women's rights movements.[35]

The Nestlé boycott revealed how Northern and Southern NGOs could work together. However, it also demonstrated that activists could not eliminate power dynamics even within their own ranks. This became clear in late 1983, when US and Canadian activists negotiated a deal with Nestlé to suspend the campaign in exchange for the company agreeing to comply with the WHO-UNICEF code of conduct. The North American groups did not include the European and Southern groups in these talks; most first learned of the suspension in their newspapers after INFACT and Nestlé publicly announced it. In February 1984, at a global meeting of activists, European and Southern NGOs vented their frustrations, insisting that they did "not need to be instruments of the campaign but active participants." Fierce arguments raged, leading US and Canadian groups to agree to European and Southern demands to ensure leadership equity in the future.[36]

---

[34] Doug Clement to DMG, November 1979, Box 31, ACA.

[35] Annelies Allain, "Fighting an Old Battle in a New World: How IBFAN Monitors the Baby Food Market," *Development Dialogue* 2 (2002).

[36] INBC and IBFAN, "Record of Proceedings: The International Baby Milk Campaign: Strategies for Action," minutes, February 2–5, 1984, M97-182, Box 1, Wisconsin Historical Society.

Even with these conflicts, the activists' apparent success in tackling Nestlé inspired many to see the breast milk substitutes fight as a promising model. In 1980 and 1981, public health and corporate accountability activists approached Fazal about backing similar efforts directed at the pesticide and pharmaceuticals industries. With the resources of IOCU at his disposal, Fazal gladly obliged, providing funds and other resources to create the Pesticide Action Network (PAN) and Health Action International (HAI), both NGO networks modeled on IBFAN.

This expansion of NGO organizing met mixed results. Early hopes of converting the United Nations into a global regulatory body soon fell to the wayside, given structural challenges at the UN and opposition from the United States. However, PAN and HAI scored concrete victories. For instance, in 1982 Bangladesh instituted a dramatic reform of its pharmaceutical industry to promote safety, affordability, and local production. NGOs from around the world lauded this move and successfully defended it against multinationals and rich nation governments who saw it as a global threat, given how the law challenged free market principles. In the years since PAN and HAI's formations, their members made important strides, winning bans and regulations of some pesticides and helping to create more equitable health policies.[37]

DEBT AND DISILLUSIONMENT IN THE 1980S

While in the 1970s, activists often expressed a reasonable (albeit cautious) optimism about the future, such hopes all but disappeared in the 1980s. This sense of despair arose in the late 1970s and early 1980s driven by events such as Ronald Reagan's election and the fall of leftist, pro-NIEO governments.[38] Yet, even as they observed "fundamental transformations within the power structures" occurring in the 1980s, many Southern activists also saw much continuity.[39] For them, the austerity measures and debt crisis of the 1980s appeared less a sea change and more an intensification of long-standing trends. As a gathering of NGO International leaders in Penang put it in 1984, "During the colonial era,

---

[37] Paul Adler, "Planetary Citizens: U.S. NGOs and the Politics of International Development in the Late Twentieth Century" (PhD diss., Georgetown University, 2014): 149–163; 215–227.

[38] Michael Moffitt to TNI Planning Board, March 23, 1981, Box 107, Folder 4, IPSP.

[39] Jorge Sol and Robert Borosage, "International Economic Order Project Proposal for Fiscal Year 1985–1986 and Report on Activities for Fiscal Year 1984–1985," undated, Box 30, Folder 39, IPSP.

the wealth taken out of the colonized territories helped to develop the colonial master countries. Today, this is even more true."[40]

The specific factors depressing the members of the NGO International reflected the confluence of multiple disillusionments – the collapse of the NIEO drive, the Third World debt crisis and the austerity that came with it, and rising anger with Third World governments who they accused of "perpetuating an outmoded form of development."[41] Lamenting in the mid-1980s that there no longer existed "'a common vision which can mobilize Third World peoples,'" key organizers at the Consumers Association of Penang decided to create one.[42] In November 1984, the CAP staff convened a meeting that gave rise to a crucial member of the NGO International: the Third World Network (TWN). Beginning operations in 1985, the Third World Network rapidly evolved into a critical hub of policy analysis and political strategizing for Southern activists and governments.[43]

The Third World Network's founding meeting found Southern activists proclaiming independence from the idea that Third World governments would usher in the new world order. Rather, the Network declared that "people's movements and organisations in the Third World" would lead the way as a force "for the sake of more justice, equity, and participation in the development process." TWN defined its particular mission as creating "closer co-operation among NGOs in Third World countries in order to ... build up an organisational framework which in terms of analysis, conscientization, and action can cope with the transnationalisation of the development dilemma."[44] Differentiating their vision from the NIEO (which still sought industrial modernization), TWN insisted that "Developing countries should not think of taking the same development path as the industrial countries."[45] Rather, they should emphasize production for basic needs, appropriate technologies, internal wealth redistribution, and programs to preserve and promote indigenous cultures.

[40] *Third World: Development or Crisis?* (Penang: Third World Network, 1984), 10.

[41] Ibid., 78.

[42] Wayne Ellwood, "Third World: Global Coalition Seeks to Create a New Voice for the Third World," *Inter Press Service*, May 18, 1985.

[43] Graham K. Brown, "Stemming the Tide: Third World Network and Global Governance," in *Yearbook of International Co-operation on Environment and Development*, ed. Olav Schram Stokke and Øystein B. Thommessen (London: Earthscan Publications, 2003/2004), 73–77.

[44] *Third World: Development or Crisis*, 78–79.

[45] Ibid., 31.

These demands formed the core value system defining social justice development.

The emphasis on local knowledge and small-scale development projects reflected the growing importance of ecological sustainability in the thinking of NGO activists. During the 1970s, resource overconsumption, pollution, and other ecological dilemmas entered international political discourse, thanks partially to environmentalist organizing seen in events like the 1972 United Nations Stockholm Conference.[46] In 1975, an international group of scholars, policy makers, and activists – many of whom worked at think tanks focusing on the NIEO – issued the Cocoyoc Declaration, warning that "Environmental degradation and the rising pressure on resources raise the question whether the 'outer limits' of the planet's physical integrity may not be at risk."[47] However, many factors complicated sustainability politics, such as many Southern governments viewing environmentalism as a distraction from the "real" issues of development – or even as a way to shut down Third World economic growth.

In the 1980s, these dynamics shifted. From scientific studies to protests, governments, corporations, and multilateral institutions found themselves forced to acknowledge ecological worries. This change owed much to North-South NGO collaborations, facilitated by the rise of internationally networked environmentalist groups from the Global South. These groups ranged from professionalized lobbying NGOs like Brazil's Gaucha Association for the Protection of the Natural Environment (AGAPAN) to innovative grassroots organizations such as the Green Belt movement in Kenya.[48]

Penang, Malaysia once again served as a hub for Southern activists. For instance, Indian physicist, philosopher, and activist Vandana Shiva, one of the most prominent Southern critics of the Green Revolution, first entered the global activist scene after attending a Third World Network conference.[49] At gatherings organized in Penang during the mid-1980s, Southerners advanced a Third World environmentalism that influenced how Northern groups conceptualized ecology-development questions. As described by Kenyan activist Achoka Awori, Third World environmentalism contrasted a "Northern concept of environment [that] places more

[46] Macekura, *Of Limits and Growth*, 91–137.
[47] "The Cocoyoc Declaration," October 23, 1974. Available: http://helsinki.at/projekte/co coyoc/COCOYOC_DECLARATION_1974.pdf
[48] Ramachandra Guha, *Environmentalism: A Global History* (New York: Longman, 2000).
[49] Vandana Shiva, *The Vandana Shiva Reader* (Lexington: The University Press of Kentucky, 2014), 2.

emphasis on the... nonhuman component" with a Southern view that saw the environment "within the context of... human welfare."[50]

Complementing this long-term network building, a vibrant campaign targeting the multilateral development banks (MDBs), particularly the World Bank, commenced. While resistance by local populations to MDB-funded projects dated back decades, only in the 1980s did global advocates forge transnational activist networks.[51] Aiming to help bring questions of green development to the World Bank itself were many of the most prominent US environmental advocacy groups, such as the Sierra Club, the Natural Resources Defense Council, and Friends of the Earth.

In the early 1980s, several green groups decided to collaborate on a coordinated pressure campaign aimed at the MDBs. This initiative emerged from the work of a few staff members who set out to publicize the MDBs' culpability in "inflicting unspeakably harsh problems on those people who are least able to... defend their rights to... a sustainable future."[52] Beginning in 1983, US environmentalists pressed the banks to alter their lending practices to incorporate ecological questions. These included reviewing projects before implementation to assess possible ecological damage and funding projects that promoted conservation. Utilizing their ties with members of the US Congress, environmentalists organized Capitol Hill hearings and helped generate letters from members of Congress to the banks.[53]

Even as they generated domestic political pressure, US environmentalists also recognized the need for transnational ties. At first, US groups mainly saw Southern NGOs as sources of information about MDB-

[50] Asia Pacific People's Environment Network, *Asia Pacific Environment* 4, no. 2 (1986), Container 10, Folder 43, Sierra Club International Program Records, BANC MSS 71/290 c, The Bancroft Library, University of California, Berkeley (hereafter SCIP); Achoka Awori, "The Environmental Movement: An Africa Perspective," undated, Container 5, Folder 23, SCIP.

[51] See, for example, Charles Drucker, "Dam the Chico: Hydropower Development and Tribal Resistance," in *Tribal Peoples and Development Issues: A Global Overview*, ed. John H. Bodley (Mountain View, CA: Mayfield Publishing Company, 1988), 151–166.

[52] Testimony of Brent Blackwelder, House Committee on Banking, Finance, and Urban Affairs, *Environmental Impact of Multilateral Development Bank-Funded Projects*, 98th Cong., 1st sess., 1983, 39.

[53] See Robert Wade, "Greening the Bank: The Struggle over the Environment, 1970–1995," in *The World Bank: Its First Half Century, Volume 2: Perspectives*, ed. Devesh Kapur, John P. Lewis, and Richard Webb (Washington, D.C.: The Brookings Institution Press, 1997), 611–734.

financed projects.[54] For generating more direct political pressure overseas, US environmentalists prioritized reaching out to Western European activists in "key donor countries" who could push their governments to "support the US initiatives" around reforming the MDBs' lending policies.[55] This approach fit with most Northern environmental NGOs' reliance on elite policy advocacy to make change. By the mid-1980s however, a global campaign evolved. It taught Northern NGOs an important lesson: international political pressure can take many forms. While US and European groups could appeal more directly to the upper echelons of the banks, in rural areas of Brazil and India particularly, grassroots groups not only monitored MDB-financed projects, but fought against them with a mix of lobbying and protests.

In forging these relationships, middle-class Southern activists played key interlocutor roles between the Southern grassroots and Northern advocacy organizations. Each segment of the activist community gained something from these relations. As US advocates noted in a 1988 report, their own "ability to apply pressure... depends on the extent to which they can draw information from affected peoples and advocate positions... formulated or strongly supported by Third World organizations." Meanwhile, Southern organizations used the influence of Northern NGOs to "be heard and seen by the hierarchical, closed bank bureaucracies... and to receive current information from First World colleagues about bank projects."[56] To formalize these relationships, in September 1986 US environmentalists hosted the first of what became an annual tradition of NGO "parallel meetings" occurring concurrently with the IMF and World Bank's yearly meetings.[57]

This multifaceted activism shined during the multiyear fight over the Sardar Sarovar Dam. Part of a massive irrigation and hydroelectric infrastructure drive in western India, the dam's construction threatened to displace tens, if not hundreds of thousands of people and wreak ecological havoc. The World Bank offered partial financing of the project despite

---

[54] Thomas B. Stoel, Jr., "Proposal for Support of the NRDC International Program," September 1985, Box 697, Folder 4175, RG 3.1, Rockefeller Brothers Fund Archives, Rockefeller Archive Center, Sleepy Hollow, New York (hereafter RBF.)

[55] Jim Barnes and Bruce Rich, "Extending the World Bank-Multilateral Development Bank Reform Campaign European Trip," December 18, 1985, Container 10, Folder 39, SCIP.

[56] EDF, NWF, EPI, NRDC, and Sierra Club, "Strategy Document: Multilateral Banks Campaign," December 13, 1988, Box 1427, Folder 8930, RBF.

[57] Environmental Policy Institute, "Citizens Conference on Tropical Forests, International Environment, and the World Bank," September 28–30, 1986, Container 2, Folder 13, SCIP.

lackluster measures by Indian state governments to consult with or resettle affected communities. Meanwhile, the World Bank essentially ignored its own social and environmental safeguards to keep the project moving.[58] As the Sardar Sarovar project continued, activists around the world labeled it the "emblematic" World Bank project, stating that it would "be difficult to believe in any possibility of introducing changes to the Bank if that project cannot be stopped."[59]

As hundreds of thousands living along the Narmada River discovered that their lives would soon be uprooted, many began to mobilize. Some wished to have more input into the project while others opposed it outright. Local organizers were joined by activists from elsewhere in India, such as social worker Medha Patkar, who became a leader in the anti-dam movement. In 1989, several of these grassroots groups combined to form a social movement organization, Narmada Bachao Andolan (NBA). The NBA represented a mass-based organization that combined "professionalized" forms of policy advocacy with Gandhian protest tactics.[60]

In one of their most dramatic actions, in late December 1990, a group of 5,000 people conducted a 250-kilometer "Long March" from the state of Madhya Pradesh to the Sardar Sarovar site in Gujarat. Blocked by Gujarati authorities at the border, activist leaders embarked upon a hunger strike.[61] As the strike continued for days and then weeks, World Bank officials felt increasing pressure to quiet the situation. At the same time, the Bank's leaders remained resistant to the NBA's demand that an independent entity conduct a review of the project – a demand crafted in collaboration between the NBA and Northern environmentalists. As the hunger strike continued, Northern NGOs facilitated the NBA's contacts with the World Bank. The NBA hunger strike finally came to an end when Northern advocates arranged a five-hour phone call linking Bank officials in Washington, D.C., Oxfam Great Britain personnel in Oxford, and

[58] See Sanjeev Khagram, *Dams and Development: Transnational Struggles for Water and Power* (Ithaca: Cornell University Press, 2004).

[59] International NGO Forum on World Bank and IMF Lending, "Continuing the Challenge: Report on the 1990 International NGO Forum," undated, Container 7, Folder 13, Mark Dubois Papers, BANC MSS 2003/314 c, The Bancroft Library, University of California, Berkeley.

[60] For more on the NBA, see Asha Thomas, "Framing the State: Social Movement in the Narmada Valley" (PhD diss., The University of Chicago, 2013).

[61] Hans Staffner, *Baba Amte: A Vision of New India* (Mumbai: Popular Prakashan, 2000), 58.

Indian activists that ended with the World Bank acquiescing to an independent review.[62]

Overall, the MDB campaign offered a mixed set of experiences and lessons for activists. In some ways, it marked one of the most successful initiatives undertaken by members of the NGO International. In the spring of 1987, the World Bank revamped its Environmental Department, greatly increasing the number of staff. In a spurt of activity driven by escalating NGO and social movement pressure, in the early 1990s the World Bank instituted further reforms. These included establishing a procedure for conducting impact assessments and the formation of a new lending mechanism, the Global Environment Facility. The protests around the Sardar Sarovar Dam also forced the World Bank to create an independent Inspection Panel to provide communities a mechanism for raising their concerns with Bank staff. Imperfect though they have been, these reforms indicated that the NGO International represented not just a voice of dissent but a force capable of winning policy changes.[63]

Beyond the specifics of the MDB campaign, activists' experiences with it also helped point the way for NGO International leaders to deal with an important internal movement dilemma. For as much as the members of the NGO International criticized elitist assumptions about development, most of the key activists came from middle-class backgrounds and boasted significant higher education, especially as lawyers or economists.[64] This fact left them open to criticism for being disconnected from what people "on the ground" truly wanted. Connecting with social movements offered a partial solution, by giving NGO leaders a conduit for communicating and strategizing directly with those most affected by development programs.

BECOMING THE VOICE OF OPPOSITION IN THE 1990S

What brought the various strands of the NGO International, from consumer groups to environmentalists, together was the creation in the early 1990s of the World Trade Organization (WTO). As an institution aspiring

---

[62] Robert H. Wade, "Muddy Waters: Inside the World Bank as It Struggled with the Narmada Projects," *Economic & Political Weekly* XLVI:40 (October 1, 2004): 54.

[63] See *The Struggle for Accountability: The World Bank, NGOs, and Grassroots Movements*, ed. Jonathan A. Fox and L. David Brown (Cambridge, MA: The MIT Press, 1998).

[64] International Forum on Globalization, "Spokesperson Bios," undated. Available: http://204.200.203.35/pdf/cancun/IFG-media;bios.pdf

to write what its first director called "the constitution of a single global economy," a constitution that would promote private enterprise and economic liberalization, the WTO embodied much of what the NGO International contested.[65] Talks to create the WTO started in 1986, with negotiations to expand the mandate of the General Agreement on Tariffs and Trade (GATT) from a body concerned with a rather narrow range of trade issues into an institution mandated to set the "rules of the road" for global economic relations.[66]

Of grave concern to activists like Nestlé boycott veteran Mark Ritchie or the Third World Network's Martin Khor was the WTO's relationship to multinational corporations.[67] Building on the corporate accountability fights spearheaded by Anwar Fazal, by the early 1990s a consensus formed within the NGO International that multinational corporations, not governments, were the most powerful players in development politics. "What is happening at the GATT talks," explained Martin Khor, a mentee of Anwar Fazal's who cofounded and directed the Third World Network, "is that the industrial countries – representing the transnational companies' viewpoint – are saying that we must remove the regulatory powers that governments now have over the transnational companies."[68]

By the early 1990s, NGO International activists saw the creation of the WTO as a distinct political and ideological project to put "in place a New International Economic Order more unjust and more inequitable to the peoples of the South than even the present order."[69] For Global South activists, this new order, which they shorthand called "neoliberalism," seemed like a new phase of imperialism. In this new economic order, institutions like the WTO, the IMF, and the World Bank would be used to dismantle regulation and social welfare programs and open the way for foreign capital.[70]

[65] United Nations Conference on Trade and Development, "UNCTAD and WTO: A Common Goal in a Global Economy," TAD/INF/PR/9628, October 7, 1996, http://unctad.org/en/pages/PressReleaseArchive.aspx?ReferenceDocId=3607.

[66] *From GATT to the WTO: The Multilateral Trading System in the New Millennium* (Geneva: The WTO Secretariat, 2000).

[67] Susan Aaronson, *Taking Trade to the Streets: The Lost History of Public Efforts to Shape Globalization* (Ann Arbor: The University of Michigan Press, 2001), 143.

[68] Jane Ayers, "Martin Khor: Fighting to Save Rain Forests and the World Environment," *The Los Angeles Times,* July 29, 1990: M3.

[69] Chakravarthi Raghavan, *Recolonization: GATT, the Uruguay Round & the Third World* (Penang: Third World Network, 1990), 294.

[70] "Recolonization – GATT & The Third World: An Interview with Martin Khor Kok Pen," *The Multinational Monitor* 11:11 (November 1990), http://www.multinationalmonitor.org/hyper/issues/1990/11/interview-khor.html

Pushing back against multinationals, members of the NGO International looked not to governments or the United Nations, but to themselves as the primary voices for social justice in the global economy. To become such a force required organizing, with the fight around the Uruguay Round negotiations that created the WTO presenting "possibilities to sustain such progressive international connections so as to counter the globalization of capital."[71] The existence of a multifaceted critique, combined with the ability of disparate NGO communities to align in common, illustrated the growing sophistication and institutionalization of the NGO International. Unlike in the 1970s and 1980s, when coalition building started anew with each campaign, by the early 1990s organizations such as the Third World Network existed that could quickly facilitate internationalist exchanges.[72]

As important for the NGO International's messaging and internal cohesion as the fight over the Uruguay Round proved to be, their agitation failed to block the formation of the WTO. Yet, the fact that serious discussions occurred over environment or equitable development at the WTO showed that activists' critiques could not be ignored.[73] In subsequent years, the NGO International scored important victories – from defeating the proposed Multilateral Agreement on Investment treaty to contributing to the ongoing deadlock in the WTO to creating the contentious political environment around trade politics seen, for instance, in the ongoing controversies over the Trans-Pacific Partnership.[74]

CONCLUSION

Assessing the international development historiography, historian Joseph Morgan Hodge proposes that this scholarship is especially important because it can help nudge "international development agencies and analysts to be more reflexive about what they do by making a sustained effort

---

[71] Michael Windfuhr to NGO-GATT Steering Committee, August 4, 1992, Global Trade Watch Papers, Washington, D.C. (hereafter GTWP.)

[72] "Minutes of Meeting of GATT-Activists during the G7 Summit in Munich," July 6, 1992, GTWP.

[73] Peter Willetts, "Representation of Private Organizations in the Global Diplomacy of Economic Policy-Making," in *Private Organizations in Global Politics*, ed. Karsten Ronit and Volker Schneider (New York: Routledge, 2000), 52–54.

[74] See Ruth Reitan, *Global Activism* (New York: Routledge, 2007). On the TPP, see *Third World Resurgence* 275 (July 13, 2014).

to understand the problematic history of their own profession."[75] In writing these words, Hodge focused on practitioners at institutions like the World Bank or the Agency for International Development. However, the thrust of his comments equally applies to left-leaning activists who for the past forty years have critiqued development – and pushed for alternative ideas and policies. Just as understanding the inadequacies and complexities of modernization, community development, or sustainability is important, so too is understanding the stories of those who have long critiqued these policies and attempted to change them.

This is made all the more relevant as, in recent years, the NGO International has become a leading force in showing the connections between development and climate change. Under the banner of dealing with climate change's ongoing and worsening effects, which are and will continue to hit the Global South particularly hard, activists of the NGO International have found new causes that might rejuvenate old demands. Just as the infusion of dependency theory ideas in the 1970s cemented the NGO International's analysis of inequality rooted in history, today's climate justice activists emphasize the "historical record and responsibility of industrialized countries" for the crisis.[76] Thus, understanding the NGO International's history not only can enrich studies of the past, but may clarify the future.

[75] Joseph Morgan Hodge, "Writing the History of Development (Part 2: Longer, Deeper, Wider)," *Humanity* 7:1 (Spring 2016): 159.

[76] Alliance Sud, "Interview with Martin Khor," October 13, 2009. Available: http://www .alliancesud.ch/en/policy/other/interview-martin-khor.

16

Epilogue: Development Dreams

Jeremy Adelman

In January 1959, revolutionaries toppled the Cuban strongman Fulgencio Batista, icon of everything wrong about how Washington was treating its neighbors to the south. The rebels promised to put an end to under-development and usher in a new era of progress – with equity and national independence from imperialism. "The Cuban revolution," Fidel Castro thundered to a massive crowd in Havana a few weeks later, "can be summed up as an aspiration for social justice, within the fullest freedom and absolute respect for the people's rights."[1] A few months later, Castro paid a visit to the United States. He pointedly did not ask for aid. Eisenhower made for the golf course, and left it to his Vice President, Richard Nixon, to meet the bearded *guerrillero*. The two did not hit it off. Thereafter, Havana and Washington stood at either end of a spectrum of a debate that would heat up: what was – what is – development?

If Nixon and Castro were sure of their answers, within five years, confidence was draining away in all camps. In late 1964, the Argentine revolutionary, Che Guevara, traveled from Cuba to Algeria to denounce "the bestiality of imperialism." He returned to Havana to pen his farewell letter to Fidel and prepare for his suicide missions to Congo and Bolivia. Oozing with nostalgia for a different development, Che reminded his compañero of the day they met in Maria Antonia's house in Mexico, and of the spirit of sacrifice to which they had vowed to create a new Latin American future. "In a revolution," wrote Che, "one wins or dies." Now it was time to take his hopes elsewhere. "I carry to new battlefronts

---

[1] Fidel Castro Speaks before Havana Rally, January 21, 1959, http://lanic.utexas.edu/pro ject/castro/db/1959/19590121.html

the faith that you taught me, the revolutionary spirit of my people, the feeling of fulfilling the most sacred of duties: to fight against imperialism wherever it may be. This is a source of strength, and more than heals the deepest of wounds."[2] That year, the Cuban writer Edmundo Desnoes struck a less defiant, more resigned tone in his novel, *Memories of Underdevelopment*. Echoing Dostoevsky's prose of doubt and isolation, Desnoes' rendition of development uprooted his protagonist, Sergio, without giving him new ground. Far from living in Marxist or modernizationist certainties about phases and stages explored in this book, Sergio wanders Havana in a state of limbo. Underdevelopment has become a state of mind. Once upon a time, dreams of development were supposed to overcome old traps and frustrations of a "backward" past; all that was left were living memories of underdevelopment. Sergio sighed: "the truth is I feel washed out, sad with my new liberty-solitude."[3] By 1964, the "Development Decade" was only a few years old. But already, believers were having doubts. Many of the doubts were now splattered over the front pages of newspapers, such as stories about South Vietnam's "Strategic Hamlet Program," euphemistically called "villagization." It aimed to cordon off peasants from North Vietnamese forces in the name of agrarian reform, was a public debacle, and was mothballed after the embarrassing coup of November 1963.

In retrospect, what is remarkable is that so many people and institutions remained committed to their ideas of development and to fathoming the causes of underdevelopment. This should remind us, as the editors of this book do in their introduction, that development has been sown into the modern experience for a very long time. And, despite its many disasters and disappointments catalogued in this book, the idea of "development" remains amazingly resilient. The Development Decade was unofficially written off as a flop. Still, a half century later, the United Nations was back at it with "Millennium Development Goals" – whose "era" came to a close in 2016, packed away to clear the ground for a new campaign, with an updated slogan, for our anthropocentric times, "Sustainable Development Goals," another to-do list for the planet. Whether these pronouncements had much effect is the source of debate. If that were not enough, and despite the World Bank's rhetoric of "do no harm" principles of lending and the stigma around "villagization," the

---

[2] https://www.youtube.com/watch?v=86YaCAdRcz4 for the Algeria speech; The Farewell Letter can be found in: https://www.marxists.org/archive/guevara/1965/04/01.htm

[3] Edmundo Desnoes, *Memorias del subdesarrollo* (Havana: 1965), 14.

practice is back – even in name. In Ethiopia, thousands of households have been relocated under the villagization umbrella in the name of development, and investigative journalists are back in the trenches revealing wrongdoings about lenders and clients.[4] What cannot be denied is the appeal of large-scale promises to right basic, global, wrongs and injustices with sweeping plans and uplifting talk, and follow-up reports of dashed hopes and repression.

This book gives us many clues as to why development dreams keep getting reborn. While historians have played their part in making development into a narrative about social change and turning, as Nick Cullather noted in a sweeping tour of the field coinciding – perhaps unintentionally – with the Millennium Summit in 2000, development into an age best bracketed into the past, it's been a heroic and tragic saga all rolled into one.[5] After reading the chapters in this book, one is tempted to say that development has been as much a determinant and idyll of the modern experience as the quest for freedom or peace – a motive for large-scale social mobilization and disenchantment alike, and as immortal as it is frustrating.

This book lays out three important innovations. The first is to enlarge the development era, to free it from the constraints of being a Cold War venture. Until relatively recently, the view from the United States in particular, and to some extent Western Europe, treated development as the umbrella for how what used to be called the Third World folded into a narrative of ideological bipolarity from 1945 to 1989. The contest over global hegemony activated "aid" – and with the rise and fall of Cold War bellicosity went aid, and therefore development. Aid was the civilian counterpoint to counterinsurgency, the economic side of the security coin, the exercise of soft power where the Cold War got hot.

Cold War narratives of development not only erased anything developmental about what came before, and what endures after 1989, they reduced the idea of development to policies of assistance from have to have-not countries, the former the superpowers, the latter the basket cases. The result was a paternalistic and one-sided narrative to mirror the paternalism and one-sided practice of aid. In fact, development has an

---

[4] https://www.icij.org/project/world-bank/evicted-and-abandoned-explore-stories-around-world

[5] Nick Cullather, "Development? It's History," *Diplomatic History* 24:4 (Fall 2000): 641–653. For an update, see Joseph Morgan Hodge, "Writing the History of Development (Part 2: Longer, Deeper, Wider)," *Humanity* 7:1 (Spring 2016).

older vintage. For Amanda Kay McVety in this book, it goes back to Adam Smith and the Scottish Enlightenment; for others, it begins with the discovery of relief. What can be said is that development, the ideas, practices, and policies that bundle it were the effects of global economic integration – development reflected one way in which observers, policy makers, and social scientists made sense of how global integration produced unevenness, inequality, and unfairness. And since these three features were indelible markers of global integration, manifest since at least the 1840s, development was one way of framing interdependence across borders, a way of framing that contrasted with a more euphoric story about the natural convergence of societies to some modern, prosperous mien. Mill and Marx disagreed on many things. But they did not, in mid-century, disagree over the basic inescapable nature of global integration and therefore convergence. But for others, inescapable did not mean convergence. It could mean divergence. Japanese thinkers behind the Meiji Restoration after 1868 did not believe that if Edo-Tokyo opened the Shogunate, Japan would be inducted into the benevolence of market integration. Rather, Japan had to play catch up, first through aggressive internal reforms and protectionism, and by the 1880s through expansion and acquisition of its own colonies, like Europe, like the United States. The Japanese model, from the late nineteenth century, and especially after the defeat of China in 1895, became a powerful export – including for Chinese themselves, who framed it in the vernacular of "development."[6]

Reaching beyond Cold War framings also captures the various waves of enchantment and disenchantment. If late nineteenth-century Japan loomed large for many countries as a developmental option to emulate in an age of empire, there was an echo of disillusionment as well. Dadabhai Naoroji, an early Indian nationalist and newspaper editor who became the first Indian member of the British Parliament (representing the London constituency of Finsbury for the Liberal Party in the 1890s), published *Poverty and Un-British Rule in India*. The work was a sensation; it questioned the presumption that Britain was in India to instill order and create wealth *for* the colony. Advocating a "drain" theory of Indian finances, Naoroji catalogued the many ways in which financial and commercial rules sucked wealth from the colony. Yes, India benefited from schools, laws, and new economic norms – but Britain was milking

---

[6] Yukiko Koshiro, *Imperial Eclipse: Japan's Strategic Thinking about Continental Asia before August 1945* (Ithaca: Cornell University Press, 2013); Pankaj Mishra, *From the Ruins of Empire: The Intellectuals Who Remade Asia* (New York: FSG, 2012).

the colony and was the cause of "famine, plagues, destruction and impoverishment." India may have been lagging behind, but due to empire it was now *becoming* poor. For his part, after the *Manchester Guardian* sent the liberal reformer John A. Hobson to cover the Boer War, Hobson came away aghast at the hypocrisy of British imperial claims to be uplifting the continent of Africa and instead keeping it under its thumb for the sake of a small minority. Development through "colonization" was simply an expression of what Hobson called "earth hunger."[7] By the end of World War I, it was unclear whether development was a euphemism for closing the gap between haves and have-nots, or whether it was a justification for the haves to preserve their status in the global hierarchy. There is a sense of ambiguity and melancholy, for instance, in Sun Yat-sen's *The International Development of China*, a compilation of essays he had been writing for the Guomintang magazine *Jianghe* (*Reconstruction*) between 1918 and 1920.[8] Ever since, the rhetoric of development has been cleaved over whether the practice perpetuates or challenges colonial rule. By the 1960s, the debate would break out in the open; for Fidel Castro, to develop meant breaking away from imperialism; for Walt W. Rostow, avatar of US-style modernization, development could only really unfold by being part of the First World system because it was, ultimately, all about the universalization of mass consumption. One might say that the Cold War was but one chapter in the epic of development, simply part of a much larger debate about empire and global order, a debate sparked not in 1945 with the decolonization of Asia and Africa, but with the start of the nineteenth century.

There is a second, vital, contribution in this book. If President Harry Truman's Point Four Program of technical assistance, unveiled at his 1949 inaugural address, has to some also been a declaration of the birth of the development age, it has been treated as an American export. He and his entourage worried about the rising anti-colonial movements in Asia and Africa, especially after the independence of India, the turn to economic nationalism in Latin America, and the imminent victory of Mao in China. Development and technical assistance represented a strategy for preserving some integration into the multilateral trading and financial system

---

[7] John A. Hobson, *Imperialism: A Study* (London: John Nisbett, 1902), 13; Dadabhai Naoroji, *Poverty and Un-British Rule in India* (London: Swan Sonnenshein & Co., 1901), v-x, 31–38.

[8] Sun Yat-sen, *The International Development of China* (London, 1922); Marie-Claire Bergère, *Sun Yat-sen* (Stanford: Stanford University Press, 1998), 280.

after the end of empires. Apologists and critics alike, from Gilbert Rist to Arturo Escobar, have tended to agree; development was an American export to integrate postcolonial societies into a wider, postwar multilateral order; for apologists, it's a liberation of, and for critics, a burden on, the rest.[9]

This book illuminates the ways in which Point Four was more the effect than the cause of rising development consciousness. This has important implications not just for development, but for thinking about US power on the global stage, and how much the United States got drawn into, rather than pushing, the development game. Not long after Truman's address, the Russian economic historian Alexander Gerschenkron gave a famous paper to a gathering of social scientists in Chicago at the behest of Bert Hoselitz. What came of that was a legendary essay about economic backwardness in historical perspective. The essay is often recalled as a critique of the emerging modernization view that there was only one way to convergence; it's true that Gerschenkron was making the point that societies that were behind could not, by definition, follow the "stages" laid out by the pioneers. But what's often forgotten is the historical content of the paper, which accents the ways in which latecomers like Germany, Japan, and what was close to his heart, Russia, had been trying to skip stages and close the gap through active development policies from the time they recognized that they were behind in the middle of the nineteenth century. Even as modernization theory was taking off, the Odessa-born skeptic noted that the half-truth of stagist history concealed an awkward other half – "that is to say, in several very important respects the development of a backward country may, by the very virtue of its backwardness, tend to differ fundamentally from that of an advanced country." How useful can any partial truth be? The history of leapfrogging in Russia, Germany, and Japan suggested, for Gerschenkron, not much. It was the fact that they found their own pathways that allowed them to progress.[10]

The point is: the world beyond the United States was playing the development game long before American social scientists and policymakers fastened on it as a way to integrate Asia and Africa after their

---

[9] Arturo Escobar, *Encountering Development: The Making and Unmaking of the Third World* (Princeton: Princeton University Press, 2011); Gilbert Rist, *The History of Development* (London: Zed, 2014).

[10] Alexander Gerschenkron, "Economic Backwardness in Historical Perspective," (1952) in his *Economic Backwardness in Historical Perspective: A Book of Essays* (Cambridge, MA: Harvard University Press, 1962), 7.

imperial uncouplings. But what is more, there is growing evidence that Washington was importing development ideas, taking cues from the rest of the world, cues it would translate and refract into the language of its own ideas of progress. First, there was the threat to old imperial orders. The 1945 Vietnamese Declaration of Independence began with some immortalized words: "All men are created equal. They are endowed by their Creator with inalienable rights; among these are Life, Liberty, and the pursuit of Happiness." Ho Chi Minh held out hope for a brokered separation to keep Vietnam out of any empire's – Beijing's as well as Paris's – orbit. But the French pressure to keep Indochina in an older fold led to war. The same happened in Indonesia. In Malaya, a peasant revolt erupted in the spring of 1948. Increasingly, claims about material injustice layered onto the demands for political sovereignty; it was not enough to be free; decolonized countries wanted to be equal; to be equal meant catching up; and increasingly, catching up meant reversing the flow of resources. In 1945, the Argentine economist Raúl Prebisch started to refer to the plights of the "periphery" in letters to friends, an indication of how the vocabulary was starting to label global injustice.[11] By then, Washington had scotched any idea of an inter-American development bank and the Truman administration wanted nothing of the hotheads questioning the global economic principles of Bretton Woods. Congress, meanwhile, was gearing up to reject the 1948 International Trade Organization. In the UN Economic Commission for Latin America offices in Santiago, an unsure and frustrated Prebisch poured his frustrations into *The Economic Development of Latin America and Its Principal Problems*, a declaration of discontent against the global economic order. Though couched in technicalities about elasticities of demand and business cycles, the normative purpose came through; all the slights from Washington were now bearing fruit in a mélange of objective data and righteous anger. Not only were primary exporters stuck in a historic rut and condemned to diminishing rewards for their staples, but unequal exchange would fossilize them there.[12]

Concern about global inequity, the need to catch up, and practices of development as a way to reverse the flow of resources from "peripheries" to "core" countries were on the table for some time, thanks to Latin

---

[11] Edgar J. Dosman, *The Life and Times of Raúl Prebisch 1901–1986* (Montreal: McGill-Queen's University Press, 2008), 180–181, 214.

[12] Andrew J. Rotter, *The Path to Vietnam: Origins of the American Commitment to Southeast Asia* (Ithaca: Cornell University Press, 1987), 17–19.

American economists and statesmen working with colleagues in the Treasury Department in the late 1930s. They came to the fore at Bretton Woods in 1944, where the postwar economic architecture was supposed to be hammered out. American officials like Harry Dexter White and Henry Morgenthau, swayed by Latin American pressures, were already on board with the idea of lending institutions that did more than "reconstruct" but also got into the "development" business. When Morgenthau presented the first drafts of the IMF and the IBRD to Roosevelt in May 1942, he argued that the institutions were necessary "to supply the huge volume of capital that will be needed abroad for relief, for reconstruction, and economic development essential for the attainment of world prosperity and higher standards of living." White pushed for a Bank that would "help stabilize the prices of essential raw materials and other important commodities" and floated an "International Commodity Stabilization Corporation to stabilize the price of important commodities." He even endorsed the support of infant industries in the periphery to help poor countries out of their lot. At Bretton Woods, Morgenthau announced that "poverty, wherever it exists, is menacing to us all." We now know that these initiatives went nowhere, scotched especially by British delegates who wanted no meddling in colonial affairs.[13]

Washington could only thwart demands to address international injustices for so long. On January 20, 1949, Truman – on the heels of a surprise electoral result – addressed the public to outline a global approach to counter "the false philosophy" of communism. The war was over in a divided Europe, but much of the rest of the planet hung in the balance. "We are moving on with other nations," Truman announced, "to build an even stronger structure of international order and justice. We shall have as our partners countries which, no longer solely concerned with the problem of national survival, are now working to improve the standards of living of all their people." The Point Four Program (as it eventually became called) signaled a more global awareness rooted in the perceptions of the risks of yawning inequities in a world Truman and his men wanted to make safe for liberal capitalism. Linking poverty to stability had come up in 1947 when Truman grappled with Greece and Turkey. There was also the short-lived and never realized Asiatic Recovery Program, which

---

[13] Eric Helleiner, *Forgotten Foundations of Bretton Woods: International Development and the Making of the Postwar Order* (Ithaca: Cornell University Press, 2016), 197–199.

borrowed from the Marshall Plan. But the idea that assistance would be part of diplomacy came from Benjamin Hardy, a State Department deputy who'd cut his teeth watching Brazilians tackle poverty as press officer for Nelson Rockefeller at the Office of Inter-American Affairs. He took his lessons to his bosses in the State Department who initially brushed them off. The White House gave him a better reception for "a program that will hold out to these people the hope of acquiring the things that science and know-how of the twentieth century can provide them." This would prevent the clamor for sovereignty and a way out of poverty from going down radical roads. There were also some domestic inspirations, like the example of the Tennessee Valley Authority. By November 1948, the provision of "technical resources" in poor countries had worked its way into memo format. Still, State and the White House insisted that any policy that favored aid was a sign of weakness, not strength. In the end, and urged by his wife, Hardy had his day. Truman's special counsel, Clark Clifford, grasping for new ideas to bake into the inaugural, liked the idea and worked it into the speech. It was far from a clear, Cold War doctrine hatched from some Ivy League workshop that subsequent historians have argued. Dean Acheson first heard of Point Four when he listened to the address.[14]

It does not take a microscope to find the language of development all over the global view from Washington. "More than half the people of the world," Truman told his citizens, "are living in conditions approaching misery. Their food is inadequate. They are victims of disease. Their economic life is primitive and stagnant. Their poverty is a handicap and a threat both to them and to more prosperous areas." What is worth signaling is that Truman identified a relationship between welfare and security at home and other people's misery. Development provided a new framework tying the haves and have-nots in a more benevolent codependent relationship. "The old imperialism-exploitation for foreign profit has no place in our plans. What we envisage is a program of development based on the concepts of democratic fair-dealing. All countries, including our own, will greatly benefit from a constructive program for the better use of the world's human and natural resources. Experience shows that

---

[14] The beginnings are told in somewhat heroic fashion in Jonathan B. Bingham, *Shirt-Sleeve Diplomacy: Point 4 in Action* (New York: John Day, 1954). For more context, see Elizabeth Borgwardt, *A New Deal for the World: America's Vision for Human Rights* (Cambridge, MA: Harvard University Press, 2005); Kiran Klaus Patel, *The New Deal: A Global History* (Princeton: Princeton University Press, 2016).

our commerce with other countries expands as they progress industrially and economically."[15]

By embedding American power within a longer time frame and a wider circulation of ideas and models, this book also offers a multisited, decentered – "global" – account of the forces that generated development and resisted it. But what made it global was not just that the idea of development had multiple sources and responded to many local and regional forces, but that development was a response to global integration. While many of the chapters in this book focus on relief and aid, both were immersed within a wider set of policies and efforts to redress the most galling inequities produced by the assembly of the world market for labor, capital, and commodities. That is, since the middle of the nineteenth century, the distribution of rewards from integration was never even or fair – and never seen as fair or even. While there was always some effort to argue that, in the long run at least, rising waters of global wealth might lift all boats, the domestic consequences and global reactions more often compelled the agents of integration either to find meliorative reforms or to advocate fundamental changes under the capacious roof of development. Colonialism, as Hobson and/or Japanese scholars of the 1890s such as Nitobe Inazo made clear, was one unstable model of development by integrating fringes; for others, decolonization *was* development. But the same expectation could boomerang, and create a sense that development required decolonization. When the African-American writer living in Paris, Richard Wright, was planning a trip to Spain he read in the newspaper about plans for leaders of 29 countries from Asia and Africa to gather in Bandung, Indonesia, in 1955. It was "a meeting of the rejected," he noted, and changed his plans. What he witnessed was a summit of yearning, yearning for industrialization, consumption, freedom from want, independence from empire. Throughout, Wright noted the "molten

---

[15] Observers have polarized widely over what to make of this declaration. For some, it was a natural step in American leadership. For others, it was symptomatic of a "top-down, ethnocentric and technocratic" (Escobar, 44) solution to problems around the world. Others have seen the propulsion of the Cold War behind the development turn. Mark Mazower, for instance, has depicted the United States turning to the United Nations and embracing the development mandate "not to reach out to the USSR but to combat its influence," he has argued. "The idea that America had a special mission to transform societies across the world was an integral part of this new conception of its role. In the great ideological confrontation with Soviet communism, the Truman administration believed it had to demonstrate that capitalism had the better tools for improving the lives of the world's poor and underprivileged." Mark Mazower, *Governing the World: The History of an Idea, 1815 to the Present* (New York: Penguin, 2013), 273–274.

wounds" of Europe's legacies; Bandung was a collage: "everybody read into it his own fears; the conference loomed like a long-buried ghost rising from a muddy grave."[16]

This helps explain the durability of the lure of development. It never goes away as long as global integration, whether under Victorian-era empires or post-1989 globalization, frames interdependent relationships between societies; it gets summoned to redress in some ways what the world economy so unfairly apportions. This is why someone like Fidel Castro could see himself so easily as the heir to the nineteenth-century Cuban patriot, José Martí, who argued that Cuban freedom required its capacity to enhance human capacities, without which backwardness and inertia would keep it in a subaltern relationship to the "Monster" to the north. This is why, as Nathan J. Citino illustrates in this book, Nasser could likewise see himself as the heir to Muhammed Ali Pasha for similar reasons. Their amalgam of developmentalism, socialism, and their flirtation with Moscow were of a piece that tapped into a memory of development attached to the sense of global injustice. This helps explain how development's moral language helped make it the source of so many utopian dreams and dystopian nightmares, how it could be simultaneously an effort to integrate into a wider, stratified, order, while at the same time resisting it.

Seeing development as a response to global integration also helps to explain some of its basic, contradictory, features, features that figured so prominently on the public stage during the Cold War and after – when the inequities of international integration became a more prominent part of the news cycle. Here, I think, the Vietnam War played a crucial role in the story about development, for it brought to public attention the ways in which American lives were entangled with villagers in the Mekong Delta. But this was not the only instance. It is worth recalling that a different kind of humanitarian horror broke out in Biafra in 1967, and it played an important role in the creation of a global gallery of suffering, visible for all to see. A year earlier, the cosmopolitan economist Albert O. Hirschman went to evaluate the World Bank's development projects. They included the Bornu rail line that crossed Nigeria's Hausa-Igbo frontiers. His report, called *Development Projects Observed,* called upon his fellow economists not to let the mystique of abstract theory get in the way. No sooner did the

---

[16] Richard Wright, *The Color Curtain: A Report on the Bandung Conference* (Jackson: University of Mississippi Press, 1956), 92–93.

book come out than Nigeria erupted in a brutal civil war that would kill three million people. Hirschman was alarmed: how could I have not anticipated this disaster? What made him alarmed, however, was the scene played out on televisions and especially in newspapers. The Biafran war, and the spectacle of horror, became the first globally televised and mediatized civil conflict that led to a humanitarian disaster. Donald McCullin, the British photographer, who'd cut his teeth in Cold War Berlin, Cyprus, and Congo, became famous for unflinching black and white shots of emaciated children and distended bellies. He and colleagues like Gilles Caron would play a key role in partnering with French doctors in the founding of Médecins Sans Frontières in 1971. And his frustration over the mounting reportage about the failures of development and the spreading visible evidence of humanitarian catastrophes led him to write a cri de coeur, *Is Anyone Taking Any Notice?*, in 1973.[17]

Yet, even as development's shine had worn off, the development game intensified. It drew in new actors, like nongovernmental organizations (NGOs), breathed new life into vintage actors like the public health crusaders described in Erez Manela's chapter, and intensified the jockeying between rivals and even relative newcomers, like European, Canadian, and Japanese "donors." It created, as Paul Adler shows, a rising internationalist coalition calling for a new international economic order (NIEO) and division of labor. And at the same time, it could also galvanize, as Stephen Macekura's recent book illustrates, a new coalition that would try to dampen the growth and development urge – in favor of conservation and population control. While the NIEO champions were calling for new rules of the global economic game that would favor industrialization of the periphery, delegates gathered in Stockholm in 1972 for the UN's first Conference on the Human Environment, under the leadership of UN Secretary-General U Thant and the Canadian diplomat Maurice Strong. There, new nongovernmental organizations, teams of scientists, and delegates from what we would now call the Global North called for rolling back the use of natural resources and slower growth to protect the planet. Delegates from the Third World howled in protest – just as they were now wanting their share of the global pie, here

---

[17] Jeremy Adelman, *Worldly Philosopher: The Odyssey of Albert O. Hirschman* (Princeton: Princeton University Press, 2013), 387–397; Donald McCullin, *Is Anyone Taking Any Notice?* (Cambridge, MA: MIT Press, 1973).

were the do-gooders wanting to shrink it! All in the name of development.[18]

Development has been a landmark of the way thinkers and practitioners have been debating global integration since the middle of the nineteenth century. It has provided the language, motivated the actors, and framed the models for considering how integration across borders has produced inequality at the same time. Its resilience in part reflects its utility and necessity. But development has done something more: it has had that strange, alchemical property of being simultaneously visionary and practical, normative, and positive. And so long as global integration is with us, the development age is not over.

---

[18] Stephen J. Macekura, *Of Limits and Growth: The Rise of Global Sustainable Development in the Twentieth Century* (New York: Cambridge University Press, 2015), chapter 3.

Index

Printed in the USA
CPSIA information can be obtained
at www.ICGtesting.com
LVHW012012170124
768960LV00003B/39